THE AMERICAN MIDWEST IN FILM AND LITERATURE

THE AMERICAN MIDWEST IN FILM AND LITERATURE

Nostalgia, Violence, and Regionalism

ADAM R. OCHONICKY

INDIANA UNIVERSITY PRESS

This book is a publication of

Indiana University Press
Office of Scholarly Publishing
Herman B Wells Library 350
1320 East 10th Street
Bloomington, Indiana 47405 USA

iupress.indiana.edu

© 2020 by Adam R. Ochonicky

All rights reserved
No part of this book may be reproduced or utilized in any form or by any means, electronic or mechanical, including photocopying and recording, or by any information storage and retrieval system, without permission in writing from the publisher. The paper used in this publication meets the minimum requirements of the American National Standard for Information Sciences—Permanence of Paper for Printed Library Materials, ANSI Z39.48-1992.

Manufactured in the United States of America

Cataloging information is available from the Library of Congress.

ISBN 978-0-253-04596-6 (hardback)
ISBN 978-0-253-04597-3 (paperback)
ISBN 978-0-253-04599-7 (ebook)

1 2 3 4 5   24 23 22 21 20 19

CONTENTS

Acknowledgments   vii

    Introduction: Nostalgia and Regionalism   1

  Part I: Twentieth-Century Narratives of Nostalgia and the Midwest

  1. Nostalgic Spatiality   29

  2. Spatial Constriction, Race, and Midwestern Stagnation   55

  3. Nostalgic Violence, Nebulous Spaces, and Blank Identities   84

  Part II: The Millennial Midwest on Film

  4. Masculinity, Race, and Violence   123

  5. Locating Sincerity, Disillusionment, and Paranoia   151

  6. Nostalgic Atonement   178

    Conclusion: Nostalgic Frontiers   203

    Afterword: Regionalism and Politics   211

Bibliography   231
Index   245

ACKNOWLEDGMENTS

Simply writing the acknowledgments for this project has left me, indeed, in a nostalgic state. I produced the first draft of this book during a portion of my ten years living in Milwaukee, Wisconsin. Having moved north from St. Louis, I quickly came to love the Cream City's many charms. I'm grateful for the lasting friendships that developed with my colleagues, neighbors, and others from the local film, music, literary, and art communities. There are many, many individuals to whom I owe a hearty "thanks."

At the University of Wisconsin-Milwaukee (UWM), I was fortunate to have worked with an array of incredible faculty and staff members. First, I wish to thank Patrice Petro, who has enriched my scholarly career in so many ways. Her speedy and invaluable feedback helped to give shape to this book during the initial drafting process, particularly in terms of maintaining focus on big picture issues. I'm also appreciative of the opportunity that she provided for me to work at UWM's Center for International Education (CIE), her inclusiveness in both professional and social settings, and simply her ongoing kindness and support.

When I was first conceptualizing this project, Andrew Kincaid recommended—and I paraphrase—"writing about what you know," at least in terms of place: in this case, the Midwest. Andrew continued to provide many helpful insights as the project evolved. Jason Puskar's rigorous critiques of my writing were immensely useful for streamlining chapters and spotlighting my own arguments. Elena Gorfinkel provided essential feedback as I prepared this manuscript for publication, and her work on temporality in cinema influenced my treatment of nostalgia in this project. I'm grateful to Andrew Martin for his steady presence and generosity during my time at UWM.

Along with Patrice, Andrew, Jason, Elena, and Andy, I wish to thank several additional people currently and formerly with UWM, especially those in the Film Studies program. In particular, I would like to express my gratitude to Gilberto Blasini, Tami Williams, Ben Schneider, Tasha Oren, Peter Paik, Pete Sands, and Jamie Poster. I'm indebted to the Film Studies program's faculty committee for giving me the leeway to develop and regularly teach an undergraduate course on the Midwest in film; my work on that course greatly influenced the organization and substance of this book. I also appreciate the faculty committee enabling me to serve as archivist of the program's collection of holdings for several years and for their initial invitation to teach in the Film Studies program. On that latter note, I'm thankful to Tasha, Ben, and Jamie for generously sharing insights about film pedagogy. In UWM's Department of English, Kristie Hamilton has given continual support and guidance since I first arrived in Milwaukee.

There are numerous other professional colleagues and associates who deserve recognition. Special thanks go to Victoria Johnson, whose friendship and advice I've greatly valued over the past several years. It's difficult to overstate the importance of Vicky's work for my own project; her book, *Heartland TV: Prime Time Television and the Struggle for U.S. Identity*, is a milestone in linking Midwestern studies with television and media studies. I'm grateful to Zoran Samardzija, who has given constructive feedback on several chapters in my book. Zoran also invited me to speak about my project as part of the Chicago Film Seminar lecture series at DePaul University; that talk occurred just as I received my book contract, and Zoran's prepared response (and the comments of audience members) informed my manuscript revisions. Susan Kerns provided many useful recommendations about films to address in this project and to include in the course that I taught about the Midwest on film.

In my current position at the University of Wisconsin-Oshkosh (UWO), I have many wonderful colleagues in the Department of English. Extra thanks go to Roberta Maguire, Don Dingledine, Pascale Manning, Stewart Cole, and Stephen McCabe. Roberta served as department chair when I was hired, and I've benefited from her sage guidance on a wide variety of matters.

As an undergraduate at Saint Louis University (SLU), Vince Casaregola introduced me to the study of film at the college level; in recent years, I've enjoyed a renewed friendship with Vince after crossing paths at conferences. From my undergraduate years, I also wish to thank Fred Arroyo, who significantly influenced my career and life. At SLU, I took two of Fred's seminars; both courses were highly formative for my ongoing interests in memory, nostalgia, and place. The seeds of this very book can be traced to the undergraduate writing that I produced for Fred, and I remain grateful for his careful, detailed feedback and general encouragement to make sense of the past through writing.

As an instructor at both UWM and UWO, I've had the opportunity to teach Midwestern content in multiple contexts. It's been a pleasure to work with, respectively, Film Studies majors and English majors at those institutions, and I'm grateful for their enthusiastic response to the materials that I've curated for several different courses. Their lively and critical engagement with Midwestern narratives and iconography—as depicted in films, literature, graphic novels, and television series—has inspired new directions in my own thinking about such materials. Encountering such passionate students has been one of the many rewarding aspects of my work on regionalism.

I've been quite pleased to serve on the editorial board of *Middle West Review* (*MWR*) since the journal first launched in 2014. Along with thanking Jon K. Lauck and the other members of the board, I'd like to express my gratitude to Paul Mokrzycki Renfro for his stewardship of *MWR* as editor-in-chief during its first five volumes, for inviting me to join the board when the journal was in its developmental stage, and for backing my efforts to further bring film, television, and media scholarship into the interdisciplinary purview of *MWR*. It's been exciting to help establish *MWR* as a scholarly journal and to collaborate on the renewal and expansion of the interdisciplinary study of the Midwest. On a similar note, I'm especially appreciative of the other scholarly journals, publication venues, and conferences that have been receptive to my scholarship on the Midwest in film, television, and other forms of media. While completing this book, I curated a short piece on *NewsRadio* (NBC, 1995–1999) for a theme week on "Flyover States and Representations of the U.S. Midwest" at *In Media Res*; thanks to Emily Kofoed for organizing the theme week and accepting my proposed piece, as well as to my fellow curators, particularly Tony Harkins. An earlier, shorter version of chapter 4 of this book—which focused on *A History of Violence* (2005) and *Boys Don't Cry* (1999)—was published in the *Quarterly Review of Film and Video* (QRFV), volume 32, issue 2. My thanks to the editors of QRFV and to the Taylor & Francis Group for granting permission to reprint that material. I previously published a review of *Two American Families* (PBS, 2013) in *Middle West Review*, volume 1, issue 1. Thanks to the University of Nebraska Press for granting permission to reproduce that piece in a revised and expanded version as part of the Afterword of this book. Over the past several years, I've presented content from nearly every chapter of this book at numerous conferences. The comments of my fellow panelists and the audience members helped this book to reach its current state. Further, I'm grateful to the organizers who accepted my proposals on Midwestern topics for the conferences of the following organizations and journals: the Society for Cinema and Media Studies (SCMS), the Modern Language Association (MLA), the Literature/Film Association (LFA), Film & History, and the Midwest Modern Language Association (MMLA). At the MLA and MMLA conferences, I presented on several panels affiliated with the Society for the Study of Midwestern Literature (SSML); thanks to Marilyn Atlas for organizing those panels and finding a place for my work on film alongside the literary topics of the other presenters.

The editorial board and staff at Indiana University Press have been incredibly supportive (and patient!) throughout the process of preparing my manuscript for publication. In particular, I owe a great debt to both of the Acquisitions Editors with whom I've worked—Raina Polivka and Janice Frisch—as well as Gary Dunham. After pitching my book to Raina at an SCMS conference, she sent it out for review by anonymous readers and brought the project before the board to secure a contract. As I was completing revisions, Raina took a position elsewhere; Janice then became my primary contact at the press, and she skillfully guided the book to publication while also responding to my steady stream of questions. I'm thankful that Raina saw promise in my project and advised me during the early stages of the publication process, and I'm exceptionally grateful to Janice for all of her work to finalize this book. In addition, my two anonymous reviewers—who I was later informed were Wheeler Winston Dixon and Douglas Reichert Powell—provided me with invaluable criticism and suggestions for revision. I'm especially appreciative of the time and energy that Douglas expended on my work, as he produced a second reader report on a revised draft of the full manuscript. The combined contributions of Janice, Raina, Wheeler, and

Douglas were instrumental in transforming this book from a rough version into its present form.

In hindsight, I can't imagine writing this book without the experience of living in Milwaukee and encountering many wonderful people during my time there. Alberto Aldana regularly visited me in Milwaukee and hosted me in Chicago; those occasions were recurring highlights of my years in the former city. I'm grateful for Alberto's calming presence, for introducing me to many aspects of Chicago culture, and for our friendship that stretches back nearly two decades. At UWM, I was surrounded by an amazingly talented set of peers. Their passion and ambition inspired me, and their friendship carried me through the challenges of developing and drafting this project. Among many others, I particularly wish to thank (in no particular order): Ali Sperling, Paul Gagliardi, Kal Heck, Mary Clinkenbeard, Ron Felten, Shawna Lipton, Bridget Kies, Molly McCourt, Eric Herhuth, Mike MacDonald, John Raucci, Drew Anastasia, Katie Malcolm, Lee Abbott, Ava Hernandez, John Couture, Katie Morrissey, Nick Proferes, Sarah Pemelton, and Niamh Wallace. Outside of the university, I'm grateful to the late Dave Monroe, who provided enthusiastic and detailed notes over a draft of my Introduction chapter and who was an iconic fixture of the local film and music communities. I was pleased to have been able to serve the Milwaukee Film organization in several capacities, including leading post-screening discussions with audience members during the annual film festival. The films assigned to me often focused on the Midwest and helped to further refine my thoughts on regionalism and cinema. Many thanks to my friends at the Comet Cafe and Colectivo Coffee (formerly Alterra Coffee). From mornings to late nights, these two Milwaukee institutions were welcoming spaces that felt like extensions of my apartment. And, of course, I'm thankful for my many kind neighbors: the self-described Irving Place gang. Our little stretch of E. Irving Place was a true community; I miss the block parties that we organized and just the friendly chats while passing one another on the street. This book is about nostalgia, and I have decidedly nostalgic associations with the neighborhood where I lived in Milwaukee.

Two longtime friends have greatly impacted my personal and professional interests in film and nostalgia. Since eighth grade, Joe Havermann's devoted cinephilia has enhanced my own love of film, and his passion for writing has been a source of motivation. My oldest friend, Jeff Lewis, has been a constant in my life for three decades. I've long appreciated Jeff's advice on matters big and small; in addition, the nostalgia that we share (and often discuss) for our childhood homes in south St. Louis has significantly shaped my thinking about nostalgia and location.

Finally, I couldn't have completed this project without the love and encouragement of my parents and my partner, Liz. When I was a child, my parents instilled a sense of curiosity about the world; I'm grateful for their unceasing enthusiasm for my academic pursuits. From grade school through graduate school and beyond, my parents have supported me in every possible way. To Liz, I cannot fully express my gratitude for all that you give to me each day. Just in terms of this project, you've continually offered insights about the Midwest and nostalgia, and you've patiently listened to my complaints regarding the slow grind of revisions. But far surpassing such concerns, I'm thankful for your presence in my life. You've been with me even when we lived in different locations, and it's now my ongoing joy to experience life together with you. And, lastly, Esther arrived just as I was completing this book, but I'm already nostalgic for each day that you've been with us.

THE AMERICAN MIDWEST IN FILM AND LITERATURE

Introduction:
Nostalgia and Regionalism

In 1996, an article in a weekly newspaper announced a startling find: "'Midwest' Discovered Between East, West Coasts."[1] The periodical in question was *The Onion* (1988–), a satirical newspaper founded in Madison, Wisconsin, in the late 1980s. Since its inception, *The Onion* has offered a sharp critique of contemporary American culture and has regularly commented on how its region of origin, the Midwest, is widely perceived. Revised and republished several times since its first appearance, the "discovery" article directly engages with the popular conception of the Midwest as "flyover country," that is, as a vacant, nondescript space—both geographically and culturally—between the two coasts.

While reporting on the Midwest's "wild lands full of corn and wheat," the article knowingly reproduces regional stereotypes, such as that of elitist coastal inhabitants and their uncultured, mysterious counterparts who occupy the center of the nation. The anonymously penned piece dutifully explains, "Though the Midwest is still largely unexplored, early reports depict a region as backwards as it is vast." One member of the fictitious "exploratory team" recounts, "The Midwestern Aborigines are ruddy, generally heavy-set folk, clad in plain nondesigner costumery.... And though coarse and unattractive, these simple people were rather friendly, offering us plain native fare such as 'Hotdish' and 'Casserole.'"[2] In an updated version of the article, a "Los Angeles-based anthropologist" details the Midwest's inherent cultural deficiencies by observing, "Many of the basic aspects of a civilized culture appear to be entirely absent.... There is no theater to speak of, and their knowledge of posh restaurants is sketchy at best. Further, their agricentric lives seem to prevent them from pursuing high fashion to any degree, and, as a result, their mode of dress is largely restricted to sweatpants and sweatshirts...."[3] Within just a few lines of text, the article showcases several reductive signifiers of the Midwest, which are accentuated in an illustrated map published with the piece. These traits include: a limited range of body types; skin complexion that indicates habitual outdoor activity (and, potentially, is intended to produce racial associations with whiteness); clothing that is functional rather than stylish; an absence of highbrow entertainment; exclusively agricultural labor; a diet that has distinct class connotations; and an indeterminate sense of the region's spatial parameters.

A high degree of self-awareness informs *The Onion*'s humorous portrait of the Midwest's "crude and provincial" inhabitants, but such bleak depictions of the region are hardly confined to late twentieth-century satire.[4] For example, in *Winesburg, Ohio* (1919), Sherwood Anderson begins his collection of stories with "The Book of the Grotesque," a short piece in which a sleepless, unnamed writer has "a dream that was not a dream" about the occupants of the titular Midwestern town.[5] While "still conscious," the old man imagines "a long procession of figures before his eyes.... All of the men and women the writer had ever known had become grotesques." Despite this transformation, the writer qualifies, "The grotesques were not all horrible. Some were amusing, some almost beautiful."[6] Among the many meanings found in Anderson's cryptic piece on the relationship between individuals and "truth," a commentary on regional identity may be inferred: if nothing else, the Midwesterners of *Winesburg, Ohio* are a profoundly damaged population living in a realm of ever-encroaching "darkness," as described in stories throughout the collection. Several decades later, in *Beloved* (1987), Toni Morrison uses the Midwest as a staging ground for an expansive meditation on cultural memory and the ongoing legacy of slavery.[7] Set in Ohio, protagonist Sethe's home is haunted by traces of past violence, including the death of her young daughter Beloved, who Sethe herself had killed in a self-described attempt to keep the child "safe" from being captured and returned to slavery in the South.[8] Within the narrative, this traumatic history inexplicably materializes in the form of a young woman who may or may not be an older version of Beloved. In the Midwest, it seems, the past may become tangible. A more contemporary and lighthearted depiction of outlandish Midwesterners appears in *Parks and Recreation* (2009–2015), a television series that follows the lives of public worker Leslie Knope (Amy Poehler) and her fellow local government employees in the fictional town of Pawnee, Indiana.[9] Whenever the genial, multiethnic cast interacts with local townspeople at public meetings, chaos and discomfort ensues, largely due to the Pawnee constituents' typically inscrutable behavior and non sequiturs. From at least as early as Mark Twain's accounts of Tom Sawyer and Huckleberry Finn's exploits in the latter half of the nineteenth century to Anderson and Morrison's reflections on experience and memory in the twentieth century to the daily trials of Leslie Knope in the twenty-first century, the Midwest has been constructed as a space of simultaneous attraction and repulsion.

The American Midwest in Film and Literature: Nostalgia, Violence, and Regionalism provides a critical overview of the evolution, contestation, and fragmentation of the Midwest's symbolic (and often contradictory) meanings in American culture. Beginning with the frontier writings of Frederick Jackson Turner, this book establishes a succession of Midwestern texts stretching from the late nineteenth century through the first two decades of the twenty-first century. With a primary focus on cinematic depictions of the region, my objects of analysis also include literature, television series, historical writings, journalism, and sociological studies. A general line of inquiry informs my agenda: how do texts such as *Sister Carrie* (1900), *Native Son* (1940), *Meet Me in St. Louis* (1944), *Halloween* (1978), and *A History of Violence* (2005) imagine, reify, and reproduce Midwestern identity, and what are the repercussions of such regional narratives and images circulating in American culture?[10] I argue that the manifold properties of nostalgia have continually transformed popular understandings and ideological uses of the Midwest's place-identity. Accordingly, nostalgia itself is as much the subject of this book as regionalism. Overall, my project offers new conceptualizations of nostalgia and reveals how an under-examined area of regional study—the Midwest—has received critical attention throughout the history of American cinema, as well as in other mediums and discourses. In doing so, I more broadly demonstrate how film and literature have been—and remain—vital forums for illuminating the complex interplay of regionalism and nostalgia.

In this book, I identify and theorize three primary modes of nostalgia: "nostalgic spatiality," "nostalgic violence," and "nostalgic atonement." Nostalgic spatiality refers to nostalgia being projected onto a physical landscape, thus changing how that space and its accompanying cultural sphere are perceived, understood, and/or experienced. Nostalgic violence is a cultural force that manifests through actions intended to regulate the behaviors, identities, and appearances of both individuals and communities. Nostalgic atonement denotes the progressive potential of nostalgia to generate an acknowledgement and possible rectification of ways in which the flawed past continues to negatively affect the present. In addition to encapsulating the elusive spatiotemporal operations of nostalgic desire within Midwestern texts, these three concepts have applications for understanding nostalgia across national cinemas, periods, and genres, as well as for the study of nostalgia in other cultural contexts. First, these concepts foreground recurrent aesthetic conventions and thematic motifs that are deployed in the textual representation of nostalgia; second, they articulate ways in which nostalgia exerts a substantial influence on cultural formations and historical knowledge.

One of my goals is to elevate the "Midwest" as an additional category for framing and interpreting texts among more established groupings within film, literary, television, and media studies. Therefore, I situate my primary textual objects—and ways in which they have been interpreted or ascribed meanings—in a regional context that is linked to nostalgia. In realizing this objective, I revise the regional "discovery" narrative detailed in *The Onion* article by sketching out a chronology or, to emphasize continuity, a lineage of the complex ways in which the Midwest has been depicted across a variety of texts. Rather than an awareness of Midwestern identity constituting a new "discovery," this book represents a recovery—or a rediscovery—of key textual objects that shaped past perceptions of the region and that continue to inform its meaning in American culture.

The Midwest: Blank Identity, Nebulous Territory

A major assumption underlying *The American Midwest in Film and Literature* is the notion that by setting fictional narratives within the Midwest, a given text is participating, intentionally or not, in a long tradition of producing, contesting, and complicating regional identity. Consequently, this project's textual objects were chosen because they reflect and engage with Midwestern representational conventions. Such texts either work against common regional stereotypes or further reproduce essentialized images of the Midwest (or, as is often the case, do both at the same time). With these materials, I examine how Midwestern narratives create and transmit regional myths that shape collective understandings of American spaces and that also may affect the lived experiences of Midwesterners themselves.

Media scholar Victoria E. Johnson challenges academics "to raise regional mythology . . . to a shared level of attention, within media studies, to those categories of identity and capital relations with which it crucially intersects and critically informs (including race, class, gender, sexuality, and generation)."[11] Following this summons, I consider an especially notable point of overlap between identity categories and regional definitions: the recurring primacy of white masculinity across numerous Midwestern narratives. Many of the texts in which I identify some blend of nostalgic spatiality, nostalgic violence, and/or nostalgic atonement feature white, male protagonists. As I discuss in later chapters, this linkage of nostalgia, violence, regional mythos, and white masculinity is hardly coincidental. Since Frederick Jackson Turner first elevated frontier settlers of European origin to a mythical stature in his writings, subsequent representations and discussions of the Midwest have regularly presented the figure of the white male as having an enduring and outsized position of prominence within the region's identity.[12] Yet such cultural narratives overlook the diversity of the Midwest's demographics. For instance, in an opinion piece pointedly titled "Stop Pretending Black Midwesterners Don't Exist" (2018), Tamara Winfrey-Harris acknowledges the ongoing association of the region "with whiteness," but then reminds the reader, "Approximately seven million people who identify as African-American live in the Midwest. That means there are more black people in the Midwest than in the Northeast or the West."[13] In light of the contrast between lasting regional perceptions and actual conditions, this book addresses the treatment of fundamental identity categories in relation to ideological conceptions of the Midwest. Before delving into such topics, a clearer sense of the Midwest's physical and cultural parameters is necessary. The seemingly self-evident task of merely identifying a text as Midwestern is not the straightforward endeavor that it might appear to be.

Although inextricably attached to nostalgia, the Midwest's identity has fluctuated over time, due to nebulous and shifting definitions of the region. For some observers, the "Midwest" is merely a geographic territory, while for others, the term designates a cultural category that refers to certain types of people, practices, values, and so on. Technically, the United States Census Bureau separates the nation into four regions, and the Midwest is composed of twelve states: North Dakota, South Dakota, Nebraska, Kansas, Minnesota, Iowa, Missouri, Michigan, Wisconsin, Illinois, Indiana, and Ohio.[14] While selecting objects of study for *The American Midwest in Film and Literature*, I identified texts with narratives that took place in one of these twelve states. Confirming that a narrative is located within the Midwest, though, is only the beginning of assessing a text's regional engagement.

As with the multiple, competing versions of the Midwest, the term "region" also resists singular, cartographic definitions. Throughout this book, my analysis of the Midwest as a discrete entity is based upon an understanding of regional identity as an outcome of cultural perceptions that are shaped by storytelling: the recurring narrative conventions, formal aesthetics, and ideological positions employed to represent a particular space. From this perspective, a region's physical borders and geological surface function as something of a canvas or stage on which the contentious negotiations of regional culture unfold. Rather than denoting stability and cohesion, "region" thus involves an ongoing evolution of meaning. The disparate texts and narratives that circulate about various regions attest to the dynamic condition of such spatial constructions.

My methodology for studying regional texts is influenced, in part, by the work of Raymond Williams and Michel de Certeau. In the revised edition of *Keywords: A Vocabulary of Culture and Society* (1985), Williams calls attention to the inherent conflicts within the term "region." He writes, "There is an evident tension within the word, as between a distinct area and a definite part. Each sense has survived, but it is the latter which carries an important history. Everything depends, in the latter sense, on the term of the relation: a part of what?"[15] This definition introduces an important determining factor regarding the parameters of a region: in terms of both geographic space and cultural traits, a region is "a part of" a larger whole, as well as simply "apart." A region thereby comes to be defined by its difference from the larger whole of which it is a component. The spatial and cultural parameters of a regional territory also coalesce through storytelling. As de Certeau explicates in *The Practice of Everyday Life* (1984), "Stories . . . traverse and organize places; they select and link them together; they make sentences and itineraries out of them. They are spatial trajectories." In short, "every story is . . . a spatial practice."[16] Elsewhere, de Certeau adds that "a narrative activity . . . is continually concerned with marking out boundaries."[17] Beyond the existence of mere geographical borders, narratives delineate additional dimensions of a territory, such as the Midwest.

Historians Andrew R. L. Cayton and Susan E. Gray bridge the concepts from Williams and de Certeau referenced in the paragraph above. Cayton and Gray explain that "regional identity is a form of storytelling . . . regionality is about how people locate themselves intellectually and emotionally within complicated landscapes and networks of social relations."[18] Similarly, Douglas Reichert Powell argues that "a region is not a stable, finite thing, but a concept that emerges cumulatively from the circulation of texts about a region."[19] Expanding on this definition, Reichert Powell writes, "A region . . . is a way of describing the relationship among a broad set of places for a particular purpose; the larger identity of a region is not defined by any single definition but emerges from the dynamic, historical relationship of these acts of definition."[20] These passages indicate that understanding a region is dependent upon recognizing how regional storytelling expresses sets of relations, such as the individual to the region and the region to neighboring spaces. In other words, more than simply being a collection of states clumped together on a map, the Midwest is a blend of its physical territory, the daily material lives of its inhabitants, *and* the narratives produced in an attempt to make sense of the region (which are disseminated through mediums including cinema and literature). It is this latter grouping—the realms in which perceptions of Midwestern identity are produced and circulated—that is my primary area of focus. What, then, are some of the stories told about the Midwest or the ways in which Midwesterners "locate themselves" within the region?[21]

"The Camel," a second season episode of *Parks and Recreation*, is an excellent example of the challenges involved in attempting to construct a coherent narrative of the Midwest. At the start of the episode, each department of the local government is tasked with creating a design for a new mural in the City Hall building because citizens continually deface "The Spirit of Pawnee" painting in protest of its racist imagery. Throughout the series, the building's numerous murals (said to have been designed by government employees in the 1930s) are recurring visual jokes, as they depict troublesome occurrences and regressive attitudes from the town's past. In this instance, "The Spirit of Pawnee" features overtly racist caricatures of Chinese, Irish, and Native American individuals, and a train bears down on two members of the latter group. As Leslie Knope observes about the image, "We . . . need better, less-offensive history."[22]

Over the course of the episode, Leslie and her coworkers struggle to define "The Spirit of Pawnee" in the twenty-first century. Each character produces a bizarre potential replacement for the problematic mural: Tom Haverford (Aziz Ansari) pays an art student to produce a painting, which is an abstract blend of random shapes and colors; Ann Perkins (Rashida Jones) crafts a poorly illustrated park, complete with pictures of animals cut from magazines; Donna Meagle (Retta) makes a collage inspired by Leonardo da Vinci's *The Last Supper*, but with "famous people" born in Indiana replacing the original figures (after struggling to find thirteen notable individuals from the state, Donna substitutes "a NASCAR" for a human being); Jerry Gergich (Jim O'Heir) produces a pointillist image in which "each dot is a photo of a citizen of the town"; intern April Ludgate (Aubrey Plaza) designs a multimedia installation made from garbage, replete with video monitors of knee surgery and an oversized hamster wheel in which a man would run, scream, and be fed raw meat; finally, Leslie presents a photograph of the town's worst disaster, a fire at the Pawnee Bread Factory that killed several people in 1922. These competing designs exemplify the uncertainty of the Midwest's identity. Is a Midwestern community reducible to its most tragic moments or most visibly successful inhabitants? Is the Midwest defined by the refuse created by its occupants or by the aggregate lives of those individuals? *Parks and Recreation* further affirms the indeterminate nature of Midwestern identity through the characters' solution for their sharply contrasting murals. Leslie suggests that they cut out "the best parts of all of [their] designs" and piece together an unwieldy mosaic—the "camel" of the episode's title—that reflects their incongruous attempts to capture the meaning of Pawnee. At the episode's conclusion, none of the new designs are chosen as a suitable replacement. Instead, the racist imagery of "The Spirit of Pawnee" mural is given a revisionist title: "The Diversity Express."[23]

Such debates about regional identity are made explicit in numerous studies of the Midwest. While reflecting on being a professional writer living in the Midwest, David Radavich addresses the region's blank image: "The Midwest has a reputation of being the 'not' place—not the impassioned South, not the establishment East, not the romanticized West. It seems to fall between, an absence that stays the rest of the country, that holds other regions together like a gluing block in carpentry."[24] Journalist Richard C. Longworth disregards the "official" twelve-state definition of the region and writes, "The Midwest presents a blurry landscape, a squishy concept, an area with no real boundaries. It doesn't begin or end so much as it oozes into the East on one end and the Great Plains on the other. In the north, it looks like Canada. In the south, it sounds like Arkansas."[25] As such, Longworth describes the Midwest as "a region with no regional feel."[26] He later opines, "Most Midwestern states don't really hang together— politically, economically, or socially."[27] Cayton and Gray similarly observe that "the Midwest lacks the kind of geographic coherence, historical issues, and cultural touchstones that have informed regional identity in the American South, West, and New England."[28] Despite the Midwest's apparent incoherence—or perhaps because of it—Cayton and Gray write that the space "is generally considered both the most American and the most amorphous of regions."[29] Elsewhere, Cayton labels the Midwest as an "anti-region" that had "so thoroughly embodied the fictions of the *national* discourse that there was . . . no urgent need for regionality in the Midwest."[30] According to Cayton, Midwesterners lack a "discourse of regionality," which ensures that "the Midwest's reputation has to do with empty normalcy."[31] In the introduction to a special issue of *GLQ* organized around the topic of "Queering the Middle," Martin F. Manalansan IV, Chantal Nadeau, Richard T. Rodríguez, and Siobhan B. Somerville assert, "The middle creates less a magisterial panoramic perspective than a queer vantage—a troubled, unstable perch buttressed by the dominance of the coasts and the 'South.'"[32] Finally, historian Jon K. Lauck identifies the Midwest as a "lost region" that "has become a foreign country, seldom visited or discussed while serving as a periodic source of exotica, but largely off the main map of American historiography and lost to the main channels of historical inquiry."[33]

Together, these descriptions—"blurry landscape," "anti-region," "empty normalcy," "'not' place," "an absence," "a troubled, unstable perch," "lost region"— configure the Midwest as a geographic and cultural void that is staid and utterly unremarkable. This perceived absence of Midwestern distinctiveness results in the region having malleable meanings in American culture. Like a regional version of a black hole, the Midwest's impenetrable blankness seems to siphon culture and attributes from elsewhere while obscuring its own constitutive properties, which leads to the divergent meanings of Midwestern identity on display in texts such as the *Parks and Recreation* episode previously discussed. Furthermore, by virtue of (supposedly) having few or no defining traits, the concept of the "normal" Midwest is susceptible to being appropriated in support of extraregional ideological and political agendas; the Midwest's meaning in American culture changes at different moments in history as attitudes about the region fluctuate in response to broader national circumstances. To some degree, then, the region may represent whatever observers want it to represent, from being culturally backwards to serving as the most idealized of American spaces. In this way, the Midwest's ill-defined identity situates it as a contested space.

Media coverage of the Midwest during national elections provides a clear illustration of the region's flexible meaning in American culture. For example, while discussing the 2000 presidential election, journalist Thomas Frank exposes how the electoral map becomes a text by which this reductive regional dynamic is visually represented. Through the blunt image of a "red" and "blue" state electoral map, large geographic portions of the United States were identified solely as Republican or Democratic, regardless of how close the polls may have been.[34] Frank writes,

> From this one piece of evidence, the electoral map, the pundits simply veered off into authoritative-sounding cultural proclamation. Just by looking at the map, they reasoned, we could easily tell that George W. Bush was the choice of the plain people, the grassroots Americans who inhabited the place we know as the "heartland," a region of humility, guilelessness, and, above all, stout yeoman *righteousness*. The Democrats, on the other hand, were the party of the elite. Just by looking at the map we could see that liberals were sophisticated, wealthy, and materialistic. While the big cities blued themselves shamelessly, the *land* knew what it was about and went Republican, by a margin in square miles of four to one.... The red-state narrative brought majoritarian legitimacy to a president who had actually lost the popular vote. It also allowed conservatives to present their views as the philosophy of a region that Americans—even sophisticated urban ones—traditionally venerate as the repository of national virtue, a place of plain speaking and straight shooting.[35]

The electoral map depicted a vast swath of red cutting across the country, encompassing much of the Midwest and becoming a new defining image of the region. As a widely circulated text, the electoral map served to enclose and mark off ideological territories in the public consciousness. Even as the region of "national virtue" was shaded red by the media in 2000, though, the Illinois Senate was the launching point for the career of Bush's Democratic presidential successor, Barack Obama.

The close results of recent presidential elections in the Midwest—as well as the status of many states as key "swing states"—points to the inherent heterogeneity of Midwestern culture, despite a persistent tendency within the media to impose essentialist narratives on the region. Ohio and Iowa, for instance, were won by Bush in 2004, by Obama in 2008 and 2012, and by Republican Donald Trump in 2016. Wisconsin and Michigan twice went to Obama before swinging back to the GOP. Given the close polling results within several of these Midwestern states—in some cases, Trump and Democratic nominee Hillary Clinton were separated by only one or two percentage points—the 2016 election especially demonstrates the Midwest's fragmented cultural condition, which is belied by the homogenizing visual of "red" or "blue" on the electoral map. Indeed, media fascination with the belligerent campaign and surprising election of Trump led to numerous think pieces on the identities and values of his purportedly invisible supporters, particularly those living in the Midwest. Twenty years after *The Onion* satirically "discovered" the Midwest, mainstream news outlets belatedly embarked on exploratory missions into the nation's central region. Pieces appeared in publications such as the *New York Times*, the *Washington Post*, *The Atlantic*, and *The Guardian* that related narratives of Midwestern communities and individuals who felt forgotten and ignored by politicians or were otherwise marginalized by economic, social, and racial factors.[36] In the wake of the election, swing states remained sites of exceptional fascination; for instance, a variety of articles covered Wisconsin's patchwork identity. From the simmering resentment running throughout rural white areas of the state to a deep sense of disillusionment among African Americans in an impoverished Milwaukee neighborhood, such articles collectively created a more nuanced portrait of the turmoil and contrasting experiences that mark both Wisconsin and the Midwest.[37]

Both explicit and implicit notions of authenticity cling to narratives about the Midwest, from works of fiction to ostensibly empirical accounts, such as election coverage. Moreover, the recurring ascription of authenticity to the region has nostalgic connotations that confine the Midwest within a peculiar temporal state. Midwestern culture is consistently rendered as anachronistic because the region is said to exemplify idealized (i.e., "authentic") American traits and values that no longer are detectible elsewhere—if they ever existed at all. In this book, I trace the historical trajectory of the Midwest as an American space of nostalgia by identifying and analyzing changing iterations of the region's nostalgic identity across the twentieth and early twenty-first centuries. To provide context for the chapters that follow, a more precise understanding of nostalgia is necessary.

Nostalgic Spatiality, Nostalgic Violence, and Nostalgic Atonement

In forums ranging from popular culture to academia, nostalgia is regularly asserted as intrinsic to the Midwest's default identity. Yet within both fictional narratives and scholarly studies of the region, nostalgia itself is treated in a rather limited manner, if any critical discussion of the term is even broached at all.[38] Often, the linkage between nostalgia and the Midwest is attached to those categories of identity and ideology that are configured as "traditional" in American culture. More specifically, a standard image of Midwesterners consistently is that of a white, middle-class, heteronormative, conservative populace that resembles the change-adverse inhabitants of Gopher Prairie in Sinclair Lewis's *Main Street* (1920) and the mundane Heck family in ABC's *The Middle* (2009–2018).[39] By reducing nostalgia solely to the domain of cultural categories, however, nostalgia's complex temporal and spatial dimensions are obscured. My project intervenes in this established regional discourse by unearthing the spatiotemporal properties of nostalgia within Midwestern texts and by revealing how multiple iterations of nostalgia shape the popular identity of the Midwest.

I use the term "nostalgia" to refer to a general preoccupation with idealized imagery of the past and a related desire to reenact or somehow to relive that past which has been lost or potentially is entirely fabricated. My emphasis on the possibility (or even probability) that nostalgia revolves around a fictional, invented past is influenced by Susan Stewart and Svetlana Boym, both of whom theorize the problematic narratives that nostalgic subjects are prone to creating. For Boym, "reflective nostalgia" and "restorative nostalgia" are two "tendencies" or "ways of giving shape and meaning to longing."[40] Whereas reflective nostalgia is a rather innocuous concern "with historical and individual time, with the irrevocability of the past and human finitude," restorative nostalgia seeks to construct an "invented tradition" that "knows two main narrative plots—the restoration of origins and the conspiracy theory. . . ."[41] As a "conspiratorial worldview," restorative nostalgia envisions that the desired "home" remains "forever under siege, requiring defense against the plotting enemy."[42] Similar to Boym's restorative nostalgia, Stewart argues, "By the narrative process of nostalgic reconstruction the present is denied and the past takes on an authenticity of being, an authenticity which, ironically, it can achieve only through narrative. . . . Nostalgia, like any form of narrative, is always ideological: the past it seeks has never existed except as narrative."[43] The nostalgic subject desires an imagined past that is elevated as more authentic than the lived present. In a similar manner, American popular culture produces visions of the Midwest that inevitably carry and transmit ideological values, particularly through the juxtaposition of the central region with other spaces. By considering questions of region and temporality alongside with one another, the process by which nostalgia conjures up fanciful, subjective impressions of time and spaces alike becomes more transparent.

To avoid the vague treatment of nostalgia that characterizes much commentary about the Midwest, I refine nostalgia as a critical framework for regional analysis with my concepts of nostalgic spatiality, nostalgic violence, and nostalgic atonement. The textual foundations for these forms of nostalgia bridge various disciplines and mediums, including historical, sociological, geographic, journalistic, literary, and filmic materials. Building on the theories of Boym and Stewart, my work on nostalgia emerges in conjunction with an examination of the Midwest's cultural formation in such disparate texts as *The Onion*, *Native Son*, and *Gran Torino* (2008).[44] Across a broad spectrum of materials, I identify a recurring presentation of the Midwest as a spatial abstraction; further, this regional image is frequently intertwined with the violent regulation of behaviors and appearances within Midwestern narratives. Although my focus is on underexamined elements within various discourses about the Midwest, this project is not intended as a refutation of prior commentary on the region. Instead, my work expands upon critical studies of the Midwest in order to show how understandings of the region's physical and cultural parameters have been shaped by the spatiotemporal and violent aspects of nostalgia, as exhibited in multiple types of texts (with a particular emphasis on cinema).

Nostalgic spatiality is evident in nearly every primary textual object that I consider in this book. From the disastrous migration eastward in Theodore Dreiser's *Sister Carrie* to filmmaker David Lynch's extensive use of dissolves to distort space and time in *The Straight Story* (1999), nostalgic spatiality is a regular component of Midwestern representational conventions.[45] The operations of nostalgic spatiality, though, are not always readily apparent on the surface of a given text. Within Midwestern narratives, nostalgic spatiality is an altered sense of space that corresponds to the nostalgic experience of time; this merging of spatial and temporal elements exacerbates the feeling that an untraversable distance separates present circumstances from a desired ideal located elsewhere or "else-when." Upon recognizing the recurrent effects of nostalgic spatiality on the region's identity, a crucial task becomes clear: locating the origins of the linkage between nostalgia and the Midwest. As with the lost objects of nostalgic desire, identifying the textual bases of nostalgic spatiality necessitates beginning in the near-present and working backwards to a distant point of origin.

For my project, the most influential region-oriented media scholarship is Victoria Johnson's *Heartland TV: Prime Time Television and the Struggle for U.S. Identity* (2008).[46] In this book, Johnson examines how popular perceptions of the Midwest have been shaped through the content of network television and the television industry's development over the course of the twentieth century. As background for this undertaking, Johnson addresses fluctuating cultural attitudes about the Midwest's defining "Heartland myth." She writes:

> Positively embraced as the locus of solid dependability, cultural populism, and producerist, "plain folks" independence, the Midwest as Heartland, in this iteration, symbolizes the ideal nation (in other words, "We the People" are, ideally, midwesterners). Conversely, the Midwest Heartland also functions as an object of derision—condemned for its perceived naiveté and lack of mobility as a site of hopelessly rooted, outdated American past life and values, entrenched political and social conservatism, and bastion of the "mass," undifferentiated, un-hip people and perspectives—and in this iteration, the Midwest becomes the "other" against which the ideal nation is defined by relief ("We the People" are *not* midwestern, in principle).[47]

Within this insightful passage, I identify traces of the atemporal nostalgic properties that are integral components of so many texts about the region. Of particular note is Johnson's assertion that Midwesterners are perceived as having a "lack of mobility" and that the region perpetuates the "past life and values" that no longer exist elsewhere in the country. These observations touch on how the Midwest's spatial centrality grants it a sort of elliptical status, at once separated from the rest of the nation by its physical expanse and by its anachronistic cultural qualities. Pushing this notion further, it may be extrapolated that the Midwest is not simply understood as old-fashioned in terms of its inhabitants' tastes and behaviors; rather, the regional landscape itself contains the past by virtue of being a geographic and temporal bubble.

Cultural geographer James R. Shortridge provides an additional segment of the historical connection between nostalgia and the Midwest. Shortridge claims that the region became defined as a "pastoral ideal—a haven midway between the corruptions of urban civilization and the dangerous, untamed wilderness" in the early years of the twentieth century.[48] This understanding of the Midwest gained cultural traction due to "a natural tendency for an Eastern-dominated popular press to report about Middle-western events that differed from life in the East. . . ."[49] Over the course of the twentieth century, media outlets effectively sculpted the popular image of the Midwest by nostalgically reducing it to a pastoral, nonurban space.[50]

Shortridge elaborates on the nostalgic implications of the pastoral label by articulating a provocative spatial metaphor for the Midwest that continues to inform the region's popular identity. During the 1950s, "small towns and traditional farms, indeed the entire Middle-western culture, began to be labeled quaint."[51] As Shortridge explains, this nostalgic reassessment became "perhaps the dominant image that outsiders held about the region. From this perspective, the Middle West had become a museum of sorts. No up-and-coming citizen wanted to live there, but it had importance as a repository for traditional values. The Middle West was a nice place to visit occasionally and to reflect upon one's heritage. It was America's collective 'hometown,' a place with good air, picturesque farm buildings, and unpretentious 'simple' people."[52] The notion of the Midwest as a nostalgia museum situates the region outside of a linear flow of time, and this temporal dynamic is accentuated by the peculiar spatial properties that recur in numerous Midwestern texts. As a "museum of sorts," the Midwest is imagined to be a space in which the past is accessible; many of the Midwestern narratives considered in the following chapters reflect this perception by depicting the temporal convergence of past and present within the spatial boundaries of the region. Clearly, the Midwest-as-museum label is an overt example of nostalgic spatiality, yet it only emerges in the middle of the twentieth century. The roots of nostalgic spatiality extend even further into the past.

From 1893 to 1918, Frederick Jackson Turner set about determining the meaning of the United States' western expansion, as well as defining the identities of the nation's regions, particularly the Midwest.[53] Although Turner's claims have been disputed on multiple fronts, his mythologization of the frontier and regional spaces endures within the American consciousness. Historian Richard Slotkin outlines how myth damages historical knowledge and asserts, "What is lost when history is translated into myth is *the essential premise of history—the distinction of past and present itself.* The past is made metaphorically equivalent to the present; and the present appears simply as a repetition of persistently recurring structures identified with the past."[54] Although Slotkin never uses the term "nostalgia," his critique essentially suggests that conflating mythology and history produces the temporal goal of nostalgia: to collapse the past and the present into a form of simultaneity. In this light, Turner's mythological account of the frontier and his idealized descriptions of the Midwest together perform the nostalgic task of bringing the past into the present. Significantly, Turner's writings in the late nineteenth and early twentieth centuries overlap with the term "Midwest" gaining popular usage and a common understanding in American discourse.[55] Beyond being a mere coincidence, this concurrent scholarly and cultural attentiveness to regional identity enables the multifaceted linkage between nostalgia and the Midwest—in terms of both culture and spatiality—to solidify.

I read Turner not only as a historian but also, crucially, as an inadvertent theorist of nostalgia. Again and again, Turner projects his own desires onto the spaces and historical developments that he details. Throughout Turner's writings, he invents idealistic narratives about "civilization," race, individualism, labor, and family. Across these topics, Turner compulsively returns to an allegedly "lost" state of existence located only in the unique temporal and spatial conditions of the frontier. By the end of the nineteenth century, Turner frames his nostalgic dismay over the closing of the frontier as a national crisis and writes, "This, then, is the real situation: a people composed of heterogeneous materials, with diverse and conflicting ideals and social interests, having passed from the task of filling up the vacant spaces of the continent, is *now thrown back upon itself*, and is seeking an equilibrium."[56] Essentially, Turner crafts a model of western expansion that functions as a spatial version of nostalgia's temporal dynamic: linear progress to a point and then a looping return inward. In subsequent essays that span the first two decades of the twentieth century, Turner further expounds the effects of the traumatic frontier closure by transferring his idealized frontier qualities onto the Midwest, which occupies a position midway between the established East and the developing West. By Turner's reasoning, the Midwest is the closest remaining approximation to the space and culture of the lost frontier.

These aspects of Turner's writings have major repercussions for the study of nostalgia and the Midwest. In addition to spatializing nostalgia's looping temporality as described above, Turner uses this model of nostalgia to project his frontier "ideals of equality, freedom of opportunity, [and] faith in the common man" onto the entirety of the Midwest.[57] For Turner, western expansion is no longer possible, but the Midwest's central location enables the region to house the lost qualities of the frontier. As such, Turner links nostalgic perceptions of space with nostalgic understandings of culture through a mythologized conceptualization of the Midwest. The importance of the Midwest's spatial status becomes clearer when considered in relation to de Certeau's observations about the properties of frontier spaces within stories. De Certeau identifies "a paradox of the frontier: created by contacts, the points of differentiation between two bodies are also their common points. Conjunction and disjunction are inseparable in them.... A middle place, composed of interactions and inter-views, the frontier is a sort of void, a narrative sym-bol of exchanges and encounters."[58] In addition to having numerous points of spatial contact with other regions, Turner's version of the Midwest as the embodiment of frontier culture also features points of temporal contact. Within this Midwestern context, a revised "paradox of the frontier" would specify that for a frontier with both spatial and temporal points of contact—a *nostalgic* frontier—the "two bodies" in contact with one another might also be two temporalities: past and present. Well before the mid-twentieth-century recognition of the Midwest as a nostalgia museum, Turner establishes the middle region as a void-like space of nostalgia for American culture and history—a region defined by a paradoxically internal "conjunction and disjunction" of different temporal moments.[59] At the same historical period when the Midwest becomes recognized as a twelve-state territory within the American popular discourse, Turner fixes the region's identity as a culturally anachronistic realm with abstract spatiotemporal properties. From this point through the early decades of the twenty-first century, nostalgic spatiality permeates the form and content of Midwestern narratives across medium and genre.

Along with this nostalgic experience of space, a second, more destructive iteration of nostalgia is detectible in Midwestern texts during the latter half of the twentieth century. Since the early 1970s, representations of the Midwest repeatedly depict nostalgic spatiality as instilling the region's inhabitants—especially white males—with violent impulses. In response to texts such as *Badlands* (1973) and *Halloween* (1978), I formulate the concept of nostalgic violence, which functions as an analytical framework for understanding instances in which nostalgia transforms from a perceptual phenomenon into a regulatory activity.[60] More than simply being an altered perception of space or time, nostalgic violence is an active manipulation of individuals and communities so that the present might *appear* as the nostalgic subject *imagines* the desired past to be. For instance, as detailed in chapter 4, Kimberly Peirce's *Boys Don't Cry* (1999) depicts how a disruption to the normalized authority of white, heterosexual men subsequently prompts brutal acts of violence against the film's transgender protagonist in a destructively nostalgic attempt to regulate gender identity and sexual orientation within the film's Nebraska setting.[61] In the same chapter, I identify David Cronenberg's *A History of Violence* as another prime example of nostalgic violence being deployed in order to manipulate and sustain the illusion of a Midwestern community's placid surface. In *A History of Violence*, the protagonist masks his criminal background by brutally killing former associates who threaten to expose the invented fiction of his nostalgic identity as a small-town Midwestern family man and proprietor of a local diner. As these examples demonstrate, portrayals of nostalgic violence complement and extend the impacts of nostalgic spatiality by more overtly spotlighting the often-regressive ideological values attached to desire for the past.

After examining nostalgic violence, I felt that it was necessary to consider how nostalgia might also produce progressive outcomes, which led me to conceptualize nostalgic atonement. By imagining a flipside to the paranoiac and conspiratorial dimensions of Boym's restorative nostalgia, I began to recognize a form of nostalgia in selected Midwestern texts that inverts the typical nostalgic relationship to the past. Instead of yearning for a mythical version of the past, nostalgic atonement acknowledges the lingering effects of the past's flaws within the present; it produces desire to repair the damaged past, rather than reactionary efforts to reshape the present in the image of an idealized, mythologized past. Perhaps the purest example of nostalgic atonement is *The Straight Story*, a film that depicts the real-life occurrence of Alvin Straight travelling across the Midwest on a riding lawnmower in order to reconcile with his estranged brother. David Lynch portrays Alvin's journey as a transcendent experience that is contingent upon his nostalgic atonement for personal failings.

With the concepts of nostalgic spatiality, nostalgic violence, and nostalgic atonement, I show how the Midwest's popular identity is forged across a broad lineage of texts that stretch back to Turner's frontier writings. Despite the Midwest often being defined solely in terms of cultural categories, such attributes actually materialize in conjunction with the configuration of the region as an abstract spatiotemporal realm. In the chapters that follow, the selected Midwestern texts serve as models for reconceptualizing nostalgia in terms of its effects on the perception of space, its insidious potential to inspire acts of regulatory violence, and its ability to generate a reparatory attitude toward the past. *The American Midwest in Film and Literature* details how the immense, veiled power of nostalgia manifests and is made discernable in depictions of the Midwest, as well as how the region's identity, in turn, is a product of those nostalgic operations.

Nostalgia, Location, Cinema

The concepts of nostalgic spatiality, nostalgic violence, and nostalgic atonement are this book's contributions to the robust, diverse area of film, television, and media studies that is concerned with nostalgia. While ruminating on the outcomes of studying nostalgia and cinema, film scholar Pam Cook asserts that such work "is a question of analysing the complex, transformative relationship of the texts to history itself, of reading and interpreting what they have to tell us about that relationship, so that our knowledge of historical representation is advanced."[62] As Cook advocates, my attention to the multiple forms of nostalgia in Midwestern narratives constitutes an effort to make sense of the imbricated dynamics of cultural memory, textual representation, and actual historical circumstance. To the extent that such an endeavor is possible, these three concepts begin to disentangle the overlapping, mutually-influencing ways in which the past is processed as a narrative and an idea—that is, how individual and cultural perceptions of the past influence beliefs and actions in the present. Although I develop nostalgic spatiality, nostalgic violence, and nostalgic atonement within a region-specific framework, it is my hope that these analytical tools will be of value for engaging with the operations of nostalgia in numerous contexts and textual objects.

Contained within the academic study of nostalgia in cinema, television, and media is a growing subsection of work that examines such topics in rather precise geographic contexts. This exciting panoply of scholarship coheres around spatial constructs that range from national cinemas to continental scales to more compact, intranational locales, such as regions or cities. Rather than attempting a lengthy overview of this corpus, it will suffice to simply cite a few examples that speak to its manifold nature. For instance, Rey Chow analyzes Stanley Kwan's *Rouge* (1987) in order to explicate a late twentieth-century "upsurge of nostalgia in Hong Kong" culture and cinema.[63] Jean Ma expands upon Chow's work by identifying and theorizing "a problematic of temporal dislocation underlying contemporary Chinese cinema" that results, in part, from cultural nostalgia.[64] In a study of Turkish cinema since the mid-1990s, Asuman Suner identifies a spectrum of political positions manifesting in "popular nostalgia films" that "emphasize subjective accounts of memory shaped around a strong sense of nostalgia."[65] Such texts "enable the audience to revisit their own past and consider new ways of representing their cultural identity."[66] While detailing temporal critique in cinema, Bliss Cua Lim eschews the "imagined unity of a national cinema" in favor of a methodology that juxtaposes films produced in numerous Asian nations; throughout Lim's project, nostalgia reappears as an impactful temporal force in various case studies.[67] Among the diverse national origins of films that Cook considers in her discussion of nostalgia and memory, a major section of her book focuses more narrowly on such topics within key segments of British film history.[68]

To varying degrees, scholarship on nostalgia in the cinema and culture of the United States features approaches that complement those described above. For example, Vera Dika primarily writes about American films while interrogating how the nostalgic re-appropriation of "past media images" and "old generic elements" may yield meaningful "confrontations with the present."[69] Christine Sprengler similarly envisions a productive outcome of recognizing and assessing nostalgia in American cinema. Sprengler concludes her project by reasserting the ongoing importance of a millennial-era "cycle of nostalgia films" because such texts "are valuable cultural objects with the potential to source critical engagements with the past and testify to the nature and limits of our present historical consciousness."[70] Beyond exclusively filmic examples, Lynn Spigel considers a group of twenty-first-century television series—*Mad Men* (2007–2015) being the most successful case study—that depict American culture in the 1960s.[71] Such series undermine "previous forms of baby-boom nostalgia" partly because "this nostalgia for the *Mad Men* era is all about imagining a future where feminism never happened, but where somehow miraculously, without political struggle, everyone gets a great job, great clothes and great mixed drinks."[72] Spigel addresses this apparently contradictory sense of history by observing that "the greatest paradox of this new form of nostalgia is the fact that the future it imagines is precisely the future that contemporary young women are not likely to achieve. . . . This is a strange temporal structure of desire—a longing for a past that looks like a better future than the one they will achieve."[73] Here, as in so many texts, nostalgic visions of the past produce desire for objects or socioeconomic standings that remain forever out of reach.

Once again, this concise review of scholarship is not intended to be comprehensive, and I certainly do not wish to conflate the uniqueness or oversimplify the complexities of these disparate contexts and approaches to studying nostalgia in film, television, and media. While seeking to avoid limiting notions of equivalency, my purpose is to reflect upon recurrent methods and postulates across the ever-expanding body of work on nostalgia and location. An important point of continuity that emerges from these diverse examples is a shared conviction that nostalgia—as a force that shapes textual objects and culture—has the potential to alternately elide or shine a light on ideologies that inform the construction of history and propel the cultural trajectory of a given space. With this book, I bring representations of the Midwest into this running discourse.

Midwestern Narratives and Nostalgic Problematics

The American Midwest in Film and Literature is divided into two halves based on chronology and methodology. The first three chapters form "Part I: Twentieth-Century Narratives of Nostalgia and the Midwest," and the last three chapters form "Part II: The Millennial Midwest on Film." Each of the six chapters examines the nostalgic dynamics that structure Midwestern narratives produced or set in periods of upheaval in American culture. The first three chapters address Midwestern identity during, respectively, the turn of the twentieth century, the Great Depression and World War II era, and the 1970s. Part II features an extended consideration of the years surrounding the dawn of the twenty-first century; this moment of renewed turmoil has prompted widespread consternation regarding the Midwest's declining economic and cultural status.

Both halves of this book are further distinguished by their primary textual objects. Part I considers twentieth-century understandings and representations of the Midwest across a variety of disciplines and mediums, while Part II primarily focuses on filmic depictions of the Midwest from the late 1990s into the second decade of the new millennium. The purpose of this distinction is to show how certain recurring elements in cinematic depictions of the Midwest (including, in Part I, twentieth-century films produced after the onset of the sound era) are variations on and expansions of representational conventions that first were established in historical, sociological, and literary texts. For instance, over the first three chapters, I analyze materials such as Turner's writings and *Middletown: A Study in Modern American Culture* (1929) in order to illustrate how those texts influenced subsequent representations of the Midwest by establishing racial and class aspects of the region's nostalgia-based identity.[74] The nostalgic problematics of the Midwest's identity are especially visible in filmic depictions of the region, which invariably contain traces of previous Midwestern narratives.

Chapter 1, "Nostalgic Spatiality," focuses on the turn of the twentieth century. This is the period during which popular awareness of the Midwestern label develops in American culture and the region's identity becomes linked to nostalgia. The chapter's key textual objects are selected writings by Frederick Jackson Turner, Theodore Dreiser's novel, *Sister Carrie* (1900), and filmmaker Vincente Minnelli's musical, *Meet Me in St. Louis* (1944). Although this latter film was not produced at the turn of the century, its narrative is set in 1903 and 1904; as such, the film complements the older texts by providing insights into how the early twentieth-century Midwest is perceived in popular culture nearly fifty years later. The central concern of this chapter involves rereading Turner as a nostalgia writer in order to reveal how his work helps to establish the Midwest as a space of nostalgia. Through my analysis of Turner, I develop the concept of "nostalgic spatiality." As detailed earlier, Turner's theories about western expansion (particularly its eventual completion) provide a spatial analogue to the temporal paradigm of nostalgia. *Sister Carrie* and *Meet Me in St. Louis* both feature narratives full of anxiety regarding spatial and temporal dislocation, as well as nostalgia for a sense of stability that characters believe to be located in the Midwest.

Chapter 2, "Spatial Constriction, Race, and Midwestern Stagnation," examines Turner's conception of the Midwest and its relationship to what he claims is the spatially constricted United States during the Great Depression and World War II era. Turner predicts that, due to the inability of the United States to further expand across the continent, American culture will stagnate. In the 1930s and 1940s, the Midwest suffers a declining image in the midst of worldwide turmoil. This chapter's primary textual objects are Robert S. Lynd and Helen Merrell Lynd's *Middletown: A Study in Modern American Culture* (1929), which is a sociological study of Muncie, Indiana, that resembles Turner's work in terms of its lasting influence and troubling methodology; Preston Sturges's satirical film, *The Miracle of Morgan's Creek* (1944); and Richard Wright's forceful novel, *Native Son* (1940).[75] These texts each generate a sense of spatial constriction through the presentation of their respective Midwestern settings as closed-off, isolated locales. Such conditions contribute to the region's overall image as a space of cultural rot and stagnation, and these Midwestern spaces are further linked with oppressive gender and racial norms. Sturges and Wright's narratives feature protagonists who desperately yearn to escape their restrictive Midwestern environments, but cannot. Moreover, these texts frame the Midwest as an antimodern space due, in part, to a regressive culture that is removed from the transformations of modernity occurring elsewhere.

Chapter 3, "Nostalgic Violence, Nebulous Spaces, and Blank Identities," analyzes materials produced during (or that comment on) the 1970s. These texts present the Midwest's physical territory as a nebulous realm filled with blank inhabitants who nostalgically seek to merge the past and present. After beginning with a brief discussion of Michael Lesy's *Wisconsin Death Trip* (1973) and Tim O'Brien's *In the Lake of the Woods* (1994), this chapter traces how Terrence Malick's *Badlands* (1973), Werner Herzog's *Stroszek* (1977), and John Carpenter's *Halloween* (1978) depict the Midwest as a space of temporal collapse, which has disastrous consequences for the region's inhabitants.[76] Of particular note is the representation of deviant white male characters who perpetrate brutal acts of violence. Through these examples, I develop my concept of "nostalgic violence," which refers to violent actions that manipulate the visible present so that it might *appear* as a nostalgic subject *imagines* the desired past to be. In other words, nostalgic violence is deployed in an effort to regulate the surface appearance of a particular space and its inhabitants—in these texts, the Midwest and its blank occupants. Whether a native Midwesterner (as in *Badlands* and *Halloween*) or a transplant (as in *Stroszek*), these three films suggest that dwelling within the region's nostalgic landscape results in a fundamental loss of identity and a violent, insatiable desire to restore subjective visions of the past.

Chapter 4, "Masculinity, Race, and Violence," marks the beginning of the second half of *The American Midwest in Film and Literature*, which focuses primarily on Midwestern films produced from the final years of the twentieth century into the second decade of the twenty-first century. This chapter expands upon my earlier discussion of performativity and nostalgic violence by examining such elements in three films: Kimberly Peirce's *Boys Don't Cry* (1999), Clint Eastwood's *Gran Torino* (2008), and David Cronenberg's *A History of Violence* (2005). These films exemplify a recurrent millennial-era Midwestern narrative that counters the often utopic rhetoric about the localized benefits of emergent digital technologies. The Midwestern communities on display in these three films remain largely provincial and culturally isolated. Consequently, geographic proximity and intimate social networks retain a substantial influence on the identities of these films' Midwestern characters. Each film spotlights various cultural forces that help to perpetuate the region's normalized popular image and surface-level placidity. Under the threat of nostalgic violence, rigid norms relating to gender performance, racialized hierarchies of power, and regional identity are enforced across a spectrum of Midwestern communities.

Chapter 5, "Locating Sincerity, Disillusionment, and Paranoia," analyzes a set of texts that engage with the Midwest's increasingly degraded image in the twenty-first century. I begin the chapter by considering the short-lived proclamations about the "end of irony" that circulated throughout the media in the immediate wake of 9/11. The supposed divide between "ironic" and "sincere" entertainments actually mirrored longstanding perceptions of regional stereotypes. As such, this debate about authenticity in the media also reactivated a national dialogue about the meanings of American regions. Soon after this national trauma, though, the "sincere" Midwest quickly regained its status as anachronistic and out-of-touch, especially once the region's identity became associated with the generic "Main Street" victimized by the East's predatory "Wall Street" during the economic crisis in the latter part of the decade. Alexander Payne's *About Schmidt* (2002), Jason Reitman's *Up in the Air* (2009), and Jeff Nichols's *Take Shelter* (2011) respond to this context (or somewhat predict it, in the case of the first film) by depicting disillusionment and paranoia across the Midwest.[77] More precisely, these films challenge the long-elevated primacy of white masculinity in Midwestern imagery and narratives by destabilizing components of the essentialist racial, gender, and class elements that have traditionally informed the Midwest's popular identity. Each film presents troubled white male Midwesterners who seek to restore faltering senses of individual purpose and meaning. The first two films feature protagonists who embark on nostalgic tours of sites with personal significance in order to forge new identities; however, both men ultimately are left with a profound sense of meaninglessness that stems from the region's general decline and their own specific fears of growing irrelevancy. *Take Shelter*'s protagonist, Curtis LaForche, experiences visions of impending destruction, which leads to a fanatical obsession with home security. Compelled by these visions, Curtis obsessively works on a storm shelter, which jeopardizes the safety and financial stability of his family. During this tumultuous historical period, the shared despair of these fictional Midwesterners reflects that of the region as a whole. In these films, the Midwest is imagined as a space in which past potentialities now appear to be foreclosed.

Chapter 6, "Nostalgic Atonement," continues to survey films depicting the millennial Midwest. Here, though, I investigate the progressive potential for nostalgia by introducing a third category of nostalgia: "nostalgic atonement." Early in the chapter, I conceptualize nostalgic atonement by returning to Boym's "restorative nostalgia" and analyzing the climactic scenes in Debra Granik's *Winter's Bone* (2010) and Gregg Araki's *Mysterious Skin* (2004).[78] Nostalgic atonement flips the dynamic of how nostalgia typically juxtaposes the past and the present. Rather than the unsatisfactory present producing desire for the past, nostalgic atonement instead recognizes—and attempts to correct or repair—ways in which the flawed past troubles the present. In films with an element of nostalgic atonement, the past is revisited not because it is preferable to the present, but because it is damaged and has lingering repercussions that must be addressed and demystified. After my preliminary discussion of nostalgic atonement, I turn to Sofia Coppola's *The Virgin Suicides* (1999) and David Lynch's *The Straight Story* (1999).[79] Both of these films are extended ruminations on ways in which nostalgia affects memory and history. In addition, I use *The Virgin Suicides* and *The Straight Story* to further consider the aesthetics of nostalgia: how cinema as a medium represents nostalgia on the level of form. In the case of these two films, the dissolve edit produces brief instances of spatial and temporal simultaneity—a basic desire of nostalgic subjects. Lynch's film especially makes use of the dissolve, and he renders the Midwest as a nostalgic space comprising overlapping temporalities.

A brief conclusion chapter provides an overview of the book. Following the conclusion is an afterword, "Regionalism and Politics," that has two primary areas of focus. First, the afterword examines the nostalgic and regional dimensions of the 2016 presidential election. I survey assessments of the election that address cultural narratives of nostalgia, failure, and resentment. From this starting point, I show how the contemporary confluence of regional mythologies and politics may be traced backwards across textual representations of the Midwest. In particular, a short story from Hamlin Garland's *Main-Travelled Roads* (1891)—entitled "Up the Coulé: A Story of Wisconsin"—offers insights about twenty-first-century cultural dynamics through its depiction of rural/urban tensions, issues of race and gender, and ideological debates about failure and success.[80] Second, I discuss a growing documentary tradition that covers aspects of Midwestern history and culture. Beginning with Michael Moore's *Roger & Me* (1989), numerous documentaries have addressed many of the Midwest's problems and challenges in the late twentieth and early twenty-first centuries.[81] Often, the subjects of these films explicitly comment on forms of Midwestern failure during this era. Rather than extensively analyzing these documentaries, my purpose is to sketch out the parameters of an alternate way in which the Midwest is interrogated in American cinema. I also briefly discuss a handful of fictional films that, to varying degrees, utilize documentary-like methods while representing the Midwest. Finally, I provide an extended look at *Two American Families* (2013), a PBS documentary that follows two working class Milwaukee families over a twenty-two-year span.[82] The financial struggles of these families, one white and one black, reflect the millennial-era status of the Midwest and serve as a critique of neoliberal economic policies. Of particular relevance for my project is the distinctly nostalgic sense of temporality that informs these families' relationships to their personal histories and future aspirations. By turning to contemporary politics and the Midwestern documentary tradition, this book concludes by further bringing to light the far-reaching impacts of nostalgia and regional narratives within American culture.

The American Midwest in Film and Literature develops theories of nostalgia in conjunction with a new history of regional identity. I track the evolution and continuity of Midwestern representational conventions across materials produced between the late nineteenth century and the second decade of the twenty-first century. Through analyses of a diverse collection of textual artifacts, the Midwest is revealed as a space of fluctuating meanings. Rather than the staid realm it is often reputed to be, the Midwest is actually a dynamic construct upon which the complexities of cultural identity are contested. Against a backdrop stretching from the closing of the western frontier to the contemporary era of unceasing connectivity, the Midwest is continually imagined as an anachronistic, past-oriented space. This status results, in part, from the projection of abstract spatiotemporal qualities onto the Midwest; indeed, the heavy influence of nostalgia is inextricable from the region's identity. While examining the textual contours of the Midwest, multifarious forms of nostalgia emerge: nostalgic spatiality, nostalgic violence, and nostalgic atonement. Ultimately, along with the specificity of the Midwest and nostalgia as primary areas of study, this book is a contemplation of "past-ness," or how the weight of both cultural and individual memory is brought to bear on the present.

Notes

1. Portions of this chapter have been previously published as Adam Ochonicky, "The Millennial Midwest: Nostalgic Violence in the Twenty-First Century," *Quarterly Review of Film and Video* 32, no. 2 (2015): 124–140, doi: 10.1080/10509208.2013.780937, reprinted by permission of Taylor & Francis, http://www.tandfonline.com; "'Midwest' Discovered Between East, West Coasts," *The Onion*, September 4, 1996, https://www.theonion.com/midwest-discovered-between-east-west-coasts-1819564009.
2. Ibid.
3. "'Midwest' Discovered Between East and West Coasts," *The Onion*, July 6, 2005, https://www.theonion.com/midwest-discovered-between-east-and-west-coasts-1819567923.
4. Ibid.
5. Sherwood Anderson, *Winesburg, Ohio* (1919; repr., New York: Viking Press, 1967), 23.
6. Ibid.
7. Toni Morrison, *Beloved* (1987; repr., New York: Vintage International, 2004).
8. Ibid., 193.
9. *Parks and Recreation* (New York City: NBC, 2009–2015), DVD.

10. Theodore Dreiser, *Sister Carrie*, ed. Claude Simpson (1900; repr., Boston: Houghton Mifflin Company, 1959); Richard Wright, *Native Son* (1940; repr., New York: Harper Perennial Modern Classics, 2005); *Meet Me in St. Louis*, directed by Vincente Minnelli (1944; Burbank, CA: Warner Home Video, 2004), DVD; *Halloween*, directed by John Carpenter (1978; Troy, MI: Anchor Bay Entertainment, 2000), DVD; *A History of Violence*, directed by David Cronenberg (2005; Los Angeles: New Line Home Entertainment, 2006), DVD.

11. Victoria E. Johnson, "The Persistence of Geographic Myth in a Convergent Media Era," *Journal of Popular Film and Television* 38, no. 2 (July 2010): 59, doi: 10.1080/01956051.2010.483341.

12. For extensive commentary on the symbolic meanings of whiteness within the broader contexts of American history and contemporary culture, see: Ta-Nehisi Coates, *We Were Eight Years in Power: An American Tragedy* (New York: One World, 2017).

13. Tamara Winfrey-Harris, "Stop Pretending Black Midwesterners Don't Exist," *New York Times*, June 16, 2018, https://www.nytimes.com/2018/06/16/opinion/sunday/black-midwesterners-trump-politics.html.

14. United States Census Bureau, "Census Regions and Divisions of the United States," United States Census Bureau, last modified February 9, 2015, https://www.census.gov.

15. Raymond Williams, *Keywords: A Vocabulary of Culture and Society*, rev. ed. (New York: Oxford University Press, 1985), 264.

16. Michel de Certeau, *The Practice of Everyday Life*, trans. Steven Rendall (1984; repr., Berkeley: University of California Press, 1988), 115.

17. Ibid., 125.

18. Andrew R. L. Cayton and Susan E. Gray, "The Story of the Midwest: An Introduction," in *The Midwest: Essays on Regional History*, ed. Andrew R. L. Cayton and Susan E. Gray (Bloomington: Indiana University Press, 2001), 4.

19. Douglas Reichert Powell, *Critical Regionalism: Connecting Politics and Culture in the American Landscape* (Chapel Hill: University of North Carolina Press, 2007), 36.

20. Ibid., 65.

21. Cayton and Gray, "The Story of the Midwest," 4.

22. *Parks and Recreation*, season 2, episode 9, "The Camel," directed by Millicent Shelton, aired November 12, 2009, on NBC, DVD.

23. Ibid.

24. David Radavich, "Midwestern Dramas," in *In the Middle of the Middle West: Literary Nonfiction from the Heartland*, ed. Becky Bradway (Bloomington: Indiana University Press, 2003), 186.

25. Richard C. Longworth, *Caught in the Middle: America's Heartland in the Age of Globalism* (2008; repr., New York: Bloomsbury, 2009), 17.

26. Ibid., 21.

27. Ibid., 222.

28. Cayton and Gray, "The Story of the Midwest," 1.

29. Ibid.

30. Andrew R. L. Cayton, "The Anti-region: Place and Identity in the History of the American Midwest," in *The Midwest: Essays on Regional History*, ed. Andrew R. L. Cayton and Susan E. Gray (Bloomington: Indiana University Press, 2001), 157, emphasis in original.

31. Ibid., 158, 142.

32. Martin F. Manalansan IV et al., "Queering the Middle: Race, Region, and a Queer Midwest," *GLQ* 20 no. 1–2 (2014): 1, doi: 10.1215/10642684-2370270.

33. Jon K. Lauck, *The Lost Region: Toward a Revival of Midwestern History* (Iowa City: University of Iowa Press, 2013), 82, 7.

34. Thomas Frank, *What's the Matter with Kansas? How Conservatives Won the Heart of America* (2004; repr., New York: Henry Holt, 2005), 16.

35. Ibid., emphasis in original.

36. The following examples are not intended to be comprehensive, but simply to provide a sampling of this journalistic trend. See: Greg Jaffe and Juliet Eilperin, "Tom Vilsack's Lonely Fight for a 'Forgotten' Rural America," *Washington Post*, September 26, 2016, https://www.washingtonpost.com/politics/tom-vilsacks-lonely-fight-for-a-forgotten-rural-america/2016/09/26/62d7ee64-7830-11e6-ac8e-cf8e0dd91dc7_story.html; Alec MacGillis and ProPublica, "The Original Underclass," *The Atlantic*, September 2016, https://www.theatlantic.com/magazine/archive/2016/09/the-original-underclass/492731/; Kate Linthicum, "'I Feel Forgotten': A Decade of Struggle in Rural Ohio," *The New Yorker*, October 2016, https://www.newyorker.com/culture/photo-booth/i-feel-forgotten-a-decade-of-struggle-in-rural-ohio; Charles M. Blow, "Trump's Rural White America," *New York Times*, November 14, 2016, https://www.nytimes.com/2016/11/14/opinion/trumps-rural-white-america.html; Jane Lindsay, "I Am a Democrat in Rural, Red-State America. My Party Abandoned Us," *The Guardian*, November 15, 2016, https://www.theguardian.com/commentisfree/2016/nov/15/rural-america-working-class-voters-democrats-donald-trump; Richard Cohen, "'Real America' Is Its Own Bubble," *Washington Post*, December 12, 2016, https://www.washingtonpost.com/opinions/real-america-is-its-own-bubble/2016/12/12/e8ba60c2-c09f-11e6-b527-949c5893595e_story.html; Robert Leonard, "Why Rural America Voted for Trump," *New York Times*, January 5, 2017, https://www.nytimes.com/2017/01/05/opinion/why-rural-america-voted-for-trump.html.

37. See: Katherine Cramer, "How Rural Resentment Helps Explain the Surprising Victory of Donald Trump," *Washington Post*, November 13, 2016, https://www.washingtonpost.com/news/monkey-cage/wp/2016/11/13/how-rural-resentment-helps-explain-the-surprising-victory-of-donald-trump/; Sabrina Tavernise, "Many in Milwaukee Neighborhood Didn't Vote—and Don't Regret It," *New York Times*, November 20, 2016, https://www.nytimes.com/2016/11/21/us/many-in-milwaukee-neighborhood-didnt-vote-and-dont-regret-it.html; Rick Romell, "In Western Wisconsin, Trump Voters Want Change," *Milwaukee Journal Sentinel*, November 27, 2016, https://www.jsonline.com/story/news/politics/elections/2016/11/26/western-wisconsin-trump-voters-want-change/94436384/; Jenna Johnson, "This Deeply Blue Wisconsin Village Still Seems Surprised It Voted for Trump," *Washington Post*, January 19, 2017, https://www.washingtonpost.com/politics/this-deeply-blue-wisconsin-village-still-seems-surprised-it-voted-for-trump/2017/01/19/9e9777ca-dd26-11e6-918c-99ede3c8cafa_story.html; Michael Kruse, "'What Do You Do if a Red State Moves to You?': Letter from Pepin County," *Politico*, January/February 2017, https://www.politico.com/magazine/story/2017/01/blue-red-state-democrats-trump-country-214647.

38. For example, Longworth makes several comments about Midwesterners generally having strong nostalgic desire for the past, particularly a version of the past that includes lost industrial labor and idealized rural lifestyles. Although Longworth attributes the longing for rural life to aged Midwesterners, his overall treatment of nostalgia in the Midwest ignores the fact that the region contains urban spaces with heterogeneous populations; elsewhere, Longworth even spends several chapters addressing diverse groups of Midwesterners, yet he does not associate them with the region's supposed nostalgia. Essentially, Longworth's form of Midwestern nostalgia—as with most

discussions of the Midwest and nostalgia—reaffirms perceptions of the rural Midwest's homogeneity and elides the daily experiences of individuals who do not conform to the region's small town image of white, heterosexual, blue-collar workers. See: Longworth, *Caught in the Middle*, 15, 32, 88.

39. Sinclair Lewis, *Main Street* (1920; repr., New York: New American Library, 1980); *The Middle* (New York City: ABC, 2009-2018), broadcast television.

40. Svetlana Boym, *The Future of Nostalgia* (New York: Basic Books, 2001), 41.

41. Ibid., 49, 42-43.

42. Ibid., 43.

43. Susan Stewart, *On Longing: Narratives of the Miniature, the Gigantic, the Souvenir, the Collection* (1993; repr., Durham, NC: Duke University Press, 2007), 23.

44. *Gran Torino*, directed by Clint Eastwood (2008; Burbank, CA: Warner Home Video, 2010), DVD.

45. *The Straight Story*, directed by David Lynch (1999; Burbank, CA: Walt Disney Home Video, 2000), DVD.

46. Victoria E. Johnson, *Heartland TV: Prime Time Television and the Struggle for U.S. Identity* (New York: New York University Press, 2008). Johnson uses the terms "Heartland" and "Midwest" somewhat interchangeably, although the former term encompasses a less precise geographic area than the latter term. As noted earlier, the United States Census Bureau defines the Midwest as twelve states: Ohio, Michigan, Indiana, Illinois, Missouri, Wisconsin, Minnesota, Iowa, North Dakota, South Dakota, Nebraska, and Kansas. For Johnson, the "Heartland" also includes states such as Oklahoma, while I limit my own work to texts that address and/or narratives that are set within one of the Midwestern states as specified by the Census Bureau. Such overlapping but alternate conceptions of the central region reflect common inconsistencies regarding the criteria by which the Midwest is defined (symbolic/cultural traits versus spatial/geographic boundaries).

47. Ibid., 5, emphasis in original.

48. James R. Shortridge, *The Middle West: Its Meaning in American Culture* (Lawrence: University Press of Kansas, 1989), 27-28.

49. Ibid., 56.

50. This version of the Midwest renders the region as an ill-defined territory that varies in relation to how it is perceived. For example, Shortridge discusses a 1980 survey of college students who were asked to create cognitive maps of the Midwest. The participants consistently shifted the Midwest's center westward into the open, less-urban spaces of the Great Plains—a relocation that ignores the region's "official" definition as twelve states. These maps reflect how the region's ostensibly fixed geographic parameters are disconnected from cultural perceptions that realign the Midwest in accordance with nostalgic ideals (such as pastoralism). See: Ibid., 82-96. As I discuss in later chapters, texts such as *The Miracle of Morgan's Creek* (1944) and *Badlands* (1973) depict the Midwest as having similarly nebulous, shifting borders that produce cultural and geographic isolation for the region's (fictional) inhabitants.

51. Ibid., 67.

52. Ibid., 67-68.

53. See: Frederick Jackson Turner, *The Frontier in American History* (1920; repr., Charleston: BiblioBazaar, 2008). This book is a collection of Turner's work that ranges from his most famous and influential piece, "The Significance of the Frontier in American History" (1893), to "Middle Western Pioneer Democracy" (1918).

54. Richard Slotkin, *The Fatal Environment: The Myth of the Frontier in the Age of Industrialization, 1800–1890* (1985; repr. Middletown: Wesleyan University Press, 1986), 24, emphasis added.

55. According to Shortridge, around 1912, the term "Middle West"—and its more common variant, Midwest—gained popular usage as a shared referent to the twelve states of the region. See: Shortridge, *The Middle West*, 24.

56. Turner, *The Frontier in American History*, 186, emphasis added.

57. Ibid., 133.

58. de Certeau, *The Practice of Everyday Life*, 127.

59. Ibid.

60. *Badlands*, directed by Terrence Malick (1973; Burbank, CA: Warner Home Video, 2010), DVD.

61. *Boys Don't Cry*, directed by Kimberly Peirce (1999; Beverly Hills, CA: Twentieth Century Fox Home Entertainment, 2000), DVD.

62. Pam Cook, *Screening the Past: Memory and Nostalgia in Cinema* (London: Routledge, 2005), 16–17.

63. Rey Chow, *Ethics After Idealism: Theory—Culture—Ethnicity—Reading* (Bloomington: Indiana University Press, 1998), 134.

64. Jean Ma, *Melancholy Drift: Marking Time in Chinese Cinema* (Hong Kong: Hong Kong University Press, 2010), 8.

65. Asuman Suner, *New Turkish Cinema: Belonging, Identity and Memory* (London: I. B. Tauris, 2010), 25–26.

66. Ibid., 40.

67. Bliss Cua Lim, *Translating Time: Cinema, the Fantastic, and Temporal Critique* (Durham, NC: Duke University Press, 2009), 34.

68. Cook, *Screening the Past*, 67–112.

69. Vera Dika, *Recycled Culture in Contemporary Art and Film: The Uses of Nostalgia* (Cambridge: Cambridge University Press, 2003), 224.

70. Christine Sprengler, *Screening Nostalgia: Populuxe props and Technicolor aesthetics in contemporary American film* (2009; repr., New York: Berghahn Books, 2011), 172–173.

71. *Mad Men* (New York City: AMC, 2007–2015), DVD.

72. Lynn Spigel, "Postfeminist Nostalgia for a Prefeminist Future," *Screen* 54, no. 2 (Summer 2013): 270, 275, doi: 10.1093/screen/hjt017.

73. Ibid., 274.

74. Robert S. Lynd and Helen Merrell Lynd, *Middletown: A Study in Modern American Culture* (1929; repr., San Diego, CA: Harcourt Brace Jovanovich, 1957).

75. *The Miracle of Morgan's Creek*, directed by Preston Sturges (1944; Hollywood, CA: Paramount Pictures, 2005), DVD.

76. Michael Lesy, *Wisconsin Death Trip* (New York: Pantheon Books, 1973); Tim O'Brien, *In the Lake of the Woods* (1994; repr., New York: Penguin Books, 1995); *Stroszek*, directed by Werner Herzog (1977; Troy, MI: Anchor Bay Entertainment, 2001), DVD.

77. *About Schmidt*, directed by Alexander Payne (2002; Los Angeles: New Line Home Entertainment, 2003), DVD; *Up in the Air*, directed by Jason Reitman (2009; Hollywood, CA: Paramount Pictures, 2010), DVD; *Take Shelter*, directed by Jeff Nichols (2011; Culver City, CA: Sony Pictures Home Entertainment, 2012), DVD.

78. *Winter's Bone*, directed by Debra Granik (Santa Monica, CA: Lionsgate, 2010), DVD; *Mysterious Skin*, Unrated Director's Edition, directed by Gregg Araki (2004; Culver City, CA: Strand Releasing Home Video, 2006), DVD.

79. *The Virgin Suicides*, directed by Sofia Coppola (1999; Hollywood, CA: Paramount Classics, 2000), DVD.

80. Hamlin Garland, *Main-Travelled Roads* (1891; repr., New York: Holt, Rinehart and Winston, 1965).

81. *Roger & Me*, directed by Michael Moore (1989; Burbank, CA: Warner Home Video, 2003), DVD.

82. *Frontline*, season 31, episode 14, *Two American Families*, written by Kathleen Hughes and Bill Moyers, featuring Bill Moyers, aired July 9, 2013, on PBS, https://www.pbs.org/wgbh/frontline/film/two-american-families/.

Part I
Twentieth-Century Narratives of Nostalgia and the Midwest

1 | Nostalgic Spatiality

In "To Be a Native Middle-Westerner" (1999), Indiana-born Kurt Vonnegut reflects on the identity of his home region and writes, "What geography can give all Middle Westerners, along with the fresh water and topsoil, if they let it, is awe for an Edenic continent stretching forever in all directions."[1] Due to the Midwest's centrality, Vonnegut suggests that Midwesterners are uniquely capable of perceiving what he glowingly describes as the uncorrupted expanse of the North American continent. Imagined in this way, the Midwest functions as a transitional space that accentuates the enviable qualities of bordering regions. In other words, the perimeter of the Midwest may be understood as a circular frontier of sorts through which Midwesterners gaze in "awe" at neighboring locales. Such sentiments about the middle region are hardly unique, as Vonnegut's reflections are yet another variation on recurring conceptions of the Midwest as a blank space that effectively defines other regions by comparison. Notably, visions of continental emptiness or vacancy are also dependent upon a troubling elision of indigenous populations whose mere existence belies the sense of "original" or "first settlement" implicit in the "Edenic" label. Of further significance, Vonnegut's statement at the cusp of the new millennium echoes how Frederick Jackson Turner nostalgically linked the Midwest and the vanishing western frontiers roughly a century earlier.

Nostalgia is the key factor in shaping the Midwest's identity in American culture, and Turner's writings on the frontier and the Midwest are crucial foundations for my study of Midwestern identity in popular culture.[2] Later chapters will consider the lingering influence of Turner on regional representations even in the twenty-first century. Here, I use Turner's work to establish the early twentieth century as the period in which the Midwest first became widely acknowledged as a space of nostalgia within American culture. One assumption underlying my arguments is that Turner was not just a historian but also a nostalgia writer—that is, a figure who projected his own desires onto the spaces and historical developments that he detailed. Analyzing this nostalgic impulse within Turner's theories enables me to formulate the concept of "nostalgic spatiality." I broadly define nostalgic spatiality as instances in which nostalgia is projected onto a physical environment, thereby altering the perception, understanding, and/or experience of that space and its accompanying cultural sphere. Nostalgic spatiality may be an individual or collective phenomenon. Within Midwestern narratives, nostalgic spatiality often is depicted as producing a sense of spatial constriction or untraversable boundaries, which I address in the second and third chapters.

Early in this chapter, I examine two significant nostalgic elements in Turner's work that influence my theorization of nostalgic spatiality. First, Turner's descriptions of the United States' western expansion feature a spatial trajectory that corresponds to the inward-looping temporal dynamics of nostalgia. In this way, Turner inscribes historical circumstances with nostalgic overtones, which is a development that has lasting repercussions on the popular identity of the Midwest. Second, after Turner asserts that there are no remaining frontier spaces, he sets about defining the Midwest as a geographic *and* cultural territory that preserves the national ideals he once detected in the frontier.[3] Consequently, the trauma of the United States' lost potential for further continental growth is partly alleviated by the establishment of the Midwest as a regional substitute for the frontier spaces that housed his idealized pioneer values. The Midwest thus comes to serve as a nostalgic symbol of the possibilities that Turner argues were available for western settlers of European origin, but that now only exist in the past. Turner's work, then, is a major contributing factor in binding the Midwest's identity to nostalgia.

Following this analysis of Turner, I turn to two texts from popular culture that provide instructive examples of nostalgic spatiality, particularly as it relates to the Midwest. Theodore Dreiser's naturalistic novel *Sister Carrie* (1900) and filmmaker Vincente Minnelli's musical *Meet Me in St. Louis* (1944) both illustrate many of Turner's concerns with movement, nostalgia, and regional identity.[4] Although Minnelli's film was produced near the middle of the century, its narrative unfolds in 1903 and 1904. This setting reveals lingering cultural perceptions of the Midwest's status during the early years of the twentieth century. Major tensions in *Sister Carrie* and *Meet Me in St. Louis* hinge on traumatic moves eastward from the Midwest to New York City. Through various narrative complications, Dreiser and Minnelli engage with Turner's claim that the western frontier was closed and that the nation was forced to turn inward. In *Sister Carrie*, nostalgia is shown to be a debilitating disorder that consumes the novel's most prominent male character through a delusion-inducing fixation on the past. In *Meet Me in St. Louis*, nostalgic desire is presented in a more positive light by functioning as a stabilizing element within families and society in general. Together, these two texts affirm Turner's configuration of the Midwest as a space of nostalgia, while further entrenching the region's nostalgic identity in American culture.

Frederick Jackson Turner

Within the thirteen essays collected in *The Frontier in American History* (1920), Turner presents his influential theories on the western frontier, while also stressing the importance of regions (or "sections," a term he often uses synonymously) in shaping American culture.[5] From the famous arguments of "The Significance of the Frontier in American History" (1893) to "Middle Western Pioneer Democracy" (1918), the mythologizing historian presents evolving nostalgic narratives about the frontier and regional identity.[6] In Turner's initial frontier essay, he links American history and the nation's general development to western expansion or, as he puts it, "the colonization of the Great West." This ability to steadily progress across the continent produces multiple frontier spaces, each of which grants a "perennial rebirth" to its occupants and to "American social development" in general.[7] However, even as Turner writes that "each frontier did indeed furnish... a gate of escape from the bondage of the past," he gloomily predicts that "never again will such gifts of free land offer themselves" to the United States.[8]

Throughout his writings, Turner laments the closing of the frontier, and this nostalgic impulse retains a strong influence within American culture, particularly in terms of how regions are perceived. As historian Jon Gjerde observes, "The long shadow cast by the work of Frederick Jackson Turner continues to inform the discussion [concerning region]. Prior to the invention of the Middle West, Americans folded the states that would become Middle Western into the broad West."[9] Turner's views have been attacked for a variety of reasons, including his idealized descriptions of pioneer life, his racist distinctions between "civilization" and "wilderness," and even his primary argument about the frontier actually being "closed" in the late nineteenth century.[10] Yet, the "long shadow" of these writings lingers partly because Turner transforms the loss of the geographic conditions enabling western expansion into abstract qualities that he nostalgically binds to regional identity.

Turner's *The Frontier in American History* contains work that spans nearly three decades. Over this stretch of time, Turner keeps returning to his initial conceptualization of the frontier—and the regions forged through the frontier experience (especially the Midwest)—as an Americanization factory of sorts, taking in misshaped individuals and churning out idealized, uniform citizens. In "The Significance of the Frontier in American History," Turner writes that "the frontier promoted the formation of a composite nationality for the American people" and that by experiencing the frontier environment, "immigrants were Americanized, liberated, and fused into a mixed race, English in neither nationality nor characteristics."[11] Three years after delivering his famous frontier thesis, Turner further elaborates on the ongoing primacy of the frontier's role in American culture. In "The Problem of the West" (1896), Turner predicts that cultural turmoil will result from the United States' lack of additional physical spaces for continued expansion. Much like the term "frontier," Turner uses "West" to refer to a set of conditions rather than a precise geographic territory, and he locates these conditions at the most distant western perimeter of American settlements at particular historical moments. Once a frontier is populated and "older institutions and ideas" begin to infiltrate that space, Turner asserts, "The wilderness disappears, the 'West' proper passes on to a new frontier, and in the former area, a new society has emerged from its contact with the backwoods. . . . Decade after decade, West after West, this rebirth of American society has gone on, has left its traces behind it, and has reacted on the East."[12] Such is the cycle of "perennial rebirth" in Turner's formulation.

Two key aspects of Turner's frontier writings are worth highlighting because of the ways in which they overtly link space, movement, and culture: first, the mutually influential dynamics of regional territories; second, the circular nature of that influence. In other words, settlers from the East are reshaped by the frontier, which is itself altered by the influx of Eastern institutions; these new "Westerners" then proceed to expand into other frontiers and revise the Eastern society from which they came. As Turner states, "The history of our political institutions, our democracy . . . is a history of the evolution and adaptation of organs in response to changed environment, a history of the origin of new political species."[13] For Turner, the major problem is that this process is dependent on "new" territories to enable continual evolution, adaptation, growth, and revision of social and political institutions.

The "problem of the West" is, in essence, a problem of space. Turner believes that the "dominant fact in American life has been expansion" and that such movement is no longer possible. Consequently, he argues that "all this push and energy is turning into channels of agitation. Failures in one area can no longer be made good by taking up land on a new frontier; the conditions of a settled society are being reached with suddenness and with confusion"[14] Turner grimly concludes, "This, then, is the real situation: a people composed of heterogeneous materials, with diverse and conflicting ideals and social interests, having passed from the task of filling up the vacant spaces of the continent, is *now thrown back upon itself*, and is seeking an equilibrium. The diverse elements are being fused into national unity. The forces of reorganization are turbulent and the nation seems like a witches' kettle."[15] Setting aside Turner's problematic mention of a "vacant" continent (this racist elision of Native American societies pervades Turner's work), this passage provides crucial insights into the frontier theorist's nostalgic inclinations. Rather than the romantic vision of America as a melting pot, Turner uses the sinister image of a "witches' kettle" to describe the newly constricted and suffocating nation. From Turner's perspective, after years of expansion, the American people have finally delimited the outermost boundaries of their nation, and that terminus is revealed to be the concave edges of a heated cauldron, one that produces internal tensions due to a lack of additional space. Hence, the United States is "now thrown back upon itself" in a movement with tumultuous repercussions.

The above passage merits further attention for two reasons. First, by considering the nostalgic undercurrents of Turner's work, correspondences emerge between his preoccupation with movement, boundaries, and idealized past states and certain functions of nostalgia, as conceptualized by Susan Stewart and Svetlana Boym. While discussing the nostalgic desire to eliminate "the gap between nature and culture," Stewart writes, "The nostalgic's utopia is prelapsarian, a genesis where lived and mediated experience are one, where authenticity and transcendence are both present and everywhere."[16] Clearly, Turner crafts ideological narratives that locate the nation's most "authentic" status solely within the formerly shifting and now lost conditions of the frontier; in doing so, Turner saturates a vanished spatiotemporal coordinate with nostalgia. Using Boym's terms, Turner may superficially appear to be engaging in "reflective nostalgia"—contemplating the loss of the desired past—but his work veers more toward "restorative nostalgia" in that he seeks to "conquer and spatialize time" by reestablishing expired frontier conditions within the Midwest.[17] Turner's claim that the United States is "now thrown back upon itself" thus functions as a spatial equivalent to the temporal operation of nostalgia. I classify this form of nostalgia as nostalgic spatiality.

For the nostalgic subject, time is experienced in a linear fashion until a point at which progress ceases, and desire doubles back on itself in a looping spiral. No version of the present or the future may be deemed as satisfactory as the idealized, distant, and possibly fictive past. Turner reveals himself as a nostalgic figure throughout his writings by continually expressing dissatisfaction with the present, while mythologizing a desired past located only in the highly specific conditions of the frontier. Of even greater importance, Turner's discussion of western expansion is a spatialized version of the nostalgic temporal paradigm. According to Turner, settlers of European origin moved steadily—and linearly— across the West until met by the Pacific Ocean, and this traumatic moment propelled American culture "back upon itself." Just as with nostalgic desire, Turner describes linear progress until an abrupt inward turn—only he projects this dynamic onto American culture as a whole, rather than it simply functioning as an individualized affliction.

The second reason why the above passage is so crucial concerns how it situates the Midwest within Turner's nostalgic model of the United States looping backwards into itself. A cartographic visualization of the nation being "thrown back upon itself" would involve rolling the left edge of a map of the United States toward its center. Such a motion situates the Midwest as the fulcrum of this nostalgic turn inward—that is, the point at which the nation begins to coil back into itself. This imaginary map's compression neatly reflects how Turner brings the Midwest into contact with his nostalgic conception of the frontier. By spatializing the nostalgic turn inward, Turner locates what is typically an abstract aspect of nostalgia—the temporal period for which the nostalgic subject longs—within a precise physical space: the Midwest. As a result of the nostalgic spatiality that permeates Turner's work, the geographic territory of the Midwest is reimagined as a nostalgia-infused ideological construct.

Turner's efforts to establish the Midwest as the nation's space of nostalgia extend beyond this mapped image of spatial return. In Turner's writings, each frontier begat its successive frontier until no additional spaces remained on the continent; the Midwest's significance in relation to this frontier lineage is that the region was the last western frontier from which there remained seemingly limitless additional frontiers. When the territories that became the Midwest were still frontiers, a great expanse of "vacant" (to use Turner's problematic description) space existed beyond them. The object of Turner's nostalgia, then, is the historical moment that he believes contained the potential for continued progress westward—the period in which the space that became known as the Midwest was still a frontier. By virtue of being in the middle of the United States, the Midwest retains some primal element of what Turner considers to be the key quality of the frontier: the potential for ongoing expansion and movement. Hence, the Midwest is framed as the space from which the continent still may be perceived as "stretching forever in all directions," to repeat Vonnegut's phrasing, and that unique characteristic also enables the region to serve as a nostalgic storehouse for past (and potentially imagined) aspects of American culture.[18]

By the early twentieth century, Turner further affirms the nostalgic character of the Midwest by transferring almost wholesale his idealized western frontier traits onto the United States' central region in his writings. Significantly, Turner's efforts to define the region overlap with the period in which usage of the term "Midwest" became common. Cultural geographer James Shortridge states that public recognition of a distinctly Midwestern territory solidified around 1912, thereby indicating "an expansion of the perceived importance of that region to American society."[19] Shortridge adds that a "flattering image of the Middle West as a mature rural paradise filled with wholesome, progressive people" circulated during the first two decades of the twentieth century and came to define the region.[20] Such regional perceptions dovetail with the essentialized Midwestern traits that Turner outlines around the turn of the twentieth century.

In an essay simply titled "The Middle West" (1901), Turner's ascription of frontier characteristics onto the Midwest is especially pronounced. Turner writes,

> The ideals of the Middle West began in the log huts set in the midst of the forest a century ago. While his horizon was still bounded by the clearing that his ax had made, the pioneer dreamed of continental conquests. The vastness of the wilderness kindled his imagination. His vision saw beyond the dank swamp at the edge of the great lake to the lofty buildings and the jostling multitudes of a mighty city.... The men and women who made the Middle West were idealists, and they had the power of will to make their dreams come true.[21]

This passage establishes a narrative of regional progress from frontier conditions to the "mighty city"—presumably Chicago, given its location on Lake Michigan and its nineteenth-century skyscrapers—that replaced such wilderness. To further emphasize the connection between the frontier and the Midwest, Turner adds that Midwesterners embodied "the pioneer's traits—individual activity, inventiveness, and competition for the prizes of the rich province that awaited exploitation under freedom and equality of opportunity.... It was 'every one for himself.'"[22]

Turner's praise for the Midwest is even more effusive in a subsequent passage: "Almost every family was a self-sufficing unit, and liberty and equality flourished in the frontier periods of the Middle West as perhaps never before in history.... Both native settler and European immigrant saw in this free and competitive movement of the frontier the chance to break the bondage of social rank, and to rise to a higher plane of existence."[23] Setting aside the disputed claim about fully self-sufficient frontier families, Turner's hyperbolic descriptions of the Midwest assign symbolic value to both the region's inhabitants and its geographic territory.[24] The Midwest's physical environment itself is imbued with idealistic qualities because the region bears the traces of its "frontier stage," such as supposedly self-sufficient families and individualistic settlers. As such, Turner writes, "The ideals of equality, freedom of opportunity, faith in the common man are deep rooted in all the Middle West." Furthermore, Turner perceives "a vigor and a mental activity among the common people" of the Midwest that reveals a sort of predestination for greatness."[25] Turner consistently seeks to dissociate the supposedly "average" white settler from any larger support apparatus so that this figure might be elevated to an aggrandized status. Throughout his work, Turner's "common man" is depicted as anything but common, and such exceptionalism is necessary to support the outsized ideals that are hung on this mythic figure.

Almost two decades after "The Middle West" essay was published, Turner continues valorizing the Midwest with "Middle Western Pioneer Democracy." In this 1918 speech, Turner describes the individuals who settled the Midwest as "social idealists" who "based their ideals on trust in the common man and the readiness to make adjustments, not on the rule of a benevolent despot or a controlling class."[26] These "self-sufficing pioneers" were "devoted to the ideal of equality" and "objected to . . . arbitrary obstacles, artificial limitations upon the freedom of each member of this frontier folk to work out his own career without fear or favor. What they instinctively opposed was the crystallization of difference, the monopolization of opportunity and the fixing of that monopoly by government or social customs." According to Turner, these "slashers of the forest" yearned for a space of equal economic opportunity free from regulation and dependent solely on an individual's work ethic.[27]

A curious contradiction is detectable within the pioneer values that Turner outlines. Nineteenth-century Midwesterners supposedly work against the "crystallization of difference" and doggedly embrace a dedication to individualism. In fairness to Turner, he clarifies that at least part of the opposition to difference refers to economics and a desire among settlers to avoid "hopeless inequality, or rule of class."[28] But this economic justification only provides a partial explanation of how difference is opposed. Overall, the underlying ideal that emerges through this particular statement—and Turner's work in general—is the importance of a lack of differentiation among people. Essentially, Turner's ideal Midwestern settlers are a collection of individualistic individuals who share identical values, aspirations, lifestyles, and skin color. As I detail throughout this book, the qualities that Turner perceives in Midwesterners have stuck to the Midwest's image since the early twentieth century when, importantly, Turner first attributed such traits to the region and the term "Midwest" gained common usage in American culture.

The uniform ideals that Turner perceives in Midwestern settlers were not necessarily brought to the region by those individuals. Throughout "Middle Western Pioneer Democracy," Turner reiterates that it was the actual physical environment that shaped and fostered such values. Upon entering the Midwest, Turner writes, "The winds of the prairies swept away almost at once a mass of old habits and prepossessions."[29] This anthropomorphism of the landscape recalls (or predicts, as it were) how the Midwest is frequently configured as an absent, blank space. For instance, in *Main Street* (1920), Sinclair Lewis similarly ascribes transformative qualities to the Midwestern landscape, but in a far less idealized manner than Turner.[30] Protagonist Carol Kennicott, a dissatisfied transplant to the fictional Minnesota town of Gopher Prairie, remarks that in "the prairie—all

Nostalgic Spatiality 35

my thoughts go flying off into the big space."[31] With this brief quote, Lewis cautions that the Midwest's spacious environment may disperse intellectual self-possession, rather than improve one's capabilities. By contrast, Turner celebrates the Midwest's physical terrain as a normalizing mechanism that continually restores the region to a blank state and naturally irons out difference among its inhabitants.

This equalizing process becomes clearer in Turner's descriptions of what occurs when diverse groups encounter one another within the Midwest. Turner writes that the region "was made up of various stocks with many different cultures, sectional and European; what is significant is that these elements did not remain as separate strata underneath an established ruling order, as was the case particularly in New England. All were accepted and intermingling components of a forming society, plastic and absorptive."[32] Through such "intermingling," Turner claims, "In this society of pioneers men learned to drop their old national animosities."[33] He summarizes this development in typical grandiose fashion: "Thus the Middle-West was teaching the lesson of national cross-fertilization instead of national enmities, the possibility of a newer and richer civilization, not by preserving unmodified or isolated the old component elements, but by breaking down the line-fences, by merging the individual life in the common product—a new product, which held the promise of world brotherhood."[34] Here, the Midwest is put forth as an American utopia, one that is possible due to the region's erasure of difference. The fantasy advanced by Turner is not one in which individuals and groups of different classes, ethnicities, and values truly intermingle, but one in which the Midwest's physical environment softens and eradicates difference until a singular "common product" emerges.

In Turner's work, the purportedly unique temporal and spatial conditions of the frontier produce its exceptional status. Regardless of the veracity of Turner's theories, the ideological aspects of his nostalgic narratives persist in the American consciousness, perhaps most notably his yearning for the "lost" state of existence located only in the time and space of the frontier. Turner imbues this vanished pioneer life with an authenticity lacking in the present and mourns his imagined version of the past by inventing place-specific narratives about "civilization," race, individualism, labor, and the family. Across such narratives, Turner crafts a model of western expansion that functions as a spatial version of nostalgia's temporal dynamic: linear progress to a point and then a looping return. Finally, Turner further focuses this nostalgic spatiality by transferring his idealized frontier qualities onto the Midwest, which was acquiring an identity in American culture just at the time of his writing. Hence, the Midwest came to be known as a national space of nostalgia—a homogenizing environment that is alternately disparaged and celebrated for being a linear time-defying embodiment of the past. The remaining sections of this chapter demonstrate how nostalgic spatiality is expressed in two disparate examples of literature and film: Dreiser's naturalistic novel *Sister Carrie* and Minnelli's highly stylized musical *Meet Me in St. Louis*. By examining this pairing, the multifarious iterations of nostalgic spatiality become clearer, as the concept's malleable nature enables it to manifest across a range of textual forms and cultural discourses.

Sister Carrie

Theodore Dreiser's *Sister Carrie* (1900) offers a complementary illustration of the nostalgic spatiality that emerges from Turner's writings. In fact, the narrative of *Sister Carrie* exemplifies Turner's contemporaneous nightmare vision of a nation "thrown back upon itself" with each American urban space existing as a "witches' kettle" of unrest.[35] Throughout the novel, Dreiser presents cities as simmering with the potential to destroy individuals and turn people against one another, partly because of perpetual competition for degrading and mechanized jobs. In Chicago, factory girls perform rote work that barely permits subsistence living; in New York, Dreiser references thousands who are unemployed, while showing that others face exploitative working conditions. At the same time, an elevated leisure class indulges in the niceties of urban living. For the purposes of studying the novel's treatment of the Midwest and nostalgic spatiality, the character arc of white, middle-aged George Hurstwood proves to be key; by the end of the narrative, the Chicago native is exiled in New York City and nostalgically longs for his past life in the Midwest. Crucially, this consuming sense of nostalgia takes hold when Hurstwood flees Chicago and is forced eastward, rather than simply disappearing into a western frontier that no longer exists.

In *Sister Carrie*, Indiana-born Dreiser presents the story of Caroline Meeber, a naïve eighteen-year-old from Columbia City, Wisconsin, who eventually becomes a star on Broadway. The narrative begins in 1889 with Carrie moving to Chicago and meeting Charles Drouet, a young traveling salesman who soon begins paying for Carrie's apartment, wardrobe, and food. Carrie subsequently has an affair with Drouet's married friend, Hurstwood, who manages a successful bar in Chicago. After Hurstwood's wife discovers the affair, he moves out and, without prior intent, impulsively steals $10,000 from the bar's safe. Hurstwood and Carrie elope to the East and settle in New York City. Over the course of several years, Hurstwood's fortunes decline steadily, while Carrie achieves fame and financial success as a theater star. With their respective statuses moving in opposite directions, Carrie leaves Hurstwood, who is absorbed into the ranks of the city's homeless population and ultimately commits suicide.

Hurstwood's theft and the accompanying fallout are the narrative developments that most directly speak to the connections among the Midwest, nostalgia, and Turner's claims that the supposedly bountiful opportunities of the West were expired by the turn of the twentieth century. Following Hurstwood's theft, the Midwesterner's thoughts immediately turn to flight, but he curiously does not consider fleeing to the West. Instead, Hurstwood's escape from Chicago brings him to the East Coast, where he plans to forge a new identity in New York City. With the frontier being "closed," Hurstwood "was thinking if he could only get [to Detroit] and cross the river into Canada, he could take his time about getting to Montreal" and then proceed to New York.[36] Hurstwood believes that in New York, "it was easy to hide. He knew enough about that city to know that its mysteries and possibilities of mystification were infinite."[37] Moreover, Dreiser writes, "Whatever a man like Hurstwood could be in Chicago, it is very evident that he would be but an inconspicuous drop in an ocean like New York.... The sea was already full of whales. A common fish must needs disappear wholly from view—remain unseen. In other words, Hurstwood was nothing."[38] Much as Turner does with frontier spaces, in these passages, Dreiser attaches issues of visibility, opportunity, and identity to a physical environment: crowded New York City, rather than the formerly open West.[39]

Upon arriving in New York City, Hurstwood's fantasy of anonymity rapidly fades into the reality of unequal opportunity within the urban maelstrom. Hurstwood and Carrie struggle financially, which prompts Hurstwood "to see as one sees a city with a wall about it. Men were posted at the gates. You could not get in. Those inside did not care to come out to see who you were. They were so merry inside there that all those outside were forgotten, and he was on the outside."[40] In contrast to Turner's unrestricted western territories, Dreiser renders the space of the city as a claustrophobic cluster of impenetrable fortresses that are guarded by a rigid class structure. Indeed, throughout *Sister Carrie*, the populations of urban spaces are presented as being split cleanly between haves and havenots, with little chance for upward mobility. Carrie's rise is a clear exception, but Dreiser still concludes his novel with Carrie feeling discontent and sorrowful, despite her financial success on the stage.[41]

Dreiser depicts the long-settled, urban East as presenting daily challenges because of desperate competition for the few jobs available and the amplification of class divisions. Carrie's prosperity takes several years to achieve, during which time she and Hurstwood struggle to subsist and to come to terms with the disparity between their lifestyles in New York City and in Chicago. Upon the fugitive couple's initial arrival on the East Coast, Dreiser writes that "as [Hurstwood] faced the city, cut off from his friends, despoiled of his modest fortune, and even his name, [he was] forced to begin the battle for place and comfort all over again."[42] This passage connects *Sister Carrie*'s spatialized narrative progression to Turner's claim that the nation was "now thrown back upon itself." Here, Dreiser echoes Turner's view that each new frontier reset civilization for western settlers, but *Sister Carrie* inverts the dynamic of the frontier bringing civilization to wilderness by showing that the urban East has regressed to unforgiving survivalist conditions. Even worse, the frontier myth of the self-sufficient man proves to be entirely unsustainable in a harsh city that necessitates social connections and a minimal financial baseline simply to find employment. Unlike Turner's mythic class-free frontier spaces, Dreiser presents New York City as an enclosed cauldron of discontent that ultimately dehumanizes and destroys Hurstwood.[43]

In conjunction with the distinctive spatial dynamics of *Sister Carrie*'s narrative, Dreiser emphasizes another form of distance: the temporal chasm that separates Hurstwood's present and past. Soon after Carrie leaves Hurstwood, he achieves the absolute anonymity he had sought when moving to New York City by sinking into the "cold, shrunken, disgruntled mass" of the impoverished population.[44] Reduced to begging for food and shelter, Hurstwood is left as a broken and tragically nostalgic figure, desperately yearning for his past life in Chicago. From the moment that Hurstwood first leaves Chicago, Dreiser depicts him as racked with nostalgia for the last moments before his life was irreversibly changed. As early in Hurstwood's exile as the train ride to Detroit, he reflects on being "shut out from Chicago—from his easy, comfortable state" and promptly "began to think that he would try and restore himself to his old state."[45] This emphasis on restoring Hurstwood's "old state" aligns with Boym's "restorative nostalgia" in which the nostalgic subject goes beyond merely reflecting on what has been lost by actively seeking to recreate an idealized past or "to rebuild the lost home."[46] To some degree, restorative nostalgia may be framed as a denial of culpability for the flawed present, and Hurstwood remains in this deluded state for the remainder of the novel.

Dreiser continually underscores Hurstwood's cleavage from the past. While in Montreal, Hurstwood "forgot that he had severed himself from the past as by a sword, and that if he did manage to in some way reunite himself with it, the jagged line of separation and reunion would always show."[47] Hurstwood's brief memory lapse calls attention to the unattainable goal of nostalgia: to seamlessly eliminate the division between the utterly irreconcilable past and present. Despite—or perhaps because of—the impossibility of Hurstwood being restored to his formerly elevated status in Chicago, he begins to suffer from nostalgic delusions near the end of the novel. Following Hurstwood's two-day tenure as a scab driver during a Brooklyn streetcar operator's strike (a job that he quits after being assaulted by a mob), he is pathetically reduced to reenacting nostalgic memories in moments of delirium. For instance, while in his apartment after the traumatic Brooklyn experience, Hurstwood "sat, gazing downward, and gradually thought he heard the old voices and the clink of glasses.... All at once he looked up. The room was so still it seemed ghostlike."[48] With these nostalgic retreats into memory, Hurstwood futilely—and perhaps even unconsciously—attempts to restore his desired past existence in Chicago.

During the final chapters of *Sister Carrie*, nostalgic fantasies of the past continue to intrude into Hurstwood's present. When Hurstwood takes up residence in a budget lodging house, Dreiser describes him as follows:

> his preference was to close his eyes and dream of other days, a habit which grew upon him. It was not sleep at first, but a mental hearkening back to scenes and incidents in his Chicago life. As the present became darker, the past grew brighter, and all that concerned it stood in relief.
>
> He was unconscious of just how much this habit had hold of him until one day he found his lips repeating an old answer he had made to one of his friends. They were in Fitzgerald and Moy's. It was as if he stood in the door of his elegant little office, talking. . . .
>
> The movement of his lips aroused him. He wondered whether he had really spoken. The next time he noticed anything of the sort he really did talk.[49]

As personal and financial failures mount, nostalgic phantasms infiltrate Hurstwood's daily life in an increasingly overwhelming manner. The debilitating nostalgia brought on by Hurstwood's flight from the Midwest prevents him from achieving contentment in the present or even mustering the energy to pursue a new job. Instead, Hurstwood reframes the present as the result of a system that has been rigged against him, and, in his increasingly deranged state of mind, he comes to deny the various personal failures that have accumulated since leaving Chicago. This delusional retreat inward is a nostalgic refutation of temporal progress since the moment that he stole money from the bar and irreversibly changed his life.

Hurstwood's inability to comprehend his physical environment further aligns *Sister Carrie* with nostalgic spatiality, which, in shorthand, refers to nostalgia profoundly altering one's relationship to space. One particular moment stands out as the apex of Hurstwood's confused slippage between perceiving the desired past and dissatisfactory present. While stumbling down Broadway, Hurstwood sees "blazing, in incandescent fire, Carrie's name" on a theater marquee, as well as "a large, gilt-framed poster-board, on which was a fine lithograph of Carrie, life-size." Because Hurstwood's "mind was not exactly clear," he addresses the image as if it actually is Carrie and says, "That's you. . . . Wasn't good enough for you, was I? Huh!" Dreiser writes that Hurstwood "lingered, trying to think logically. This was no longer possible with him."[50] Strangely, Hurstwood perceives the two-dimensional replica of Carrie as if she is actually present.[51] Such a surface-level engagement with his environment reveals the extent of his nostalgic derangement.

As a result of Hurstwood's extreme nostalgic state, he experiences the present as if it is a set of images, just as he relives the past through delusions. In Hurstwood's mind, the past and present become equivalent in terms of both temporality and spatiality—moments from his personal history in Chicago seep into the present in New York City. Yet, in this instant, Hurstwood is confronted with proof that his imagistic perception of the present is false; he currently exists as a degraded version of his better self that is located elsewhere and "else-when": in Chicago several years prior. Hence, this scene functions as a final refutation of Hurstwood's nostalgic reverie. Hurstwood is forced to acknowledge the temporal separation of past and present because Carrie's contemporary success cannot occupy the same moment as Hurstwood's previous contentment in Chicago. Carrie's image thus reaffirms Hurstwood's failed status in the present, which disrupts his nostalgic conflation of the past and the present. Ultimately, this encounter serves as the final catalyst that pushes Hurstwood to commit suicide.

The character of Hurstwood represents an extreme possible outcome of Turner's dire prediction about a nation "thrown back upon itself."[52] After Hurstwood's actions cause him to lose his family and career in the Midwest, he flees to the urban East and swiftly is destroyed (instead of following the previous waves of pioneers into the mythic western frontier, which supposedly no longer has vacant space). Moreover, this movement eastward also effects a delusional turn inward, as Hurstwood devolves from charming socialite to depressive nostalgic.

Dreiser's linkage of space, desire, and the transformation of Hurstwood reveals the power of nostalgic spatiality. As debilitating nostalgia for the past increasingly overwhelms Hurstwood's perception of the present, the possibility of spatial escape becomes inconceivable. Until his eventual death, an overpowering sense of nostalgic spatiality traps and suspends Hurstwood between desired past and degraded present. In sharp contrast with *Sister Carrie*, the narrative of *Meet Me in St. Louis* revolves around enacting a suspension of temporal progress. The Midwestern Smith family's fear of impending spatial dislocation prompts a preemptive state of nostalgia for the contemporary moment and its promise of a pleasant future, which is dependent on physical stasis.

Meet Me in St. Louis

While examining "the dreamlike power" of dance within the musical comedy, Gilles Deleuze celebrates director Vincente Minnelli for revealing that "there are as many worlds as images" in film.[53] Deleuze elaborates on this "plurality of worlds" in Minnelli's films and writes, "In Minnelli, every world and every dream is shut in and on itself, closed up around everything it contains, including the dreamer. . . . Musical comedy has never come as close to a mystery of memory, of dream and of time, as a point of indiscernibility of the real and the imaginary, as in Minnelli."[54] By foregrounding themes of enclosure and slippages among reality, perception, and fantasy, Deleuze's discussion of Minnelli recalls the temporal and spatial dynamics of nostalgia. This critical framework serves as a starting point for my analysis of Minnelli's *Meet Me in St. Louis* (1944), which depicts the Midwest of the early twentieth century as a fantastical realm populated by characters who resist the passage of time via nostalgic memory and desire.[55] Moreover, on a narrative and formal level, *Meet Me in St. Louis* provides an important demonstration of ways in which nostalgic spatiality may appear in film.

Meet Me in St. Louis shares several major themes with Turner's work, including his preoccupation with movement, boundaries, idealized past states, and, in a more indirect manner, the supposed cultural effects of the nation's traumatic turn inward due to the closure of the western frontier. Taking place from the summer of 1903 to the spring of 1904—roughly a decade after Turner first publicly presented his frontier thesis and just a few years after the publication of *Sister Carrie*—*Meet Me in St. Louis* details the affluent Smith family as they anticipate the arrival of the 1904 World's Fair. Major tensions mount as a result of the family's impending move from the Midwest to New York City. Following patriarch Alonzo's (Leon Ames) announcement of this relocation, the other members of the Smith clan desperately yearn to preserve their present status in St. Louis by halting spatial movement and temporal progress. However, unlike the destructive flight eastward in *Sister Carrie*, *Meet Me in St. Louis* concludes with the establishment of a static nostalgic interval within the film's Midwestern setting. In this case, nostalgic spatiality is presented as a stabilizing, positive factor for the Smith family.

Meet Me in St. Louis unfolds across four seasons, and its springtime conclusion suggests that nostalgia has a rejuvenating effect on both the Smiths and their environment. Minnelli's use of seasonal title cards accentuates the film's nostalgic themes. These cards each feature a sepia-toned photograph of the Smiths' home surrounded by a decorative floral border, and they identify the various settings as Summer 1903, Autumn 1903, Winter 1903, and Spring 1904. During each appearance of the cards, the camera zooms in on the photograph, and the image dissolves into a colorized establishing shot full of movement.[56] Minnelli thus creates the illusion that the camera is entering the photograph in order to animate and recreate the past.[57] Throughout *Meet Me in St. Louis*, Minnelli presents the past as brighter and more vivid than is possible in historical documents and mere photographs from the era; he replaces the distant, foggy past with an improved cinematic version that is colorful and glamorous.[58]

With the Technicolor imagery of *Meet Me in St. Louis*, Minnelli develops a Midwestern environment that is based on a nostalgic conception of the region. As context for understanding this particular vision of the Midwest, it is worth reviewing film scholar Rick Altman's explanation of the musical genre's distinctive temporal dynamics. In *The American Film Musical* (1987), Altman writes, "Traditional notions of narrative structure assume that chronological presentation implies causal relationship . . . in the musical, chronological presentation and causal relationships alike are at climactic moments eschewed in favor of simultaneity and similarity."[59] In other words, Altman suggests that distinctions between past and present are collapsed within crucial moments in musicals, as the genre regularly operates in a temporal vacuum of sorts. Regarding temporality, then, the musical is a form that readily enables the creation of atemporal or nonlinear spaces—precisely those qualities so often attributed to the Midwest.

Altman also addresses how the musical genre functions in relation to American culture. He frames the musical as "a cultural problem-solving device" that engages with society's

> fundamental paradox: both terms of the oppositions on which [society] is built (order/liberty, progress/stability, work/entertainment, and so forth) are seen as desirable, yet the terms are perceived as mutually exclusive. Every society possesses texts which obscure this paradox, prevent it from appearing threatening, and thus assure the society's stability. The musical is one of the most important types of text to serve this function in American life. By reconciling terms previously seen as mutually exclusive, the musical succeeds in reducing an unsatisfactory paradox to a more workable configuration, a concordance of opposites. Traditionally, this is the function which society assigns to myth.[60]

Although Altman suggests that "the American courtship ritual" is the primary stabilizing myth in musicals, *Meet Me in St. Louis* instead asserts the primacy of the family unit in general.[61] Certainly, eldest daughters Rose (Lucille Bremer) and Esther (Judy Garland) have romantic entanglements in the film, but these relationships are intertwined with a nostalgic fixation on geographic stasis—that is, maintaining spatial proximity to the Smiths' home in St. Louis—and a desire to slow temporal progress in order to preserve the family's idealized present lifestyle. Like Turner's preoccupation with the vanished frontiers, *Meet Me in St. Louis* designates a precise space and time as the Smith family's most desired object of nostalgia: their shared state of sustained anticipation throughout 1903 for the opening of the 1904 World's Fair.

Because the Smiths' fear of spatial and temporal dislocation results from Alonzo's decision to take a promotion in New York City, the family patriarch is, accordingly, a crucial figure for understanding nostalgic spatiality in *Meet Me in St. Louis*. Alonzo does little except to introduce the major problem of migrating eastward and then to resolve it by abruptly choosing to stay in St. Louis. Yet these decisions produce the ongoing tension between desiring and dreading the future that looms over all of the other domestic and romantic proceedings. The possibility of moving represents an acceleration of the already-changing dynamics within the Smith household, which are partly due to the eldest daughters approaching adulthood. Given these burgeoning domestic fissures, the potential relocation further unsettles the family. In response to the impending trauma of moving, the members of the Smith household (excluding Alonzo) nostalgically brood over the idealized perfection of their hometown. Alonzo's status as an outsider is persistently reaffirmed until he finally is swayed by the family's collective nostalgic mindset. For nearly the entirety of the film, Alonzo is set apart, both with dialogue and through meticulous shot compositions.

The first onscreen appearances of the film's main characters reflect Alonzo's lack of synchronicity with the other members of the Smith clan. As *Meet Me in St. Louis* begins, Minnelli provides a remarkable introduction to the family via the camera meandering through the Smith household, which is established as a space of domestic bliss and song. Even with mother Anna Smith (Mary Astor) and maid Katie (Marjorie Main) disagreeing over the flavoring of the ketchup they are making, the Smiths are shown to be a harmonious unit during this introductory sequence. Adult son Lon Jr. (Henry H. Daniels Jr.) enters the kitchen humming a few notes from "Meet Me in St. Louis," which second youngest daughter Agnes (Joan Carroll) also sings while on her way upstairs. There, Agnes encounters Grandpa (Harry Davenport) singing the same song while shaving. Outside, Esther returns home on a horse-drawn carriage with several friends, who all are singing "Meet Me in St. Louis." Oldest daughter Rose soon arrives at the house, where she and Esther discuss their romantic designs on, respectively, Warren Sheffield (Robert Sully) and John Truett (Tom Drake), the latter of whom is literally the boy next door.

Both Alonzo and the brash youngest daughter Tootie (Margaret O'Brien) notably are absent from this sequence.[62] When Alonzo finally returns home (and is shown onscreen for the first time), he interrupts Rose and Esther singing "Meet Me in St. Louis" and grumpily declares, "For heaven's sake, stop that screeching. That song. The fair won't open for seven months. That's all everybody sings about or talks about. I wish everybody would meet at the fair and leave me alone." Alonzo's presence disrupts the mirthful domesticity within the Smith home and ends the family's collective singing of the title theme. As patriarch, Alonzo has the authority to uproot the family, but he is otherwise marginalized and excluded from the household's daily dramas. For example, early in the film, the Smiths initiate a humorous conspiracy to keep Alonzo from knowing that Warren is expected to call Rose from New York City and possibly propose marriage. As Grandpa wryly observes, "[Alonzo is] not supposed to know. It's enough that we're letting him work hard every day to support the whole flock of us. He can't have everything." Upon discovering that he was the last person to be aware of Rose's potential engagement, Alonzo exasperatingly wonders aloud, "Just when was I voted out of this family?" Beyond Alonzo's exclusion from domestic drama, he is further isolated by his gruff attitude about the potential relocation to the East Coast.

On Halloween night, Alonzo declares his intentions to move the Smiths to New York City. For the duration of this scene, Minnelli's blocking visually distances Alonzo from the family within the frame. Alonzo most often is shown alone in a medium shot, separated from other family members in an unbalanced frame, or occupying a different plane of action. As the scene begins, the family gathers for cake and ice cream in the dining room, where Alonzo sits alone at the head of the table and is flanked on his left side by Anna, Rose, and Esther, with Katie, Tootie, Grandpa, and Agnes grouped across the table. Throughout the ensuing conversation, the family is horrified by the prospect of moving, and Alonzo's bafflement at their response is reinforced by his visual separation. For example, one portion of this scene begins with a medium shot that features Alonzo listening to the family's protestations. Alonzo is seated at the far left of the frame with empty space in the middle, while Anna is seated on the right of the frame with Rose and Esther standing behind her. As the shot progresses, Alonzo rises and asserts, "It's all settled. We're moving to New York." He then turns and retreats to the background of the shot, where he states, "I've got the future to think about. The future for all of us. I've got to worry about where the money is coming from, with Ron in Princeton and Rose going to college." Alonzo's dialogue creates emotional distance between himself and the family, which is underlined by Minnelli's careful shot composition. In addition, Alonzo's concern with the long-term future sharply contrasts with the family's short-term fixation on the present and the near-future arrival of the World's Fair.

The scene continues with Alonzo cutting a cake while the family critiques New York City. Rose emotionally asserts that in New York, "Rich people have houses. People like us live in flats, hundreds of flats in one building." Framed in a medium shot with Agnes, Grandpa, and Katie, Tootie dejectedly states, "I'd rather be poor if we could only stay here." Minnelli then cuts to a medium shot across the table of a seated Esther looking up at Alonzo and lamenting that they will be moving "Just when St. Louis was going to be the center of attraction of the entire universe." Every family member either declines to have a piece of cake or accepts a piece without eating it, and they subsequently vacate the table except for Alonzo and Anna, who are left in a medium close-up with the cake between them. Alonzo then stands, walks to the living room, and sarcastically asks Anna, "Aren't you afraid to stay here alone with a criminal? Well, that's what I'm being treated like. After all, I'm trying to earn more money to give my grateful family everything they deserve. That's worse than murder. I'm wrecking everybody's life." The scene eventually concludes with a duet between Alonzo and Anna that draws the children back to the cake, although Minnelli's framing continues to cluster the other family members apart from Alonzo (with the exception of Anna).

Despite Alonzo explaining that his preoccupation with the future emerges from a concern for the collective well-being of the Smiths, the other family members' negative reactions reflect a different engagement with space and time. Alonzo has a long-term conception of the future as progressing indefinitely and requiring careful planning; conversely, all of the other Smiths only envision a short-term future that does not extend beyond the arrival of the World's Fair. This nostalgic engagement with time informs the behavior of every family member (aside from Alonzo, of course), as they seem to believe that time will halt once the greatly anticipated World's Fair arrives in St. Louis. Similarly, everyone but Alonzo associates familial unity and sociality with the space of the Midwest itself. The East is feared as a site of ongoing economic trials and perpetual challenges to the stability of the family. *Meet Me in St. Louis* thus presents an alternative to the degrading character arc of the eastbound Hurstwood in Dreiser's pessimistic *Sister Carrie*; rather than risk destruction on the East Coast, the Smith family's heightened sense of nostalgic spatiality impels them to preserve the present dynamics of their idyllic Midwestern lifestyle.

Beyond the relationship to nostalgia, *Meet Me in St. Louis* expresses additional categorical distinctions between the Midwest and New York City. Altman observes a gendered quality informing the film's attitudes about regions, and he writes, "*Meet Me in St. Louis* identifies all the happy-go-lucky women folk with the Midwest, while their ambitious men yearn for college or a job in the East."[63] Within Altman's taxonomy, the tranquil, harmonious Midwest—the nation's space of nostalgia—is feminized. Obviously, the character of Grandpa belies this gendered split, as his dependent status and attachment to the Midwest is at odds with Altman's dichotomy. On a related note, J. P. Telotte offers an alternate explanation for the rift between Alonzo and the rest of the Smiths based on the musical genre's "two distinct impulses: one affirming the group or celebrating society, and another acknowledging a necessity for *self*-expression."[64] Telotte writes that Alonzo's announcement "comments upon two possibilities facing the family— either to follow the individual's desires and abandon the world in which they are so comfortably immersed, or to remain and participate in that celebration of cultural harmony promised by the fair."[65] Whereas Altman feminizes the Midwest and masculinizes New York City, Telotte assigns collective harmony to the central region and individualism to the East Coast. Such classifications correspond with Dreiser's depiction of the East as a volatile urban wilderness in which every individual must fend for one's self.

It is, in part, the ongoing comparison of St. Louis and New York City that eventually persuades Alonzo to keep the Smiths in their Midwestern home. On Christmas Eve, the Smith home is packed up in preparation for the impending

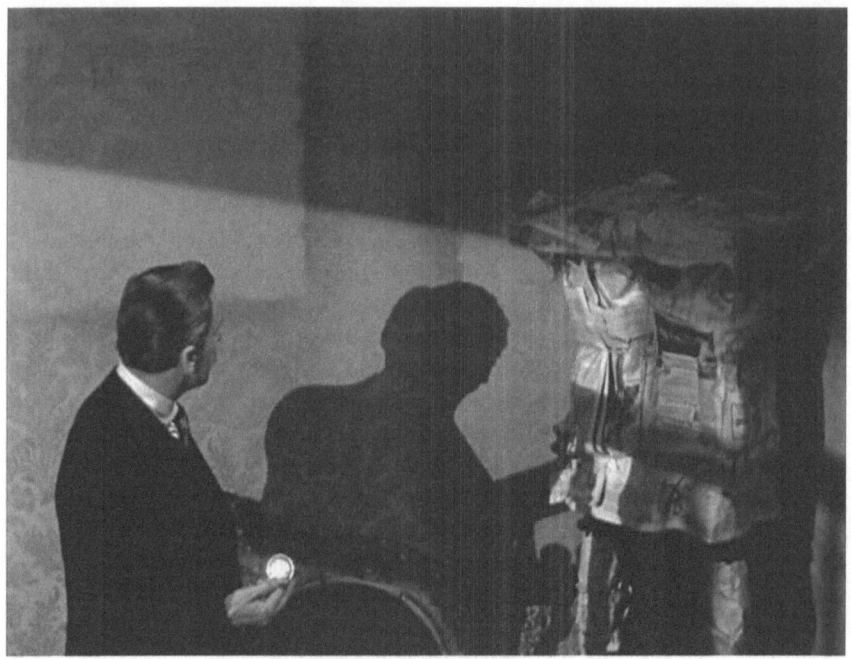

Fig. 1.1. Alonzo contemplates the stopped clock and his pocket watch. Screen capture, *Meet Me in St. Louis* (1944).

move, and Esther delivers her iconic performance of "Have Yourself a Merry Little Christmas."[66] Full of emotion, Tootie races outside the house and smashes a family of "snow people" that had been built earlier in the film. Esther attempts to console the child by saying, "New York is a wonderful town. Look, everybody dreams about going there. But we're luckier than lots of families because we're really going." Alonzo witnesses this exchange from an upstairs window and then solemnly walks downstairs. While pausing on the staircase to check his pocket watch, Alonzo gazes at a grandfather clock that is covered with packing material; notably, Minnelli frames the shot so that Alonzo's shadow is centered between himself and the longcase clock (see fig. 1.1). This important shot visually juxtaposes the film's two competing temporalities: Alonzo's preoccupation with the future and moving forward in time versus his family's nostalgic desire to halt time and/or return to the past. Moreover, the film's pervasive nostalgic spatiality is once again made clear by linking temporal progression with New York City and a paused temporality with St. Louis. In this climactic moment, Alonzo's contemplation of a stopped clock and the unceasing ticking of his own pocket watch functions as the final catalyst that prompts him to embrace—or succumb to, depending on the perspective—the powerful pull of the nostalgic spatiality that has overcome the Smith family.

Upon observing his children's despair and passing a symbol of paused time on the staircase, Alonzo abandons his future-oriented mentality in favor of the

46 *The American Midwest in Film and Literature*

looping temporality of nostalgia. The Smith patriarch immediately calls the rest of the family into the living room and proclaims, "I've got a few words to say. We're not moving to New York. And I don't want to hear a word about it. We're going to stay right here. We're going to stay here till we rot. . . . New York hasn't got a copyright on opportunity. Why, St. Louis is headed for a boom that'll make your head swim. This is a great town. The trouble with you people is, you don't appreciate it because it's right here under your noses. The grass is always greener in somebody else's yard." To this point in the film, Minnelli consistently depicts Alonzo's discordance with his family via his isolation in the frame, such as the patriarch being the only figure in a shot, separated by space between himself and other characters, or situated on a different plane of action. During this scene, for the first time in the film, Minnelli places Alonzo in the same frame and on the same plane as the entire Smith family. This visual solidarity reaffirms the stability that the Smiths will enjoy because Alonzo has canceled the move, and he now shares the family's nostalgic fondness for their present status in St. Louis.

Alonzo's speech about future opportunities in St. Louis, however, must have seemed curious to the film's initial wartime audiences. Regarding Alonzo's earlier enthusiasm for moving to New York City, James Naremore writes, "He is . . . wrong about where one can find progress or modernity, which lie in the new west."[67] But the Smith family is not heading to the West or the East; rather, they are staying in the Midwest until they "rot." By the time that *Meet Me in St. Louis* was released, the nation had experienced World War I and was in the midst of emerging from the Great Depression while entering into another massive global conflict. Together, these events conspired to reduce the popular assessment of the Midwest in American culture. Shortridge observes that "the longer-term impact of [the Great Depression and World War II] on the region's image was negative. Both crises led to increased portrayals of the Middle West as a rural place. . . . By 1950, even Middle Westerners had largely accepted the earlier Eastern view of their region not only as rural but also as a place that was somewhat backward culturally. . . ."[68] Accordingly, Alonzo's claims about rotting and economic booms take on an ironic quality when considered in relation to the Midwest's popular status in 1944.

The historical circumstances during the initial release of *Meet Me in St. Louis* are notable in relation to the film's conclusion, particularly because of the contrast between the temporal context of audience members and that of the Smith family. For audiences living through the continuous turmoil of the first half of the twentieth century, *Meet Me in St. Louis* offers an appealing fantasy: that a desired moment may be occupied indefinitely, rather than expiring when the uncertain future consumes it. The commitment to nostalgically preserving such a moment is evident in the final scene of *Meet Me in St. Louis*. Throughout the narrative, the future oscillates between being a source of dread (due to the potential New York move) and excitement, but the desired World's Fair remains conspicuous in its absence for the majority of the film. In total, barely two minutes of the film's nearly two-hour duration are spent at the Fair, a curious fact in light of how much anticipation the Fair generates.[69] For the most part, the

World's Fair remains an object of desire situated at a temporal moment that is removed from the film's present. Even the lyrics to "Meet Me in St. Louis" emphasize the temporal distance of the Fair, as the song's narrator promises to dance and to "be your tootsie-wootsie" only "*if* you *will* meet me in St. Louis" (emphasis added).[70] Essentially, the vast majority of the film unfolds within a state of sustained desire for an idealized future event. Yet the Smith family anticipates a future moment already located deep in the nation's collective past and, presumably, prior to many of the film's audience members even being born. In this light, the Smiths' mirthful ability to desire the future would itself be an object of nostalgic yearning for audiences aware of the worldwide turmoil following the moments of optimism depicted in *Meet Me in St. Louis*.

The nostalgic desire to preserve the lengthy period of anticipation for the World's Fair strongly informs the film's conclusion, which presents the Smiths finally entering this long-awaited spectacle. Altman writes that "the World's Fair is at the same time a dream image and a hometown reality for the Smith family."[71] This observation calls attention to the way in which the longing produced by temporal distance seems to have caught up to its desired object in *Meet Me in St. Louis*. Like a nostalgic individual yearning for the past, though, the Smiths appear more preoccupied with experiencing desire than attaining the actual object of desire—in this case, the arrival of the World's Fair. When the Fair finally opens, the present reality matches the characters' desire, which prompts not satisfaction, but astonishment and a revised goal: to preserve the initial moment of contact with this long-desired spatiotemporal coordinate.

This updated desire is made evident by the Smiths' reaction to the spectacle of the World's Fair. In the film's final scene, the entire family gathers together as the electric lights of the World's Fair blink on and illuminate the festival grounds. Minnelli concludes *Meet Me in St. Louis* with a series of medium shots, each of which features different groupings of the family with the World's Fair lights reflecting across their faces, while an instrumental version of the title song rises on the soundtrack. Standing alongside Lucille, Lon Jr., and Alonzo, Anna states, "There's never been anything like it in the whole world." Minnelli cuts to a two-shot of Sheffield and Rose, who proclaims, "We don't have to come here on a train or stay in a hotel. It's right in our own hometown." This is followed by a shot of Agnes, Grandpa, and Tootie. The latter asks, "Grandpa, they'll never tear it down, will they?" and Grandpa replies, "Well, they'd better not." The last shot is of John and Esther, who gushes, "I can't believe it. Right here where we live. Right here in St. Louis." The scene then fades out and a title card stating "The End" appears onscreen.

Despite Tootie and Grandpa wishing for the World's Fair to be preserved, it was built to be ephemeral. With their desire for the Fair's permanence clearly unrealized at the time of the film's release, *Meet Me in St. Louis* itself serves as a nostalgic restoration of what was torn down once the World's Fair ended. Understood in this way, the form of nostalgic spatiality that I identify in Turner and Dreiser—that of progress to a certain point and then a looping return inward or backwards—is very much present in *Meet Me in St. Louis*, albeit in a much more positive iteration. The film's climax is Alonzo's announcement of the decision not to move so that the Smith family's present lifestyle may be sustained, and the film ends rather abruptly once the much-anticipated World's Fair opens. Not only is this the end of the narrative, but it also is the end of temporal progress for the Smiths. The Midwestern family does not wish to experience anything beyond that final scene, and the narrative reflects their desire to remain unchanged in a precise locale at an idealized moment by simply ending. Following the World's Fair, the uncertain future can only suffer by comparison, so Minnelli leaves viewers with an image of the resolutely immobile Smith family in an indefinite state of nostalgic rapture.

The desire for temporal simultaneity—of the lost past occupying the same moment as the present—is a key element of nostalgia, particularly within the context of Midwestern texts produced during (or that represent the region at) the turn of the twentieth century. Just as in Turner's writings and *Sister Carrie*, the true object of nostalgia in *Meet Me in St. Louis* is the last moment at which the future was not yet considered to be predetermined or limited. These three texts each express nostalgia for the ability to perceive the future as full of opportunity and positive potential, and they locate this idealized perceptual state within the Midwest. In other words, nostalgic spatiality continually emerges as a significant influence on—and element within—depictions and discussions of Midwestern locales.

From Turner transferring idealized frontier traits onto the Midwest to Dreiser's Hurstwood dementedly conjuring up past memories in his temporally confused present to Minnelli leaving the Smith family at the desired World's Fair for an indefinite duration, these texts all offer a fantasy of the Midwest as a nostalgic realm with overlapping temporalities. The disparity between the medium and tone of each text—historical writing that merges actual occurrence and spatiocultural mythology, naturalistic fiction that is socially engaged and pessimistic about the nation's trajectory, and a vivid, highly artificial cinematic musical full of optimism and familial cheer—further speaks to the deep influence of nostalgic spatiality in the American consciousness. Since the earliest years in which "Midwest" gained recognition and popular usage as a term referencing a collection of twelve states, that regional designation has been marked by nostalgia, regardless of the forum or discourse. Following Turner's initial projection of nostalgic conceptualizations of space and culture onto the Midwest, texts such as *Sister Carrie* and *Meet Me in St. Louis* have helped to calcify such regional associations—and to reveal varying manifestations of nostalgic spatiality—by rearticulating them in different mediums. Configured as a locale in which temporal simultaneity is possible, the Midwest thus comes to be defined as a space of nostalgia within American culture. This identity has remained stubbornly attached to the region even in the twenty-first century.

Notes

1. Kurt Vonnegut, "To Be a Native Middle-Westerner," 1999, Indiana Humanities Council, NUVO Cultural Institute, accessed July 28, 2019, http://www.indianahumanities.org/pdf/Vonnegut.pdf.

2. Frederick Jackson Turner, *The Frontier in American History* (1920; repr., Charleston: BiblioBazaar, 2008).

3. Turner does not define the frontier as one single space; instead, the frontier is a set of conditions detectable in many spaces. Turner describes "a continually advancing frontier line" that creates multiple frontier spaces succeeding one another whenever the "line" of American settlement moves westward. Because Turner theorizes that each progressive frontier features the same rejuvenating qualities, he discusses these shared characteristics in singular terms. As such, "the frontier" actually refers to numerous frontiers located in different spaces at different moments. See: Turner, *The Frontier in American History*, 14.

4. Theodore Dreiser, *Sister Carrie*, ed. Claude Simpson (1990; repr., Boston: Houghton Mifflin, 1959); *Meet Me in St. Louis*, directed by Vincente Minnelli (1944; Burbank, CA: Warner Home Video, 2004), DVD.

5. For instance, in a 1909 address about the Ohio Valley, Turner states, "In short, the real federal aspect of the nation, if we penetrate beneath constitutional forms to the deeper currents of social, economic and political life, will be found to lie in the relation of sections and nation, rather than in the relation of States and nation.... But even if the States disappeared altogether as effective factors in our national life, the sections might, in my opinion, gain from that very disappearance a strength and activity that would prove effective limitations upon the nationalizing process." Here, Turner posits that the nation's "real" character emerges through regional (or sectional) differentiation to a greater degree than through the individual states that comprise the United States. This belief that some degree of underlying authenticity may be located within regional constellations helps to expose Turner's underlying nostalgic tendencies. As detailed in the introduction chapter, Susan Stewart links a nostalgic desire for "authenticity" to the production of narratives that merely reproduce the distance between a past ideal and the inadequate present. Turner's longing for vanished frontier spaces clearly fits Stewart's conception of nostalgic narratives—which, she notes, are "always ideological"—and his discussion of the frontier in relation to the Midwest further exposes a strong current of nostalgia running through what are purportedly empirical histories. See: Turner, *The Frontier in American History*, 137–138; Susan Stewart, *On Longing: Narratives of the Miniature, the Gigantic, the Souvenir, the Collection*. (1993; repr., Durham, NC: Duke University Press, 2007), 23.

6. The former was first presented publicly at "the meeting of the American Historical Association in Chicago, July 12, 1893," while the latter was delivered at a building dedication for the State Historical Society of Minnesota in 1918. See: Turner, *The Frontier in American History*, 39, 298.

7. Ibid., 13–14.

8. Ibid., 38.

9. Jon Gjerde, "Middleness and the Middle West," in *The Midwest: Essays on Regional History*, eds. Andrew R. L. Cayton and Susan E. Gray (Bloomington: Indiana University Press, 2001), 181.

10. In the 1990s, historian John Mack Faragher expressed a sense of befuddlement upon reading a report that Turner's theories about the American West were being refuted by several historians. Faragher's surprise stems not from this critique of Turner, but because he believes it is well established that some of Turner's viewpoints are erroneous. For Faragher, such a perspective on the frontier theorist should not have been notable in the 1990s or even the middle of the twentieth century. Regarding the frontier theory, Faragher writes that the "argument for the closing of the frontier has not held up well," as the maps upon which Turner based his theories turned out to be "less a work

of science than of the imagination. A century later, the West has yet to fill up." More public land in the West was claimed after 1890 than before that year, the "frontier line" reappeared on census maps in 1900 and 1910, and there remained western counties in the late twentieth century that fit Turner's criteria of "unsettled." When corresponding with a colleague, Turner himself later qualified his theories by admitting, "Of course the frontier did not come to an end 'with a bang' in 1890," although he maintained that "the importance of the frontier movement as a large factor in American history did reach its close about that time." See: John Mack Faragher, afterword to *Rereading Frederick Jackson Turner: "The Significance of the Frontier in American History" and Other Essays*, by Frederick Jackson Turner, ed. John Mack Faragher (New York: Henry Holt, 1994), 225–226; John Mack Faragher, introduction to *Rereading Frederick Jackson Turner: "The Significance of the Frontier in American History" and Other Essays*, by Frederick Jackson Turner, ed. John Mack Faragher (New York: Henry Holt, 1994), 6–7.

11. Turner, *The Frontier in American History*, 27.
12. Ibid., 174.
13. Ibid.
14. Ibid., 185.
15. Ibid., 186, emphasis added.
16. Stewart, *On Longing*, 23.
17. Svetlana Boym, *The Future of Nostalgia* (New York: Basic Books, 2001), 49.
18. Vonnegut, "To Be a Native Middle-Westerner."
19. James R. Shortridge, *The Middle West: Its Meaning in American Culture* (Lawrence: University Press of Kansas, 1989), 27.
20. Ibid., 35–36.
21. Turner, *The Frontier in American History*, 132.
22. Ibid.
23. Ibid., 132–133.
24. Historian Stephanie Coontz observes that the frontier family and the "1950s suburban family" typically are "held up as models of traditional American independence.... In fact, these two family types probably tie for the honor of being the most heavily subsidized in American history." Significantly, both of these family types have been associated with the Midwest at various points in history. Regarding western settlers, Coontz writes, "In reality, prairie farmers and other pioneer families owed their existence to massive federal land grants, government-funded military mobilizations that dispossessed hundreds of Native American societies and confiscated half of Mexico, and state-sponsored economic investment in the new lands." Coontz elaborates, "Even after [the] generous, government-funded head start, pioneer families did not normally become self-sufficient. The stereotypical solitary western family, isolated from its neighbors and constantly on the move, did exist, but it was also generally a failure. Economic success in nineteenth-century America, on the frontier as well as in the urban centers, was more frequently linked to persistence and involvement in a community than to family self-reliance or the restless 'pioneering spirit.'" See: Stephanie Coontz, *The Way We Never Were: American Families and the Nostalgia Trap* (1992; repr., New York: Basic Books, 2000), 73–74.
25. Turner, *The Frontier in American History*, 133–134.
26. Ibid., 289–290.
27. Ibid., 284–285.
28. Ibid.
29. Ibid., 289.
30. Sinclair Lewis, *Main Street* (1920; repr., New York: New American Library, 1980).

31. Ibid., 171.
32. Turner, *The Frontier in American History*, 291.
33. Ibid.
34. Ibid., 292.
35. Ibid., 186.
36. Dreiser, *Sister Carrie*, 223.
37. Ibid., 238.
38. Ibid., 245.
39. Jeff Jaeckle provides an insightful reading of *Sister Carrie* that addresses themes of growth and destruction in the novel. Jaeckle describes the novel's "universe" as "a system of perpetually changing processes of evolution and dissolution, which give rise to inscrutable disjunctures not only within the universe itself but between various human beings and between human beings and the universe." Jaeckle's analysis of the novel draws on the work of proto-evolutionary theorist and philosopher Herbert Spencer, who was a major influence on Dreiser's personal beliefs. Jaeckle explains that "Spencer's universe [is] characterized by a perpetual struggle between 'evolution' and 'dissolution.' According to Spencer, motion and change virtually constitute the bulk of existence—motion signals a difference in place, while change indicates a shift in direction . . . at almost all times, there exist varying degrees of evolution and dissolution." The key terms that Jaeckle highlights in Spencer's work—evolution and dissolution—may be adapted in relation to Turner's frontier theories, which also feature a preoccupation with the evolutionary potential in movement and an accompanying prediction of individual and social entropy resulting from stasis. See: Jeff Jaeckle, "Dreiser's Universe of Imbalance in *Sister Carrie*," *Dreiser Studies* 33, no. 2 (Fall 2002): 4–6, Academic Search Complete (8874442).
40. Dreiser, *Sister Carrie*, 275.
41. Nina Markov suggests that Carrie's unhappiness stems, in part, from the fact that her material wealth does not provide her with the cultivated high-culture tastes and symbolic wealth of the more established upper class. Interestingly, Markov reads an almost self-reflexive element into Carrie's in-between class status by observing that "her experience parallels Dreiser's in many ways." Markov explains, "In attempting to gain entry into New York's elite literary establishment, Dreiser encountered the symbolic barriers that [love interest and cultural authority Robert] Ames unconsciously erects before Carrie, a classism all the more effective because it masquerades as moral and aesthetic superiority. . . ." Another possible layer to this classism is the Midwestern origin of Dreiser and the fictional Carrie; the region has a long history of being considered the paragon of low-culture tastes. As I discuss in chapter 5, filmmaker Alexander Payne is perceived similarly as an individual whose Midwestern roots are detectable in the very form and content of the films that he writes and directs. See: Nina Markov, "Class, Culture, and Capital in *Sister Carrie*," *Dreiser Studies* 36, no.1 (Summer 2005): 17, 22, Academic Search Complete (19637685).
42. Dreiser, *Sister Carrie*, 246.
43. Philip Fisher provides insights on the relationship between environment and identity—particularly within urban spaces—in Dreiser's writing. Despite focusing on Dreiser's *An American Tragedy* (1925), Fisher's basic claims about Dreiser's presentation of selfhood are relevant to the identity transformation experienced by Hurstwood in *Sister Carrie*. Fisher writes, "In the city man's world confronts him as his own product and in the end his life confronts him, in verdict, as his own product too. . . . Under modern conditions, the conditions no longer of nature, the self is now outside the body, around the body at a distance that, once felt, creates a desire for the possession or

appropriation of an assembled self in material, external form. This desire with its inversion, flight, becomes visible in the two categories of possession of what is distant—sexual desire and money." Certainly, there is some straightforward correspondence and causality among Hurstwood's sexual desire for Carrie, his accompanying need for money, and his flight to New York City. Moreover, Fisher observes that the unnatural city environment cleaves one's "self" from the physical constraints of the body, thus creating a "distance" between the two. Such a perception of distance regarding present circumstances and identity recalls the nostalgic belief in temporal and spatial separation from what is "authentic." See: Philip Fisher, "Looking Around to See Who I Am: Dreiser's Territory of the Self," *ELH* 44, no. 4 (Winter 1977): 730–731, JSTOR.

44. Dreiser, *Sister Carrie*, 414.
45. Ibid., 231.
46. Boym, *The Future of Nostalgia*, 41.
47. Dreiser, *Sister Carrie*, 241.
48. Ibid., 358.
49. Ibid., 382.
50. Ibid., 410.
51. Paula Geyh discusses this scene in relation to issues of class and describes the way in which Hurstwood's "misidentification heightens his own sense of lack, evokes in him a desire for what she's 'got'—wealth, fame, social acceptance—all symbolized by that sign." Geyh adds, "Having lost the real Carrie, Hurstwood is reduced to negotiating with her sign. While his confusion signals the depth of his disorientation and despair, it also points to how, in many ways, Carrie's real identity is now not much more than this sign." With these observations, Geyh highlights the reduction of identity that occurs in New York City for both Hurstwood and Carrie. For Geyh, these two characters steadily are stripped of complexity until they exist merely as signs representing categories such as age, class, gender, and culture. See: Paula Geyh, "From Cities of Things to Cities of Signs: Urban Spaces and Urban Subjects in *Sister Carrie* and *Manhattan Transfer*," *Twentieth-Century Literature* 52, no. 4 (Winter 2006): 424, JSTOR.
52. Turner, *The Frontier in American History*, 186.
53. Gilles Deleuze, *Cinema 2: The Time-Image*, trans. Hugh Tomlinson and Robert Galeta (1985; repr., Minneapolis: University of Minnesota Press, 2010), 62–63.
54. Ibid., 63–64.
55. Despite referencing several of Minnelli's other musicals, Deleuze does not directly comment on *Meet Me in St. Louis* in *Cinema 2: The Time-Image*.
56. I present a lengthier consideration of the dissolve's nostalgic properties when discussing *The Virgin Suicides* (1999) and *The Straight Story* (1999) in chapter 6.
57. This aspect of the film somewhat matches Boym's claim that restorative nostalgia renders history as "a perfect snapshot." See: Boym, *The Future of Nostalgia*, 49.
58. Beth Genné writes, "Minnelli's aim was not simply to be historically accurate. Rather, his goal was to create pictures that were aesthetically satisfying as well." Such vibrant images fit a nostalgic understanding of the past as being superior to the drab present. Scott Higgins directly comments on these seasonal title cards and writes, "Minnelli explained that he intended these illustrations, resembling turn-of-the-century greeting cards, to help set the film's nostalgic tone." See: Beth Genné, "Vincente Minnelli's Style in Microcosm: The Establishing Sequence of 'Meet Me in St. Louis,'" *Art Journal* 43, no. 3 (1983): 252, Academic Search Complete (5492363); Scott Higgins, "Color at the Center: Minnelli's Technicolor Style in *Meet Me in St. Louis*," *Style* 32, no. 3 (Fall 1998): 458, JSTOR.

59. Rick Altman, *The American Film Musical* (Bloomington: Indiana University Press, 1987), 28.

60. Ibid., 27.

61. Ibid.

62. During this introductory sequence, Tootie is revealed to be riding along with the ice delivery man. Tootie has a delightfully morbid sensibility that reappears throughout the film, and these tendencies appear to set her apart from the more staid desires of the other members of the Smith family. For instance, during a much-analyzed Halloween celebration later in the film, Tootie explicitly embraces being declared the "most horrible" child in the neighborhood. James Naremore assesses this scene by writing that "Halloween momentarily inverts the patriarchal and heterosexual values of the film, confusing genders and setting domestic property afire. . . . Tootie wears a floppy business suit, wire-rimmed glasses, and a rat's nose with long gray whiskers dangling from the nostrils; she is supposed to represent a 'horrible ghost,' but she looks more like . . . a parody of her father." Despite Tootie's wild streak and participation in a temporary disruption of the film's normative ideology, Naremore notes that "Tootie is seldom a rebel against convention. Her favorite city is St. Louis, and in some respects she is the most conservative character of them all." As such, the film's true "most horrible" figure remains Alonzo, whose values diverge from his family until the climactic scene. See: James Naremore, *The Films of Vincente Minnelli* (Cambridge: Cambridge University Press, 1993), 82–85.

63. Altman, *The American Film Musical*, 48.

64. J. P. Telotte, "Self and Society: Vincente Minnelli and Musical Formula," *The Journal of Popular Film and Television* 9, no. 4 (1982): 181, emphasis in original, Academic Search Complete (31127942).

65. Ibid., 185.

66. The lyrics to this melancholy song reiterate the nostalgic character of the film in several lines that suggest a relationship between contingency and happiness by highlighting spatial and temporal distance. For instance, the song's final verse is "*Someday* soon/We all will be together/*If* the Fates allow/*Until then*/We'll have to muddle through somehow/So have yourself a merry little Christmas *now*" (emphasis added). These sentiments indicate that the uncertainty of the future necessitates a preservation of—and appreciation for—the present, an attitude that the Smith family embraces throughout *Meet Me in St. Louis*.

67. Naremore, *The Films of Vincente Minnelli*, 74.

68. Shortridge, *The Middle West*, 62.

69. Of course, as Naremore notes, the visual absence of the World's Fair may be attributed to practical reasons, such as production costs: "wartime restrictions on sets forced MGM to economize on the design of the fair; the idyllic glow of the film's conclusion is achieved entirely through our memory of the Smith women." See: Naremore, *The Films of Vincente Minnelli*, 89.

70. While the lyrics present such merrymaking as a condition located in an undetermined future rendezvous, they also construct the World's Fair as a singular spectacle: "Don't tell me the lights are shining/Any place but there." Much as nostalgia invents a fictional and perfected past, the characters singing the song all reproduce the image of a fantastical future that will exist exclusively at the World's Fair.

71. Altman, *The American Film Musical*, 80.

2 | Spatial Constriction, Race, and Midwestern Stagnation

Near the conclusion of Victor Fleming's *The Wizard of Oz* (1939), Dorothy Gale (Judy Garland) famously learns that she can return to her life in Kansas simply by repeating, "There's no place like home."[1] Having journeyed across the Technicolor landscape of Oz, Dorothy still yearns for the sepia-tinted hues of the stark Kansas terrain shown during the film's opening and closing scenes. Before departing from Oz, Dorothy makes an overtly nostalgic resolution by promising, "[If] I ever go looking for my heart's desire again, I won't look any further than my own backyard because if it isn't there, I never really lost it to begin with." Released just five years later, Vincente Minnelli's *Meet Me in St. Louis* (1944)—another Judy Garland vehicle—is also marked by a preoccupation with preserving a threatened Midwestern lifestyle.[2] In Minnelli's film, the mere possibility of moving from St. Louis to the East Coast is enough to cause panic within the Smith household until patriarch Alonzo (Leon Ames) finally declares, "We're going to stay here till we rot." These two films' shared emphasis on nostalgically embracing provincialism must have been intended as a comforting sentiment to help audiences escape the troubled world of the Great Depression and World War II outside of the theater. Regarding Garland's MGM musicals set in the Midwest, Patricia Oman observes, "The midwestern setting of [these] films allows for a safe separation between their problematic contemporary culture and the safety of the past, but they all acknowledge this separation.[3] In this way, films such as *The Wizard of Oz* and *Meet Me in St. Louis* "work through a variety of American cultural anxieties of the World War II era, [but] their imagined resolutions to these conflicts demonstrate social exclusion."[4] Many other Midwestern texts from this period further reveal the problematic effects of stability by depicting the disturbing outcomes that stem from spatial constriction. Such narratives counterpose the nostalgic fear of movement (as exemplified by George Hurstwood in *Sister Carrie* [1900] or the Smith family in *Meet Me in St. Louis*) by prominently showcasing characters who yearn to break free from varying forms of restriction and entrapment in the Midwest.[5]

This chapter's three primary texts were released during a fifteen-year period of national and global crisis—from 1929 to 1944—that overlaps with the Great Depression and the majority of World War II. In popular representations of the Midwest from this era, the region frequently is depicted as having devolved into the very "rot" that Alonzo boldly predicts at the climax of *Meet Me in St. Louis*. Indeed, Robert S. Lynd and Helen Merrell Lynd's sociological project, *Middletown: A Study in Modern American Culture* (1929), Richard Wright's novel *Native*

Son (1940), and Preston Sturges's film *The Miracle of Morgan's Creek* (1944) all envision the Midwest as a stagnating realm, largely due to the region's constricted status in terms of both culture and geography.[6] The claustrophobic regional spaces of these three texts undermine positive nostalgic associations with the Midwest and affirm Frederick Jackson Turner's prediction that the inability to expand further into the West would produce cultural turmoil by transforming the nation into "a witches' kettle" of discontent.[7] As will become clear in this chapter, spatial constriction is interconnected with issues of race and gender within Midwestern narratives, particularly in relation to the complex ways in which white masculinity has been attached to the region's default popular identity.

Building upon my earlier analysis of nostalgic spatiality and Turner, this chapter has two purposes: first, to consider—within a Midwestern context—the lingering cultural repercussions of Turner's claim that the United States was "thrown back upon itself" when frontier expansion theoretically ended in the late nineteenth century, and, second, to reveal the contrasting ways in which the Lynds, Wright, and Sturges each identify nostalgia as a significant factor in restricting social mobility and physical movement in the Midwest, especially within racial and gendered frameworks.[8] Moreover, *Middletown*, *The Miracle of Morgan's Creek*, and *Native Son* all portray the Midwest as a space that is often isolated from the modern culture unfolding elsewhere. In other words, these texts present either the entire Midwest, precise regional communities, and/or individual Midwestern characters as what could be described as "antimodern" on some level.

If the Midwest is indeed out of sync with the creative and destructive processes of modernity, then it is necessary to briefly identify some general qualities of this historico-cultural context. While describing modernity as a state of "permanent revolution," Marshall Berman comments on the "kinds of people" who are able to endure such circumstances.[9] Berman elaborates,

> In order for people, whatever their class, to survive in modern society, their personalities must take on the fluid and open form of this society. Modern men and women must learn to yearn for change: not merely to be open to changes in their personal and social lives, but positively to demand them, actively to seek them out and carry them through. They must learn not to long nostalgically for the "fixed, fast-frozen relationships" of the real or fantasized past, but to delight in mobility, to thrive on renewal, to look forward to future developments in their conditions of life and their relations with their fellow men.[10]

Here, Berman asserts that thriving in modernity necessitates a lack of nostalgia, which is the very quality that rapidly comes to define the Midwest in the first half of the twentieth century. The future-oriented disposition required by modernity also contrasts with cultural narratives that link the Midwest to the past, such as Turner's transference of "vanished" frontier traits onto the heartland. Accordingly, the Midwest's anachronistic and nostalgic popular identity renders the region as incompatible with modernity's transformative drive.

Of particular pertinence for this chapter is Berman's insistence that "modern men and women" continually adapt to change and "delight in mobility." An unwillingness or inability to embrace change—especially those changes produced by modernity—pervades many Midwestern narratives from the 1920s through the 1940s. For instance, in a study of the various film adaptations of Edna Ferber's novel *Show Boat* (1926), Oman argues that this era's "discourses of region and nation not only are bound up with those of race and gender but also reflect anxiety about modernity. This fear of modernity is the single defining feature of all versions of *Show Boat* . . . [which foreground] the juxtaposition of modern urban spaces to nostalgic rural spaces."[11] Similarly, in films such as *The Wizard of Oz* and *Meet Me in St. Louis*, Midwestern characters are committed to preserving stable, nostalgic formations of home. In the texts considered in this chapter, the Midwest is imagined as an environment that prevents geographic mobility and locks its inhabitants into rigidly fixed identities. The Midwesterners subjected to these restrictive pressures—as evident in *The Miracle of Morgan's Creek* and *Native Son*—experience great anxiety and distress, which physically manifest through bodily dysfunction or violent outbursts. Before examining the damaged protagonists developed by Sturges and Wright, it is instructive to survey how the Midwest's popular image was shaped in the decades prior to the 1940s.

Middletown and Midwestern Literature of the 1910s and 1920s

The first half of the twentieth century features a fluctuating spectrum of American attitudes toward the Midwest. James Shortridge claims that "1920 marks a clear apogee" in favorable assessments of the Midwest, while the region's "nadir came about 1950."[12] Significantly, the downturn from the high-water mark of the Midwest's popular estimation coincides with the emergence of the so-called "revolt from the village" writers, whose ranks include Midwesterners Sherwood Anderson and Sinclair Lewis.[13] While analyzing this regionally engaged literature, Tom Lutz describes the beginning of the 1920s as a moment that features a "new, demythologizing approach to the American village"—which regularly is depicted as being located in the Midwest—in texts such as Anderson's *Winesburg, Ohio* (1919) and Lewis's *Main Street* (1920).[14] Lutz explains that Anderson and Lewis detail and criticize "the standardizing small-mindedness of provincialism" by crafting small town characters who are "complicit in their own oppression."[15]

With *Main Street* and *Babbitt* (1922), Lewis especially is harsh in his evaluation of the Midwest.[16] In these novels, Lewis indicates that the region's small town inhabitants willfully foster social insularity, which exacerbates the homogenizing effects of their geographic seclusion. For example, while reflecting on "the surface ugliness" of seemingly interchangeable small towns, Carol Kennicott—the frustrated protagonist of *Main Street*—asserts, "The universal similarity—that is the physical expression of the philosophy of dull safety."[17] Over the course of the narrative, Carol's attempts to introduce even a mild bit of cosmopolitanism through activities such as upscale parties or the development of a local theater group are stymied by Gopher Prairie's inhabitants, who are resolute in their resistance to change. In contrast to Carol, *Babbitt*'s titular protagonist embraces the provincialism that often characterizes the Midwest in popular representations of the region. During one especially longwinded speech, George Babbitt pronounces that

> the ideal of American manhood and culture isn't a lot of cranks sitting around chewing the rag about their Rights and their Wrongs, but a God-fearing, hustling, successful, two-fisted Regular Guy, who belongs to some church with pep and piety to it, who belongs to the Boosters or the Rotarians or the Kiwanis, to the Elks or Moose or Red Men or Knights of Columbus or any one of a score of organizations of good, jolly, kidding, laughing, sweating, upstanding, lend-a-handing Royal Good Fellows, who plays hard and works hard, and whose answer to his critics is a square-toed boot that'll teach the grouches and smart alecks to respect the He-man and get out and root for Uncle Samuel, U.S.A.![18]

Along with endorsing these conservative values and limited notions of masculine identity, George also recognizes only a sanitized version of his fictional Midwestern hometown, Zenith. As George drives through Zenith, his willful blindness to any less-than-ideal sections of the midsize city is made clear when Lewis writes, "As always [George] ignored the next two blocks, decayed blocks not yet reclaimed from the grime and shabbiness of the Zenith of 1885."[19] In this brief passage, Lewis subtly reveals how Midwestern environments are selectively imagined through the omission or obscuring of elements that do not correspond to idealized regional imagery.

Just a few years before Lewis and Anderson's critiques were published, Willa Cather's *O Pioneers!* (1913) captured the Midwest in the process of transitioning from a harsh, isolated frontier space to a more ordered and populous environment.[20] Over the thirty-year span of the narrative, Cather details tensions within the immigrant community that inhabits a segment of the Nebraska prairie. Protagonist Alexandra Bergson continually advocates for more sophisticated farming techniques and business practices despite the frequent protestations of her two eldest brothers, Lou and Oscar. They, in turn, harbor resentment toward Alexandra's successful stewardship of the family's land because she is a woman. At one crucial moment, the brothers effectively sabotage her marriage plans with longtime friend, Carl Linstrum, by claiming that "everybody's laughing to see you get took in; at your age, too. Everybody knows he's nearly five years younger than you, and is after your money. Why, Alexandra, you are forty years old!"[21] Throughout the novel, Cather associates the brothers' general resistance to modern farming practices and their lack of business acumen with regressive attitudes about gender, sexuality, and marriage.

Earlier in the narrative, Alexandra and Carl debate the merits of living in rural Nebraska versus New York City. For Carl, the benefits of being "near the heart of things" are outweighed by his own feelings of insignificance, anonymity, and failure, as well as simply "the exorbitant rent."[22] Alexandra responds by ruminating on the "high rent" of rural life that is physically taxing and culturally isolated, which allows "minds [to] get stiff."[23] This conversation makes explicit the novel's continual oscillation between celebrating the resourcefulness and resilience of the prairie inhabitants while also acknowledging the limitations of such provincial spaces. Lutz posits that Cather's work is in a dialogue with modernity. He writes, "*O Pioneers!* is antimodern in its rejection of mass culture, promodern in its respect for agricultural science and psychology, antimodern in its respect for old Ivar [an eccentric character who is devoted to individualistic, hybrid religious beliefs and is associated with animals and the natural world], promodern in its rejection of social convention."[24] Such clashing dynamics recur across Midwestern literature of this era and speak to the region's peculiar status in the American popular imagination. From the brutal mechanization of the Chicago stockyards detailed by Upton Sinclair in *The Jungle* (1906) to the more pastoral settings of literature by Cather, Anderson, and Lewis, the Midwest slides on a spectrum that includes urban sites of dehumanizing technological advances and rural spaces of outdated social and cultural values.[25]

Significantly, Robert S. Lynd and Helen Merrell Lynd conducted their research for *Middletown* during 1924 and 1925 in the immediate wake of the literary assaults on Midwestern culture by Anderson and Lewis, as well as Cather's more ambivalent portrait of the region.[26] Although the "revolt from the village" authors had antecedents in earlier writings by figures such as Hamlin Garland and Mark Twain, a key distinction is that the Midwest did not achieve popular recognition as a discrete region until the early twentieth century. As such, the work of these later writers was produced within a still-developing regional context that permitted them to react against the Midwest's popular identity as it was evolving. The Lynds, interestingly, appear to have been influenced by the limited cultural associations with the Midwest that Lewis and others sought to trouble and critique.

Despite the pretense of being an objective sociological study of Muncie, Indiana, *Middletown* actually participates in a mythologizing discourse about the Midwest that dates back to at least Frederick Jackson Turner's nostalgic vision of the region.[27] Similar to Turner's writings, the Lynds' analysis of Muncie is shaped by preexisting assumptions about culture, demographics, and Midwestern identity. In short, *Middletown* reflects ideological notions of what constitutes "averageness" or the "typical" in both the United States and the Midwest. Certainly, the Lynds provide a variety of insights about the culture of Muncie, including commentary on tensions stemming from class differences, the effects of technological change on socialization, and other issues in the community. The Lynds, however, rather explicitly select Muncie and develop their methodology with problematic racial factors in mind. Consequently, I read the Lynds' work not for its ostensibly empirical content, but for how it affirms and reifies certain elements of the Midwest's reductive popular image, particularly in terms of race. For the purposes of my project, I situate *Middletown* as one of many influential accounts of the Midwest produced during the 1920s.

While outlining criteria for the selection of Muncie as the focus of *Middletown*, the Lynds reveal several significant biases about the Midwest and American culture. To ensure that "the city be as representative as possible of contemporary American life," the Lynds determine that their object of study should feature seven qualities:

> (1) A temperate climate. (2) A sufficiently rapid rate of growth to insure the presence of a plentiful assortment of the growing pains accompanying contemporary social change. (3) An industrial culture with modern high-speed machine production. (4) The absence of dominance of the city's industry by a single plant, i.e., not a one-industry town. (5) A substantial local artistic life to balance its industrial activity; also a largely self-contained artistic life ... (6) The absence of any outstanding peculiarities or acute local problems which would mark it off from the mid-channel sort of American community ... a seventh qualification was added: the city should, if possible, be in that common-denominator of America, the Middle West.[28]

This seventh desired trait shows that the Lynds assume the "average" nature of the Midwest is self-evident and a preexisting condition, rather than being a cultural association that their project is complicit in further reproducing. Moreover, for the Lynds, the Midwest's generic quality extends into the realms of the cultural, the economic, and the natural environment itself. With Muncie, then, the Lynds identify a locale featuring an abstract "middle-of-the-road quality" that is presumed to be a defining element of the entire Midwest.[29] Clearly, the Lynds' project is predicated on a presumption of Midwestern averageness and standardization.[30]

Even as the Lynds proclaim Muncie's status to be a "representative" city within the nation's "common-denominator" region, they quickly undermine such synecdochic presuppositions. Regarding Muncie, the Lynds confusingly qualify that, "although it was its characteristic rather than its exceptional features which led to the selection of Middletown, no claim is made that it is a 'typical' city, and the findings of this study can, naturally, only with caution be applied to other cities or to American life in general."[31] Here, as is often the case, the Midwest is presented as a space onto which any qualities may be projected, however contradictory they might be. At once "representative," yet not "typical," the Lynds' version of Muncie (and the Midwest) is that of a malleable space, one that may be constructed to affirm preexisting perceptions instead of reflecting actual circumstances.

Another primary consideration directing the Lynds' methodology casts further doubts on their pretense of objectivity. The Lynds specify that Muncie was chosen for being "compact and homogeneous enough to be manageable," which is a rather loaded statement.[32] Although the Lynds' desire for manageability may appear to be innocuous and related to issues of scale, the term also suggests some manipulation of their object of study; in this sense, Muncie as a "manageable" space configures the city as something akin to a block of clay that might be molded into a desired shape. Such an evaluation of *Middletown* is affirmed when the Lynds detail how they assessed the desired "compact and homogenous" character of potential cities for their project.

For the Lynds, three characteristics were identified as necessary "to secure a certain amount of compactness and homogeneity" regarding the city that they would study:

> (1) A city of the 25,000–50,000 group. This meant selection from among 143 cities, according to the 1920 Census. A city of this size ... would be large enough to have put on long trousers and to take itself seriously, and yet small enough to be studied from many aspects as a unit. (2) A city as nearly self-contained as is possible in this era of rapid and pervasive inter-communication, not a satellite city. (3) A small Negro and foreign-born population. In a difficult study of this sort it seemed a distinct advantage to deal with a homogenous, native-born population, even though such a population is unusual in an American industrial city. Thus, instead of being forced to handle two major variables, racial change and cultural change, the field staff was enabled to concentrate on cultural change. The study thus became one of the interplay of a relatively constant native American stock and its changing environment.[33]

In the context of Midwestern representational conventions, particularly those of this period, two elements assume a high degree of significance in this passage. First, the Lynds express a general concern with the cultural effects of movement and containment. The requirement for stasis and provincialism—for the city to be "self-contained" and to have limited "inter-communication" with other communities—certainly would produce a more "manageable" object of study, but it also reflects an attitude that imagines the Midwest as removed or detached from the rest of the nation. Through this emphasis on geographic and cultural boundaries, nostalgic spatiality is detectable in the Lynds' work. Their version of the Midwest retains a proximity to idealized past modes of living, due to its perceived cultural isolation and lack of contact with other locales.

The second major element in this passage is, of course, the Lynds' highly problematic engagement with race and regionalism.[34] The Lynds note that Caucasians "compose 92 per cent. [sic] of the total population" in Muncie, which might otherwise explain their decision to limit the study to the city's "native whites"; however, the fact that they sought a locale with limited diversity for their project exposes how *Middletown* serves to reaffirm racially exclusionist definitions of what constitutes a small Midwestern city.[35] Revealingly, the Lynds' dismissal of the heterogeneous elements of Muncie's demographics recalls the pervasive racism of Turner's writings. Indeed, aspects of the work by the Lynds and Turner correspond to what Eric Hinderaker describes as "liberating contrivances."[36] Hinderaker's valuable descriptor includes "rhetorical practices that have allowed Midwesterners, and those who have written about Midwestern experience, to elide the moral problem of conquest," as well as regional narratives that "allowed later residents of the Midwest to cultivate and sustain their myths of reconciliation and pluralist democracy in a conquered, debatable land."[37] Turner describes the frontier as "the meeting point between savagery and civilization," and this dichotomy is based upon both physical terrain and racial distinctions.[38] For Turner, North America's supposed past vacancy (which enabled

European settlers to expand across the continent) was contingent on defining Native Americans as "the savage lords of the boundless prairie" who stubbornly "resist the march of civilization."[39] Throughout Turner's work, Native Americans are configured as simultaneously present and absent. Native Americans exist, but because they are not part of "civilization," the spaces that they occupy remain "vacant." By means of a racist classificatory system, Turner invents a version of the continent to support his theories. This overt erasure of difference portends the troubling racial absences in both *Middletown* and the ongoing popular identity of the Midwest.

For contemporary readers, the Lynds' description of Muncie's white population as "native American" stands out for multiple reasons.[40] Obviously, the term "Native American" now is commonly used to denote the continent's indigenous people rather than individuals of European origin. Furthermore, both the separation of "racial change" from "cultural change" and the concomitant exclusion of African Americans and immigrants from the status of "full" American are rather egregious presuppositions upon which the Lynds build their study. Along with the Lynds' association of a white population and the "native" label, these foundational aspects of *Middletown* echo the rhetoric and values of nativist political movements throughout American history.[41] Although such correspondences with nativism are presumably unintentional, the Lynds' methodology clearly invites scrutiny. For the purposes of the present discussion, equating Midwesterners with "native" status signals a major change in perceptions of the Midwest and its inhabitants as the 1930s approached. Between Turner's earliest writings and the Lynds' study of Muncie, the Midwest's identity evolves from western frontier territory to American region, which is a development that reframes its popular identity. This identification shift of the white Midwesterner from "settler" to "native American" requires a sort of cultural amnesia about how the regional space previously had been understood. No longer is the Midwest dutifully transforming individuals into "Americans" as Turner claims; now, "native-born" white Midwesterners are perceived as not only intrinsically "American," but the most exemplary incarnation of American citizens.[42]

That social scientists such as the Lynds unquestioningly accept and repeat the conflation of whiteness and native status reveals the extent to which this association is absorbed into American culture by the mid-1920s. Even with the literary critiques of the period—or perhaps because of their success in imagining the region as a discrete space—the Midwest's identity as the nation's "common-denominator" is affirmed. Beyond *Middletown*'s status as an influential, if problematic, classic in the field of sociology, the Lynds' study also serves as evidence of essentialist regional narratives permeating cultural perceptions of place and becoming ingrained in history. As the remainder of this chapter will demonstrate, notions of the Midwest's averageness and homogeneity prove to be an ongoing target of satire and critique in subsequent works of film and literature. *The Miracle of Morgan's Creek* depicts the disorder masked by proclamations of the Midwest's "average" or undistinguished identity, while *Native Son* revolves around an impoverished African American protagonist whose mere existence draws attention to the racial omissions of the Midwestern narratives discussed above.

The Miracle of Morgan's Creek

In sharp contrast to the ways in which Turner and the Lynds create and disseminate reductive visions of the Midwest, writer/director Preston Sturges overtly calls attention to the mechanisms that produce normalized regional narratives with his subversive wartime comedy, *The Miracle of Morgan's Creek*. Blending slapstick and screwball conventions, *The Miracle of Morgan's Creek* links nostalgic Midwestern imagery, limiting gender norms, and restricted movement. Sturges addresses these topics through the film's narrative and form: Norval Jones (Eddie Bracken) and Trudy Kockenlocker (Betty Hutton) struggle with conformist pressures endemic to their small Midwestern community, and a series of lengthy tracking shots accentuates the social and spatial constriction of Morgan's Creek.[43] With *The Miracle of Morgan's Creek*, Sturges strips Midwestern imagery of nostalgic associations and shows it to be a space of odious cultural stagnation.

The Miracle of Morgan's Creek revolves around a series of escalating deceptions, as the narrative features characters scheming to create an illusion of conformity to the social mores repeatedly endorsed by the Midwestern town's inhabitants and public institutions. Despite multiple attempts to enlist in the army, Norval's crippling anxiety leaves him stuck in Morgan's Creek, much to his dismay. Norval is infatuated with Trudy, a young woman who attends a military party that culminates with her getting drunk, married, pregnant, and unable to remember the name of the soldier whom she wed, much less the act of consummation.[44] Eventually, Trudy gives birth to sextuplets, who comprise the titular "miracle" of the film. Prior to the birth, Trudy and her younger sister Emmy (Diana Lynn) collaborate to coerce Norval into participating in a series of plans designed to obscure Trudy's indiscretions so that her marriage and pregnancy will appear as "legitimate" in the eyes of the townspeople. These plans are foiled until the last-minute intervention of Governor McGinty (Brian Donlevy), who pardons the jailed Norval, gives him an honorary position in the State Guard, and has marriage documents falsified so that Trudy's sextuplets are on the record as having been born into wedlock. The film concludes with Norval embracing his marriage to Trudy, only to convulse wildly upon discovering that he now is responsible for six children.

The sense of disorder that Sturges brings to the Midwest in *The Miracle of Morgan's Creek* is typical of the films that he wrote and directed. Andrew Dickos writes that Sturges "utilized Hollywood as a tool to complicate, cynicize, as well as contradict, the myths and vision of America that directors such as Capra, Ford, and Griffith propagated."[45] The very "compositions" in Sturges's films, Dickos suggests, "belie the delusion that there is much harmony in the world."[46] Regarding *The Miracle of Morgan's Creek*, Dickos writes, "Sturges' vision of small-town life in 1940s America confirms certain cultural myths and values as much as it debunks others. The idyllic harmony one envisions about provincial America becomes little more than a delusion in the chaotic world of Morgan's Creek. All of the same elements are there—the setting, people, and activities; however, they are constituted differently, invested with qualities of frenzied anxiety, contradiction, and paradox."[47] Leger Grindon similarly observes, "The film portrays failure or success as inadvertent: the individual is essentially a helpless plaything of circumstances and the unpredictable ebb and flow of social sympathy, condemnation or praise."[48] Unlike Turner's conception of the Midwest as a space that retains the frontierlike conditions for individual success based on merit, Sturges argues that the region is a disorderly realm of chance and uncertain opportunity.

Aside from merely presenting chaos within the supposedly staid environment of the Midwest, Sturges also exposes the highly constructed nature of the idealized narratives that circulate about the region. From the earliest frames of the film, Sturges's subversive critique emphasizes gaps between actual events and official records, thus exposing the machinations involved in sustaining the deceptively bland surface of Midwestern small town imagery. The majority of *The Miracle of Morgan's Creek* is presented as a flashback from framing scenes in which an unnamed newspaper editor (Victor Potel) informs Governor McGinty of an unfolding crisis in Morgan's Creek. At the start of the film, Sturges cuts between the newspaper editor and McGinty in order to obscure details of the crisis, but the governor's hyperbolic reaction suggests a potentially devastating catastrophe. McGinty proclaims, "This is a matter of state policy, state pride. National pride," and he quickly appends, "This is the biggest thing to happen to this state since we stole it from the Indians." These comments are notable for two reasons. First, the explicit acknowledgment of land theft from Native Americans—not to be confused with the Lynds' white Midwestern "native" Americans—is a surprising admission that belies any pretense of moral superiority on the part of the government agencies that continually attempt to regulate the behavior of the residents of Morgan's Creek. Second, McGinty immediately links the "crisis" to "pride" on both a local and national scale, as well as, curiously, to "state policy." As the narrative proceeds, this governmental concern with the private lives of the state's constituents recurs; again and again, authority figures articulate and enforce a linkage between individuals and the broader identities of the town, state, and even nation.

Sturges sporadically cuts back to this phone conversation throughout the film, and McGinty's ongoing preoccupation with Trudy's status further foregrounds the connection between private life and public regulation. During one segment of the conversation, the governor interrupts the editor and proclaims, "Wait a minute, never mind the details. Is the girl married or isn't she married? It's a matter of state honor. . . . Well, she's got to be married, that's all there is to it. We can't have a thing like that hanging over our fair state, besmirching our fair name." Eventually, McGinty rectifies the "problem" of Trudy's pregnancy by simply rewriting the official account of what occurred. Regarding the irregularities of the marriage license, McGinty shouts, "What's the matter with the marriage? She's married to Norval Jones, she always has been," and so it is recorded as such.[49] Here,

Sturges presents a process by which the governor reinscribes a potentially disruptive development—Trudy's drunken military marriage to an unknown soldier and her accompanying pregnancy—into a sanitized "official" narrative.

Within the film, reconciling Norval's spasmodic body with idealized masculine traits proves to be just as great of a challenge as explaining away Trudy's indiscretions, even with his earnest desire to conform.[50] Part of what makes Norval such a subversive character is the wartime context in which *The Miracle of Morgan's Creek* was produced. James Harvey notes that "it was not a good time for the romantic comedy" because of "the spreading atmosphere of religiosity-cum-patriotism."[51] Harvey elaborates, "Hollywood—at least as submissive to the State propaganda system as it was to the Catholic Church—was off to war well before the country was."[52] Consequently, Hollywood films—particularly comedies—began to function as recruitment tools "with the heroine inciting the hero not to romance but to enlistment."[53] Trudy herself does not seem particularly interested in marriage until she discovers her unexpected pregnancy, and she justifies her desire to attend the military party with the pretense of being patriotic. As Trudy explains to Norval, the soldiers are "fine, clean, young boys from good homes and we can't send them off maybe to be killed and rockets' red glare and bombs bursting in air without anybody to say goodbye to them, can we?" This statement reveals an awareness, conscious or not, of rigid gender roles in the town, as men are "supposed" to go fight, while women are "supposed" to encourage the men to do so.

Norval, however, upends wartime romantic comedy conventions through his inability to embody masculine ideals, as do Trudy's early flirtations with numerous soldiers. Grindon writes, "The soldiers represent the ideal of strong, self-sacrificing men ready to defend their country; however, the romantic comedy needs to embody these virtues in a sterling individual, a move the film refuses. As the handsome soldiers depart, they are replaced by Norval Jones."[54] Even though Norval claims to have a strong desire to enlist in the army, his body physically revolts against the intense social pressure to conform to masculine ideals. As Dickos notes, Norval "craves order in his life . . . but his hyper-dysfunctional behavior belies any possibility for physical, let alone mental order."[55] Beyond Bracken's spasmodic performance functioning as physical comedy, Norval's anxious behavior indicates that bodily dysfunction is a potential outcome of failed attempts to adhere to compulsory gender norms.

Sturges attaches additional critical dimensions to Norval's uncontrollable body and faltering masculinity. Dickos explains, "For Sturges, the art of slapstick is less a matter of the mind exercising control over the body than a case of making one's convulsiveness conform to the desires and intentions one would like to express. Physical movement, in this sense, necessarily plays against linear, logical thinking and undermines such thinking to make us see that the comedy of an orderly existence lies precisely in our dogged attempts to make such an existence possible."[56] In other words, through the chaos of his body, Norval reveals the extent to which efforts to conform to restrictive ideals produce social disorder and individual discontent. Exposing this dynamic—and, notably, attaching it to military recruitment during wartime—is one of Sturges's most scandalous acts of subversion in the film. Reminiscent of the social critique expressed through the superficial platitudes of Lewis's George Babbitt character, Sturges consistently exposes the negative outcomes of the collective conformity at work within Morgan's Creek. Norval's failure to embody a masculine archetype produces a sense that, by contrast, perhaps all of the town's characters are successfully and even unconsciously performing some type of standardized identity. Because of Norval's deficiencies, the character serves as a device that disrupts the order produced by other townspeople abiding by normalized cultural scripts about gender roles and sexual mores.

The marriage plot in *The Miracle of Morgan's Creek* is another way in which Sturges introduces tensions related to motifs of movement and entrapment.[57] Prior to ensnaring Norval in their schemes, Trudy and Emmy consult the town lawyer, Mr. Johnson (Al Bridge), for advice about attaining an annulment or divorce. Mr. Johnson's brusque response reaffirms the restrictive gender roles enforced within Morgan's Creek and directly equates marriage with entrapment: "Responsibility for recording a marriage has always been up to the woman. If it wasn't for her, marriage woulda disappeared long since. No man is gonna jeopardize his present or poison his future with a lot of little brats hollerin' around the house unless he's forced to. It's up to the woman to knock him down, hogtie him, and drag him in front of two witnesses immediately, if not sooner. Anytime after that, it's too late." Mr. Johnson's brief lecture links gender, temporal concerns, and movement in the regulatory role ascribed to women, who occupy an important but contradictory status in Morgan's Creek. Throughout the film, traditional marriage is identified as an institution that stabilizes society, but men apparently are resistant due to supposed temporal restrictions on their "present" and "future" (except, of course, when getting married will enable them to have sex before departing for combat). Sturges repeatedly highlights the townspeople's general anxiety about young women potentially disrupting society by deviating from their designated roles as protectors of social order. Consequently, the women of Morgan's Creek are scrutinized so that they, in turn, will regulate the young men whose disregard for conservative social conventions presumably could lead to chaos.

Following this scene with the lawyer, Emmy concocts a plan to trick Norval into proposing. The younger Kockenlocker sister explains to Trudy, "It would hurt me just as much as it would you to have you hurt and miserable and ashamed and everything. That's the only reason I want you to get married. You can't tell how a town is going to take things.... All suspicious and suspecting the worst in everything." In this speech, the fear of judgment—and being socially ostracized as a result of the town's gossipy surveillance culture—is shown to be the true motivation for marriage. Accordingly, Trudy's efforts to pressure Norval into proposing to her are couched in appeals to the normative values that create the imperative to marry. When Trudy claims that "a woman's place is in the home," a surprised Norval responds, "That sounds kind of old-fashioned and domestic coming from you, Trudy." Norval's statement prompts Trudy to elaborate on why she abruptly is embracing "old-fashioned" values: "Sometimes you just naturally feel old-fashioned and domestic, Norval. I guess no girl ever gets away from it, really. She thinks she is, and then one day something happens, and then she finds out she isn't." A sense of proximity and distance is apparent in Trudy's explanation—albeit one of a temporal, rather than spatial, variety. When younger (or at least prior to the soldiers' going away party), Trudy felt distanced from domestic aspirations, but now that she is older (and pregnant), she has been pushed closer to such conservative values.

By the end of the film, Trudy's affection for Norval goes beyond mere appreciation of his status as available dupe and appears to be genuine. When the couple finally reunites just after the birth of the sextuplets, Trudy declares that she is "so happy," and she lovingly tells Norval, "You're a papa now. . . . You are one. A papa gives love, protection." With these words, their assimilation into "proper" society and conformity to approved gender roles is complete, as Trudy and Norval are bound in marriage, which the governor backdates so that the sextuplets are identified as "legitimate" in the town's official records. No longer a wild youth, Trudy expresses satisfaction in marriage, and Norval attains some degree of masculinity by virtue of his status as a "papa." Not content to leave the protagonists in such a content and blissful state, Sturges ends the film with Norval's physical disarray returning upon the discovery that he is responsible for six children. An onscreen postscript emphasizes the artificiality of the couple's newfound respectability. Attributed to Shakespeare, the quote reads, "Some are *born* great, some *achieve* greatness, and some have greatness *thrust upon them*" (emphasis in original). Both Trudy and Norval are indicted by this innuendo-laden sentiment, as neither one has done much to attain "greatness." After Trudy becomes pregnant, they both readily acquiesce to being folded into the normalizing narratives and restrictive gender roles from which they each previously had been excluded.

The mechanisms that "thrust" such a status on the couple extend beyond the behind-the-scenes machinations of the governor, as the national newspaper industry also works to normalize the "miracle" results of Trudy's deviant pregnancy.[58] Near the end of the film, Sturges includes a montage of newspaper headlines, the first of which declares, "SEXTUPLETS BORN IN MID-WEST," while another proclaims, "SIX! ALL BOYS! SIX!" An additional newspaper links the sextuplets to the war effort with the headline, "NATURE ANSWERS TOTAL WAR," and the article's explanatory subheadline reads, "PLATOON BORN IN MIDWEST." These newspapers assign the Midwest a very particular identity within the 1940s context. First, labeling the sextuplets as "nature" responding to the manmade destruction of World War II echoes the perception of the Midwest as an anachronistic, past-oriented space. Only a region closely linked to nature could produce such a "miracle," and the diametrical opposition of the pastoral Midwest to modernity persists in these headlines. The "miracle" of a large birth conjures up associations with bountiful harvests, so it must occur in a region often represented with images of rural labor. Second, the newspapers immediately declare that the male sextuplets are to be a platoon. Although the headline may be attributed to the wartime context, this prediction of patriotic self-sacrifice is yet another allusion to the region's symbolic role as the "most" American of spaces. By including this brief montage of headlines, Sturges outlines the scope of the mutually supporting mechanisms that produce a sanitized, "official" narrative about the Midwest: from gossipy neighbors to the state governor to the national media, the identities of Midwesterners are intensely regulated and managed. Any deviance from such gender and labor ideals is subsumed beneath a veneer of normativity.

A motif of restricted movement recurs throughout *The Miracle of Morgan's Creek*. Although spatial constriction produces a superficial semblance of order within the Midwestern community, Sturges actually shows that social and bodily disorder result from confinement.[59] With the exception of the departing soldiers, the borders of the town are seemingly impermeable by the remaining townspeople. Beyond these narrative details, Sturges also accentuates the theme of spatial constriction via a fascinating use of tracking shots. Sturges generally adheres to classical Hollywood shooting conventions and keeps his camera stationary for most of *The Miracle of Morgan's Creek*; however, there are five major scenes in which the camera is untethered, as Sturges strategically utilizes lengthy tracking shots to integrate his concern with movement into the very form of the film itself. Each scene with extended camera movements—tracking shots that are absent elsewhere in the film—depicts characters physically moving while plotting ways in which they might resolve personal problems in the face of various social restrictions (see fig. 2.1). These scenes feature the following durations and narrative events: a nearly four-minute long take in which Trudy embarks on a date with Norval as a cover to attend the military dance which her single father Edmund (William Demarest) had forbidden her from attending; a one-and-a-half-minute long take in which Emmy and Trudy create a plan to trick Norval into proposing to Trudy; a three-minute sequence comprised of several tracking shots featuring Trudy confessing to Norval that she is married and pregnant; a two-minute long take that concludes with Norval developing an ill-fated proxy marriage scheme (the plan involves posing as Trudy's unknown husband so that she can use the falsified marriage certificate to attain a divorce and then remarry Norval under his own name); finally, a two-minute long take that functions as a pseudotracking shot in which Norval and Trudy finalize the details of the false marriage plan while seated in a car with rear projection used to suggest motion.

The tracking shots in these five scenes are formal manifestations of the continually unrealized desire to escape from the oppressive values imposed on the inhabitants of Morgan's Creek, as well as from the accompanying cultural stagnation within the town. Perhaps Sturges's most subtle critique in *The Miracle of Morgan's Creek* is the fact that the lengthy onscreen movement of the characters during these scenes never actually produces distance or separation from sources of conflict. Instead, these characters' movements—dutifully tracked by Sturges's camera—expose the fishbowl quality of Morgan's Creek, as the wandering sequences consistently lack spatial progression and typically circle back to where the characters began. Because of this looping movement, the tracking shots provide a visualization of nostalgic spatiality. The inability to transcend the spatial

Fig. 2.1. A moment of anxiety during a looping stroll. Screen capture, *The Miracle of Morgan's Creek* (1944).

boundaries of Morgan's Creek reflects the temporal frustrations of the nostalgic subject, whose yearning for the past produces a looping desire circuit. Sturges thus spatially represents the neurosis-producing effects of the town's restrictive social mores and gender norms (in addition to showing how they activate Norval's physical spasms). The Midwesterners subjected to such values are compelled into motion, but perpetually find that their movement is stifled.

Following the critique of the Midwest in literature of the 1920s, cinematic depictions of the region featured a great deal of variance. In *Meet Me in St. Louis*, the Midwest is a domestic idyll, while in Orson Welles's famously truncated adaptation of *The Magnificent Ambersons* (1942), the region teeters between outmoded customs of the past and a more mechanized future, as represented by the profitable growth of the automobile industry.[60] Another perspective is evident in Chicago-based crime films such as *The Public Enemy* (1931) and *Scarface* (1932), which depict the urban Midwest as a seedy space of violence.[61] These contrasting viewpoints are somewhat typical of the era. Shortridge explains, "The decades of the 1930s and 1940s are difficult to assess in terms of regional imagery, for the period clearly was a transitional one, and the arguments are often contradictory."[62] Overall, Shortridge notes that "the consensus of observers throughout the late 1930s and the 1940s was that there had been a loss of regional vitality."[63] With *The Miracle of Morgan's Creek*, Sturges joins this chorus by depicting the many layers of confinement and restriction that are brought to bear on his fictional Midwestern town's residents. Nearly all of the major characters spend time scheming about, for instance, how to trap one another in marriage or how to escape persecution by the watchful eyes of their fellow citizens and white male community leaders (such as the lawyer, newspaper editor, and state governor). Sturges also exposes the constructed nature of the popular narratives that circulate about the Midwest, particularly during the framing scenes with the intrusive Governor McGinty, who rewrites history in order to erase deviation from standardized ideals and gender roles. Moreover, Sturges critiques the deranging effects of compulsory conformity through Norval's physical dysfunction and with numerous wandering tracking shots, the duration of which belies the fact that actual spatial progress is inhibited. Overall, the claustrophobic space of Morgan's Creek provides one of the most thorough interrogations of the restrictive spatial dynamics and regional narratives that contributed to the Midwest's stagnating image as the middle of the twentieth century approached. The final section of this chapter examines how *Native Son* filters these concerns with space and movement through the prism of race in Chicago.

Native Son

Published in 1940, but set in the 1930s, Richard Wright's *Native Son* engages with forms of spatial constriction and issues of race, gender, and class in a Midwestern context. Within this chapter's historical timeframe, *Native Son* has added significance as a text that belies essentialized images of the Midwest during the first half of the twentieth century in two ways: the narrative is confined to the urban space of Chicago, and it details the tribulations of an African American protagonist, Bigger Thomas. The works of authors such as Cather, Anderson, and Lewis are overtly region-oriented, but those narratives predominantly revolve around rural or small town settings and white characters. By reading Wright's novel as a Midwestern text, *Native Son* provides a necessary correction to narrow, exclusionary conceptions of the Midwest, while still speaking to broader regional issues.

The disassociation of the Midwest's identity from its urban spaces and the diversity of its population stretches back to at least as early as Turner's attribution of frontier traits to the region. Once the Midwest was associated with pastoralism in the early twentieth century, its whitewashed image became even more fixed in American culture. For instance, Shortridge observes that Midwestern cities have been considered to be "outside the context of regional labels," partially because of "racial conflict and industrial collapse" in those urban spaces as the twentieth century progressed.[64] To acknowledge such conditions as "Midwestern" would be to challenge the region's dominant pastoral and white image.[65] Victoria Johnson also expounds the peculiar relationship between the Midwest's popular identity and race over the latter half of the twentieth century and the early years of the twenty-first century. According to Johnson, the region simultaneously "symbolizes the ideal nation" and "functions as an object of derision."[66] These dual and seemingly irreconcilable roles relate to the Midwest's perceived racial character. Johnson explains that

> the persistent association of "midwesternness" *as* "white" is critical to the region's revaluation—particularly in moments of social upheaval and trauma—as 'home' of 'authentic' cultural populism and traditional U.S. values.... Imagined in this way, the Heartland Midwest underscores the nation's historic and ongoing, systemic racism while also functioning as the site upon which to transfer or "locate" the culture's possessive investment in whiteness. The Heartland thus offers a myth through which the nation reifies racism as the status-quo, *and* by which national discourse disavows racism, proclaiming enlightened ideals that stand in direct contrast to those imagined to inhere in the region.[67]

By being mythologized as "white" and lacking racial heterogeneity, the Midwest is configured as a space that contains the most regressive elements of the nation, but is also contradictorily elevated as the locus of "authentic" American values. With the racial and spatial regional perceptions detailed by Shortridge and Johnson firmly established in the cultural imagination, the necessity of resituating African American narratives that unfold in urban environments—such as *Native Son*—within Midwestern discourses is clear.

Wright himself expresses some connective threads between *Native Son* and Midwestern contexts. His description of the narrative's Chicago setting links the novel to Turner's frontier theories. In "How 'Bigger' Was Born" (1940), an oft-referenced companion piece to *Native Son*, Wright describes the Midwestern metropolis of Chicago as

> the fabulous city in which Bigger lived, an indescribable city, huge, roaring, dirty, noisy, raw, stark, brutal; a city of extremes: torrid summers and sub-zero winters, white people and black people, the English language and strange tongues, foreign born and native born, scabby poverty and gaudy luxury, high idealism and hard cynicism! A city so young that, *in thinking of its short history, one's mind, as it travels backward in time, is stopped abruptly by the barren stretches of wind-swept prairie*! But a city old enough to have caught within the homes of its long, straight streets the symbols and images of man's age-old destiny, of truths as old as the mountains and seas, of dramas as abiding as the soul of man itself! A city which has *become the pivot* of the Eastern, Western, Northern, and Southern poles of the nation.[68]

Wright's reflection on Chicago's past prompts a nostalgic turn "backward in time," and he locates the city's origins within "the barren stretches of wind-swept prairie," which conjures up associations with both Turner and the Midwest's pastoral identity. Turner establishes the Midwest as the fulcrum of the nation's coiling turn inward, and this development purportedly results from the end of frontier expansion. In this passage, Wright affirms the Midwest's status as a nostalgic hinge by further specifying that Chicago is the very "pivot" of the United States. Chicago is described as an overwhelming city with some degree of temporal proximity to the past, and it is within this chaotic space that Wright sets the story of Bigger Thomas.

By immersing readers in Bigger's "life lived in cramped limits" throughout *Native Son*, Wright shows how racism is institutionalized via housing discrimination and geographic segregation.[69] These issues are recurring elements in texts depicting African American experiences in Chicago, from Lorraine Hansberry's play *A Raisin in the Sun* (1959) to Bernard Rose's horror film *Candyman* (1992).[70] *A Raisin in the Sun* focuses on the individual and collective aspirations of the Younger family, who live on Chicago's South Side. After receiving money from the death of her husband, Lena Younger (Mama) purchases a home in a mostly white neighborhood; while packing their apartment, the Youngers are offered a bribe to not move by Karl Lindner, a representative of their prospective community. Karl disingenuously explains that, although "racial prejudice simply doesn't enter into it," he and his white neighbors believe that "Negro families are happier when they live in their *own* communities."[71] Ultimately, the play concludes with adult son Walter Lee triumphantly informing Karl that the Youngers will, in fact, move to the home they purchased. *Candyman* also addresses segregation along the lines of race and class in Chicago. The narrative is centered on the infamous (and now-demolished) Cabrini-Green housing project in which a supernatural entity known as "Candyman" is believed to reside and to perpetrate violence as retribution for his murder at the hands of a white lynch mob decades earlier. In addition to affirming Cabrini-Green as a failure of modernist architecture, Rose also calls attention to the layout of the highways cutting through Chicago; such roads function as borders between wealthy and poor neighborhoods. Much like these later narratives, Wright presents Bigger and all of the members of his impoverished African American community as enmeshed in a restrictive network of systematized racism. The first scene of *Native Son* immediately introduces this dynamic by showing Wright's troubled protagonist along with his mother, brother, and sister as they contend with a rat invading their tiny, one-bedroom apartment. Beyond mere discomfort, Wright links this claustrophobic space to the fragmentation of Bigger's sense of identity.

Bigger's fractured persona results in compulsive, violent behavior, as well as ongoing fluctuations in his self-presentation to others. Matthew Elder explores the causes of this divided self and explains that Bigger "struggles with negotiating the different formulations of his identity, which are thrown into disarray by a segregated, inequitable, and frequently hostile society."[72] As such, Elder argues that Wright's novel reveals "the psychological pressure of existing in an environment that demands the artificial adoption of so many different roles."[73] Over the course of the narrative, Wright emphasizes the varying degrees of disconnect between Bigger's internal and external states.[74] At times, Bigger uses violent threats to mask fear around his friends; at other moments, he adopts an inarticulate and inexpressive façade in the presence of wealthy white people such as the Dalton family, for whom he works as a chauffeur. After inadvertently killing Mr. Dalton's adult daughter, Mary, and then disposing of her body in the family's furnace, Bigger develops a fake ransom scheme to account for the disappearance.[75] These ill-advised machinations force Bigger to oscillate among personas at a more rapid pace, which causes further anxiety.

Bigger partly justifies his extortion scheme by noting Mr. Dalton's involvement in Chicago's exploitative real estate market. The Dalton family perpetuates and profits from racial segregation due to their ownership of multiple buildings on the South Side, including Bigger's decrepit tenement. Bigger reflects, "Even though Mr. Dalton gave millions of dollars for Negro education, he would rent houses to Negroes only in this prescribed area, this corner of the city tumbling down from rot." Later in the novel, Bigger returns to the topic of housing discrimination and suggests that rich white people "had shunted him off into a corner of the city to rot and die."[76] Bigger's choice of the word "rot" in these passages implies a link between movement and decay; when motion is inhibited, rot is produced. Here, Wright echoes Turner's sentiments regarding the debilitating effects of limited expansion, but Wright also provides a necessary revision to the frontier theorist's persistent racism by highlighting racialized restrictions on movement—both socioeconomically and geographically—in the urban Midwest.

Wright further accentuates the relationship between racial inequality and spatial constriction after Bigger is identified as Mary's killer. Bigger attempts to hide from the police with his girlfriend Bessie, but the city grid is easily transformed into an ever-tightening surveillance network. Cut off from any escape outside of Chicago, Bigger moves among the abandoned, dilapidated "houses on the South Side" that were "homes once of rich white people, [but are] now inhabited by Negroes or standing dark and empty with yawning black windows." As the police close in on Bigger, Wright narrates, "How easy it would be for him to hide if he had the whole city in which to move about! They keep us bottled up here like wild animals, he thought. He knew that black people could not go outside of the Black Belt to rent a flat; they had to live on their side of the 'line.' No white real estate man would rent a flat to a black man other than in the sections where it had been decided that black people might live." During Bigger's trial, his lawyer Boris Max confronts Mr. Dalton about the discriminatory practice of redlining. The latter simply replies that "it's an old custom" to segregate and that he would be "underselling my competition" if he charged lower rent in areas of the city populated by white inhabitants. Like the character of Karl Lindner in Hansberry's later *A Raisin in the Sun*, Mr. Dalton asserts, "I think Negroes are happier when they're together."[77] By citing the influence of "custom" on his rental policies, Mr. Dalton attaches a nostalgic element to racial segregation. This, then, is yet another iteration of nostalgic spatiality. In Wright's novel, the wealthy white real estate men cultivate a troubling sense of nostalgia for segregation and inequality; crucially, this nostalgia has a spatial dimension, as evident by the active regulation of racial demographics across Chicago neighborhoods.

Native Son's theme of constriction extends beyond the depiction of housing segregation along the lines of race and class. Throughout the novel, Wright mirrors the issue of spatial constriction by regularly confining readers within Bigger's paranoid perspective.[78] As Wright explains, "Wherever possible, I told of Bigger's life in close-up, slow-motion, giving the feel of the grain in the passing of time. I had long had the feeling that this was the best way to 'enclose' the reader's mind in a new world, to blot out all reality except that which I was giving him."[79]

Wright's use of the phrasing, "close-up, slow-motion," to describe his portrait of Bigger has a decidedly cinematic connotation, which frames the novel as a pictorial experience in which the reader-as-spectator is forced to gaze upon horrifying images projected at an agonizing speed. In this way, Wright's desire to "enclose" the reader mimics the spatial constriction that deranges Bigger. Whether due to racism, class inequality, or the police systematically surveying Chicago, Bigger is enmeshed in a network of forces that collectively restrict his physical movements and the development of his identity. By narrating Bigger's internal subjective perspective, Wright compels readers to share in the intense anxiety produced by these circumstances.

In addition to influencing Wright's narrative technique, the cinema also serves as a formative space for Bigger's damaged psyche. The full importance of the cinema, in fact, relates to the novel's historical context. Morris Dickstein writes that "fantasy culture of the 1930s" is about "movement that suggests genuine freedom."[80] He adds that "the real dream of the expressive culture of the 1930s was not money and success, not even elegance and sophistication, but mobility, with its thrust toward the future."[81] According to Dickstein, this era's escapist media reflects a yearning for movement and mobility that, in turn, is attached to a future-oriented sense of time. Such elements ostensibly function as a reassuring "denial of the depression" for audiences.[82] For figures such as Bigger, whose desires and movements are continually curtailed, the contemporary dreams of autonomous motion identified by Dickstein are impossible fantasies.

Wright displays an acute awareness of the power of mass culture during the 1930s to create and shape desire. When discussing the numerous real-life incarnations of Bigger Thomas that led to the creation of *Native Son*'s fictional composite, Wright suggests that these violently rebellious figures were "trying to react to and answer the call of the dominant civilization whose glitter came . . . through the newspapers, magazines, radios, movies, and the mere imposing sight and sound of daily American life."[83] Wright's statement indicates that Bigger's struggles to attain a coherent identity in the face of systemic racism are, to some degree, exacerbated by popular media. Rather than being a stabilizing or soothing influence, the fantasy images within the dark, isolating space of the cinema skew Bigger's personal desires and engagement with the city space that surrounds him.[84] For instance, when Bigger travels to the Dalton residence for the first time, Wright notes, "While walking through this quiet and spacious white neighborhood, he did not feel the pull and mystery of the thing as strongly as he had in the movie."[85] In this moment, Bigger considers the filmed images of the neighborhood (which he had seen onscreen earlier in the novel) to be more affecting than the physical environment itself, and this affinity for fantasy greatly informs his ever-shifting desires.

Bigger's many unrealized desires partly contain a nostalgic dimension because of his perpetual sense of longing. Just as the nostalgic subject yearns for an inaccessible sensation of authenticity located in an alternate space and time, Bigger's changing desires remain forever unavailable. Early in the novel, Bigger is asked by his friend Gus what he desires, and Wright describes his response: "'Anything,' Bigger said with a wide sweep of his dingy palm, a sweep that included all the possible activities of the world." Later, Bigger simply has "an overwhelming desire to be alone." Following the death of Mary, Bigger wants "the power to say what he had done without fear of being arrested; he wished that he could be an idea in their minds, that his black face and the image of his smothering Mary and cutting off her head and burning her could hover before their eyes as a terrible picture of reality which they could see and feel and yet not destroy." While evading the police, Bigger reflects on how modern culture influences his desires. Wright narrates, "It was when he read the newspapers or magazines, went to the movies, or walked along the streets with crowds, that he felt what he wanted: to merge himself with others and be a part of this world, to lose himself in it so he could find himself, to be allowed a chance to live like others, even though he was black."[86] Images of physical dissolution—of Bigger transcending his body's corporeality and becoming a symbol of an unseen "reality" or blending seamlessly into Chicago's crowded mass—abound in these passages. Much like Bigger's view that filmed images have a more substantive "pull and mystery" than reality, his fantasy involves achieving an incorporeal status that will enable an escape from physical restraints and permit a newfound ease of movement.

The desires detailed above reveal a deeply ambivalent attitude toward the urban space of Chicago, as Bigger alternately wishes to be apart from and to be absorbed by the city and its inhabitants. According to Wright, Bigger "was hovering unwanted between two worlds—between powerful America and his own stunted place in life—and I took upon myself the task of trying to make the reader feel this No Man's Land.... [Bigger] felt the *need* for a whole life and *acted* out of that need; that was all."[87] The relationship between Bigger's internal disjuncture and marginalized cultural status is key to understanding why his initial desire for a nebulous "anything" produces violent tendencies. Bigger's desires are clearly shaped by the mass culture that he consumes and encounters in Chicago, yet realizing those desires seems impossible within that same space. As such, Wright presents incommunicability and alienation as a product of the Midwest's cultural capital, Chicago.[88]

Being confined within the desire-producing modern space of Chicago compounds the daily racism that Bigger experiences and heightens his rage.[89] Wright argues, "The urban environment of Chicago, affording a more stimulating life, made the Negro Bigger Thomases react more violently than even in the South. More than ever I began to see and understand the environmental factors which made for this extreme conduct.... Chicago's physical aspect—noisy, crowded, filled with the sense of power and fulfillment—did so much more to dazzle the mind with a taunting sense of possible achievement that the segregation it did impose brought forth from Bigger a reaction more obstreperous than in the South."[90] In this passage, Wright makes explicit the deep influence of place upon the collective psyches of the original "Bigger Thomases." Beyond providing insights into the development of his fictional protagonist, Wright also presents an argument about the transformative powers of Chicago itself. In this regard, *Native Son* functions as an urban-based analog to the persistent environmental determinism that characterizes much commentary about the "pastoral" Midwest, as evident in Turner's claims about the "Americanizing" properties of the region. Wright's forceful depiction of racism and classism in Chicago thus overlaps with the critiques of less urban Midwestern locales in other texts from this general period, including Sturges's *The Miracle of Morgan's Creek*. Whereas the small town inhabitants of Morgan's Creek are limited by being geographically distant from the modern culture of contemporary cities, Wright's protagonist is immersed within the dynamic environment of urban Chicago; this physical proximity to modern amenities, though, merely serves to accentuate the confined parameters of Bigger's life.

Middletown, The Miracle of Morgan's Creek, and *Native Son* each show that the Midwest's status as a past-oriented space is produced through reductive regional narratives that delimit parameters for Midwestern behaviors and identities. Moreover, these restrictive norms are symbolically mirrored by physical enclosures within all three texts. Since the early twentieth century, the Midwest is repeatedly imagined to be a blank space that operates on and reshapes the "blank slates" who occupy it. Such transformative properties may superficially appear to be aligned with the rapid changes of modernity. Yet depictions of the Midwest from this period present the region as a static space that resists change. The Midwestern spaces of *Middletown* and *The Miracle of Morgan's Creek* are (or are assumed to be, in the case of the Lynds' study) cut off from modern developments elsewhere, and their inhabitants cannot breach each locale's seemingly impenetrable borders. In *Native Son*, spatial constriction results from housing discrimination and racial segregation. Finally, various works by Cather, Anderson, and Lewis configure the rural and small town Midwest as a closed-off, isolated realm that inhibits those within its boundaries.

As this chapter's materials demonstrate, a preoccupation with movement and mobility—both socially and geographically—deeply informs many Midwestern texts produced from the 1910s through the 1940s. During the Great Depression and World War II, numerous works of fiction depict Midwesterners seeking to transcend restrictive regional boundaries. Together, such texts provide an image of the Midwest as a space that is impervious to or incompatible with the transformations of the modern world due to, among other factors, an oppressive sense of spatial constriction that isolates the region and its inhabitants.

At the turn of the twentieth century, Turner predicted that the "forces of reorganization" resulting from the nation's turn inward were transforming the United States into "a witches' kettle."[91] *Middletown, The Miracle of Morgan's Creek*, and *Native Son* each affirm this foreboding vision at a remove of several decades. In artificially constructing a "typical" version of the Midwest, the Lynds exclude all racial categories that are not "white" from their conception of what constitutes an "average" Midwestern—the region that is the supposed "common-denominator of America"—demographic.[92] Sturges depicts how regressive values about gender, sexuality, and Midwestern families constrain movement and produce social and bodily turmoil. Wright examines the deranging effects of systemic racial and class-based discrimination, particularly the resultant forms of physical, intellectual, and emotional entrapment. Across these texts, the inability to adapt—whether by choice or by circumstance—to changing environmental factors looms large and forecloses the potential for the entire region to be recognized as "modern."[93] Exceptions, of course, include urban sites such as Chicago, which is frequently disassociated from the regional label of "Midwestern." Overall, the Midwestern imagery on display in this chapter's three primary texts bolsters perceptions that the Midwest was a stagnating space as the twentieth century approached its midpoint. This representational trend becomes increasingly prominent in depictions of the Midwest from the midcentury forward, and later Midwestern texts establish a more direct connection between nostalgic spatiality and violence, as detailed in the next chapter.

Notes

1. *The Wizard of Oz*, directed by Victor Fleming (1939; Burbank, CA: Warner Home Video, 2009), DVD.

2. *Meet Me in St. Louis*, directed by Vincente Minnelli (1944; Burbank, CA: Warner Home Video, 2004), DVD.

3. Patricia Oman, "Judy Garland and MGM's Nostalgic Midwestern Home," *Middle West Review* 4, no. 1 (Fall 2017): 227–228.

4. Ibid., 228.

5. Theodore Dreiser, *Sister Carrie*, ed. Claude Simpson (1900; repr., Boston: Houghton Mifflin, 1959).

6. Robert S. Lynd and Helen Merrell Lynd, *Middletown: A Study in Modern American Culture* (1929; repr., San Diego, CA: Harcourt Brace Jovanovich, 1957); Richard Wright, *Native Son* (1940; repr., New York: Harper Perennial Modern Classics, 2005); *The Miracle of Morgan's Creek*, directed by Preston Sturges (1944; Hollywood, CA: Paramount Pictures, 2005), DVD.

7. Frederick Jackson Turner, *The Frontier in American History* (1920; repr., Charleston, SC: BiblioBazaar, 2008), 186.

8. Ibid.

9. Marshall Berman, *All That Is Solid Melts Into Air: The Experience of Modernity* (1982; repr., New York: Penguin, 1988), 95.

10. Ibid., 95–96.

11. Patricia Oman, "'Here Comes the Show Boat!': *Show Boat* and the Case for Regionalism," *Cinema Journal* 56, no. 1 (Fall 2016): 64.

12. James R. Shortridge, *The Middle West: Its Meaning in American Culture* (Lawrence: University Press of Kansas, 1989), 38–39.

13. It is worth noting that such critiques were not uniform among regional writers. Jon K. Lauck points out that the "revolt thesis" actually "obscures a large body of work produced by midwestern regionalist writers who were neither alienated nor rebellious and who possessed a genuine affection for their home region." See: Jon K. Lauck, *From Warm Center to Ragged Edge: The Erosion of Midwestern Literary and Historical Regionalism, 1920–1965* (Iowa City: University of Iowa Press, 2017), 9, 11–67.

14. Tom Lutz, *Cosmopolitan Vistas: American Regionalism and Literary Value* (Ithaca, NY: Cornell University Press, 2004), 138; Sherwood Anderson, *Winesburg, Ohio* (1919; repr., New York: Viking, 1967); Sinclair Lewis, *Main Street* (1920; repr., New York: The New American Library, 1980).

15. Lutz, *Cosmopolitan Vistas*, 140.
16. Sinclair Lewis, *Babbitt* (1922; repr., New York: Bantam Classic, 2007).
17. Lewis, *Main Street*, 260.
18. Lewis, *Babbitt*, 207.
19. Ibid., 58.
20. Willa Cather, *O Pioneers!* (1913; repr., New York: Vintage Classics, 1992).
21. Ibid., 86.
22. Ibid., 62.
23. Ibid., 63.
24. Lutz, *Cosmopolitan Vistas*, 114.
25. Upton Sinclair, *The Jungle* (1906; repr., New York: The Modern Library, 2006).
26. Although Lewis emphasizes the problematic elements of Midwestern communities, the Minnesota native's true object of critique is American culture in general. In *Main Street*'s one-page prologue, Lewis notes that even though the novel is set in the fictional Gopher Prairie, Minnesota, "its main street is the continuation of Main Streets everywhere. The story would be the same in Ohio or Montana, in Kansas or Kentucky or Illinois, and not very differently would it be told Up York State or in the Carolina hills." Near the end of the novel, Carol is exasperated by her life in Gopher Prairie and flees to Washington, DC. Of her time there, however, Lewis writes, "Always she was to perceive in Washington (as doubtless she would have perceived in New York or London) a thick streak of Main Street. The cautious dullness of a Gopher Prairie appeared in boarding-houses . . . in the Sunday motor procession, in theater parties, and at the dinners of State Societies." Eventually, Carol concludes that "institutions are the enemies. . . . They insinuate their tyranny under a hundred guises and pompous names, such as Polite Society, the Family, the Church, Sound Business, the Party, the Country, the Superior White Race. . . ." These passages clarify that, while Lewis's critique is born and centered in the Midwest, *Main Street* actually is a much broader indictment of the United States as a whole. Hence, Lewis's version of the Midwest is representative of "average" or "typical" American culture by virtue of the fact that it most clearly reveals the inherent flaws of the nation. See: Lewis, *Main Street*, 6, 410–413.
27. The identity of "Middletown" initially was not revealed by the Lynds in order to preserve the anonymity of Muncie's inhabitants. A follow-up study, *Middletown in Transition: A Study in Cultural Conflicts* (1937), was published several years later, and a documentary miniseries simply titled, *Middletown* (1982), returned to Muncie roughly five decades after the Lynds produced their influential first study of the community. See: Robert S. Lynd and Helen Merrell Lynd, *Middletown in Transition: A Study in Cultural Conflicts* (1937; repr., San Diego, CA: Harcourt Brace Jovanovich, 1965); *Middletown* (Arlington, VA: PBS, 1982), broadcast television.
28. Lynd and Lynd, *Middletown*, 7–8.
29. Ibid., 9.
30. The perception of Midwestern averageness persists in many ways across the twentieth and twenty-first centuries, but consumer culture is one of the clearest categories in which the region is believed to have nondescript preferences. Victoria Johnson discusses how "the Midwest has been a particularly problematic region in network history. It is simultaneously understood to be the most reliable, 'mass,' 'all-American' market—as an aggregate class of consumers with presumptively popular, commercial tastes—*and* to be a risky investment, considering its lower population density and weaker, more rural market strength. . . ." Thomas Frank also touches upon this supposed Midwestern taste for the generic and writes that Kansas

is anti-exotic, familiar even if you've never been there. As a tourist destination, Kansas ranks dead last among the states but it remains a popular proving ground for test marketers of every kind. It has been a prolific birthplace of chain restaurants—Pizza Hut, White Castle, and Applebees, to name a few—and it supplies the nation with anchormen, comedians, and actors of wholesome visage and accent inoffensive. Kansas City is the home of Hallmark Cards and the nation's very first suburban shopping center. Thanks to its unerring sense for the middle, the state is a politician producer of the first rank, a reliable wellspring of down-home statesmen.

As evident in these passages by Johnson and Frank, the Lynds' assumptions about the Midwest's "common-denominator" quality remains attached to the region and has been used strategically by marketers in order to predict the potential for mass consumption of television shows, chain restaurants, and other products. See: Victoria E. Johnson, *Heartland TV: Prime Time Television and the Struggle for U.S. Identity* (New York: New York University Press, 2008), 7, emphasis in original; Thomas Frank, *What's the Matter with Kansas? How Conservatives Won the Heart of America* (2004; repr., New York: Henry Holt, 2005), 29–30.

31. Lynd and Lynd, *Middletown*, 9.
32. Ibid., 7.
33. Ibid., 8.
34. Two anthologies published around the turn of the twenty-first century respond to the Lynds' omissions of Muncie's African American and Jewish populations. See: Luke Eric Lassiter et al., eds., *The Other Side of Middletown: Exploring Muncie's African American Community* (Lanham, MD: AltaMira, 2004); Dan Rottenberg, ed., *Middletown Jews: The Tenuous Survival of an American Jewish Community* (Bloomington: Indiana University Press, 1998).
35. Lynd and Lynd, *Middletown*, 9.
36. Eric Hinderaker, "Liberating Contrivances: Narrative and Identity in Midwestern History," in *The Midwest: Essays on Regional History*, ed. Andrew R. L. Cayton and Susan E. Gray (Bloomington: Indiana University Press, 2001), 50.
37. Ibid.
38. Turner, *The Frontier in American History*, 14.
39. Ibid., 125.
40. Lynd and Lynd, *Middletown*, 8.
41. Such movements include the Know Nothings of the mid-nineteenth century and the various incarnations of the Ku Klux Klan. For an extensive history of nativism within the United States, see: David H. Bennett, *The Party of Fear: From Nativist Movements to the New Right in American History* (Chapel Hill: University of North Carolina Press, 1988).
42. Lynd and Lynd, *Middletown*, 8.
43. As with many films set in small towns, there is a general lack of specificity regarding where Morgan's Creek is located in terms of both state and region. Near the end of the film, though, there is diegetic confirmation of the town's placement within the Midwest, as Sturges includes shots of newspaper headlines announcing that the "miracle" sextuplets were born in the region. Of small towns in American film, Kenneth MacKinnon writes that "individual small towns in Hollywood movies have no resonance of the sort analogous to that of New York or Los Angeles in the movies and that such associations as are imported into individual small towns seem to be those created by an amalgam of elements much less to do with actual American small towns than with manifold literary descriptions and repeated cinematic treatments." According to MacKinnon, then, there is a lack

of precision afforded issues of verisimilitude regarding onscreen small towns, and such locales often are depicted as spaces located potentially anywhere or nowhere in particular. In a curious way, such vagary links most cinematic small towns to ways in which the Midwest has been configured as an absent space without clearly defined characteristics beyond being generically "American." See: Kenneth MacKinnon, *Hollywood's Small Towns: An Introduction to the American Small-Town Movie* (Metuchen, NJ: Scarecrow, 1984), 18.

44. Leger Grindon notes, "The Sturges dialogue plays upon the implied substitution of the forbidden for the respectable. The equation of sex with 'marriage' is a repeated gag that becomes a pivot for humor." See: Leger Grindon, *The Hollywood Romantic Comedy* (Hoboken, NJ: Wiley-Blackwell, 2011), 108.

45. Andrew Dickos, *Intrepid Laughter: Preston Sturges and the Movies* (Metuchen, NJ: Scarecrow, 1985), 112.

46. Ibid.

47. Ibid., 106.

48. Grindon, *The Hollywood Romantic Comedy*, 115–116.

49. Because Trudy cannot remember who she married after the farewell party for the soldiers, she and Norval concoct a convoluted scheme to attain a proper marriage license. Basically, Norval plans to assume the identity of the absent soldier and marry Trudy under that name; they then will secure a divorce and remarry one another with Norval's real name listed on a new license. This plan fails almost immediately when they attempt to implement it at the Honeymoon Hotel.

50. Norval continually laments his inability to join the military and embody masculine ideals due to his extreme anxiety. For instance, when Trudy initially turns down Norval's request for a date because of the military party, he dejectedly mutters, "You'd think they'd give a party someday for those who have to stay behind. They also serve, you know, who only sit and . . . well, whatever they do, I forget." Later, Trudy asks for a favor, and Norval enthuses, "Except maybe getting into the army, I can't think of anything that makes me more happy than helping you out. I almost wish you'd be in a lot of trouble sometime, so I could prove it to you." Again and again, Norval reveals a deep longing to be "more" masculine or to have the opportunity to "prove" his conformity to gendered ideals.

51. James Harvey, *Romantic Comedy in Hollywood, from Lubitsch to Sturges* (1987; repr., New York: Da Capo, 1998), 413.

52. Ibid.

53. Ibid.

54. Grindon, *The Hollywood Romantic Comedy*, 108.

55. Dickos, *Intrepid Laughter*, 106.

56. Ibid., 108.

57. Harvey observes that such thematic elements became common in the romantic comedies of this era. He explains, "Romantic comedy shifted from a fantasy of freedom to a joke about entrapment: women by their nonsense, and men by their women; she trying to escape her nature, and he trying to fulfill it, and both without success." Harvey suggests that "the whole feeling was different" within this genre, as each film increasingly "had become less a comedy about falling in love than about trapping a man," See: Harvey, *Romantic Comedy in Hollywood*, 415–416.

58. Incidentally, the Lynds also note the conforming function of the newspapers that circulate in Muncie. They write, "It is largely taken for granted in Middletown that the newspapers, while giving information to the reading public as best they may, must not do it in any way that will offend their chief supporters," namely, the "business class."

The Lynds observe a suppression of "adverse news about prominent business class families," and they write that "in any given controversy the two leading papers may be expected to support the United States in any cause, the business class rather than the working class, the Republican party against any other, but especially against any 'radical' party." Through this selective and biased reporting, the Muncie newspapers shape the values of the citizens, who are made to imagine that an ideological consensus exists within the community. This dynamic is a micro version of Benedict Anderson's discussion of the newspaper's role in forming national identity. Anderson describes the individual "ceremony" of reading the daily newspaper as one in which the reader "is continually reassured that the imagined world is visibly rooted in everyday life ... fiction seeps quietly and continuously into reality, creating that remarkable confidence of community in anonymity which is the hallmark of modern nations." See: Lynd and Lynd, *Middletown*, 475–477; Benedict Anderson, *Imagined Communities: Reflections on the Origin and Spread of Nationalism* (1983; repr., London: Verso, 2006), 35–36.

59. Such dynamics somewhat correspond with Turner's theories about the frontier, regional identity, and cultural stagnation. Turner views the closing of the frontier as a turn inward for the United States, one in which the Midwest is the fulcrum of this motion. By being a space of nostalgia, the Midwest is seemingly especially susceptible to the cultural rot or decay that ensues from limitations on the nation's ability to expand.

60. *The Magnificent Ambersons*, directed by Orson Welles (1942; Burbank, CA: Warner Home Video, 2011), DVD.

61. *The Public Enemy*, directed by William A. Wellman (1931; Burbank, CA: Warner Home Video, 2005), DVD; *Scarface*, directed by Howard Hawks (1932; Universal City, CA: Universal Studios Home Entertainment, 2007), DVD.

62. Shortridge, *The Middle West*, 62.

63. Ibid., 64.

64. Shortridge, *The Middle West*, 56, 68.

65. By contrast, Oman details a complicating perspective on race and the Midwest in the multiple versions of *Show Boat* and certain other regional discourses from the 1920s through the 1940s: an "assumption of black rurality" that "associate[es] racial blackness with the supposedly authentic rural life of the nineteenth century" and generally ignores "Chicago's large population of Southern black migrants." See: Oman, "'Here Comes the Show Boat!,'" 67–69.

66. Johnson, *Heartland TV*, 5.

67. Ibid., 18, emphasis in original.

68. Richard Wright, "How 'Bigger' Was Born," in *Native Son* (1940; repr., New York: Harper Perennial Modern Classics, 2005), 453, emphasis added.

69. Wright, *Native Son*, 338.

70. Lorraine Hansberry, *A Raisin in the Sun* (1959; repr., New York: Vintage, 1994); *Candyman*, directed by Bernard Rose (1992; Culver City, CA: Columbia TriStar Home Entertainment, 2004), DVD.

71. Hansberry, *A Raisin in the Sun*, 118, emphasis in original.

72. Matthew Elder, "Social Demarcation and the Forms of Psychological Fracture in Book One of Richard Wright's *Native Son*," *Texas Studies in Literature and Language* 52, no. 1 (Spring 2010): 31.

73. Ibid., 35.

74. For instance, when Bigger first reports for work as the chauffeur for the wealthy and white Dalton family, the boisterous personality on display around his friends is replaced by a much more stoic performance. As Elder observes, "The change, though

not unexpected, is unsettling nonetheless and all the more striking here because these scenes are proximately juxtaposed with the vivid scenes of Bigger's volatile aggression and reckless bravado. He speaks the simpleton dialect expected of him and appropriate to the role that white society has circumscribed for him." Masaya Takeuchi also addresses how "Bigger's identity splits into two conflicted selves, an assertive one among blacks and a submissive one in front of whites." Takeuchi elaborates, "Bigger attempts to balance his submissive self, which is thoroughly conditioned by whites, by asserting control over others.... [His] sadistic behaviors are the product of a frustrated manhood that ultimately seeks expression in a violent sexual assault." Although Bigger is quite distinct from Norval in *The Miracle of Morgan's Creek*, both characters are compelled to adopt unnatural mannerisms because of normalized expectations relating to race and gender, respectively. See: Elder, "Social Demarcation," 40; Masaya Takeuchi, "Bigger's Divided Self: Violence and Homosociality in *Native Son*," *Studies in American Naturalism* 4, no. 1 (Summer 2009): 56, 63.

75. Kate Marshall provides a fascinating reading of the "infrastructural modernity" evident through Wright's attentiveness to physical structures and their effects on movement. Marshall writes,

> Circulation in *Native Son* is always double-sided, and so it follows that the circulation system of the furnace relies on another form of circulation to operate. It also makes sense that in a novel so invested in movement, enclosure, and communication, a fiery furnace becomes both a way to locate these things explicitly and the occasion to reflect upon how they work. When the circulation of heat halts in the novel, it draws attention to the fact that the outside of the circulation system is another circulation system, albeit engaged with another medium. As the furnace reveals ventilation and combustion to be two aspects of a larger circulatory dynamic, the clogging of the furnace with body parts ensure that the embeddedness of persons within these circulation systems will not go unnoticed.

Even the infrastructure of buildings, as Marshall details, reflects the restrictive forces at work throughout *Native Son*. See: Kate Marshall, "Sewer, Furnace, Air Shaft, Media: Modernity Behind the Walls in *Native Son* and *Manhattan Transfer*," *Studies in American Fiction* 37, no. 1 (Spring 2010): 56, 67.

76. Wright, *Native Son*, 174, 240.

77. Ibid., 182, 248–249, 327–328.

78. Many critics have commented on the vast range of restrictions in Bigger's life. For instance, Sara D. Schotland writes, "Bigger is closed off from all avenues that lead out of the ghetto into the privileged world of meaningful work, political power, and material wealth." Eric Van Hoose perceives constriction within the very progression of the narrative, and he writes, "*Native Son* is built upon the structural principle of reversal ... the relative freedom of movement utilized by Bigger and his friends at the novel's opening has, by the novel's end, been replaced by his literal confinement and death." See: Sara D. Schotland, "Breaking Out of the Rooster Coop: Violent Crime in Aravind Adiga's *White Tiger* and Richard Wright's *Native Son*," *Comparative Literature Studies* 48, no. 1 (2011): 16; Eric Van Hoose, "Native Sun: Lightness and Darkness in *Native Son*," *The Black Scholar* 41, no. 2 (Summer 2011): 51.

79. Wright, "How 'Bigger' Was Born," 459.

80. Morris Dickstein, "Depression Culture: The Dream of Mobility," in *Radical Revisions: Rereading 1930s Culture*, ed. Bill Mullen and Sherry Lee Linkon (Urbana: University of Illinois Press, 1996), 238.

81. Ibid., 239.
82. Ibid., 240.
83. Wright, "How 'Bigger' Was Born," 439.
84. The cinema works as both a temporary salve and damaging stimulus for Bigger's ongoing frustrations. For example, Edward J. Ahearn writes that, inside the cinema, Bigger is inculcated with "distorted information about race and financial success," which produces desires that will remain unrealized in the harsh space of the city. By contrast, Jacqueline Stewart explains the concept of "reconstructive spectatorship, a formulation that seeks to account for the range of ways in which black viewers attempted to reconstitute and assert themselves in relation to the classical cinema's racist social and textual operations." Stewart goes on to discuss the "reconstructive spectatorship" of Bigger and Pauline Breedlove, the protagonist of Toni Morrison's novel, *The Bluest Eye* (1970). Stewart writes that the fictional pair "use the cinema to fill spaces in their lives that result from both their status as working-class African Americans with few social options and their status as migrants struggling to (re)construct themselves—physically and metaphysically—in new and often hostile urban environments." As evident by these varied interpretations, the precise effects of Bigger's encounters with the cinema and other aspects of mass culture are rather muddled, while still exerting a major influence on his perception of the world. See: Edward J. Ahearn, *Urban Confrontations in Literature and Social Science, 1848–2001: European Contexts, American Evolutions* (Burlington, VT: Ashgate, 2010), 80; Jacqueline Stewart, "Negroes Laughing at Themselves? Black Spectatorship and the Performance of Urban Modernity," *Critical Inquiry* 29, no. 4 (Summer 2003): 653, 669–670.
85. Wright, *Native Son*, 43.
86. Ibid., 20, 41, 130, 240.
87. Wright, "How 'Bigger' Was Born," 451, emphasis in original.
88. Sarah Relyea writes, "*Native Son* unfolds from a basic premise: in the modern world, one cannot grasp the complex whole or the lived experience of others." See: Sarah Relyea, *Outsider Citizens: The Remaking of Postwar Identity in Wright, Beauvoir, and Baldwin* (New York: Routledge, 2006), 22.
89. Nicole Rafter discusses films that provide "bad-environment" justifications for criminality, and her explanation is applicable to how Wright depicts Chicago in *Native Son*. Rafter observes that the criminals in such narratives "initially . . . are like everyone else: blank slates on which the social environment engraves behavioral patterns. Films of this type are highly deterministic; arguing that escape from one's situational fate is unlikely or impossible, they offer their characters few alternate courses of action, a point they drive home with images of entrapment." See: Nicole Rafter, *Shots in the Mirror: Crime Films and Society* (Oxford: Oxford University Press, 2006), 65–68.
90. Wright, "How 'Bigger' Was Born," 442.
91. Turner, *The Frontier in American History*, 186.
92. Lynd and Lynd, *Middletown*, 7–8
93. As mentioned at the beginning of this chapter, Berman describes the flexibility, willingness, or even eagerness to be continually altered as a necessary condition of the modern subject.

3 | Nostalgic Violence, Nebulous Spaces, and Blank Identities

Terrence Malick's debut feature, *Badlands* (1973), enters its final act with protagonists Kit Carruthers (Martin Sheen) and Holly Sargis (Sissy Spacek) driving across the barren landscape of the Great Plains in order to escape the South Dakota police.[1] In their attempted flight from the Midwest, the lethal couple is encumbered by the vast flatness of the borderlands between South Dakota and Montana, and their constant forward motion strangely seems to yield no actual spatial progress. As Kit and Holly journey farther into this regional border, it increasingly appears to be an untraversable space that expands indefinitely in all directions. With the desired "mountains of Montana" perpetually in the distance, Holly laments, "We lived in utter loneliness, neither here nor there. Kit said that 'solitude' was a better word, 'cause it meant more exactly what I wanted to say. Whatever the expression, I told him we couldn't go on livin' this way."

"Neither here nor there" is a particularly apt phrase for describing the nostalgic spatial and temporal properties featured in key cinematic depictions of the Midwest during the 1970s. Holly's narration imagines that the region is an indeterminate space, and she experiences its physical terrain as a nebulous environment impervious to the passage of time. Indeed, Holly alternately might have qualified that she and Kit were occupying a time "neither now nor then." Along with announcing the arrival of a major American director, *Badlands* also introduces a new variation on the Midwest's long association with nostalgia, especially as shown on film. In this decade, several films emphasize the region's nostalgic identity in at least two notable ways: by presenting the Midwest as a realm in which distinctions between past and present become impossible to discern; by depicting Midwesterners as blank slates who mask an underlying absence of identity by conforming to regional stereotypes and/or by engaging in violent acts intended to infuse the present with meaning. This latter representational development is of particular significance, as it signals the emergence of a phenomenon that I conceptualize as "nostalgic violence," which refers to a violent act committed in an attempt to manipulate the surface appearance of a particular space and its inhabitants. Nostalgic violence is used to regulate the visible present so that it might *appear* as a nostalgic subject *imagines* or *believes* the desired past to be. In this chapter and the next, textual examples of nostalgic violence reveal a latent destructive impulse within nostalgia's looping desire mechanism.

This chapter identifies *Badlands* as a singular text among popular representations of the Midwest. Malick's film introduces a new rendering of Midwesterners and the nostalgic landscape that surrounds them. Such imagery has proven to have a lasting influence on—or at least to have foreshadowed the shape of—subsequent narratives about the region. The importance of *Badlands* within a Midwestern context results from Malick merging the two approaches to depicting the region's nostalgic identity outlined above. In brief, Kit and Holly are blank slates who adopt and discard identities throughout the narrative, which unfolds in an environment that Malick presents as both spatially and temporally removed from other locales. The Midwest of *Badlands* has a physical flatness that is reflected in the deadpan personas of its protagonists. In addition to *Badlands*, this chapter also considers two later films with similar thematic content: Werner Herzog's *Stroszek* (1977) and John Carpenter's *Halloween* (1978).[2] In *Stroszek*, Herzog fills his depiction of Wisconsin with looping, circular imagery that subtly establishes the Midwestern setting as resistant to the linear progression of time; in *Halloween*, Carpenter's monstrous "boogeyman" figure Michael Myers is perhaps the blankest Midwesterner ever shown onscreen, and his shocking violence is interconnected with an underlying nostalgia that compels him to terrorize his hometown in Illinois. All three films also problematize white masculinity by prominently featuring troubled male characters with damaged, purposeless lives. For two of these characters—Kit and Michael Myers—such internal turmoil is externalized through various acts of nostalgic violence.

Although the settings of these three films resemble the sparse terrain and small town environments that often denote the Midwest on film, they actually each expose a high degree of spatial and temporal abstraction concealed beneath that traditional regional imagery. Together, these films form a distinctive branch of Midwestern representations that emerges in the 1970s. In such texts, the Midwest is brought into further alignment with nostalgia's temporal dynamics. *Badlands*, *Stroszek*, and *Halloween* overtly frame the region's physical terrain as nebulous and present various white male Midwestern characters as blanks who obscure their innate vacancy with violence and superficial enactments of identity. This blend of abstract landscape and performative inhabitants becomes particularly acute in cinematic depictions of the Midwest around the turn of the twenty-first century, as will be detailed in later chapters. Here, however, the focus is limited to the ways in which Malick, Herzog, and Carpenter set about undermining the stability of the region's normalized image as a placid environment filled with good-natured, simple individuals.

The remarkably amorphous version of the Midwest on display in *Badlands*, *Stroszek*, and *Halloween* reflects a significant change in understandings of the region since the middle of the twentieth century. James Shortridge identifies the 1950s as a period in which "a new perspective on the region emerged. This was nostalgia."[3] Shortridge argues that, as the twentieth century's second half progressed, nostalgia and the Midwest became more and more entwined in the American public's imagination. He explains,

> Small towns and traditional farms, indeed the entire Middle-western culture, began to be labeled as quaint. Support for this viewpoint quickened in the mid 1960s, and by the early 1970s it was perhaps the dominant image that outsiders held about the

region. From this perspective, the Middle West had become a museum of sorts. No up-and-coming citizen wanted to live there, but it had importance as a repository for traditional values. The Middle West was a nice place to visit occasionally and to reflect upon one's heritage. It was America's collective "hometown," a place with good air, picturesque farm buildings, and unpretentious "simple" people.[4]

This passage is a striking example of how nostalgic spatiality is attached to the Midwest's identity in American culture. By describing the Midwest as a "museum," Shortridge highlights a recurring conceptualization of the region as a realm that permits access to the past, which is a fundamentally nostalgic function. Essentially, the Midwest-as-museum image is an assertion that this regional space somehow sutures the separated past and present. Those who enter the Midwest thereby experience a sensation of temporal collapse or convergence comparable to that which occurs when contemplating artifacts in a museum.

Portrayals of the Midwest as an atemporal museum literalize ways in which older texts—such as Frederick Jackson Turner's writings and Theodore Dreiser's *Sister Carrie* (1900)—link the region and nostalgia.[5] As Shortridge observes, over the course of the twentieth century, the Midwest increasingly is perceived as actually housing the past and serving as something of an archive for American culture, rather than merely lagging behind the coasts in terms of contemporaneity and relevancy. By the 1970s, this impression of the Midwest is entrenched in the American popular discourse. As a "museum," the Midwest does not simply have an anachronistic culture; rather, the region enables and encourages a nostalgic connection to the past (or at least an imagined version of the past). Glimpses of these peculiar temporal conditions appear throughout *Badlands*, *Stroszek*, and *Halloween*, each of which is marked by a distinctly nostalgic relation to space and time. Before delving into these films, though, two additional texts provide insightful context for this era's engagement with Midwestern identity and nostalgic spatiality: Michael Lesy's *Wisconsin Death Trip* (1973) and Tim O'Brien's novel *In the Lake of the Woods* (1994).[6]

Wisconsin Death Trip remains a captivating and unnerving rediscovery of a damaged Midwest from the decades surrounding the turn of the twentieth century. Composed of period photographs, newspaper articles, and other archival documents, Lesy's reclamation of these materials refutes claims of the Midwest being a pastoral paradise. Of particular fascination are the morbid yet mundane photographs—or "records of flesh," as Lesy describes them—taken by Charles Van Schaick (the town photographer for Jackson County, Wisconsin) between 1890 and 1910.[7] By repurposing Van Schaick's stark images of death, fatigue, and madness—ranging from portraits of dead infants to the weathered faces of elderly Wisconsinites, as well as more banal scenes of everyday life—*Wisconsin Death Trip* serves as something of a corrective to Turner's mythologization of the Midwest during this period.

Lesy's project was published in the 1970s, a period in which the Midwest's staid nostalgic identity is challenged in films such as those addressed in this chapter. Notably, in the introduction to *Wisconsin Death Trip*, Lesy reveals a purpose beyond merely shining a light on a forgotten Midwestern community. Lesy writes,

> This book is an exercise in historical actuality, but it has only as much to do with history as the heat and spectrum of the light that makes it visible, or the retina and optical nerve of your eye. It is as much an exercise of history as it is an experiment of alchemy. Its primary intention is to make you experience the pages now before you as a flexible mirror that if turned one way can reflect the odor of the air that surrounded me as I wrote this; if turned another, can project your anticipations of next Monday; if turned again, can transmit the sound of breathing in the deep winter air of a room of eighty years ago, and if turned once again, this time backward on itself, can fuse all three images, and so can focus who I once was, what you might yet be, and what may have happened, all upon a single point of your imagination, and transform them like light focused by a lens on paper, from a lower form of energy to a higher.[8]

In this evocative passage, Lesy ascribes a remarkable function to what is, essentially, a collection of curated objects: that of a "flexible mirror" which has the ability to converge the past, present, and future. This sense of temporal simultaneity that Lesy hopes to achieve is both nostalgic in its connection to the past and beyond nostalgia's circular mode of desire. Through the act of recontextualizing artifacts from the past, Lesy intends for his book to produce a temporal collapse that is transformative and constructive. In other words, *Wisconsin Death Trip* symbolizes a form of nostalgia that works against regressive attempts to restore "lost" ideals, as apparent in Turner's writing or in fictional depictions of nostalgic violence.

Similar to Lesy exhuming the Midwest's forgotten past, O'Brien's *In the Lake of the Woods* establishes the region as a space "where the vanished things go"— or at least where people go when they wish to vanish.[9] O'Brien's novel details a middle-aged Midwestern couple dealing with the repercussions of history unexpectedly intruding into the present. The narrative begins after John Wade's political career is destroyed by revelations about his involvement in the 1968 My Lai Massacre during the Vietnam War. This initially hidden atrocity was publicly reported in the United States just on the cusp of the 1970s; in the novel, John's participation is not revealed until the early 1990s due to his manipulation of military records. To recuperate from the professional and personal fallout, John and his wife, Kathy, retreat to Minnesota's isolated Northwest Angle, where she promptly disappears. John, too, vanishes while searching the maze-like network of lake channels and islands. Hence, the reemergence of the obscured past prompts a return to the nostalgic space of the Midwest, which reabsorbs its disgraced inhabitants into the landscape itself.

O'Brien's novel is not a traditional detective story, and it provides no definite answers for its mysteries. Instead, *In the Lake of the Woods* is, in part, a rumination on how history lingers and the ways in which the Midwestern landscape both conceals the past and makes it present. In the novel, O'Brien presents the

Northwest Angle as a realm with abstract properties. He writes, "And in the deep unbroken solitude, age to age, Lake of the Woods gazes back on itself like a great liquid eye. Nothing adds or subtracts. Everything is present, everything is missing. . . . Thickly timbered, almost entirely uninhabited, the Angle tends toward infinity. Growth becomes rot, which becomes growth again, and repetition itself is in the nature of the angle."[10] Here, as in many texts, the Midwest is imagined as a space that reflects and produces a nostalgic impulse to look into the past and contemplate the progression of time. Rather than enable a greater awareness of "historical actuality," to borrow Lesy's phrase, O'Brien's Midwestern landscape offers a distortion of the past.[11] O'Brien explains, "The angle shapes reality . . . Partly window, partly mirror, the angle is where memory dissolves."[12] This regional space is marked by confounding physical properties in which, paradoxically, everything is simultaneously perceptible and absent. Within this perilous environment, nostalgia's repetitive desire circuit permeates both Midwestern culture and the physical territory itself. The Midwest swallows up lives, clouds the future, and is set apart from the unfolding contemporary time of other locations. As John observes, "The world was elsewhere."[13]

Both *Wisconsin Death Trip* and *In the Lake of the Woods* provide key examples of ways in which the Midwest may be configured as a domain with nostalgic spatiotemporal elements. As a nostalgia museum, the Midwest appears to be in close proximity to and a great distance from the past that the region supposedly contains. Actual historical circumstances merge with myth, personal recollection, and nostalgic desire. Lesy's engagement with neglected aspects of Midwestern history works against the regional mythology constructed by figures such as Turner. By contrast, O'Brien demonstrates how perceptions of the Midwest's atemporal status situate the region as a site of forgetting and negation of history. Since the early 1970s, attention to these qualities recurs in many important depictions of the region. Malick's *Badlands*, which was released the same year as *Wisconsin Death Trip*, is a revelatory case study for understanding the ongoing abstraction of the Midwest as a space of nostalgia and violence.

Badlands

Badlands is set in the 1950s and loosely based upon the real life exploits of Charles Starkweather and Caril Ann Fugate, a teenage couple who embarked on a killing spree across Nebraska in late 1957 and early 1958 before being apprehended in Wyoming. Despite such specific reference points, an ahistorical quality permeates *Badlands*. While discussing the film in a 1975 interview, writer/director Terrence Malick explains, "I tried to keep the 1950s to a bare minimum. Nostalgia is a powerful feeling; it can drown out anything. I wanted the picture to set up like a fairy tale, outside time, like *Treasure Island*. I hoped this would, among other things, take a little of the sharpness out of the violence but still keep its dreamy quality."[14] Curiously, by working against cultural nostalgia for the 1950s, Malick instead produces a vision of nostalgia in the abstract: that is, *Badlands* is saturated with a sense of temporal displacement that corresponds to the forever-desiring state of nostalgia. Yet, the film does not feature a typical object of nostalgic desire. Kit and Holly both seek *something*, but they appear unable to articulate precisely what that might be.

As context for my reading of *Badlands* and other texts over the remainder of *The American Midwest in Film and Literature*, a brief overview of two critical works on nostalgia and film is instructive. While addressing how "nostalgia for the past is slowly being corrupted" in *Badlands*, as well as the film's "critical attitude toward its material and the present," Vera Dika draws upon Fredric Jameson's concept of the "nostalgia film."[15] Dika describes "nostalgia films" as "reconstructions of dead or dismantled forms, genres that are now returned after a period of absence or destruction. The films are thus better understood as *copies* whose originals are often lost or little known."[16] In *Postmodernism: or, The Cultural Logic of Late Capitalism* (1991), Jameson links the replicative quality of the nostalgia film to the way in which such texts "restructure the whole issue of pastiche and project it onto a collective and social level, where the desperate attempt to appropriate a missing past is now refracted through the iron law of fashion change and the emergent ideology of the generation."[17] As such, Jameson writes that "the nostalgia film . . . approache[s] the 'past' through stylistic connotation, conveying 'pastness' by the glossy qualities of the image."[18] I include these definitions of the "nostalgia film" in order to distinguish my own arguments from such conceptualizations. Although I do not dispute framing certain uses of generic conventions in cinema since the 1970s as "nostalgic," my interest in the nostalgic qualities of *Badlands* (and other films) is separate from these concerns. As with all of my primary textual objects in this book, I explore ways in which *Badlands* represents the relationship between nostalgia (as both a spatiotemporal phenomenon and cultural force) and the film's Midwestern setting. Within the regional context of my project, Malick's appropriation and subversion of crime-film conventions is less relevant than his projection of nostalgia onto the film's Midwestern landscape and the identities of various characters.

In *Badlands*, the Midwest's nostalgic spatial and violent dimensions are most evident in two ways: first, through presenting the Midwestern landscape as a nebulous and inescapable environment that is oppressive in its flatness; second, through the characters of Kit and Holly, both of whom are obstinately "blank," even while committing murder and oscillating among various adopted personas. Throughout the film, this violent pair exhibits contradictory tendencies, as their murderous trek across South Dakota belies what appears to be an impulse to conform to "traditional" Midwestern behaviors and values, as evident by their unfailing politeness.[19] Before returning to Kit and Holly's eccentric identities, a closer examination of the regional venue for their behaviors is necessary.

A relationship among trauma, environment, and nostalgia is introduced immediately in *Badlands*, which opens with a medium shot that circles around Holly as she plays with a dog on her bed. Holly's aloof and disconnected narration—the first instance of the disjunctive voiceover that recurs across Malick's filmography—quickly complicates this brief scene by introducing the peculiar tone of the film. She states, "My mother died of pneumonia when I was just a kid. My father had kept their wedding cake in the freezer for ten whole years. After the funeral, he gave it to the yardman. He tried to act cheerful, but he could never be consoled by the little stranger he found in his house. Then, one day, hoping to begin a new life away from the scene of all his memories, he moved us from Texas to Fort Dupree, South Dakota." According to Holly, she and her father (played by Warren Oates) relocated to the Midwest so that he could escape a physical space associated with negative memories. Holly's narration suggests that her father perceives the middle region as something of a blank canvas upon which the past may be revised, elided, or erased entirely.[20] In the midcentury setting of *Badlands*, then, Mr. Sargis believes (or simply wishes) that the Midwest is enclosed within a protective barrier from traumatic memories that are located elsewhere and "else-when."

Holly's father works as a sign painter touching up advertisements that have cracked and faded—significantly, this profession entails covering up evidence of decay. Physical markers of time (such as a billboard's progressively weathered condition) are obscured, as Mr. Sargis transforms these artifacts of the past into vibrant images affirming the vitality of the present. Dika provides an insightful reading of a scene in which Holly's father works on a billboard painting that "renders all objects on the same flat representational plane. Shown in long shot against a flat prairie landscape and cloud-filled blue sky, the effect is to equate the billboard and the film image itself as pictures."[21] For Dika, this spatial flattening is one of many instances in which Malick's "concern with the 'pictureness' of the image" manifests.[22] Nostalgia is an imagistic fixation that generates desire for idealized or outright fabricated images of the past, and Mr. Sargis's restoration work mirrors the nostalgic drive. Moreover, as Dika suggests, Malick himself slyly reflects on cinema's nostalgic potential to preserve or brighten the vanished past. In this regard, both the father's labor and the mise-en-scène of *Badlands* accentuate the Midwest's designated role as a museumlike cultural archive that preserves past modes of living and outdated values (see fig. 3.1).[23]

Malick presents the Badlands as a territory with an expansive quality that has the potential to collapse boundaries between here and there, now and then. But even as this nostalgic landscape compresses Midwesterners' identities, it fails to satiate their desires. In this sense, the Midwest—as depicted in *Badlands* or *In the Lake of the Woods*—serves as the most perfect site of nostalgia. Individuals such as Mr. Sargis or O'Brien's John Wade enter this nebulous space seeking to access lost objects of desire or to forget past trauma, but these texts' regional environments merely reproduce longing and separation. Following the opening scene in which Holly describes her father's nostalgic purpose for moving to the Midwest, Malick gradually reveals an unsettling outcome of occupying the region: once inside its borders, no exit appears possible, as is evident by Kit and Holly's failed escape into the Badlands. During this sequence, their car races across the screen, often along precise x and y axes within the frame, yet they never seem to gain proximity to Montana's distant mountains (see fig. 3.2). In addition, Malick contrasts Kit and Holly's futile movements with the linearity of a train moving steadily across the same landscape. It is not until the police apprehend Kit that

Fig. 3.1. A portal in the billboard accentuates the abstract spatial properties of the Midwestern landscape. Screen capture, *Badlands* (1973).

an automobile (the police cruiser) finally parallels the train's linear motion and actually surpasses the locomotive. By continually emphasizing stymied spatial progression, Malick links the physical Midwestern environment with nostalgia's temporal dynamics, which manifest as yearning for a state of existence that is lost in the past or deferred to the future. This depiction of the Midwest is a clear example of nostalgic spatiality, as the blankness of the Badlands proves to have a transformative effect on the subjectivity of the characters caught in this space.

Beyond the flat Midwestern landscape expanding so as to be inescapable, the film's setting also reduces some of the region's inhabitants to blank slates, which is especially evident in the characters of Kit and Holly.[24] Throughout *Badlands*, this couple adopts and discards many identities, and their efforts are shaped by the Midwestern environment—in both a cultural and geographic sense—in which they reside. I categorize Kit and Holly's acts of identity construction in three general ways: (1) as attempts to infuse present events with nostalgic connotations via commemorative rituals and the fetishization of objects; (2) as replications of archetypes and icons from popular culture (such as James Dean) and of behaviors normalized as "Midwestern"; (3) as abrupt outbursts of seemingly inexplicable violence, which belies the ideological implications of those actions. Given the layered nature of these behaviors, the duo's external inscrutability may be understood as a façade that covers their interior vacancy.

The first identity construction category is most clearly apparent via the abrupt shifts in nostalgic attachments to objects that recur throughout *Badlands*, such as Holly's father unceremoniously disposing of the wedding cake. Kit habitually assigns nostalgic meaning to random objects, only to compulsively discard those items soon after. This fascination with objects is evident when Kit first appears

Fig. 3.2. Kit and Holly drive along *x* and *y* axes within a nebulous environment. Screen captures, *Badlands* (1973).

onscreen while emptying garbage cans in the back alleys of Fort Dupree. Immediately, Kit demonstrates a conspicuous interest in what others have thrown out, including a dead dog, a pair of boots, and a collection of unpaid bills. Kit scrutinizes this detritus as if he were an alien figure befuddled by human behavior, and his analysis of the discarded items focuses on how that refuse might relate to one's identity. Accordingly, Kit's own persona remains predicated upon objects, visual appearance, and actions. This externalization of identity renders Kit as something of a "past-less" character who lacks a precise history to be mourned or restored.

To compensate for his blankness, Kit injects random objects with significance and commemorates mundane occurrences with symbolic rituals.[25] Such instances include the launching of a red balloon with personal mementos early in Kit and Holly's courtship; a later moment in which Kit buries some of his and Holly's possessions in a bucket while crossing the Badlands; and a pile of rocks that Kit constructs beside his car as an impromptu monument to mark his impending capture by the police. Kit's persistent reduction of identity to exterior traits and actions is aligned with nostalgic desire, which seeks to preserve or invent an idealized veneer that glosses over the imperfections of the past. Like the Midwest's nondescript surface (as depicted in *Badlands*), the exterior of Kit's body is a hollow husk that he adorns with signs of an elusive internal identity. Whether marking the physical terrain surrounding him or incongruously wearing cowboy boots as a garbage collector, Kit's identity is continually expressed through physical tokens and the ritualistic commemoration of personal events.[26]

Kit's commemorative actions are intended to generate the meaningfulness that his existence otherwise lacks. One of the first instances of this behavior occurs after the first time that Kit and Holly have sex. Kit picks up a rock and states, "We should crunch our hands with this stone. That way we'd never forget what happened today.... I'm gonna keep [the stone] for a souvenir." Much like Kit's alterations of the landscape to mark his existence, in this scene he expresses a belief that physically branding his body (and Holly's) is necessary to mark significant moments. When Holly fails to assent to Kit's symbolic mutilation plan, he defaults to fetishizing a mundane object: in this case, the rock. Later, Kit adds a ritualistic element to his and Holly's temporary occupation of a rich man's home while evading the police. Upon entering the house, Kit rings a bell and proclaims, "Next time I ring that means it's time to clear out." Ultimately, Kit transforms his own body and personal effects into nostalgic objects. After being apprehended, Kit ceremoniously gives his comb, lighter, and a pen to various police officers. During Holly's final bit of narration, she reveals that Kit was sentenced to death in the electric chair and that he donated his body to science. In being captured and executed, Kit's body—the physical exterior that he believes displays one's identity—is transformed into an artifact, a remnant of the past akin to the various objects he sought to ascribe with nostalgic connotations.

Both the objects that Kit and Holly collect and the couple's numerous ritualistic moments are efforts to invent a past that may be nostalgically mourned and commemorated *in the future*. In other words, the blank duo seeks to transform their present into a temporal moment that one day will be nostalgically desired. Because Kit and Holly equate desire with identity, they continuously engage in a mimicry of nostalgic longing. Consequently, the murderous couple's behavior might be described as "preemptive nostalgia." For instance, regarding the buried bucket of personal objects, Holly observes that Kit "said that nobody else would know where we put 'em, and that we'd come back someday, maybe, and they'd still be sittin' here, just the same, but we'd be different. And if we'd never got back, well, somebody might dig 'em up 1,000 years from now, and wouldn't they wonder." Kit's plan to return and unearth the time capsule indicates that he believes he will become nostalgic in the future; as such, he preserves objects in the present so that a link to the current moment will be possible as time passes. Objects that are mundane in the present presumably will be bursting with nostalgic value in the future.[27] Compelled by their expectation of a nostalgic future, Kit and Holly seek to instill the present with meanings that will not be recognized until a later time, as with the time-capsule bucket. Rather than nostalgia as an outcome of the gap between desired past and unsatisfactory present, *Badlands* instead presents a nostalgic chasm between the lived present and the imagined future.

The second identity construction category that I detect in *Badlands* involves Kit and Holly absorbing and refracting the iconography of popular culture and normalized Midwestern values and imagery. As in Turner's account of American frontier spaces, white masculinity, physical labor, and heteronormative family formations remain major elements in many Midwestern narratives. With Kit and Holly's overtly performative identities, Malick offers a critique of these Midwestern associations by highlighting the violence and reactionary values that underpin such nostalgic conceptions of the region. The duo's blankness both reflects and results from the flattened Midwestern spatial environment on which they act out their adopted identities.

Kit and Holly rapidly cycle through a variety of personas that are temporarily adopted and then quickly forgotten. Their most self-consciously performative moment occurs while fleeing Fort Dupree following the murder of Mr. Sargis. In voiceover, Holly states that she and Kit adopt pseudonyms: "His name would be James, mine would be Priscilla." These chosen names reference James Dean and Priscilla Presley, and multiple characters explicitly note Kit's resemblance to the icon of teen rebellion throughout the narrative.[28] Malick undercuts these ostensibly rebellious allusions by showing the fugitive "James" and "Priscilla" recreating a domestic idyll while on the run. After shooting Holly's father, Kit burns down the Sargis home; however, the destruction of this domestic space merely precedes a reenactment of domesticity when Kit and Holly hide out in a wooded area. The blank pair build an elaborate tree house and interact as an anachronistic, frontierlike version of husband and wife. Kit installs booby traps around their living quarters and hunts, while Holly gathers water and other supplies. Yet, Holly's narration reiterates the temporary and tenuous status of this performed domestic tranquility. At one point, Holly wonders about the appearance of "the man I'll marry," who clearly is not Kit and who exists in an undetermined future moment.²⁹ As with all of the identities tried out by Kit and Holly, the domestic bliss of "James" and "Priscilla" proves to be fleeting.

Even as Kit shoots eight people, he speaks authoritatively about mundane topics and advocates social conformity.³⁰ Upon first encountering Holly, Kit asks her to take a walk with him and declares, "Oh, I got some stuff to say. Guess I'm kinda lucky that way. Most people don't have anything on their minds, do they?" Kit's near-incessant pontificating reveals few independent ideas, and he continually reaffirms his status as a reflector of generic, "traditional" values. For example, while collecting garbage, Kit critiques a woman for habitually throwing away unpaid bills. A few scenes later, he sees a bag on the ground during a walk with Holly and admonishes, "If everybody did that, the whole town'd be a mess." Later, when hiding out at a rich man's house, Kit makes a second Dictaphone recording—an additional artifact to mark his existence—and states: "Listen to your parents and teachers. They got a line on most things, so don't treat 'em like enemies. There's always an outside chance you could learn something. Try to keep an open mind. Try to understand the viewpoints of others. Consider the minority opinion, but try to get along with the majority of opinion once it's accepted. Of course, Holly and I have had fun, even if it has been rushed. And, uh, so far, we're doin' fine. Hadn't got caught. Excuse the grammar."³¹ In this baffling endorsement of conformity, Kit encourages his imagined audience to yield to authority figures, to embrace "the majority of opinion," and to use proper grammar while speaking. Clearly, such statements stand in stark opposition to Kit's murderous actions, but he does not acknowledge any contradiction between his stated values and actual behavior.

A strange relationship to authority figures complicates Kit's status as a murderous outlaw and exposes that role as a performance. Kit believes that killing is a component of playing this archetypal identity, but he generally abides by idiosyncratic rules of engagement. After Kit murders three bounty hunters who locate the tree-house hideout, Holly explains Kit's philosophy about the police: "Kit felt bad about shooting those men in the back. But he said they'd come in like that and would've played it as down and dirty as they could. . . . With lawmen, it would've been different. They were out there to get a job done, and they deserved a fair chance. But not a bounty hunter." During the climactic police chase through the Badlands, Kit extends a "fair chance" to the pursuing officers by declining to even fire his gun at their car, instead shooting haphazardly without aim through the driver side window. Following his surrender, Kit praises the police officers for having "performed like a couple of heroes." These comments and behaviors indicate that Kit is disconnected from his own violent actions and show that he has an innate respect for authority figures, despite being unlawful himself. Like the "James Dean" persona, Kit's "unlawfulness" may be considered as merely one temporary identity among many.³²

Kit's deference to authority is mirrored by his admiration for wealth. With the exception of the rich man and his maid, Kit shoots everyone else who he encounters while on the run. The lack of violence perpetrated against the rich man and his maid suggests that Kit's conformity is linked to an aspirational class-consciousness. Malick himself states that the rich man is "the only man [Kit] doesn't kill, the only man he *sympathizes* with, and the one least in need of sympathy. It's not infrequently the people at the bottom who most vigorously defend the very rules that put and keep them there."³³ Understood in this light, Kit's blankness and continual adoption of personas stem from an impulse to obscure what he actually is: an impoverished, unskilled worker living in a rural Midwestern community. As a physical laborer, Kit is socially marginalized, but by articulating generic values, emulating James Dean's image, and adopting visual signs of wealth, Kit attempts to transcend the limitations of his class status. For example, Kit and Holly steal nonessential items from the rich man in order to masquerade as having wealth. When leaving the mansion in a stolen Cadillac, Kit wears the rich man's Panama hat and Holly's head is draped in a veil.³⁴ This brief image recalls their earlier performance of domesticity at the tree house. Kit even dons the hat while awaiting capture by the police, as if to mark his body as being even more exceptional than that of a common criminal.³⁵

Given Kit's compulsion to conform, his violence initially registers as inexplicable, but I consider it to be a third method of identity construction that complements his commemorative acts and performative gestures. At the beginning of *Badlands*, Kit is an invisible figure lurking in the back alleys of Fort Dupree among discarded objects. He exists as an excluded body within society, performing necessary labor—collecting garbage—that remains hidden. Kit's attempts to perform what he perceives to be normal behaviors and to articulate supposed Midwestern values go unrecognized, which partly prompts his violent actions. Anton Blok and Slavoj Žižek each identify discrete forms of violence that, when considered in relation to one another, provide potential ways of understanding Kit's behavior. According to Blok, the charge of "senseless violence" is applied to "cases where easily recognizable goals and obvious relationships between means and ends are absent."³⁶ Blok elaborates, "Widely different forms of violence routinely labeled as 'senseless' or 'irrational' are governed by rules, prescription, etiquette, and protocol. Ritualization characterizes any number of violent operations. . . . If there are any goals involved, they can only be reached in a special, prescribed, expressive, indeed *ritualized* way."³⁷ Blok's attentiveness to the relationship between ritual and certain violent actions—even those of the ostensibly "senseless" variety—suggests that some perpetrators of violence may find meaning simply through operating within the ceremonious parameters that govern such violence. In *Violence* (2008), Žižek briefly addresses what he describes as "a zero-level protest, a violent protest act which demands nothing" in terms of material objectives.³⁸ For Žižek, such violence should be understood as "a direct effort to gain *visibility*," as it is enacted in order to achieve some degree of cultural recognition.³⁹

Throughout *Badlands*, Kit's behavior functions as a merging of (or ongoing oscillation between) Blok's ritualistic "senseless violence" and Žižek's notion of a "zero-level protest." Unlike, say, the protagonists in Arthur Penn's *Bonnie and Clyde* (1967), Kit does not explicitly frame his violence as being in the service of some sort of class conflict.⁴⁰ Instead, Kit parrots authoritative, conservative language about social mores, mimics the rich man, and plays at being an archetypal outlaw. Kit rebels so that he might gain visibility and be integrated into "normal" society, rather than lurking at its fringes. Even Kit's first several murders may be understood as efforts to remove individuals who exist as barriers to his attempts to conform more fully. Holly's father prevents Kit from engaging in a relationship with Holly, and the bounty hunters disrupt the couple's enactment of domesticity in the wilderness. Interpreted in this way, Kit's violence, at least initially, is not irrationally destructive, but is actually an attempt to gain access to and recognition through the social order that has rejected or simply ignored him. These actions are examples of nostalgic violence, as Kit deploys violence in an effort to construct an identity based on a blend of idealized masculine roles such as the domestic provider, the frontier settler, and the iconic rebel. When pursued by the police, Kit dutifully performs the prescribed elements of the outlaw role by firing his gun, but he neglects to aim because the car chase is a ritualized form of play-acting; Kit eventually just pulls over and shoots out his own tire so that the police can catch up and apprehend him peacefully and without resistance. Overall, Kit demands "nothing" materially with violence, but his violent actions reveal a deep-rooted desire for recognition that Kit himself seems incapable of articulating. So, he collects and discards nostalgic objects, while ritualistically marking his existence on the surrounding terrain and through the violence he inflicts on others. Crucially, all of these acts fail to produce a stable identity or satisfactory environment, which corresponds to the inaccessible objects and conditions of nostalgic desire.

Kit's nostalgic violence temporarily establishes performative venues that exist as spaces outside of a linear temporal progression. For instance, locales such as the tree house or the rich man's home are elliptical environments that provide a respite from the rapid identity changes that Kit and Holly undergo elsewhere. No single space proves sustainable in *Badlands*, though, and Kit apparently is unable to be content in the present; indeed, he experiences the contemporary moment as if it has already slipped into the past.[41] Even during the romanticized scene in which Kit launches a balloon filled with mementos, Holly's voiceover explains, "His heart was filled with longing as he watched it drift off. Something must've told him that we'd never live these days of happiness again, that they were gone forever." Holly later repeats this sentiment as she wanders through the rich man's neighborhood. She reflects on her disconnected status by narrating, "The world was like a faraway planet to which I could never return. I thought what a fine place it was, full of things that people can look into and enjoy." This commentary reveals how the couple's deep sense of nostalgic spatiality impacts their perceptions of the world, which they experience as an imagistic, distant realm. Ultimately, Kit and Holly's flight takes them into the nebulous space of the Badlands, an environment in which the temporal and spatial simultaneity so desired by nostalgic individuals is revealed to be a form of confinement.

Within the atemporal environment of Malick's *Badlands*, nostalgic desire transforms every moment into an experience of traumatic loss for Kit and Holly. In response, they engage in futile efforts to generate meaning in their lives by frantically adopting and abandoning numerous performed identities. As the present assumes an unsatisfactory and inauthentic quality, the perception of time becomes muddled and the Midwestern environment itself is flattened into a nearly featureless backdrop in which linear progress is halted. Kit and Holly desperately pursue an unobtainable spatial and temporal coordinate that is "neither here nor there"—a site at which their unarticulated and perhaps even unknown desires might be actualized, however fleetingly. By the conclusion of *Badlands*, nostalgic desire has become temporally dislocated, and the harsh landscape of the Badlands is revealed to be a metaphoric space that can never be traversed.

Since the release of *Badlands*, the Midwest has continued to be depicted as an anachronistic space populated by blank inhabitants. Such fictional Midwesterners often engage in violent acts in order to mask their assumed identities and prop up decaying Midwestern iconography. Instead, the region's nostalgic image is exposed as a surface-level veneer. Two films from the late 1970s, *Stroszek* and *Halloween*, memorably complicate and expand upon this dynamic that *Badlands* introduced, as detailed over the remainder of this chapter.

Stroszek

With *Stroszek*, director Werner Herzog brought his unique sensibility to bear on the Midwest. Since the beginning of his career during the New German Cinema period, Herzog has been notorious for taking on arduous film projects, from dragging a several-hundred-ton steamship over a mountain in *Fitzcarraldo* (1982) to venturing to Antarctica for the documentary, *Encounters at the End of the World* (2007).[42] In comparison to such undertakings, the Wisconsin setting for the majority of *Stroszek* appears to be exceptionally mundane. On the DVD commentary track for *Stroszek*, Herzog even praises the Midwest, stating that the central region is "the best part of America. . . . People are very kind, very big hearts, down-to-earth, hardworking, no bullshit, nothing like Hollywood, nothing like the craze in New York or whatever. Good people, solidly on the ground, generous. Everything that's good about America you'd find in the Midwest, and always the very best come from there."[43] Despite this expressed appreciation for the Midwest, in *Stroszek*, Herzog depicts the region as a soul-crushing space of deceptive surfaces from which escape is impossible once an individual enters its parameters.

To evade harassment by violent criminals and vicious pimps in Berlin, Bruno Stroszek (Bruno S.), Eva (Eva Mattes), and Scheitz (Clemens Scheitz) decide to move to America because, as Eva claims, "Everybody makes money there, and we can, too."[44] As in *Badlands*, Herzog presents the Midwestern setting of *Stroszek* as a strangely abstract environment with spatial properties that reflect the looping desire circuit of nostalgia.[45] Once inside Wisconsin, progress—in terms of both economic security and the linear flow of time—becomes an illusory fantasy for the film's trio of German immigrants. The Midwestern landscape transforms the boisterous Bruno and his optimistic companions into sullen, depressed individuals whose status in Wisconsin is equivalent to or worse than their dire circumstances in Berlin.

The ongoing regression of the characters' mental states and material conditions is reflected by a circular motif evident in the narrative and form of *Stroszek*. In fact, circular motifs are prevalent throughout Herzog's filmography; for instance, in the remarkable final shot of *Aguirre, The Wrath of God* (1972), the camera circles around the film's mad protagonist standing on a sinking raft while surrounded by monkeys and corpses.[46] Regarding this recurring motif, Eric Rentschler writes, "The circle is *the* informing structure in Herzog's cinema. . . . The circle connotes a trapped life without purpose, a human existence without meaningful activity, merely an eternal repetition of the same, motions that leave us time-bound captives, subject to the whims of inscrutable higher powers."[47] Such circularity assumes further meanings within a Midwestern context. Certainly, Rentschler's references to "a trapped life" or "time-bound captives" are applicable to the emotionally stunted and geographically constrained characters in *Badlands* or many other Midwestern narratives. In *Stroszek*, the circle motif is brought into contact with the perceived nostalgic character of the Midwest; nostalgia is antilinear and typified by desire for a looping return to the past, which is especially evident in cinematic depictions of the region's anachronistic culture and nebulous terrain. Herzog's film refracts both of these recurring Midwestern representational conventions in quite singular ways.

Even before departing for the United States, Herzog presents Bruno as something of a nostalgic character who is reluctant to leave his home, despite being subjected to constant threats. When Eva and Scheitz discuss the trio's immigration plans, Bruno observes that "if we don't like it, we can always come back." Bruno later echoes this sentiment in Wisconsin after his relationship with Eva fails, and he is unable to repay the bank loan that was used for their mobile home. Speaking in the third person, Bruno nostalgically laments, "Bruno's on the outside looking in. Stupid of him to ever have done it, coming to America, just to watch his whole world fall apart. I might as well be back where I came from." These two statements provide insights into Bruno's changing perception of the relationship between space and time. In the former statement, Bruno expresses faith that his then-present Berlin lifestyle may be restored if the journey to America proves to be unsatisfactory; once installed within the Midwest, however, Bruno no longer considers a recovery of his past self to be possible, so he nostalgically longs for what once was.

Herzog claims, "America is so open, the center of America is . . . vast and strange and open."[48] Yet, *Stroszek* repeatedly features symbolic foreclosures of movement and opportunity, along with a bank literally foreclosing on Bruno's mobile home. Herzog shoots both the delivery and repossession of the home in a long shot with a stationary camera, which has the remarkable effect of rendering Bruno's Wisconsin living space as an approximation of a point on a timeline or the x axis of a graph. When the trailer home is delivered, it enters from the left of the frame and moves toward the right; when the home is removed, it is towed

Fig. 3.3. The site of Bruno's home is transformed into a blank space. Screen captures, *Stroszek* (1977).

from the center of the frame and exits to the right. In both scenes, the rectangular home roughly bifurcates the frame horizontally, and the composition of the trailer home's sharp lines and the empty lot—initially filled by the home, and later vacated once more—suggest that Bruno is trapped in a static bubble on a timeline through which other objects and individuals pass (see fig. 3.3). Herzog's Wisconsin, then, extends the anachronistic and atemporal depiction of the Midwest that Malick also made prominent in *Badlands*.

A connection between paused temporal progress and Herzog's circular motif is evident in *Stroszek*'s Wisconsin setting, which features several frozen ponds brightening the otherwise drab landscape. For instance, in one long shot, Herzog fills the frame with the icy curves of a pond as Bruno, Eva, Scheitz, and the latter's American nephew Clayton (Clayton Szalpinski) frolic in the background. Earlier, Clayton explained that there have been several unexplained disappearances of farmers in Railroad Flats, which locals superstitiously attribute to four or five unknown murderers. Clayton scours the area with his metal detector in order to uncover clues, and the colder temperatures enable him to use the device on the iced-over surfaces of the ponds. In addition to the practical function of permitting Clayton to search for submerged artifacts of the past that otherwise would be inaccessible, these frozen bodies of water are something of a metaphor for the Midwest's nostalgic character. Within a Midwestern context, these circular ponds symbolize the region's general stasis and ability to grant its inhabitants access to the past.

The circle motif also is prominent in a brief scene during which two farmers antagonize one another over a land dispute next to Clayton's property. Each man claims ownership of a narrow strip of land. When one farmer rides on his tractor near the disputed area, the other emerges and mirrors those actions. Both farmers are armed with rifles while plowing, and they circle the same spot again and again in a counterclockwise direction. The two farmers loop back and forth, keeping one another at bay, but they never actually go anywhere or achieve a resolution to their disagreement. Their constant efforts and threats merely produce stasis.

Circling appears on *Stroszek*'s soundtrack via two distinctive forms of doubling. First, as Emily Hauze observes, "internal performances are replaced by a carefully aligned external musical soundtrack in Bruno's America. Most of this music appears twice, highlighting incongruities between events."[49] Such instances include "a vocal duet entitled 'Silver Bell' from a circa-1911 Edison cylinder [that] accompanies the arrival and removal of Bruno's mobile home."[50] Once in Wisconsin, Bruno's ability to indulge his love of music is restricted, and the soundtrack itself becomes oppressively repetitive. Various nondiegetic songs keep recurring, subtly calling attention to the Midwest's circular temporality.

The second form of doubling on the soundtrack manifests in numerous acts of translation that occur once Bruno, Eva, and Scheitz arrive in America. Bruno speaks only German, Clayton speaks only English, Eva has fluency in both languages, and Scheitz sometimes appears able to translate English into German, but frequently is shown to be incapable of communicating clearly with locals. Because of these language barriers, Eva (and occasionally Scheitz) serves as a translator and repeats statements made by Clayton and Scott (Scott McKain), a representative of the bank who harasses Bruno and Eva about repaying their loan. During these moments of translation, Herzog typically uses screen time to show a statement in one language and then its repetition in another language. One such instance involves Clayton explaining the neighboring farmers' mutual hostility toward one another, which Scheitz then relates to Bruno in German.

Repetition—through a constant doubling of verbal communication—thus informs Bruno's experiences in Wisconsin, which is a space that features an almost immediate return and re-articulation of past speech acts. By emphasizing translation, Herzog again affirms the looping nature of the Midwest.

The final act of translation in *Stroszek* is the most unusual and takes place during the film's surreal concluding sequence. Following the repossession of the mobile home and Eva returning to prostitution (and then embarking for Canada with a trucker), Bruno and Scheitz decide to rob the local bank with a rifle. Upon discovering that the bank is closed, the tragicomic duo abruptly robs the barber next to the bank before entering a supermarket across the street. Scheitz is promptly arrested, but Bruno escapes with a frozen turkey; he returns to Clayton's garage, steals an old tow truck and several cans of beer, and drives away with the turkey and rifle. Although it is unclear how far Bruno travels, he eventually arrives in a small town filled with Native Americans and tourist shops selling replicas of objects such as hunting spears.[51] As a fire ignites in the engine of Bruno's tow truck, he pulls into a parking lot where a solitary figure in ceremonial Native American garb stands.

With rifle and turkey in hand, Bruno enters a sandwich shop. Herzog uses a jump cut to move from the parking lot to inside of the shop. This edit is not a direct continuation of Bruno's movement, as might be expected. Instead, once Herzog cuts to the interior shot, Bruno is already seated at a table with an unidentified man, and the pair apparently has been conversing for an uncertain period of time. Their relationship is never explained; it seems likely that Bruno merely sat at the man's table, but, improbably, this individual speaks German. In English, he says, "So, your car is kaput. And your girlfriend is gone. And thine house they have sold." The stranger then shifts to German and declares, "I wouldn't worry about it." Bruno replies (in German, of course), "You said it. Absolutely." After the anonymous man toasts Bruno with "Prost," Herzog's camera lingers on a silent close-up of Bruno. Aside from the uncertain duration of the encounter and nature of the relationship between the two men, this scene stands out as the final moment of translation in a film filled with such occurrences. Unlike the earlier instances, though, Herzog does not depict the initial speech act that prompts the translation—in this case, Bruno's narrative of his trials in Wisconsin. Furthermore, the stranger's recitation of Bruno's ordeal in English is unwarranted, as Bruno cannot understand what the man says in any language but German, and no one else is near their table. In this odd scene, the act of translation is for no one within the diegesis. As such, the man's rote translation reflects upon the doubling and circularity throughout the film. Here, the stranger's repetitive speech act almost seems to be compelled by the Midwestern environment itself.

This mysterious interlude leads into the film's even more bizarre conclusion. Bruno exits the restaurant, hops in the tow truck cab, and sets the flaming vehicle spinning in a counterclockwise circle (see fig. 3.4). Still clutching the rifle and turkey, Bruno leaves the truck circling in the parking lot and walks into a building across the street, where he observes chickens and a rabbit in cages; he deposits coins in these cages, and the animals are prompted to pantomime various acts,

Fig. 3.4. A truck circles in the foreground as Bruno walks toward the looping chairlift in the background. Screen capture, *Stroszek* (1977).

such as steering a toy fire truck, plunking a miniature piano, or "dancing." Continuing through this building, Bruno accesses a chairlift that rises up a wooded hillside, which he turns on and then boards. On the back of Bruno's chair, a sign reads, "IS THIS REALLY ME!" The protagonist completes a full circuit on the lift—which also loops around in a counterclockwise direction—but remains seated to circle around again. Herzog's camera tilts upwards from ground level as Bruno ascends the hill, and a single gunshot rings out. Although unconfirmed, Bruno presumably has killed himself, and his corpse is left to circle around and around on the lift.

Nostalgia's looping desire circuit drives individuals to attempt to regain a lost, idealized, or perhaps even fictionalized past that is perceived as superior to the degraded present. In *Stroszek*, the Midwest's nostalgic spatiality and past-oriented culture reshape Bruno into an individual who is fixated on his own falsely-idealized past in Germany, which he wishes to restore. As Herzog makes abundantly clear in the film's early scenes, Bruno's experiences in Berlin oscillate between institutional imprisonment and routine brutality when free. Even so, Bruno claims that the openness of such violence in Germany is preferable to America, where various oppressors such as the bank representative "do it ever so politely and with a smile. It's much worse." Despite the Wisconsin environment looking more drab and desolate than Berlin, Bruno's quality of life is poor regardless of his location. What truly has changed over the course of the film is his attitude toward the past, which now resembles a distinctly Midwestern iteration of nostalgic spatial and temporal properties.

Bruno's actions and the setting of the final sequence accentuate the nostalgic aspects of *Stroszek*. Both the tow truck and the chairlift circle in a counterclockwise direction. These mechanized circles provide insights into Bruno's otherwise inexplicable actions by suggesting an internal nostalgic desire to go backwards in time. Significantly, this desire is externalized onto the physical environment itself.[52] Through meticulous camera movements, Herzog situates the truck and chairlift as points on a graph of sorts, just as the earlier shots showing the arrival and removal of the mobile home resemble a rough timeline. In the final sequence, this important shot begins on the now-immobile and flaming truck emitting copious amounts of smoke that fill the frame; the camera then pans to the right, pauses on the entrance to the chairlift, and tilts upward to the top of the hill. With these fluid movements, the camera connects the truck and chairlift by locating each object on the horizontal and vertical lines that compose an x-y axis. The convergence point of these perpendicular lines is the entrance to the chairlift, which is transformed into a symbolic point of entry to the self-negating circularity and nostalgia that pervade *Stroszek*. The circling truck leads to the looping chairlift, and poor Bruno's only response to this endless circuit is to kill himself. Echoing Bruno's terminal loop on the chairlift, the counterclockwise movement of the burning truck connotes immolation and self-destruction. The truck billows smoke, which quickly spreads throughout the scene. As smoke pours out, it clouds everything within the frame, thus obscuring the unfolding present. Together, these elements—Bruno's suicide, the linkage of the looping truck and lift, their shrouding effect on the present, and the Midwestern environment's continual production of nostalgic subjects and circular symbols—compose the thorough critique of nostalgia within *Stroszek*.

Like *Badlands*, Herzog's film concludes by affirming the abstract nature of the Midwest's seemingly nebulous geography. The fate of Bruno serves as a haunting example of the latent violence in certain incarnations of nostalgia. In contrast to *Stroszek*'s focus on the encounter between outsiders and the Midwest, *Halloween* explores the dynamics of a Midwestern town being confronted with its own dark history. Further, over the duration of *Halloween*, nostalgic violence is deployed on a wide scale that destabilizes an entire community.

Halloween

On the iconic promotional poster for John Carpenter's *Halloween* (1978), the tagline reads, "The Night *He* Came Home!" The "he" referenced in the tagline is the film's monstrous boogeyman, Michael Myers, who escapes from a mental institution and returns to wreak havoc in his fictional Midwestern hometown of Haddonfield, Illinois. Fifteen years after six-year-old Michael kills his older sister Judith (Sandy Johnson) by stabbing her to death, he now "comes home" as an adult to continue murdering (mostly) teenagers. Clearly, the tagline and narrative lend themselves to a psychoanalytic reading of Michael Myers—and his villainous brethren in subsequent slasher films—as a figure representing a return of repressed impulses: an unbound id or perhaps a rampaging super ego, given Michael's propensity for punishing youths engaged in debauchery.

Such an interpretation of *Halloween* corresponds to ways in which the horror genre in general has been theorized. For example, Robin Wood assesses American horror in the 1970s by writing, "One might say that the true subject of the horror genre is the struggle for recognition of all that our civilization represses or oppresses, its re-emergence dramatized, as in our nightmares, as an object of horror, a matter for terror, and the happy ending (when it exists) typically signifying the restoration of repression."[53] From Wood's perspective, the "collective nightmares" on display in horror films are a surreptitious engagement with the individual and cultural "conditions under which a dream becomes a nightmare . . . the repressed wish is, from the point of view of consciousness, so terrible that it must be repudiated as loathsome, and that it is so strong and powerful as to constitute a serious threat."[54] For Wood and theorists such as Carol Clover and Barbara Creed, the horror films of the 1970s and 1980s are often concerned with issues of gender and sexuality in relation to American society.[55]

While these studies convincingly demonstrate how such dynamics shape horror from this period, my reading of *Halloween* extends such analyses by foregrounding the film's regional and temporal dimensions. I propose an interpretation of *Halloween* that reframes Michael Myers as a troubled nostalgic character and that also emphasizes the film's Midwestern setting, which features temporal properties similar to how the region is presented in *Badlands* and *Stroszek*. Hence, these three films—particularly *Halloween*—reimagine nostalgic images of the Midwest as collective visions that straddle the line between dream and nightmare, to adapt Wood's formula. Much like Kit Carruthers in Malick's film, Michael Myers exemplifies the violently nostalgic white male subject frequently found in Midwestern narratives set or produced during the 1970s and beyond. Michael is a blank figure who compulsively seeks to restore the past with violence because the present is found to be unsatisfactory. Similar to Kit, Michael is knowable only through his actions, which are an exteriorized performance of identity layered over his rather overt blankness.

Director/cowriter Carpenter and producer/cowriter Debra Hill intended for Michael Myers's blankness to accentuate his unsettling presence onscreen. As Carpenter explains, their goal was to make Michael into "a blank slate that we [the audience] can project everything into."[56] To achieve this effect, Carpenter and Hill dressed the mute antagonist in a pale, featureless mask and mechanic coveralls, which reduce his identity to the level of physical action.[57] Accordingly, Michael Myers is designated as "The Shape" (Nick Castle) in the film's credits.[58] With this label, the filmmakers distinguish between Michael when he is masked and unmasked, the latter of which only occurs during two brief instances in the film. Consequently, Michael's "true" identity is established as the blank exterior that engenders the fearful projections of audience members. Whereas in *Badlands*, Kit's blankness is occasionally obscured by his charisma and adoption of personas such as "James Dean" or an archetypal criminal on the run, Michael selects attire that reinforces the inherent absence of his identity. Kit engages in performative gestures to cover up his blankness, but The Shape's very appearance confirms his lack of identity beyond a driving compulsion to kill. In addition to the gender-oriented readings of *Halloween*, it is important to examine other possible motives for Michael's violence. I suggest that The Shape may be understood as a horrific embodiment of the general nostalgic longing associated with the Midwest.

With the exception of two moments during which Michael is unmasked—after killing his teenage sister Judith (Sandy Johnson) as a child and while assaulting the teenaged babysitter (and surrogate sister) Laurie Strode (Jamie Lee Curtis) during the film's climax—none of the relentless killer's facial expressions are visible. Since the murder of Judith, Michael is mute, so he never verbalizes an explanation for his violence. That task falls to Michael's (rightly) paranoid doctor, Sam Loomis (Donald Pleasence), who repeatedly describes his patient in monstrous and supernatural terms. Following the former's escape from a mental institution, Loomis immediately predicts that Michael is returning home to Haddonfield. When Loomis and Sheriff Leigh Brackett (Charles Cyphers) tour the dilapidated Myers home, they discover evidence that Michael has reoccupied the house, which prompts the doctor to explain his relationship to the killer. Loomis recounts, "I met him fifteen years ago. I was told there was nothing left: no reason, no conscience, no understanding, and [not] even the most rudimentary sense of life or death, of good or evil, right or wrong. I met this six-year-old child with this blank, pale, emotionless face and the blackest eyes—the devil's eyes. I spent eight years trying to reach him and then another seven trying to keep him locked up because I realized that what was living behind that boy's eyes was purely and simply evil." Setting aside the overwrought labeling of Michael as "evil" or devil-like—a clear nod to genre conventions that hyperbolize the threat of monstrous beings—the fifteen-year gap between the initial murder and return home is highly significant. An attentiveness to this duration of time recurs across the film and relates to the context within which *Halloween* was produced, as well as to the narrative's engagement with nostalgic temporality.

The 1970s witnessed the emergence of widespread nostalgia for idealized versions of 1950s and early 1960s culture, as evident in films and television series such as *Grease* (1978) and *Happy Days* (1974–1984).[59] Notably, such texts sharply contrast with the gloom cast by contemporaneous events including the Watergate scandal, the final years of the Vietnam War, and the decade's economic recession.[60] Fredric Jameson posits that "one tends to feel, that for Americans at least, the 1950s remain the privileged lost object of desire—not merely the stability and prosperity of a pax Americana but also the first naïve innocence of the countercultural impulses of early rock and roll and youth gangs."[61] Similarly, Christine Sprengler suggests that the renewed fascination with the "Fifties" as a "mythic, nostalgic construct" was partly attributable to the "fiscal despair" of the 1970s.[62] Just as *Badlands* works against the nostalgia circulating in 1970s American popular culture by depicting violent, deviant, and nostalgic Midwesterners during the 1950s, so too does *Halloween* undercut nostalgia for the early 1960s.

Halloween stealthily engages with the nostalgic and conservative turn in American culture of the 1970s. Of pertinence is Michael Myers's shift between active and inactive states over the fifteen-year period that comprises all of the film's narrative events. Michael is locked away in a mental institution just after killing his sister on Halloween night in 1963. Coincidentally, this date is less than one month before the assassination of John F. Kennedy, and Michael's return occurs just a few years prior to Ronald Reagan's presidency in the 1980s.[63] In the world of *Halloween*, Michael is removed from history during some of the prime years of the civil rights movement and the counterculture's peak, and he returns on the cusp of a new conservative era.[64] Obviously, Carpenter and Hill could not have known what developments were to transpire in American culture and politics, but in hindsight, these historical events provide intriguing bookends to Michael's lengthy period of inactivity. By "coming home" in the late 1970s after a fifteen-year absence, Michael functions as a horrific parody of the decade's nostalgia for the 1950s and early 1960s. Following Malick's critique of nostalgia for that earlier era in *Badlands*, Carpenter and Hill show the destructive effects of the past intruding into the present through the violently nostalgic character of Michael Myers.

Aspects of the blank boogeyman's nostalgia are evident in his actions and the ways in which Dr. Loomis mythologizes him. For instance, late in *Halloween*, Sheriff Brackett again expresses skepticism about Michael being a threat in Haddonfield, which prompts Loomis to proclaim, "I watched him for fifteen years, sitting in a room, staring at a wall, not seeing the wall, looking past the wall, looking at this night, inhumanly patient. Waiting for some secret, silent alarm to trigger him off. Death has come to your little town, Sheriff." Loomis's emphasis on "this night," however, belies the seemingly arbitrary selection of the fifteen-year anniversary of Judith's murder as the date when Michael finally returns to his hometown (rather than, say, returning twenty or thirty years later). In effect, the extended duration between the original murder and its reenactment (through new murders) lends a nostalgic quality to the adult Michael's violence. By depicting the convergence of violence and nostalgia, *Halloween* bridges Midwestern representational norms and the still-developing conventions of the slasher subgenre of horror.[65]

Before returning to *Halloween*'s regional context, it is worth reviewing how the horror genre envisions the past in a way that overlaps with and subverts the nostalgic desire to invert temporal progress. Susan Stewart explains, "the horror story presents a repetition that is cumulative. Rather than canceling the significance of the original event by displacing it, the horror story increases that event's significance, multiplying its effect with each repetition. It articulates a paradox of reversibility and irreversibility in the given social shape of death."[66] Horror narratives depict worlds in which the distance between past and present is collapsible, which permits temporal simultaneity. Across the genre, the nostalgic desire to return to the past is reimagined as an actual potentiality fraught with horrific effects stemming from the past overlapping with the present.

The slasher subgenre features notable nostalgic repetitions through the seemingly endless status of its most popular franchises, as well as on the level of narrative within individual films. Regarding slasher franchises, Carol Clover writes that their many sequels "are better taken as remakes than sequels . . . in most cases [a sequel] simply duplicates with only slight variation the plot and circumstances—the formula—of its predecessor."[67] Carpenter himself observes, "Basically, sequels mean the same film. . . . That's what people want to see. They want to see the same movie again."[68] Interestingly, the duplicative nature of slasher sequels is mirrored by the typical narrative trajectory of such films. Vera Dika identifies a "two-part temporal structure" within slasher narratives that revolves around the relationship between a "past event" and a "present event."[69] Dika explains, "The two-part temporal structure of the stalker film first depicts an event long past, and then a resurgence of that event after a period of latency."[70] Accordingly, one of the subgenre's primary "narrative functions" includes a present "event [that] commemorates the past action."[71] This "function" requires a temporal gap of some duration in order to ensure that the present commemoration of the past is shocking (due to the unexpected return of a temporally distant trauma), as well as, crucially, nostalgic. Considered through this critical framework, the repetitions of slasher films—both within individual narratives and across franchise installments—point to regressive and potentially destructive outcomes of the nostalgic fascination with the past.

Unlike many haunted house stories and other supernatural fright narratives, slasher films—or at least popular franchises such as *Halloween*, *Friday the 13th*, and *A Nightmare on Elm Street* (the latter of which also is set in the Midwest)—typically feature a monstrous figure who originates from the relatively near past, as well as from the terrorized community itself. Rather than an ancient (and often foreign) threat, such as a mummy or vampire, major horror franchises of the 1970s and 1980s unleash monsters who symbolize a grotesque homecoming of sorts, as continually emphasized in *Halloween*. Upon returning to Haddonfield, Michael does not immediately begin killing people. Instead, Michael initially reoccupies his childhood home. During an early scene in which protagonist Laurie drops off a key at the abandoned Myers house, Carpenter's camera watches Laurie from behind the front door of the house, and Michael abruptly steps into the frame to reveal his presence.[72] On the sidewalk, young Tommy Doyle (Brian Andrews), who Laurie babysits later in the evening, recounts the mythology of the Myers home that circulates among his elementary school friends. Tommy claims that it is a "haunted house" and that "awful stuff happened there once." Within the "two-part temporal structure" of *Halloween*, "once" invariably produces a subsequent "again," as Michael's physical return portends a reactivation of the "awful" past.

Beyond merely returning to his childhood house, Michael also nostalgically seeks to commemorate—by compulsively reenacting—his murder of Judith, which marks the moment at which his identity halted development. Michael commences this nostalgic endeavor by collecting objects that are related to the murder of his sister, such as her tombstone. In addition, Sheriff Brackett is shown responding to a robbery at a hardware store in which a "Halloween mask, rope, and a couple of knives" are the only stolen items. Michael used a knife to kill his sister and wore a mask during the violent act; a key aspect of Michael's nostalgic

Fig. 3.5. A macabre—and nostalgic—tableau. Screen capture, *Halloween* (1978).

return to Haddonfield, then, is the re-creation of his final moments before being removed from the town and put into temporal stasis (during his lengthy confinement at the mental institution). As the film progresses, Michael stalks Laurie and kills two of her friends—Annie (Nancy Kyes) and Lynda (P. J. Soles)—who are clearly nostalgic substitutions for Judith.[73] Both of these murders occur in a home across the street from where Laurie is babysitting. When Laurie enters the house to investigate, she discovers that Michael has ritualistically arranged the corpses and tombstone in an upstairs bedroom (see fig. 3.5). Annie's body rests face-up on a bed with Judith's tombstone placed near the headboard and a jack-o'-lantern sitting on the nightstand. The bodies of Lynda and her boyfriend Bob (John Michael Graham) are stored in the room's wardrobe and closet. Michael has transformed the present bedroom into a space that resembles (or conjures up associations with) the site where he killed Judith as a child.

This ritualistic display of bodies and objects underscores Michael's innate nostalgic tendencies. It seems unlikely that Michael would set up the horrific scene to merely frighten Laurie (and the audience), even if that is its ultimate effect. Instead, Michael produces this macabre tableau to satisfy his own warped sense of nostalgia. A temporal gap between past event and present commemoration is necessary to produce nostalgia. After waiting fifteen years to become active once again, Michael seeks to merge the past and present. By collecting corpses and totems that recall the murder of his sister, Michael reveals the underlying nostalgic impulse that compels his violent attempt to restore the past. Moreover, Michael's violent return home to Haddonfield functions as a critique of the cultural nostalgia prevalent in numerous popular texts of the 1970s. Through the nostalgic reenactment of his first murder in 1963, Michael undermines nostalgia for the 1950s and early years of the 1960s by showing the idealized imagery of that period to be false. By contrast, Michael and his sexualized violence are products of that era, and his return troubles the nostalgic fantasy of recreating the past within the present. As *Halloween* reveals, such a temporal collapse would be a horrific and destructive development.

Significantly, *Halloween*'s depiction of nostalgic violence unfolds in the Midwest, which long has been imagined as an anachronistic space that exists as the nation's nostalgia museum. These cultural associations with *Halloween*'s Midwestern setting further correspond to conventions of the slasher film, as well as to recurring elements in Carpenter's filmography. According to Clover, a primary component of this subgenre is its typical site of horror, which generally is "not-home, at a Terrible Place."[74] Clover explains, "Into such houses unwitting victims wander in film after film, and it is the conventional task of the genre to register in close detail the victims' dawning understanding, as they survey the visible evidence, of the human crimes and perversions that have transpired there. That perception leads directly to the perception of their own immediate peril."[75] Although Clover identifies the Myers house as the "Terrible Place" in *Halloween*, the Wallace home more fully satisfies her definition of this key element of the slasher film.[76] The final images of *Halloween* gesture toward an even more expansive notion of what the film's "Terrible Place" might actually be. After Michael pursues Laurie from the Wallace house to the second floor of the Doyle residence, Dr. Loomis intervenes and shoots the masked killer, who falls to the ground outside. Loomis looks over the balcony only to discover that Michael has vanished, and *Halloween* concludes with a montage of locations from earlier in the film. Carpenter uses Michael's heavy breathing as a sound bridge across these images, which end with successive exterior shots of the Wallace, Doyle, and Myers homes. This concluding sequence produces a sense of lingering dread due to Michael's indeterminate spatial location.

By the film's end, Michael has a dual status as a nostalgic subject who seeks to restore the past and as a figure whose very presence embodies the return of the repressed past. Of particular importance, the concluding montage of domestic spaces and the unclear whereabouts of Michael (as evident by his breathing on the soundtrack) indicate that the nostalgic boogeyman has transcended his corporeal body. Despite being shot multiple times by Dr. Loomis, Michael still lives and, terrifyingly, he now appears to have the ability to manifest anywhere in Haddonfield.[77] The final montage thus configures the entirety of Haddonfield as a "Terrible Place," one in which the Midwestern community that produced Michael remains susceptible to the power of his nostalgic violence. Given the ongoing threat of Michael Myers—as well as the nostalgic connotations of his return to Haddonfield—the film's true horror ultimately is the indefinite destabilization that results from the past's unceasing invasion into the present. Uncritical nostalgia for the 1950s and early 1960s has enabled the return of a monstrous boogeyman. Michael is an entity born in that era and resolutely intent on collapsing distinctions between the past and the present through symbolic acts of nostalgic violence.

Within a Midwestern context, the supposed singularity of Michael Myers's monstrosity belies the fact that he merely makes visible the disastrous outcomes of the restrictive nostalgia attached to the Midwest. Frederick Jackson Turner established the Midwest as an important space of nostalgia, and this association culminated with the region being perceived as a nostalgia museum for American culture around the middle of the twentieth century. In the 1970s, however, films such as *Halloween*, *Stroszek*, and *Badlands* begin to imagine the deleterious consequences of reducing the Midwest's identity to this nostalgic role through critical depictions of blank white male characters occupying the atemporal regional terrain. *Halloween* especially troubles the conception of the Midwest as an anachronistic perpetuation of frontier ideals with the character of Michael Myers, whose blankness literally masks the character's unspoken compulsion to bring the past and the present into a chaotic state of simultaneity.

At the conclusion of *Halloween*, Haddonfield is an unstable environment in which violence may erupt at any moment because of Michael's seemingly supernatural mastery of that Midwestern space. Beyond fitting into horror conventions, the nebulous, violent world of *Halloween* functions as a frontier environment reimagined for the 1970s. Kendall R. Phillips writes that "the frontier serves as the location for Carpenter's vision of horror" across his filmography.[78] Whereas Turner framed the frontier as "a site of perpetual progress," Phillips observes, "In Carpenter's cinematic logic, the frontier mythology lingers, but its trajectory is reversed. His films are peopled not by pioneers but by the isolated remnants of a civilization that has begun a slow, painful withdrawal. . . . Carpenter's films provide a graphic reversal of the frontier mythology of progress . . . the emphasis is on the frontier myth in reverse: a desolate frontier encroaching on the shrinking space of civilization."[79] Regarding *Halloween*, Phillips designates Haddonfield as one such "desolate frontier," particularly because it "represents the broader sense of American suburbia as a place in which the American family had begun to disintegrate."[80] Echoing Turner's prediction that the closing of frontier spaces would result in cultural stagnation and turmoil, *Halloween* suggests that nostalgic foreclosures of the Midwest—both in terms of physical space and cultural meanings—eventually produce horrific monsters capable of perpetrating brutal acts of violence.

By the end of the 1970s, notions of the Midwest as an out-of-time remnant of Turner's frontier spaces or as the appealing "pastoral ideal" identified by Shortridge are disrupted by films such as *Badlands*, *Stroszek*, and *Halloween*.[81] Together, these texts critique perceptions of the Midwest as an atemporal, anachronistic nostalgia museum by showing the debilitating repercussions of such a cultural function being mapped onto the region and its inhabitants. In complementary ways, each of these three films abstracts the Midwest's physical territory, thereby rendering the region as a space of confinement that cannot be escaped. Rather than an idealized museum of American cultural memory, the Midwest is reimagined as a site that houses a destructive form of nostalgia.

The Midwestern settings of *Badlands*, *Stroszek*, and *Halloween* are nebulous spaces that pause temporal progress and propagate a physically demonstrative form of nostalgic desire: what I identify as nostalgic violence. This emerging linkage of nostalgia and violence is attributable, in part, to the environments in which such blank characters are confined. Major characters in these films are internally vacant subjects who nostalgically long for *something* that forever remains out of grasp (the German Bruno is an exception at the outset of *Stroszek*, but he also proves to be vulnerable to the Midwest's "blanking" effects on identity). Sooner or later, the distressing nostalgia of these white male Midwesterners compels them to commit violence in desperate attempts to imbue the unsatisfactory present with meaning or to return to the desired past. Examples of such nostalgia-influenced violence include Kit's startlingly abrupt murders which punctuate the ongoing commemoration of his blank existence with mundane objects and various ritualistic actions; Bruno's despairing of the present and future that culminates in his (presumed) suicide; and Michael's implacable drive to reenact the violent past by ravaging the youth in his hometown and restaging his first murder. Whether individuals are native Midwesterners or transplants, these films grimly propose that to occupy this purported nostalgia museum is to be denied an identity beyond a violent, insatiable desire for the past.

In the wake of the blank and damaged characters on display in *Badlands*, *Stroszek*, and *Halloween*, subsequent depictions of the Midwest continue to interrogate the complex interplay of violence, performativity, and nostalgia in shaping Midwestern identities. During the years surrounding the beginning of the new millennium, several notable films associate nostalgic violence with reactionary values relating to gender, sexuality, and race. As such, nostalgic violence shifts from being portrayed as a more isolated and individualized phenomenon (as in these 1970s films) to having more widespread effects due to its deployment as a regulatory cultural force in the "millennial Midwest."

Notes

1. *Badlands*, directed by Terrence Malick (1973; Burbank, CA: Warner Home Video, 2010), DVD.
2. *Stroszek*, directed by Werner Herzog (1977; Troy, MI: Anchor Bay Entertainment, 2001), DVD; *Halloween*, directed by John Carpenter (1978; Troy, MI: Anchor Bay Entertainment, 2000), DVD.
3. James R. Shortridge, *The Middle West: Its Meaning in American Culture* (Lawrence: University Press of Kansas, 1989), 67.
4. Ibid., 67–68.
5. Frederick Jackson Turner, *The Frontier in American History* (1920; repr., Charleston: BiblioBazaar, 2008); Theodore Dreiser, *Sister Carrie*, ed. Claude Simpson (1900; repr., Boston: Houghton Mifflin, 1959).
6. Michael Lesy, *Wisconsin Death Trip* (New York: Pantheon, 1973); Tim O'Brien, *In the Lake of the Woods* (1994; repr., New York: Penguin, 1995).
7. Lesy, *Wisconsin Death Trip*, n.p.
8. Ibid.
9. O'Brien, *In the Lake of the Woods*, 239.
10. Ibid., 286–287.
11. Lesy, *Wisconsin Death Trip*, n.p.
12. O'Brien, *In the Lake of the Woods*, 288.
13. Ibid., 281.
14. Beverly Walker, "Malick on Badlands," *Sight and Sound* 44, no. 2 (Spring 1975): 83.
15. Vera Dika, *Recycled Culture in Contemporary Art and Film: The Uses of Nostalgia* (Cambridge: Cambridge University Press, 2003), 56–58.

16. Ibid., 11, emphasis in original.

17. Fredric Jameson, *Postmodernism: or, The Cultural Logic of Late Capitalism* (Durham, NC: Duke University Press, 1991), 19.

18. Ibid.

19. Hannah Patterson observes that Kit and Holly's general politeness "signals their desire not only to be liked and accepted but also to conform to the rules of convention." Certainly, the use of polite language provides an unsettling contrast to the lethal violence wielded by Kit. For instance, when Mr. Sargis discovers Kit packing a suitcase for Holly, Kit demurely states, "Hi . . . I got a gun here, sir." Kit then shoots the unarmed Mr. Sargis, who had merely walked downstairs. Later, as Kit directs a young couple into a storm shelter at gunpoint, he respectfully inquires, "I'm gonna have to keep my eye on you, though. You don't mind?" Such politeness is cosmetic during these encounters, and the desire "to be liked" can only partially account for the behaviors of Malick's aloof protagonists. See: Hannah Patterson, "Two Characters in Search of a Direction: Motivation and the Construction of Identity in *Badlands*," in *The Cinema of Terrence Malick: Poetic Visions of America*, ed. Hannah Patterson (London: Wallflower, 2004), 34.

20. Of Holly's opening narration, Dika writes that "a hollow thud results in emotional terms, subtly distancing us from the film we are watching." See: Dika, *Recycled Culture*, 57.

21. Ibid., 60–61.

22. Ibid., 61.

23. Jack Sargeant similarly describes how Malick abstracts the Midwest with shot compositions that depict the region as a nebulous realm. He writes:

> While the narrative focuses on the transgression of the rule of law and entry into a zone of willful exclusion, of outsiderness, the *mise-en-scène* reiterates this narrative trajectory of the borderless state. This is most apparent in the scenes set in the badlands, here the great plains are shot as an almost hellish infinity of flat, empty miles, mirrored by the flatness of the sky above them. . . . The geography is filmed to emphasise [sic] its collapse, until the horizon seems to vanish into pure flatness; world and sky as one massive blank canvas. Such a landscape can only ever be identified as borderless; as infinite; the end of distinction between sky and earth merely reiterating the collapse of other borders and boundaries within the narrative.

The characteristics that Sargeant attributes to the badlands reflect the nostalgic fantasy of simultaneity: in other words, the nostalgic yearning to eliminate the temporal separation of the past and present or the physical distance from desired locales. See: Jack Sargeant, "Killer Couples: From Nebraska to Route 666," in *Lost Highways: An Illustrated History of Road Movies*, eds. Jack Sargeant and Stephanie Watson (London: Creation Books, 1999), 153–154.

24. Patterson observes that Kit and Holly "are fundamentally lacking a strong or clear sense of *their own* identity. . . . Although they may appear motiveless, it is possible to view their actions in the film as motivated by their need to find, and more fully construct, identities for themselves." Dika discusses the search for identity in relation to the nostalgic genre elements of *Badlands*, and she writes that Kit and Holly are "from 'nowhere,' but throughout the film they never get 'somewhere.' Instead these outlaws run across a landscape that does not accept them, nor does it allow them in. They stand as paper cutouts against a flat, illusory, picture plane. And since they never desired material

possessions, the only way they envisioned participating in the American dream was to *become the image*." Although Dika is correct to observe that Kit and Holly sometimes aspire to represent the "image" of outlaws in crime films, this is merely one of many identities that they adopt and discard over the duration of the film. See: Patterson, "Two Characters in Search of a Direction," 25, emphasis in original; Dika, *Recycled Culture*, 64, emphasis in original.

25. Neil Campbell addresses many of these instances and writes that "Kit marks his 'history' with symbolic gestures.... With these acts, Kit records his life by inscribing his otherwise anonymous identity into space for others to know...." See: Neil Campbell, "The Highway Kind: *Badlands*, Youth, Space and the Road," in *The Cinema of Terrence Malick: Poetic Visions of America*, ed. Hannah Patterson (London: Wallflower, 2004), 43.

26. Early in the film, Kit expresses relief about getting a job at a feedlot because he had been wearing cowboy boots as a garbage collector. With the new job, Kit says, "Well, at least nobody could [sic] get on me about wearing these boots anymore." Patterson observes that "Kit gives no clear indication as to why he wears the boots—what they may or may not symbolically mean to him," and this lack of explanation suggests that "Kit *does not know* why he wears the boots." Rather than indicating uncertain reasons for wearing boots, however, Kit's dismay at the skeptical reactions of others reflects his frustrations that adopting the appearance of an iconic figure—that of the mythic American cowboy—has not actually granted him that identity. See: Patterson, "Two Characters in Search of a Direction," 26, emphasis in original.

27. This attitude about the future reappears when Holly decides to abandon Kit and surrender to the police in the badlands. Initially, Kit becomes angry, but he then abruptly offers her a "second chance" by proposing an overtly romanticized and symbolic reunion in the future: "Twelve noon, the Grand Coulee Dam, New Year's Day, 1964. You meet me there. Now you got that?" For Kit, the future will contain the meaningfulness that he is unable to achieve in the present.

28. Kit's attire and hairstyle alternately resemble Dean's appearance in Nicholas Ray's *Rebel Without a Cause* (1955) and George Stevens's *Giant* (1956). Dika contextualizes Malick's appropriation of Dean within the film's 1970s period of production. She writes, "The allusions to James Dean in *Badlands* . . . is [sic] not meant to ridicule the original star, nor is [sic] it meant to blankly re-present his image, as might be the effect of other copies.... *Badlands* thus evokes a marginalized James Dean, one whose profession is that of garbage man, and whose rebel status is transformed to that of sociopath." Kit's appropriation of Dean is further evidence of his need to draw upon preexisting imagery and iconography for an identity. See: *Rebel Without a Cause*, directed by Nicholas Ray (1955; Burbank, CA: Warner Home Video, 2010), DVD; *Giant*, directed by George Stevens (1956; Burbank, CA: Warner Home Video, 2003), DVD; Dika, *Recycled Culture*, 58–59.

29. During the forest sequence, Holly's narration also reveals a sadistic desire to witness violence: "We had our bad moments like any couple. Kit accused me of only bein' along for the ride, while at times, I wished he'd fall in the river and drown, so I could watch." This voyeuristic statement perhaps explains why Holly is so willing to accompany Kit on his killing spree without much complaint.

30. At least five of these individuals are killed, but it is uncertain whether the other victims are dead or injured. In one scene, Kit herds a young couple into a tornado shelter and then fires blindly through the doors. He turns to Holly and says, "Think I got 'em? [. . .] Well, I'm not going down there and look [sic]." The final victim is a police officer

who lands in a helicopter near Kit and Holly in the badlands. Kit shoots him, but the extent of the officer's injuries is not clear.

31. The first recording occurs between Kit killing Mr. Sargis and burning down the house. This recording is intended to misdirect investigators. Kit states that he and Holly decided to kill themselves, and the record is left playing outside of the burning home.

32. Despite Kit being captured, Patterson claims that he "has managed ... to develop a clearer sense of identity, one which does not fit into society but is an identity nonetheless." Patterson observes that Kit's "defined role" is that of "dangerously criminal and psychologically fascinating." Perhaps from the perspective of his captors, Kit's identity is that which Patterson describes. Within the broader context of the film, however, it merely appears as the last identity shown to audiences, but not really any change from the Kit on display at the start of the film. From the beginning to the end of *Badlands*, Kit remains a blank slate who temporarily locks into an identity performance, but who also demonstrates that he will continue to oscillate among personas. See: Patterson, "Two Characters in Search of a Direction," 35.

33. Walker, "Malick on Badlands," 82, emphasis in original.

34. Campbell describes Kit and Holly as appearing like "a parodic married couple." See: Campbell, "The Highway Kind," 46.

35. Inside the police car, one of the officers abruptly lifts the hat from Kit's head and throws it out the window in a gesture that visually restores Kit to his lower class status. Kit responds in his typical deadpan intonation, "You tossed my hat out the window," but he may as well have stated that the officer deflated his flimsily performed identity as a rich man.

36. Anton Blok, "The Enigma of Senseless Violence," in *Meanings of Violence: A Cross Cultural Perspective*, eds. Göran Aijmer and Jon Abbink (Oxford: Berg, 2000), 24.

37. Ibid., 24–25 emphasis in original.

38. Slavoj Žižek, *Violence* (New York: Picador, 2008), 75.

39. Žižek formulates his notion of a "zero-level protest" in response to the 2005 French suburban riots. Essentially, Žižek believes that the protestors were responding to an intense feeling of exclusion across French culture, from government institutions to social contexts. Although Žižek's interpretation elides the complexities of the full context for these protests, his concept of the "zero-level protest" has useful applications for understanding the representation of violence in texts such as *Badlands*. It should be emphasized, though, that Kit's marginalization does not have the ethnic and religious dimensions of the French protestors. See: ibid., 77, emphasis in original.

40. *Bonnie and Clyde*, directed by Arthur Penn (1967; Burbank, CA: Warner Home Video, 2008), DVD.

41. Adrian Martin identifies a troublesome instability experienced by characters throughout Malick's filmography. He writes, "A settled life, settling down, is a constant dream for Malick's characters.... Everyone starts out displaced, or soon finds themselves displaced, from any centre in which any such settlement might actually, mythically occur.... The only experience of settlement ... is an experience of fleeting time rather than fixed place—an idyll, a rest of plateau between upheavals, between catastrophes (death is everywhere in his films)." The general lack of fixity in Malick's films is perhaps most overt in *Badlands* in which the protagonists' identities fluctuate to match their ever-shifting surroundings. See: Adrian Martin, "Things to Look Into: The Cinema of Terrence Malick," *Rouge* 10 (2007), http://www.rouge.com.au/10/malick.html.

42. *Fitzcarraldo*, directed by Werner Herzog (1982; Troy, MI: Anchor Bay, 1999), DVD; *Encounters at the End of the World*, directed by Werner Herzog (2007; Chatsworth, CA: Image Entertainment, 2008), DVD.

43. Werner Herzog and Norman Hill, "Audio Commentary," *Stroszek*, DVD, directed by Werner Herzog (1977; Troy, MI: Anchor Bay, 2001).

44. In *Stroszek*, Herzog blurs distinctions between reality and fiction in several ways, as accentuated by the coinciding names of the performers and the fictional characters they portray. The film's early scenes in Berlin are also largely based on the experiences of Bruno S. (born Bruno Schleinstein). During this portion of the film, the character of Bruno is released from prison, but his alcoholism compels him to immediately resume drinking excessively, and he struggles to make money as a street performer. According to Herzog, settings such as Bruno's apartment and the bar depicted in these early scenes were the actual living quarters and haunts of Bruno S.

45. Of Herzog's filmography, Jan Mouton claims, "What is visible on the screen will imply what is not visible, what is just beyond." Regarding *Stroszek*, Mouton claims that Herzog "draws upon the folkloric tradition . . . and in so doing he creates a fairy tale film." Consequently, Mouton reads the peculiarities of the Midwestern setting as evidence that "the marvelous" is present within the narrative. Similar to Mouton's observations about *Stroszek*, Malick himself acknowledged that *Badlands* was intended to be understood as something of a fairy tale located outside of time. This is yet another dynamic that connects these two films, along with featuring a Midwestern setting and being produced in roughly the same period. See: Jan Mouton, "Werner Herzog's *Stroszek*: A Fairy-Tale Film in an Age of Disenchantment," *Literature Film Quarterly* 15, no. 2 (1987): 100.

46. *Aguirre, The Wrath of God*, directed by Werner Herzog (New York City: New Yorker Films, 1972), film.

47. Eric Rentschler, "How American Is It: The U.S. as Image and Imaginary in German Film," *The German Quarterly* 57, no. 4 (Autumn 1984): 610, emphasis in original, doi: 10.2307/404701.

48. Herzog and Hill, "Audio Commentary."

49. Emily Hauze, "Keyed Fantasies: Music, The Accordion and the American Dream in *Stroszek* and *Schultze Gets the Blues*," *German Life and Letters* 62, no. 1 (January 2009): 90, doi: 10.1111/j.1468–0483.2008.01450.x. For Hauze, "internal" essentially corresponds to diegetic sounds, and "external" corresponds to nondiegetic sounds. While in Berlin, Bruno plays the piano, glockenspiel, signal horn, and accordion regularly; in America, Bruno's performances are limited to one blast of the signal horn and one scene in which he plays his accordion.

50. Ibid.

51. Herzog shot this final sequence in North Carolina, but it conceivably could be considered a Midwestern town within the film, especially given the Native American culture and names that are prominent in various parts of Wisconsin.

52. Brad Prager discusses the tow truck and the ski lift during the film's final sequence. Of the truck, he writes, "The vehicle now going around and around stands in for a world that has spun out of control: the journey to the Midwest has placed Stroszek in a vehicle without a driver. There is no changing course, no means by which one can approach the circle's empty centre." Prager later argues that "Herzog's characters themselves . . . turn in circles, as in the case of Bruno . . . endlessly circling the ground on a ski-lift. This 'going nowhere' can be seen as a reflection on the substance of the subject itself. It is an ever-widening spiral in which none come closer to the centre, and by

virtue of which the permanence of things is endlessly proposed and then negated." Prager's comments reiterate the primacy of circular motifs in Herzog's work and attach such symbolism to an individualized quest for a coherent sense of one's self within a troubled world. Expanding upon Prager's astute observations, the spiraling search for an undefined, subjective "centre" also has clear nostalgic connotations within the film's Midwestern setting. See: Brad Prager, *The Cinema of Werner Herzog: Aesthetic Ecstasy and Truth* (London: Wallflower, 2007), 75, 114.

53. Robin Wood, *Hollywood from Vietnam to Reagan . . . and Beyond*, revised and expanded edition (1986; repr., New York: Columbia University Press, 2003), 68.

54. Ibid., 70.

55. See: Carol J. Clover, *Men, Women, and Chain Saws: Gender in the Modern Horror Film* (Princeton: Princeton University Press, 1992); Barbara Creed, *The Monstrous-Feminine: Film, Feminism, Psychoanalysis* (1993; repr., London: Routledge, 2007).

56. *Halloween: Unmasked*, directed by Mark Cerulli (1999; Troy, MI: Anchor Bay, 2000), DVD.

57. When the filmmakers were creating Michael's "look," they narrowed down the choice of masks between that of an Emmett Kelly clown mask and a doctored William Shatner mask from *Star Trek*. Regarding the clown as a symbol of horror, Noël Carroll writes, "The clown figure is a monster . . . a fantastic being, one possessed of an alternate biology" that can sustain severe physical abuse which normal humans cannot. Michael certainly has the indestructibility of Carroll's monstrous clown, but to achieve the desired lack of individual features, the filmmakers selected the Shatner mask, which resulted in the character's eerie "blank" exterior. See: Ibid.; Noël Carroll, "Horror and Humor," *The Journal of Aesthetics and Art Criticism* 57, no. 2 (Spring 1999): 155.

58. Although Castle plays the masked Michael Myers for the majority of the film, the six-year old Michael shown during the opening scene obviously required a different actor (Will Sandin). When the adult Michael is briefly unmasked near the end of the film, Tony Moran fills in as the youthful twenty-three-year-old face beneath the killer's blank exterior. On a side note, within the film's chronology, the adult Michael—listed as twenty-three in the credits—actually should be twenty-one, based on the fifteen-year gap between killing his sister and returning to Haddonfield; this seems to be a minor continuity error in the script.

59. *Grease*, directed by Randal Kleiser (Hollywood, CA: Paramount, 1978), film; *Happy Days* (New York: ABC, 1974–1984), broadcast television.

60. David Harvey suggests that the pervasive discontent of the 1970s contributed to the emergence of the neoliberal economic policies that continue to shape the global economy and American society. See: David Harvey, *A Brief History of Neoliberalism* (2005; repr., Oxford: Oxford University Press, 2009), 42.

61. Jameson, *Postmodernism*, 19.

62. Sprengler distinguishes between the "Fifties" as "the mythic, nostalgic construct" and the "1950s" as "the actual historical period of time between 1950 and 1959 and all of its social, political and cultural complexities." See: Christine Sprengler, *Screening Nostalgia: Populuxe props and Technicolor aesthetics in contemporary American film* (2009; repr., New York: Berghahn, 2011), 39, 47.

63. David Roche also notes the significance of the opening scene's time period and writes, "It seems that the time-setting of *Halloween* (1978) identifies 1963 as the year the U.S. lost its innocence while watching a traumatic event on TV." See: David Roche, *Making and Remaking Horror in the 1970s and 2000s: Why Don't They Do It Like They Used To?* (Jackson: University Press of Mississippi, 2014), 25–26.

64. Christopher Sharrett notes that the emergence of the slasher film in the late 1970s—a subgenre that surged in popularity following *Halloween*—coincides with the dawn of a "post-liberal" period. Dika similarly observes that Michael's "murderous threat is itself presented as a return, and one now defined by specific dates [1963 and 1978]. . . . What is unavoidable in *Halloween* is a return to old values, accomplished by returning to a pre-1960s period in both style and content." See: Christopher Sharrett, "The Horror Film in Neoconservative Culture," *Journal of Popular Film and Television* 21, no. 3 (Fall 1993): 102; Dika, *Recycled Culture*, 208.

65. The numerous subsequent entries in the slasher horror subgenre display something of a nostalgic compulsion through a seemingly endless repetition of *Halloween*'s basic narrative and stylistic elements. This perpetual reproduction of *Halloween*'s "original" components—a production that also drew heavily upon prior films including Alfred Hitchcock's *Psycho* (1960) and Bob Clark's *Black Christmas* (1974)—exposes a nostalgic tendency within such horror films' "return of the repressed" narrative developments. Sarah Trencansky identifies a possible explanation for the nostalgic narrative repetitions and habitual returns of slasher villains by focusing on the historical context for these films. Trencansky writes, "None of these monsters can be eliminated unless the very nature of society is transformed and authority definitively undermined." Rick Worland similarly attaches this horror subgenre to then-contemporary historico-cultural developments. He observes that the emphasis on a "body count" in such films "suggests it was in fact the war that had come home, that the slasher film was another indirect reprocessing of Vietnam's impact on American culture [and] the accompanying tremors set off by the women's movement in particular." See: *Psycho*, directed by Alfred Hitchcock (1960; Universal City, CA: Universal Studios, 2008), DVD; *Black Christmas*, directed by Bob Clark (1974; Toronto, ON: Critical Mass Releasing, 2001), DVD; Sarah Trencansky, "Final Girls and Terrible Youth: Transgression in 1980s Slasher Horror," *Journal of Popular Film and Television* 29, no. 2 (Summer 2001): 70; Rick Worland, *The Horror Film: An Introduction* (2007; repr., Malden, MA: Blackwell, 2011), 231.

66. Each era and subgenre of horror reflects the past in distinct ways. As Paul Wells observes, "The horror genre is predominantly concerned with death and the impacts and effects of the past." Regarding *Halloween*, Kendall R. Phillips writes that "*Halloween* entails a kind of Gothic return of the past to haunt the present," while Robin Wood notes that Michael features a "compulsion to reenact the childhood crime." See: Susan Stewart, "The Epistemology of the Horror Story," *The Journal of American Folklore* 95, no. 375 (1982): 36, doi: 10.2307/540021; Paul Wells, *The Horror Genre: From Beelzebub to Blair Witch* (2000; repr., London: Wallflower, 2004), 7; Kendall R. Phillips, *Projected Fears: Horror Films and American Culture* (Westport: Praeger, 2005), 135; Wood, *Hollywood from Vietnam to Reagan*, 172.

67. Clover, *Men, Women, and Chain Saws*, 23.

68. Martin Harris, "You Can't Kill the Boogeyman: *Halloween III* and the Modern Horror Franchise," *Journal of Popular Film and Television* 32, no. 3 (Fall 2004): 107.

69. Vera Dika, "The Stalker Film, 1978–81," in *American Horrors: Essays on the Modern American Horror Film*, ed. Gregory A. Waller (Urbana: University of Illinois Press, 1987), 93–94.

70. Ibid., 96. Dika uses the term "stalker" rather than "slasher" for this category of horror. As Murray Leeder notes, the term "slasher" is most commonly used to denote this particular subgenre of horror, but it is one of several descriptors for such films. While "slasher" references the type of violent acts frequently depicted onscreen, competing terms such as "stalker" emphasize plot conventions such as an antagonist who stalks

victims, as well as the subgenre's formal conventions, which prominently feature recurring usage of first-person point-of-view camera shots while victims are being followed. *Halloween*'s opening long take is among the most famous of such sequences. See: Murray Leeder, *Horror Film: A Critical Introduction* (New York: Bloomsbury Academic, 2018), 64–65.

71. Dika, "The Stalker Film," 94.

72. Presumably, it is this chance encounter with Laurie that results in Michael fixating on her as a contemporary surrogate for his dead sister, Judith. Michael's endless pursuit of Laurie is never explained in *Halloween* beyond this possibility, although subsequent sequels in the franchise reveal that the pair are brother and sister; following the murder of Judith, Laurie apparently was given up for adoption as a baby, which explains her different last name and lack of awareness regarding familial connections to the original film's blank boogeyman.

73. Kyes is listed as "Nancy Loomis" in the credits for *Halloween*.

74. Clover, *Men, Women, and Chain Saws*, 23–24.

75. Ibid., 30–31.

76. Ibid., 30.

77. While commenting on the peculiarity of this final sequence, Leeder emphasizes how "two aural elements, the score and Michael's heavy breathing, give him presence in absence." See: Leeder, *Horror Film*, 172–173.

78. Kendall R. Phillips, *Dark Directions: Romero, Craven, Carpenter, and the Modern Horror Film* (Carbondale: Southern Illinois University Press, 2012), 123.

79. Ibid., 125–126.

80. Ibid., 142–143.

81. Shortridge, *The Middle West*, 27.

Part II
The Millennial Midwest on Film

4 | Masculinity, Race, and Violence

Set in the fictional Indiana town of Millbrook, David Cronenberg's *A History of Violence* (2005) portrays the Midwest as a space containing layered identities, deceptive tranquility, and—as the title indicates—a tradition of violent behavior.[1] At the time of the film's release, Cronenberg stated that exploring the superficially placid nature of Millbrook piqued his interest in the project: "You ... wonder what does it take to support that perfect little town? What outside of that town, and outside of that country, has to happen in order for it to exist?"[2] One form of outside "support" is the sheer repetition of idealized Midwestern imagery in American popular culture. Through the circulation of cultural myths about the idyllic nature of Midwestern small towns, the region's role as a nostalgia museum for the United States is affirmed again and again. Yet, to focus solely on conditions external to the Midwest is to elide the regulatory mechanisms at work within the region, at least as depicted in various Midwestern narratives of the late twentieth and early twenty-first centuries. Despite Cronenberg's professed interest in circumstances outside of "perfect" Millbrook, *A History of Violence* actually demonstrates that the town's "perfect" surface is maintained through distinctly nostalgic forms of performativity and violence.

This chapter begins the second half of *The American Midwest in Film and Literature*, which coheres around the topic of "The Millennial Midwest on Film." Whereas the first three chapters provide a broad history of the development and reification of the Midwest's popular identity across a wide array of twentieth-century texts, the final three chapters are an extended analysis of cinematic treatments of the region during the years surrounding the turn of the new millennium. The bifurcated organization of my project (in terms of texts and period) reveals how select twenty-first-century Midwestern films are expansions of and variations on conventions that first were established in earlier historical, sociological, literary, and cinematic texts. In other words, there is some degree of continuity connecting regional narratives from Frederick Jackson Turner's frontier theories to films such as *A History of Violence*. As always, nostalgia—especially in terms of its spatial and violent dimensions—remains a crucial component in depictions of the Midwest. To expand upon Cronenberg's queries listed above, the remainder of this book asks the imperative question: what conditions sustain the linkage between the Midwest and nostalgia in the new millennium?

Representations of the millennial Midwest speak to American cultural anxieties and conflicts during the extended turmoil of the relatively young century. To list simply a few pieces of historico-cultural context, the United States' twenty-first century has been marked by the rise of social media, unsettled perceptions of domestic security in the wake of 9/11, ongoing economic crises (including the Great Recession), conservative resistance to LGBTQ+ rights (on issues ranging from marriage equality to public restroom usage by transgender people), numerous high-profile shooting deaths of unarmed African Americans by both citizens and police officers (among others, the cases of Trayvon Martin and Michael Brown generated major public outcry and media coverage), the regular occurrence of mass shootings across the country, an overtly visible resurgence of white supremacist organizations and ideologies, and an intensely polarized political landscape. In light of this roiling context, perhaps it is unsurprising that Midwestern narratives from this period repeatedly present nostalgia as a restrictive cultural force that regulates regional identities with extreme violence. Further, such violence is often depicted as being perpetrated by white male characters. These recurring narrative elements hint that the longstanding predominance of white masculinity within Midwestern identity is eroding, yet this progressive development is accompanied by reactionary violence, paranoia, and destructive impulses among individuals from that privileged demographic. This chapter engages with these fraught historical conditions through analyses of Kimberly Peirce's *Boys Don't Cry* (1999), Clint Eastwood's *Gran Torino* (2008), and Cronenberg's *A History of Violence*.[3] In these three Midwestern texts, several major representational elements repeat and signal fluctuating understandings of the region. Such elements include perceptions of a techno-cultural lag within the Midwest that produces social isolation, as opposed to the increased connectivity promised by the proliferation of digital communication technologies; a continued emphasis on performativity, particularly in terms of gender, race, and regional identity; and multiple iterations of the nostalgic violence that emerged in Midwestern films of the 1970s. Regarding this latter quality, *Boys Don't Cry*, *Gran Torino*, and *A History of Violence* each prominently feature troubled white male characters who commit violent acts in order to nostalgically reshape and regulate the Midwestern environments in which they live.

An anxiety-driven yearning for the past in general—and idealized regional iconography in particular—appears in a wide variety of millennial-era Midwestern narratives. Moreover, many characters pursue these desires through acts of nostalgic violence. As detailed in the previous chapter, nostalgic violence is used to manipulate the present so that it might *appear* as an individual *imagines* the desired past to be. Midwestern texts that feature nostalgic violence are generally set in fading communities that have lost or are in the process of losing elements long framed as foundational for the region's identity. In 1901, Turner wrote that early Midwesterners were "idealists," nearly "every family was a self-sufficing unit," and because of diligent labor, "into this region flowed the great forces of modern capitalism."[4] Throughout his racially problematic writings, Turner consistently contrasts mythic settlers of European descent with Native Americans, who are said to "resist the march of civilization."[5] Over a century later, Victoria Johnson highlights the persistence of a regional ideology based upon narrow ideals relating to gender, race, and sexuality. She writes that "'whiteness' and heteronormativity are routinely mobilized as *belonging* in the Midwest" through depictions of the region in popular media.[6] Since at least the late nineteenth century, notions of economic opportunity (often based on physical labor), the reduction of sexual orientation solely to heterosexuality, the primacy of whiteness, and the symbolic value of the nuclear family all have strongly informed the Midwest's popular image and continue to do so in the twenty-first century.

Numerous Midwestern narratives from this era display a preoccupation with components of the region's reductive mythology. These narratives frequently revolve around the strategic use of nostalgic violence to prop up superficial signs that vanishing elements of the region's popular identity persist and remain dominant. A short (and nonexhaustive) list of films with fractured visions of the Midwest includes *A Simple Plan* (1998), *Drop Dead Gorgeous* (1999), *The Virgin Suicides* (1999), *Mysterious Skin* (2004), *Winter's Bone* (2010), *Take Shelter* (2011), and, perhaps most famously, Joel and Ethan Coen's *Fargo* (1996).[7] Some of these films will be addressed more thoroughly in later chapters. For now, the focus remains on *Boys Don't Cry*, *Gran Torino*, and *A History of Violence*, which exemplify Midwestern representational trends of this period. More precisely, these latter three films present characters using nostalgic violence in efforts to obscure the fragmentation of the Midwest's traditional identity. Because signs of regional change cannot be excised, individuals who symbolize difference are violently subsumed beneath a vast, normative Midwestern façade.

"No Environment" Outside the Virtual Frontier

An insecure fixation on Midwestern identity becomes particularly acute during the final years of the twentieth century and sharply contrasts with concurrent cultural narratives about the geography-transcending capabilities of digital communication technologies. James Shortridge observes a historical tendency among national media outlets to reduce Midwestern identity solely to that of a pastoral realm, despite the existence of major industrial cities such as Chicago and Detroit. In this way, the Midwest generally was—and continues to be—presented as lagging behind the cultural and, importantly, technological changes produced and experienced in urban centers elsewhere.[8] During the 1990s, a similar regional narrative emerges in popular texts regarding the Midwest's relationship to the cultural effects of digital technologies. In order to better understand nostalgic violence within texts such as *Boys Don't Cry*, *Gran Torino*, and *A History of Violence*, a brief survey of this intersection of regionalism and technology is instructive.

While complicating regional perceptions within American culture, many Midwestern films produced around the turn of the twenty-first century also serve as counter-narratives to assertions of the ostensibly beneficial effects of digital media, particularly for individual and communal identity. Across such texts, celebratory rhetoric about emergent technologies is at odds with the provincial and disconnected Midwest. Obviously, the actual Midwest does not lack access to the internet, but the region's image as an anachronistic space (in terms of culture and technology) lingers in the popular imagination. Millennial-era Midwestern narratives thus offer a rebuttal to the positive cultural changes predicted by many media scholars during this period. Reviewing just a few examples of such hopeful predictions highlights the separation between the optimism surrounding new digital technologies and the despair of regions perceived to be geographically and technologically isolated, such as the Midwest. For instance, Douglas Rushkoff enthuses about the utopic potential for a latter-day cultural renaissance made possible through increased interconnectivity and networks of online communities.[9] Frances Cairncross is even more overtly utopic with her prognostications that the "death of distance" will "reinforce local cultures" and that more sophisticated communication technologies will "increase understanding, foster tolerance, and ultimately promote worldwide peace."[10] Filmic portrayals of the Midwest, on the other hand, portray a decidedly isolated culture that either resists or is unable to join this technological utopia.

Media theorist Lev Manovich brings debates about the effects of rapid advances in storage and communication technologies into a specifically American context by arguing that the "flat structure of the Web" reflects what he describes as "the American ideology of democracy with its paranoid fear of hierarchy and centralized control."[11] Continuing in this vein, Manovich compares the mythic figure of the "nineteenth-century American explorer to the explorer of navigable virtual space."[12] This association relates directly to Turner's theories about the closure of the frontier in the late nineteenth century. Turner suggests that the American frontier was a space that granted "perennial rebirth" to its occupants, and Manovich borrows this utopic sentiment for his views on the new "virtual" frontier.[13] Unlike Manovich, who projects few limitations for users within digital spaces, Turner offers dire warnings about the cultural fallout from the loss of the western frontier, which is a development that produces an upended nation "now thrown back upon itself."[14] For Turner, frontier space—as opposed to the seemingly limitless parameters of Manovich's "navigable virtual space"—became filled up, which forced would-be explorers to forge their identities within demarcated regional spaces, such as the newly coalescing Midwest.

Popular culture from the late twentieth and early twenty-first centuries repeatedly presents the Midwest as an anachronistic, nostalgic space counterposed to the inclusive virtual environments praised by Manovich and others. Such regional associations reflect broader changes in how material spaces and cultural progress are perceived in relation to then-new digital technologies. Svetlana Boym's critique of online temporality provides insights for understanding this cultural dynamic. She observes, "At first glance, hypertextual organization eliminates the very premise of nostalgia—that of the irreversibility of time and of the inability to revisit other times and places. Here it is merely a matter of access. Time in cyberspace is conceived in terms of speed: speed of access and speed of technological innovation."[15] According to Boym, though, this relationship of speed, time, and space is contradictory:

> There is a hidden paradox in the Internet philosophy of time: while internally the system relies on hypertext and interaction, externally many info-enthusiasts rely on

the nineteenth-century narrative of progress with occasional eliminational pathos. The extreme version of the eliminational model of progress (which believes, for example, that [the] e-book will supplant the book altogether rather than that the two can happily cohabit in the same household) presents a kind of tunnel vision of the road toward the future. It presumes that there is *no environment around that tunnel, no context, no other streets and avenues that take a detour* from the underground speed lanes and traffic jams. Reflective nostalgia challenges this tunnel vision, backtracking, slowing down, looking sideways, meditating on the journey itself.[16]

In this passage, Boym identifies a disavowal of materiality accompanying some of the breathless hyperbole about "cyberspace" and other digital media in the late twentieth century. Beyond idealistic notions like the "death of distance," Boym suggests that such perspectives neglect to fully acknowledge the physical environments within which one accesses virtual spaces.[17] To some degree, this idea of a spatial void surrounding the internet's material infrastructure recalls the dismissal of the middle American states as "flyover country"; in both instances, physical environments are relegated to the status of unimportant, nebulous realms.[18] Regarding attitudes about regional spaces, the Midwest has been consistently situated as dependent on physical embeddedness for identity formation—while serving as a metaphorical site of the past, the region is firmly fixed in its geographic coordinates.

Boym's spatial metaphors for technology and nostalgia dovetail with ways in which popular narratives configure the millennial Midwest's past-oriented and resolutely material status in relation to a digitized online frontier. The Midwest has historically been distanced from cultural narratives of technological progress, and the region's popular image corresponds to the slower, nonlinear qualities that Boym attributes to reflective nostalgia. This purported resistance to the new has pervaded Midwestern narratives since the turn of the twentieth century, and twenty-first-century texts continue to define the Midwest as an atemporal space. Just as the Midwest once was a territory through which European settlers passed while entering Turner's most western frontier spaces, the region again is configured as a bubble removed from the ceaselessly expedited flow of information within a virtual frontier. At multiple historical moments, the middle region remains situated as a geographic interval or way station on linear trajectories to elsewhere.

Despite historical challenges to the veracity of Turner's theories, his prediction of the dire fallout from geographic constriction continues to loom large in popular representations of the Midwest. The Midwest's perceived spatial and cultural isolation is often framed as a factor that prompts Midwesterners to nostalgically look into the past for their identities. Films such as *A History of Violence, Gran Torino,* and *Boys Don't Cry* almost literalize this link to the past by depicting the Midwest as a rough and tumble space that has regressed to violent frontier conditions, which requires equally anachronistic individuals to occupy and tame the threatening environment. In this way, various twenty-first-century Midwestern narratives surreptitiously contemporize Turner at the same moment that Manovich links an emerging digital frontier with the closed western frontier from one century earlier. The tone toward this shared frontier imagery varies wildly between Manovich's quite utopic outlook on virtual environments and the regressively nostalgic flipside emerging from the fictional Midwest. These surprising, parallel allusions to Turner expose tensions relating to cultural identity within regional communities that are presented as having been left behind from the supposedly ubiquitous American entry into an expansive digital frontier. Over the remainder of the chapter, I will detail how *Boys Don't Cry*, *Gran Torino*, and *A History of Violence* provide definitive portrayals of Midwestern environments that persist outside of such immaterial realms and are shaped by nostalgic violence.

Boys Don't Cry

Boys Don't Cry has received extensive scholarly commentary and critique, but its Midwestern setting has been somewhat underexamined relative to other concerns. A renewed attentiveness to this regional context extends and complicates understandings of the film's engagement with sexuality, gender, race, and class. Within a regional framework, *Boys Don't Cry* is both a representative and singular film among a diverse group of Midwestern texts from around the turn of the millennium. Consequently, it is important to recognize ways in which Peirce's treatment of those categories corresponds with recurrent conventions and subject matter in representations of the Midwest. As in *A History of Violence* and *Gran Torino*, Peirce's film depicts the brutal regulation of a Midwestern community via nostalgic violence.

Based on actual events, *Boys Don't Cry* details the final days of Brandon Teena (Hilary Swank), a transgender man who was raped and killed by John Lotter (Peter Sarsgaard) and Tom Nissen (Brendan Sexton III) in Falls City, Nebraska, after they learned that Brandon was legally classified as female. Across several issues of *Screen* in 2001 and 2002, Patricia White, Jack Halberstam, Jennifer Devere Brody, and other scholars address issues of sexuality, gender, race, and class in Peirce's film. For instance, Halberstam identifies an internally divided "transgender gaze" and problematizes the way in which *Boys Don't Cry* "makes the transgender subject dependent upon the recognition of a woman. In other words, Brandon can be Brandon because Lana is willing to see him as he sees himself (clothed, male, vulnerable, lacking, strong, passionate), and to avert her gaze when his manhood is in question."[19] Halberstam references scenes in which Brandon's lover, Lana Tisdel (Chloe Sevigny), is called upon to affirm that Brandon's gender is male after they are both threatened by John and Tom.

Another major point of criticism is Peirce's omission of Phillip DeVine, a disabled African American man, from the film. In reality, John and Tom murdered Brandon, Lisa Lambert, and DeVine, who had been dating Lambert's sister, Leslie.[20] *Boys Don't Cry* notably features no African American characters whatsoever. Halberstam ties DeVine's absence to the film's troublesome reaffirmation of Brandon as a woman by suggesting that Peirce "sacrifices the hard facts of racial hatred and transphobia to a streamlined humanist romance."[21] Brody writes the most extensive critique of DeVine's absence and asserts that "the erasure of DeVine from the narrative places the white female bodies as the only true victims of crime; and the film's inability to show DeVine as violated rather than violator perpetuates the myth of the black man as always already a perpetrator of crime."[22] Drawing these analyses together, I contend that Peirce is operating within a cinematic tradition that has its own discrete set of representational conventions: filmic depictions of the Midwest. Johnson argues that the Midwest's "ongoing social and political relevance is *secured* via ... the imagination of the region as almost exclusively patriarchal, 'straight,' and white. Through this highly selective and partial imagination of the Midwest as affiliated—in raced, gendered, and sexed terms—with dominant cultural identifications, the Heartland remains powerful...."[23] Even when the region is perceived as a backwards realm, Midwestern imagery and narratives still retain powerful cultural uses and symbolic meanings. By oscillating between marginal and dominant status, the Midwest serves as a cultural straw man of sorts—a regional depository for negative attributes that exist within American culture in general (such as racism and heteronormativity) but are framed as endemic to a space already imagined to be lagging behind the rest of the nation in numerous ways.

Within a cultural framework that projects such normative values onto the Midwest, the horrific rape in *Boys Don't Cry* may be understood as an act of nostalgic violence. As depicted in the film, John and Tom initially assault Brandon because they perceive his gender identity as transgressive and threatening; their violence is thus enacted for the purpose of social regulation. After assaulting Brandon, John callously states, "If you keep our secret, we'll stay friends. All right, little buddy?" Despite the jarring dissonance between John's violence and promise of sustained friendship, his offer somewhat appears to be presented at face value. At the same time, the phrase "little buddy" reads as a derisive acknowledgment of Brandon's male identity in the moments following the vicious attack. Regardless of this statement's meaning, John and Tom first inflict nostalgic violence upon Brandon in response to his divergence from the restrictive norms relating to gender and sexuality that are attached to the Midwest's popular identity. Accordingly, the implication of this assault is that once Brandon's gender identity has been violently regulated by two cisgender heterosexual men, then Falls City's normative social order is symbolically restored to its default state.

In addition to the nostalgic violence perpetrated by the characters of John and Tom, DeVine's absence is also an act of violence by means of narrative elision. Peirce's decision to omit DeVine does not obviate the film's important advocacy of tolerance for transgender people and queer sexuality, but it inadvertently affirms a component of the violent discrimination to which *Boys Don't Cry* otherwise is opposed. As this representational issue demonstrates, an ideological challenge becomes apparent for filmmakers attempting to depict the Midwest: how to work against long-entrenched cultural perceptions that seemingly push regional narratives exclusively in normative or reactionary directions. One option is to highlight (or possibly exaggerate) the dysfunctional elements within standard regional imagery. Brenda Cooper claims that Peirce "challenge[s] heteronormativity and *hetero*sexed narratives . . . by dismantling the myth of 'America's heartland'" and "by problematizing heteromasculinity," among other functions.[24] Similarly, Lisa Henderson focuses on the film's portrayal of class, which results in "a gothic, elemental portrait of a dead-end community whose citizens are rarely able to act on their own behalf."[25] A general lack of mobility (in terms of class and geography) burdens the inhabitants of Falls City, and such restrictions produce a nostalgic desire to preserve identity traits that affirm a "traditional" conception of Midwestern identity. Even John and Tom—who take it upon themselves to violently enforce the perpetuation of normative gender roles and identities (most overtly in the case of Brandon)—are depicted as being unable to perceive any potential for alternate lifestyles for themselves beyond self-destructive behaviors such as excessive alcohol consumption and self-mutilation. Hence, the narrative developments of *Boys Don't Cry* are inextricable from its regional setting and require a careful consideration of the relationship between the Midwest and the identity performances that it yields.

The narrow parameters of masculinity permitted in Falls City call attention to the community's cultural and geographic disconnect. Brandon's limited financial means and an inability to communicate with individuals outside of his immediate vicinity further exacerbate his challenges. Without the ability to transcend physical distance (via, say, the emerging internet culture of the era), Brandon's identity is deeply influenced by his isolated Midwestern environment. Interestingly, within the remote Nebraska setting of *Boys Don't Cry*, Brandon (at least as depicted in this fictionalized account) may be reframed as both a gender rebel *and* as a regional conformist. The film's closed-off Midwestern community affects the very construction of its inhabitants' identities, including that of Brandon. In particular, unavoidable proximity to a small roster of deviant males—especially John and Tom—has a significant impact on Brandon's behavior. Although Lana is attracted to Brandon because of his more sensitive and considerate nature, Brandon still feels compelled to display a rougher masculinity by participating in a bar brawl early in the film and later risking serious injury while drunkenly "bumper skiing." During another scene, Brandon listens to Tom boasting about self-mutilation and his willingness to cut himself deeper than John. Tolerance for—and even pursuit of—physical pain is framed as a necessary condition of being male in this environment.

Within Falls City, to perform masculinity is to disfigure and damage one's body, to mark it as both an agent and receptacle of violence. Brandon is surrounded by constant displays of aggression that eventually tip over into brutal assault and murder. John and Tom use nostalgic violence to reinforce heteronormative gender roles by punishing Brandon, whose masculinity undermines the stability of their own gender identities (see fig. 4.1). This preoccupation with policing gender performance and identity deeply informs *Gran Torino*, as well. Throughout Eastwood's film, numerous characters explicitly articulate what they believe to be appropriate behaviors and expressions of gender. And, as with *Boys Don't Cry*, ideals about masculinity in *Gran Torino* are invariably bound to violence.

Fig. 4.1. A crowded frame accentuates the threat of violence. Screen capture, *Boys Don't Cry* (1999).

Gran Torino

Paul Verhoeven's satirical *RoboCop* (1987) remains one of the most—if not *the* most—iconic cinematic portrayals of Detroit.[26] The film's cyborg protagonist serves a decaying urban environment at the mercy of Omni Consumer Products (OCP), a corrupt corporation that privatizes the police department and seeks to raze the city. OCP collaborates with a band of criminals to accelerate the decline of Detroit so that a fantastical, consumer-oriented "Delta City" might be erected in its place. Twenty years later, *Gran Torino* retains this sense of Detroit as a lawless environment in need of violent regulation. In both popular reviews and academic articles, many observers identified *Gran Torino* as something of a capstone for Clint Eastwood's filmography, particularly in relation to his iconic roles as "The Man With No Name" in Sergio Leone's spaghetti Westerns and as the titular protagonist of *Dirty Harry* (dir. Don Siegel, 1971) and its four sequels.[27] Kate Stables, for instance, specifies that *Gran Torino* features "elements that Eastwood has explored throughout his long body of work: questions of race, masculinity, and the uses and abuses of violence."[28]

Beyond Eastwood's self-reflexive nods, however, *Gran Torino*'s Detroit setting firmly grounds the film within an expansive discourse on Midwestern identity unfolding across numerous films released around the turn of twenty-first century, including *Boys Don't Cry* and *A History of Violence*. My interest in *Gran Torino* revolves around examining how the film links ideals regarding race, masculinity, and violence to the film's Michigan setting. Such elements of the film speak to longstanding cultural perceptions about which regional inhabitants are counted as being "Midwesterners" and which are situated outside of that category. Even more importantly, *Gran Torino*'s narrative is strongly informed by a reactivated frontier mentality, which further aligns the millennial Midwest with Frederick Jackson Turner's late nineteenth- and early twentieth-century theories about the importance of the frontier in American culture. Faced with a destabilized identity, senior protagonist Walt Kowalski (Clint Eastwood) enacts a troubling nostalgic turn to the past by embodying Turner's frontier archetype of the rugged individual seeking to master an uncivilized wilderness.

Against a backdrop of racial tension, urban decay, and violence in modern-day Detroit, *Gran Torino* focuses on recent widower Walt and the changing demographics of his neighborhood. The former autoworker lives in an area of Detroit that once was occupied by white residents and now is populated primarily by African Americans and, increasingly, Mexican and Hmong immigrants. Along with the relaxed work ethic and generational disconnect within his own family, Walt perceives this influx of diverse groups as undermining the conventional notions of masculinity and whitewashed definitions of the Midwest that the retired machinist embodies. After initially labeling the new Hmong neighbors as "damn barbarians," though, Walt gradually warms to the Vang Lor family. The aging Polish patriarch soon finds himself serving as a violent protector and father figure to teenage siblings Thao (Bee Vang) and Sue (Ahney Her), who are threatened by a Hmong gang led by their cousin, Spider (Doua Moua). Of particular note, Walt instructs Thao on how to "man . . . up a little bit" through physical labor, the casual usage of racial and gendered slurs, and being more assertive with women. Eventually, Walt confronts the gang unarmed and compels them to shoot him, which results in their arrest and enables the Vang Lors to, in theory, live in peace.

Despite the twenty-first-century setting of *Gran Torino*, frontier ideology and motifs deeply pervade the film's narrative. Until just before the final encounter with the Hmong gang, the Detroit police are unseen. Antonio Machuco suggests that this conspicuous absence shows "*that all action takes place within a pre-judiciary order in which there are no rules and no mediating entities that could prevent the rising level of violence.*"[29] Walt's self-sacrifice is seemingly intended to signal an end to the neighborhood violence—Eastwood's Christlike pose after being shot is an especially obvious moment of symbolism—but the climactic scene belies all that precedes it. Prior to that point in the film, Walt eagerly embraces Detroit's "pre-judiciary order," as it permits him to indulge his violent tendencies while demonizing the ethnic "others" surrounding him. Indeed, Walt's ostensibly nonviolent self-sacrifice is possible only because his earlier violence produced the gang's expectation that he would be armed and aggressive; this self-mythologizing strategy permits Walt to die as the white savior of an ethnically diverse neighborhood. Understood in this light, Walt's plan is a nostalgic attempt to perpetuate a racial hierarchy in which white masculinity is imagined as a necessary element to maintain social order.

This racialized power structure points to a further intrusion of Turner's frontier mythology within the contemporary urban Midwest. Turner's writings retain a significant influence on depictions of the Midwest, especially in relation to race, labor, and masculinity. More than one hundred years after Turner famously declared that the American frontier was closed, *Gran Torino* presents the logic of the frontier's mythical iteration as still present in the decayed urban spaces of the Midwest.[30] While discussing the frontier and American regions, Turner valorizes the archetypical figure of the white male pioneer, situates the space of the frontier as an Americanization factory, and describes the frontier line as "the meeting point between savagery and civilization."[31] For Turner, the former term designates groups such as indigenous populations, and the latter term represents settlers of European origin. *Gran Torino* revisits Turner's racist dichotomy between savagery and civilization through its presentation of a former frontier space—the Midwest—in the early twenty-first century. In the logic of the film, because this regional environment has been vacated by its "civilized" white inhabitants, it is now susceptible to becoming "primitive" once again, due to an influx of immigrants and people of color.

To use Turner's racist terms, instead of white settlers bringing civilization to savagery in frontier spaces, Walt must recivilize his urban neighborhood that has declined into a state of violent chaos. This development situates the contemporary urban Midwest as a frontier-like environment in need of taming. Moreover, this status requires the return of Turner's archetypical pioneer figure who embodies the "traits of the frontier."[32] For Turner, these traits include "That coarseness and strength combined with acuteness and inquisitiveness; that practical, inventive turn of mind, quick to find expedients; that masterful grasp of material things, lacking in the artistic but powerful to effect great ends; that restless, nervous energy; that dominant individualism."[33] In short, *Gran Torino* establishes Walt as a latter day incarnation of Turner's frontier settler, albeit one who is defiantly immobile. Walt remains present but inactive until the neighborhood is threatened with violence by members of the newly arrived Hmong population.

Eastwood imbues Walt with a certain degree of indestructibility—until he chooses to sacrifice himself, that is—and Walt's violent efficacy plays upon a nostalgic fantasy of white masculinity. Walt is configured as the only male character who is capable of responding to the conflicts unfolding in the neighborhood. The adult Kowalski sons indulge in leisurely suburban lifestyles, while local priest Father Janovich (Christopher Carley) vacillates between encouraging forgiveness and instigating violent retribution. Such contradictory stances effectively undermine Father Janovich's authority, and the film elevates the single-minded, action-oriented Walt as a masculine ideal. Even more significantly, with the exception of the violent gang members, all of the other Hmong characters are shown to be ineffectual and in need of saving by Walt. This elevation of Walt is dependent upon a problematic and gendered presentation of Hmong culture.

Louisa Schein and Va-Megn Thoj provide a thorough examination of Hmong characters in *Gran Torino*, and it is instructive to review their findings here. They observe that *Gran Torino*'s "main cast of characters skirts around one markedly absent presence—that of the mature, productive Hmong man. The story revolves around an infantilized good boy opposite a demonized set of gangsters."[34] Early in the film, the Vang Lor family's grandmother (Chee Thao) even laments this male absence: "I'm just so brokenhearted. I want my daughter to find another husband. If she married again, there would be a man in the house. . . . Look at

[Thao] washing dishes. He does whatever his sister orders him to do. How could he ever become the man of the house?" Such scenes reflect the film's contradictory gendering of Hmong culture. On the one hand, Schein and Thoj identify a "dominant discourse" that defines the Hmong as "perpetual warriors."[35] When such "hypermasculine warriorhood" appears in the United States—either via real life events such as a 2004 incident in which a Hmong man killed "six white hunters in Wisconsin" or the depiction of a Hmong gang committing acts of violence in *Gran Torino*—then Hmong masculinity is "reviled as anachronism and failed assimilation."[36] On the other hand, the youthfulness of most of *Gran Torino*'s male Hmong characters "affirms a kind of newcomer greenness to Hmong Americans in general," while "the lack of productive Hmong men works toward creating the profile of refugee helplessness that sets Thao up for saving."[37] This version of Hmong culture is one in which "docility and assimilative desire are what remains legible, encoding Hmong Americans as feminine, vulnerable and in need of rescue."[38] As such, the attribution of feminized vulnerability to *Gran Torino*'s Hmong characters is an attempt to validate Walt's white savior status. The film indicates that the neighborhood's "white" Midwestern culture is threatened with extinction once Walt is no longer present, which creates the imperative for his mentoring of Thao. Even without Walt physically occupying the area, his values will linger.

Despite the large cast of Hmong performers in *Gran Torino*, the film's pretense of verisimilitude easily unravels. In an interview, Bee Vang (the actor who plays Thao) outlines a wide critique of *Gran Torino* and acknowledges being "repulsed" by how Thao and other Hmong characters were depicted in the script.[39] Vang claims that "there's no real reason for us to be Hmong in the script. We could be any minority."[40] He also responds to viewers who feel that the film "rings true": "Well—'rings true' for who? Maybe to people who live in a world where whites are the only heroes. Or to those who take the film as a documentary about Hmong culture. Even other Asians do this a lot. . . . Meanwhile, what a lot of us Hmong feel is that the film is distorting and *un*-true."[41] For example, late in the film, Sue and Thao depart for Walt's funeral while wearing "full Hmong festival costume."[42] As Schein and Thoj explain, the supposed authenticity of the attire is undercut by the absolutely inappropriate context, which confused many Hmong viewers who thought that "Sue was being forced to marry the gangbanger who had taken her virginity, and that the dress was part of the wedding ritual."[43] Hence, the ostensibly "authentic" specificity of the Hmong culture on display in *Gran Torino* is little more than window dressing to obscure the fact that the narrative simply requires any "othered" group to set against Walt's whiteness. So long as that group is distinguished by skin color, language, and/or attire, then they capably fill the role of a demographic that needs to be rescued and Americanized.

Many of the most widely disseminated images of the Midwest in popular culture lack all but token references to any ethnic group that is not white. Even with a predominantly Hmong cast, Eastwood's film once again affirms that Midwestern identity is predicated on whiteness. In parallel with *Gran Torino*'s fantasy of aging male potency, the reductive portrayal of the Hmong characters serves to maintain the primacy and relevance of a white Midwestern culture that itself is essentialized in terms of labor and gender, among other categories. Walt believes that without his protection—and accompanying instruction on how to achieve order in society, a status as fully American, and traditional masculine traits (particularly as exemplified by Thao)—the Vang Lors will not "find peace in this world." Such reasoning is contingent upon presenting the Hmong characters as incomplete, but eager to conform to Walt's values.[44]

Throughout *Gran Torino*, Eastwood features numerous scenes in which characters (often Walt) explicitly outline limited definitions of what it means to be American, Midwestern, and male. Early in the film, Walt and the Vang Lor family's grandmother exchange glares and muttered insults that the other presumably does not understand. Subtitles are provided for the grandmother's dialogue: "Why does that old white man stay here? All the Americans have moved out of this neighborhood. Why haven't you gone?" In this fleeting snippet of dialogue, whiteness is equated with "American" in general. A later scene further advances this limited definition of "American." Sue and Walt chat in the foreground of the frame while Thao washes the Gran Torino in the background (see fig. 4.2).[45] During the conversation, Sue declares, "It's nice of you to kinda look after [Thao] like this. He doesn't have any real role models in his life. . . . I wish our father would've been more like you. . . . He was really hard on us, really traditional, and really old-school." Walt protests that he too is "old-school," and Sue replies, "Yeah, but you're an American." Here, the conspicuously absent Hmong father—who presumably is a deceased "perpetual warrior"—is offered as a justification for Walt to proceed in his remolding of Thao.

Sue's comments also touch on a contrast between the Vang Lors and the Kowalskis that reappears throughout the film. Unlike the self-involved Kowalski sons and their children, the Vang Lor family supports one another and respects its aged members. Even Walt crudely and despondently acknowledges sharing values with the Vang Lors while gazing at his reflection in a mirror: "God, I've got more in common with these gooks than I do my own spoiled rotten family."[46] Regarding family unity, the marked traditionalism of the Vang Lors associates them with the "older" values that Walt represents and seeks to preserve. This is one additional way in which *Gran Torino* features muddled portrayals of ethnicity in relation to nostalgia and regional identity. As is evident by scenes depicting "traditional" garb or rituals, the onscreen fetishization of the Vang Lors' pastness is generally presented as a spectacle to mark their difference from Walt. At the same time, even though the importance that they place on family is framed as antiquated, that value is "old school" in a way that corresponds to Walt's views. Recognizing the ongoing fluctuation between shading pastness as a positive or negative attribute in *Gran Torino* is crucial to comprehending the conflicting interpretations that the film has provoked, as well as its millennial-era update of Turner's frontier conflict between civilization and savagery.

Gran Torino inverts Turner's racialized expansion narrative. Whereas Turner claims that the "savage" frontier occupied by Native Americans became "civilized" through an onslaught of European settlers, the sole remaining white

Fig. 4.2. Walt and Sue chat on the porch while Thao works in the background. Screen capture, *Gran Torino* (2008).

presence in *Gran Torino*'s urban Midwest—Walt—is driven to restore order within a space that has slid from stable to chaotic because it is now populated by minorities. According to the narrative's problematic logic, Walt's extralegal "white" violence echoes the "civilizing" efforts of the pioneers and thus is acceptable, while the Hmong gang's violence recalls the savage perpetual warrior image that must be abandoned in order to become the correct version of "American." In this regard, Walt's actions fit into the category of nostalgic violence. Walt is tasked not just with fighting the gang, but also with indoctrinating youth such as Thao into embracing nostalgic ideals relating to labor and masculinity in the Midwest. Due to this clear surrogate father/son subplot in the film, Schein and Thoj describe the film as a "drama of ethnic succession."[47] Whereas white settlers once displaced Native Americans, now *Gran Torino*'s Hmong immigrants displace white "natives," while nostalgically retaining elements of that supposedly vanishing white culture.

Given the loaded racial and gender content of *Gran Torino*, it should not be surprising that critical responses to this ideologically muddled film are full of contrasting viewpoints in both popular reviews and academic sources. Such mixed reactions reflect broader anxieties about the shifting identity of the Midwest in the early twenty-first century. In general, responses to Eastwood's film adopt one of three positions: ambivalence or outright anger over the essentialized and often inaccurate presentation of Hmong culture; an uncritical endorsement of the film's superficially progressive treatment of racial diversity in the Midwest; or racist anger over the perceived displacement of white culture due to multiculturalism in the United States. The first position is evident throughout Bee Vang's insightful critique of *Gran Torino*, as well as in the article cowritten by Shein and Thoj. Once again, both texts address how *Gran Torino*'s depiction of Hmong culture depends upon stereotypical, false, or misleading imagery.

The second position is a bit more complex and stems from a presumption of verisimilitude regarding *Gran Torino*'s portrayal of race.[48] Basically, the fictionalized depiction of Hmong culture is taken to be objective, and the film's conflicts are seen as representative of the growing pains that Midwestern communities experience when diverse groups encounter one another within the region. For example, Mark W. Roche and Vittorio Hösle assert that the film's "multiculturalism is not naïve."[49] In developing this assessment, they claim that *Gran Torino* "shows a time of transition" in which it is "the old America that is still bigoted and exclusive and the new America that is multicultural and diverse; an old America that still needs heroes and a new America that is seeking through institutional strategies to ensure peace and order."[50] Roche and Hösle also specify that *Gran Torino* demonstrates how "immigration can rejuvenate America, widening its vision, but only if the old citizens interact with those other cultures and learn to understand and appreciate them and if the immigrants are willing to accept basic American principles, such as the rule of law and the dignity of labor."[51] From this perspective, the mutually influencing relationship between Walt and the Hmong community points toward a peaceful future with shared values. As discussed earlier, however, such coexistence depends on an uneven power structure in which the Hmong characters still require validation from Walt. *Gran Torino* preserves the primacy of whiteness within Midwestern culture by either conditioning individuals such as Thao to enact what Walt nostalgically frames as "white" values or by asserting the fundamental otherness of various Hmong characters through an emphasis on their superstitious beliefs or violent behavior.

Gran Torino's problematic depiction of Hmong culture also provides fodder for interpretations of the film from diametrically opposed positions on the political spectrum. The third position is exemplified by a review of *Gran Torino* that appeared in *American Renaissance*, which is a white supremacist magazine that claims "race realism" as a guiding principle. Titled "Elegy for the White Man," Stephen Webster writes that Walt "shames [the Vang Lors], because they cannot do what he can" and that "his reward for trying to preserve order in his neighborhood is—at first—to be despised by the newcomers."[52] Regarding the overall message of *Gran Torino*, Webster writes, "Since [Walt] can't make his neighborhood more white, he tries to make his neighbors more white, and that is what the film is really about: white America graciously giving way to its non-white future."[53] Clearly, these assertions (and others within the published essay) are founded upon racial prejudice, but the review does not really distort the details of the film. What stands out is that Webster's racist reading of *Gran Torino* is not particularly far removed from Schein and Thoj's assessment of the film as a "drama of ethnic succession" or of Roche and Hösle's emphasis on cultural transition.[54] These authors mostly draw upon overlapping or identical textual evidence, despite the dramatically different values informing their respective interpretations of *Gran Torino*. Such variable responses indicate that Eastwood's ideologically muddled depiction of Detroit might best be understood as something of a Rorschach test for viewers. Moreover, the broad interpretability of *Gran Torino* mirrors the very manner in which the Midwest's meaning fluctuates in American culture.

Gran Torino reveals the contentiousness involved in defining the Midwest, as the film's conflicting critical reactions reflect the malleability of Midwestern imagery. In *Gran Torino*'s version of the urban millennial Midwest, the dynamics of Turner's frontier are reasserted in the face of changing demographics. The loss of Walt's white "civilizing" presence—particularly his ability to deploy nostalgic violence in response to threatening scenarios with racialized and gendered implications—is mourned even as the film suggests that such stability will be perpetuated through the newly masculinized Thao. Although Walt's white culture is presented as being threatened with extinction, a future is predicted in which those cultural values will persist and flourish. By the conclusion of the narrative, the Hmong community embodies "correct" values through Walt's guidance and the environment of the Midwest itself, which (following Turner's claims) is presented as an Americanizing space that reproduces nostalgic conceptions of racial identity, labor, family formations, and gender performance. These concerns with the impacts of a Midwestern environment on identity formation and performance are also foregrounded in *A History of Violence*, albeit in a far more overtly critical manner. Unlike the celebration of Walt's violence and self-sacrifice in *Gran Torino*, Cronenberg's multifaceted protagonist is a figure of deep ambivalence.

A History of Violence

David Cronenberg is notorious for presenting viewers with extremely graphic depictions of bodily transformations resulting from medical mishaps, scientific experiments, genetic mutations, and drug usage, among other phenomena. By contrast, *A History of Violence* tells the story of a superficially ordinary Midwestern man defending his family from Philadelphia gangsters. Adapted from a 1997 graphic novel (written by John Wagner and illustrated by Vince Locke), the film version of *A History of Violence* borrows the general premise of a Midwestern family man hiding an abandoned identity and violent past from his community.[55] Cronenberg, though, discards most of the details of the original narrative. The film instead focuses on the psychological balancing act of protagonist Tom Stall (Viggo Mortensen) as he attempts to preserve his outward performance of stereotypical Midwestern traits while dealing with the reemergence of Joey Cusack, Tom's repressed identity as a violent gangster during his youth on the East Coast. Here, the fascination with identity that Cronenberg had so often filtered through outrageous special effects manifests via subtle components of the film's lead performances, particularly that of Mortensen. With *A History of Violence*, identity mutations are effected by intentional performative acts, rather than unexpected body horror.[56]

On the film's commentary track, Cronenberg addresses the constructed nature of the fictional setting of Millbrook, Indiana, by observing, "This town is maybe too perfect. And that's part of the playing with mythology of Americana that America itself wants to believe. There's a lot of that in this movie."[57] This sense of play operates on multiple levels in the film, including Cronenberg's manipulation of regional myths, Tom's constructed identity, and the willingness of Millbrook's inhabitants to sustain a façade of normalcy that is repeatedly fractured by violence. Over the course of the film, Cronenberg sets about dismantling the Midwest's reified identity by depicting it as a nostalgic shell that not only obscures, but also is dependent upon a latent violence housed within regional narratives and iconography. To visualize such regional critiques, *A History of Violence* presents an interlocking place-bound network of Midwestern performances that collectively enact idealized conceptions of the region. Cronenberg further indicates that the community's surface-level unity is partly preserved through Tom's brutal deployment of nostalgic violence. In other words, Tom's internal division and violent actions are deeply entangled with the spatial and temporal conditions of the film's Midwestern setting.[58]

As with *Boys Don't Cry* and *Gran Torino*, the inhabitants of Millbrook remain isolated even in an era of greater connectivity. *A History of Violence*'s Indiana setting reflects perceptions of the Midwest's anachronistic status; Millbrook exists as a space of simultaneity in which multiple temporalities are seemingly accessible within its parameters. A tension thus emerges regarding which temporal conditions are considered to be "Midwestern" and which ones are representative of elsewhere, as exemplified by Tom/Joey's fragmented self. Regarding Millbrook's temporality, film scholar Mark Browning notes two shots of a clock that always displays the same time in the center of town. From this detail, Browning extrapolates, "Paradoxically, the narrative takes place within an extended frozen moment. It concerns the past but principally how this co-exists with the present *at the same time and within the same person*—Viggo Mortensen's character. . . . The past doesn't meet the present—the two have always co-existed."[59] Considered from this perspective, the overlapping Tom Stall and Joey Cusack personas connect to the Midwestern setting, which is the region where past American culture is perceived as lingering within the present. The ultimate desire of the nostalgic subject—to restore or relive an idealized (potentially invented) version of the past—is made available by the very landscape itself.

Cronenberg immediately spotlights the Midwest's peculiar temporality with a deliberately paced long take that lasts just over four minutes at the start of the film. Notably, the camera primarily tracks to the right, as if following the x axis of a linear timeline, although it occasionally deviates from this fixed trajectory by retreating backwards or moving forwards into the depth of the mise-en-scène. These camera movements suggest a disruption of linearity and create a sense of halting temporal progression. The scene begins with two men, later identified as Leland (Stephen McHattie) and Billy (Greg Bryk), exiting from a room at a small roadside motel and discussing plans to "keep heading east" and to "stay out of big cities."[60] The camera then tracks Billy as he slowly moves their convertible toward the motel office, and the first cut of the film occurs when he enters the structure to get water. Inside the office are the bodies of two people who Leland and Billy presumably murdered, and a young girl tentatively emerges from a back room. Billy calmly pulls out a pistol and shoots her; just as the gunshot explodes over the soundtrack, Cronenberg cuts to a shot of Tom's similarly aged daughter

Sarah Stall (Heidi Hayes) sitting up in bed and screaming as she awakens from an apparent nightmare. A rapid tonal shift results from the combination of the lethargic long take, the jump cut, and the sound bridge. These elements lend the opening moments a degree of uncertainty as to whether the motel scene was Sarah's dream or an actual narrative event. The sound bridge somewhat suggests temporal continuity, but the spatial proximity between the gunshot and the bedroom is unclear. Are these killers near the Stall home? Are they inventions of Sarah, and is the girl at the motel an imagined version of herself?

This narrative ambiguity is accompanied by Cronenberg's nearly parodic depiction of familial unity in which the entire Stall family—Tom, teenage son Jack (Ashton Holmes), and wife Edie (Maria Bello)—rushes to comfort Sarah. Throughout this scene, the Stalls are shot in medium close-up, and their four heads are tightly clustered in the frame, which gives a claustrophobic feel to their support for one another. Tom asserts, "There's no such thing as monsters," but Sarah insists, "They came out of my closet, and then they were in the shadows." Clearly, this dialogue foreshadows narrative developments to come, as Sarah demonstrates an intuited awareness of something sinister already existing within the Stalls' seemingly perfect domestic space: what eventually is revealed to be the "Joey" persona. Cronenberg's purpose, however, is not to construct an ironic portrait of Midwestern family life, but to contemplate what is necessary to create and preserve this idyllic domesticity. Cronenberg publicly pondered what conditions were necessary to support Millbrook; within the narrative, he shows that "support" entails a symbiotic relationship between Tom's performance and Millbrook itself. Tom's embodiment of a Midwestern everyman is sustainable only within a community that is eager to accept that fiction. Consequently, "Tom" should be understood as a product of that "perfect little town" itself. The Tom identity—the preservation of which is arguably the film's primary conflict—necessitates communal support. Maintaining this identity transformation is an endeavor that began individually, but which has become collective and interdependent.[61]

Essentially, Tom's performance of Midwestern traits operates as an amalgam of mainstream imagery that circulates about the region (see fig. 4.3). Recalling Judith Butler's emphasis on "constraint" as a key element of performativity, Tom's outward identity is predicated on the socialized constraints that dictate what is acceptable in terms of appearance, values, and behavior within Millbrook.[62] Butler's oft-referenced theories of performativity thoroughly consider gender identity, but she also specifies that the "identifications" of "race or sexuality or class or geopolitical positioning/displacement" require attention because "these identifications are invariably imbricated in one another, the vehicle for one another...."[63] Focusing on specific regional contexts enables the interplay between place and performance to become clearer. As "Tom," Mortensen uses an unassuming vocal affectation that is meek and warm, while as "Joey," Mortensen's voice remains soft spoken, but exudes menace through its emotionless, flat cadence. Such understated alterations of speech pattern are complemented by Tom's adornment of a Midwestern small town "uniform" of sorts, which consists

Fig. 4.3. Tom/Joey stares out from the shadows of his diner. Screen capture, *A History of Violence* (2005).

of jeans, a plaid shirt, and sneakers for the entirety of the film.[64] It is obvious that Tom perceives the Midwest as being the locus of the generic in nearly every conceivable way, but he did not invent such associations; rather, Tom draws on a preexisting set of images, mannerisms, and behaviors that circulate in popular culture. For instance, Tom's appearance and attire recalls that of characters in Midwestern working class sitcoms with predominantly white casts such as *Roseanne* (1988–1997, 2018) and *Grace Under Fire* (1993–1998).[65] Hence, Tom's mimicry of this regional iconography reveals that the "Tom" persona is an identity that merely had to be learned, rehearsed, and performed.

The complicated task of becoming Tom is not depicted in the film, and this development is yet another narrative omission that troubles linear temporality. Despite the knowledge that Tom came from elsewhere, he seemingly has always been in Millbrook. It is as if the Tom identity already existed, but was in stasis until being donned by Joey. Because Tom is an archetypical Midwestern figure, any absent history may simply be re-created or invented in the nostalgic regional environment. For instance, an early role-playing scene with Edie fills a gap in Tom's personal history within the Millbrook community; she dresses in a cheerleader uniform because, as she explains, "We never got to be teenagers together." In this encounter, Edie attempts to access a fictional past by performing a generic cultural symbol of youthful lust. Later in the film, Edie explicitly confronts Tom about his past as Joey. Seemingly bewildered, Tom replies, "I never expected to see Joey again. . . . I thought I killed Joey Cusack. I went out to the desert, and I killed him. I spent three years becoming Tom Stall." Again, this act of "becoming Tom" involves the rehearsal of Midwestern affectations and the adornment of apparel associated with the region in popular culture. The climactic encounter with Philadelphia mob boss Richie (William Hurt)—who is

Tom's estranged brother—echoes Edie's line of questioning. Richie sarcastically inquires, "You're living the American dream, you really bought into it, didn't you? You've been this other guy almost as long as you've been yourself. Hey, when you dream, are you still Joey?" Again, Tom dutifully insists, "Joey's been dead a long time," although to this point in the film, he has used Joey's violent faculties to kill several people.

There are four scenes in which "Joey" makes an appearance in the film, each of which features violence: during an attempted robbery at Stall's Diner by Leland and Billy; when gangster Carl Fogarty (Ed Harris) and his men threaten the Stalls at their home; in the midst of a brutal sex scene with Edie after Tom has admitted to being Joey; and while disposing of Richie and his men in Philadelphia. In all of these instances, Mortensen oscillates between the Tom and Joey personas, often with some degree of uncertainty as to which identity is dominant at a given moment. Beyond Joey's shocking acts of extreme violence, Mortensen's nuanced performance reveals fissures in the constructed "Tom" exterior through subtle shifts in mannerisms and gestures that alert viewers to the presence of Joey. Before returning to the three scenes in which Tom commits murder, the complicated encounter with Edie merits a closer look.

Following Tom's murder of Carl Fogarty's bodyguards (teenage son Jack dispatched Carl with a shotgun blast) and a second stay in the hospital, Sheriff Sam Carney (Peter MacNeill) confronts the Stall patriarch about needing to "hear the truth" regarding Tom's past. Edie returns home during this conversation and, despite her misgivings about Tom's newly revealed proclivity for violence, defends the authenticity of her husband's Midwestern identity. Sam exits, and Cronenberg presents a second sexual encounter between Edie and Tom, who both undergo rapid shifts between personas for its duration. After pursuing Edie to the staircase, Tom reaches out for his wife, who turns and slaps him in the face. Mortensen's visage then hardens into that of "Joey"—as evident by an intense glare in his eyes—and he chokes Edie, who responds by tauntingly calling him "Joey." Edie turns to escape up the stairs, but "Joey" trips her and spreads her legs. Mortensen abruptly softens his countenance and begins to separate himself from Edie, but she pulls his head toward her face and kisses him, which leads to bruising intercourse on the wooden steps. Upon climax, they gently kiss until Edie scornfully pushes Tom away and ascends the stairs, while Tom remains below and passively watches her leave.

Both characters fluctuate between identities throughout this encounter. Tom reverts to the violence-prone Joey while initially assaulting Edie, but overrides this impulse, and the more outwardly passive Tom persona quickly returns. Edie, on the other hand, performs being overwhelmed with grief in front of the sheriff, shuns Tom's emotionally needy pleas, appears both revolted and aroused by the "Joey" persona, and then pushes feeble Tom away once more. These contradictory impulses are indicative of the simultaneous attraction to and repulsion by violence in the film. Of this scene, Adam Lowenstein evocatively observes, "Their bodies speak the darkest ambivalences of their relationship."[66] A major part of Edie's ambivalence and intermittent antipathy for Tom could stem from a realization, conscious or not, that her ideal family life would not have existed had Tom not actually been Joey. Without discarding that monstrous identity in favor of a generically Midwestern one, the "perfect" Stall family would never have been. This intricate dependency of idealized Midwestern imagery upon violence—as evident by the fact that violent Joey is a necessary precondition for activating the archetypical Midwestern figure of Tom—is even more transparent in the other three scenes in which Joey appears.

Tom's earlier violence during the diner scene initially appears to be instinctual, as he simply responds to the immediate threat of death. After Tom efficiently dispatches Leland and Billy, Cronenberg tightly frames the protagonist in a close-up looking around nervously with the gun in his hand. Tom's concerned gaze glances at the gun, but then quickly looks away. He lowers the pistol out of the frame, and his eyes continue darting back and forth, as if troubled by the unanticipated exposure of his violent capabilities. The subsequent appearance of Carl and his men at the Stall home, however, prompts an intentional transformation into "Joey." To defend his family, Tom summons the latent violence that he has suppressed within himself. During this scene, Mortensen's utterances are flat and emotionless, and his gaze becomes both vacant and piercing. After the mobsters release Jack, Tom calmly declares, "I think it'd be better if you'd just leave now," and this statement assumes the tone of a warning more than a polite Midwestern request. Here, Tom's Midwestern accent is barely perceptible, and Mortensen appears to be portraying Joey performing "Tom." Even as Joey asserts control, a slight vocal trace of "Tom" persists and demonstrates the tenuous nature of both identities. Having rehearsed being "Tom" for so long, not even Joey is able to fully override this constructed identity. This Jekyll and Hyde quality is particularly evident as the "Joey" personality dissipates after Jack shoots Carl. Tom trains his intense gaze onto his stunned son and snatches the rifle from Jack's hands; while flitting his eyes between the weapon and his son, the hardened "Joey" facial expression slides away and is replaced with Tom looking concerned.

During the film's climax, Tom returns to Philadelphia, where he summons "Joey" in order to kill his brother Richie and his men. Along with the encounter with Carl on the Stalls' front lawn, this sequence indicates that Tom is developing the ability to inhabit either personality at will and for strategic purposes. The performance of "Joey" in Carl's presence functions as a warning, an announcement that the potential for violence is present; conversely, by playing up his adopted Midwestern mannerisms at Richie's home, Tom attempts to evade retribution for his violent past by demonstrating that he now is a simple Midwesterner. In this latter scene, the performance of the "Tom" personality—such as his soft-spoken vocal affectation—rings false through its exaggeration of stereotypical Midwestern traits and on account of the setting. Cronenberg continually emphasizes the duality of Tom within a Midwestern space, where there is a temporal overlap of identities. "Joey" is considered to be "past" and "Tom" is designated as the "present," but they both occupy the same body within the region. In Philadelphia, Tom does not fully exist because the conditions necessary for sustaining that identity are located elsewhere, in Millbrook.

This spatialized identity dynamic is further underscored in a brief scene the morning after Tom kills Richie. Cronenberg cuts directly from the evening murder to Tom walking to a pond behind the mansion and then washing the blood from his body in daylight. The cleansing symbolism of this scene is rather heavy-handed on the surface, but as Scott Wilson observes, the preceding elliptical edit calls attention to "an uncomfortable lack. Something has occurred during this period that the film is unable to represent, and we spectators . . . do not have the requisite information to fill in this space."[67] This narrative gap illustrates the dependency of the competing Tom and Joey personas on environment. In Millbrook, the Tom identity is visibly restored almost immediately after Joey's violence, as if to justify the savage behavior by displaying the "good" identity that has been protected. At Richie's mansion, on the other hand, the Joey persona dominates in his native Eastern environment and even performs as "Tom." Within the simultaneous temporalities of the Midwest, the Tom and Joey identities may switch back and forth rather quickly, while shifting between the two in Philadelphia requires a lengthy transitional period.[68] The unseen and delayed restoration of the Tom persona following the final murders in the film ultimately reinforces that identity's dependency on Midwestern spaces.

Because preserving the illusion of "perfect" Midwestern imagery is the overt purpose of Tom's violent actions after the diner scene, all of those instances are clear examples of nostalgic violence. In particular, the latter two scenes in which "Joey" emerges and kills people—on the Stalls' front lawn and at Richie's mansion—feature violence that is born from a nostalgic desire to sustain the idealized present state of life for the Stalls and their small Indiana community in general. The town, family, and figure of Tom himself all are shown to be dependent on the brutal violence of "Joey," as is evident by a cause-and-effect sequence that binds the film's events: the past prenarrative violence of Joey led to the creation of Midwestern Tom, whose diner violence led to the attempted retribution by Joey's former East Coast associates, which led to additional murders by the Tom/Joey hybrid in order to stabilize the appearance of the small town environment in which the Tom identity flourishes. Acts of violence perpetually precede, disrupt, and restore Tom's desired Midwestern lifestyle, and Cronenberg persistently reiterates that the isolated town's "perfection" relies upon a network of performative collaboration that is supported by nostalgic violence.

What enables Tom's past to remain undetected in Millbrook for so long is the community's willingness to embrace imagery and mannerisms that fit idealized perceptions of the Midwest. Tom looks and plays the part of a generic Midwesterner, so he is accepted as such. For instance, after Carl and his men first approach Tom at the diner, Edie phones Sheriff Carney, who intercepts the gangsters on the outskirts of Millbrook. The sheriff threatens, "Let me make something clear. . . . This is a nice town. We have nice people here. We take care of our nice people. Do you understand me?" This sentiment is repeated when Sam later asks if Tom is involved in a witness protection program. Tom refutes the notion and thanks Sam for "watching out for us." Sam responds by asserting, "Come on, Tom. You know we look out for our own here." Sam's inclusion of Tom within the categories of "our nice people" and "our own" reaffirms the successfulness of Tom's performance and is indicative of the communal preoccupation with regulating the town's identity. Visually and aurally discordant elements such as suit-wearing gangsters with Philadelphia accents must be escorted out of Millbrook, but so long as Tom *looks* and *sounds* appropriate, he is able to stay within this nostalgic space. In this way, Cronenberg illuminates the masking properties of Midwestern imagery and narratives, which obscure violent tendencies. Tom's presence has not clandestinely contaminated the town with violence; instead, violence—particularly that of Joey, whom Tom is unable to repress—is necessary for molding and supporting the collective self-image that the community wishes to publicly enact. The townspeople's acceptance and vigorous defense of Tom's performance thus is an indictment of Millbrook as a whole.

Much like the postnightmare scene that introduces the Stalls, Cronenberg concludes *A History of Violence* with a mournful final moment that is borderline parodic. Upon returning from the murderous Philadelphia excursion, Tom reenters his Indiana home while the family is eating dinner. Tom sits, Sarah sets his place, and Jack passes him a tray with meatloaf. Cronenberg's camera lingers over the detailed mise-en-scène, which allows viewers to see the Stalls' meal that includes mashed potatoes, peas, carrots, and corn. Tom's nostalgic violence has succeeded in restoring a superficial appearance of normality to the household, but his actions have also made transparent the interdependency of performativity, violence, and nostalgia for propping up that essentialized image of Midwestern normality. Now forced to contemplate the constructed nature of their identities, Tom and Edie silently weep across the table from one another. The perfection of their idealized family has been shattered, but they are compelled nonetheless to continue performing their roles (see fig. 4.4).

Millbrook's inhabitants collectively work to produce a semblance of small town "perfection" with stylized performances of stereotypical Midwestern qualities. In this regard, *A History of Violence* is a key example of representational conventions endemic to films depicting the Midwest at the turn of the twenty-first century. Films such as *Boys Don't Cry*, *Gran Torino*, and *A History of Violence* present forceful Midwestern counter-narratives that challenge utopic rhetoric about the localized effects of emerging digital technologies and increased interconnectivity. Rather than transcending distance within a virtual frontier, the geographically isolated and closed-off communities of Falls City, inner city Detroit, and Millbrook are burdened by the conforming pressures of nostalgia. Moreover, such place-specific nostalgia is linked to regressive ideals relating to masculinity, race, and violence. All three films show that a limited range of acceptable incarnations of masculinity yields pernicious effects within these Midwestern communities. Self-destructive tendencies abound, as does an overt antipathy toward individuals whose identities do not fully comply with the region's white and heteronormative popular image. The contrasting forms of masculinity embodied by *Boys Don't Cry*'s Brandon or *Gran Torino*'s Thao are eradicated through assault, murder, and/or ideological indoctrination. *A History of Violence*'s Tom/Joey hybrid is something of a disguised sentinel who springs into action when

Fig. 4.4. An uneasy reunion and family dinner. Screen capture, *A History of Violence* (2005).

the town's (and his family's) mundane operation is threatened with disruption. Notably, one of "perfect" Millbrook's defining elements appears to be homogeneity, much like the violent space of Falls City in *Boys Don't Cry*. And, of course, the more diverse populations on display in *Gran Torino* are framed as requiring either a white savior or extralegal enforcer to establish order. Whether endorsing such dynamics (as in Eastwood's film) or critiquing them (as Peirce and Cronenberg do), these texts overtly foreground the powerful influence of nostalgia on narratives of race, gender, and region.

Together, *Boys Don't Cry*, *Gran Torino*, and *A History of Violence* problematize the lingering perception of the Midwest as an atemporal museum for lost or antiquated elements of American culture. The threat of nostalgic violence constantly looms behind regional identity performances in these films, and this ever-present violence is unleashed to strike down and discipline individuals who would challenge the surface-level placidity of Midwestern iconography. Hence, nostalgic violence functions as a cultural regulatory mechanism. The convergence era may signal the death of distance for some individuals and communities, but in *Boys Don't Cry*, *Gran Torino*, and *A History of Violence*, the millennial Midwest remains stubbornly detached from other locales and shaped by a resilient conception of the region as a space of nostalgia.

Notes

1. Portions of this chapter have been previously published as Adam Ochonicky, "The Millennial Midwest: Nostalgic Violence in the Twenty-First Century," *Quarterly Review of Film and Video* 32, no. 2 (2015): 124–140, doi: 10.1080/10509208.2013.780937,

reprinted by permission of Taylor & Francis, http://www.tandfonline.com; *A History of Violence*, directed by David Cronenberg (2005; Los Angeles: New Line Home Entertainment, 2006), DVD.

2. Brian Johnson, "Violence Hits Home," *Maclean's* 118, no. 42, October 17, 2005.

3. *Boys Don't Cry*, directed by Kimberly Peirce (1999; Beverly Hills, CA: Twentieth Century Fox Home Entertainment, 2000), DVD; *Gran Torino*, directed by Clint Eastwood (2008; Burbank, CA: Warner Home Video, 2010), DVD.

4. Frederick Jackson Turner, *The Frontier in American History* (1920; repr., Charleston, SC: BiblioBazaar, 2008), 132–133.

5. Ibid., 125.

6. Victoria E. Johnson, *Heartland TV: Prime Time Television and the Struggle for U.S. Identity* (New York: New York University Press, 2008), 19, emphasis in original.

7. *A Simple Plan*, directed by Sam Raimi (1998; Hollywood, CA: Paramount Pictures, 1999), DVD; *Drop Dead Gorgeous*, directed by Michael Patrick Jann (Los Angeles: New Line Home Entertainment, 1999), DVD; *The Virgin Suicides*, directed by Sofia Coppola (1999; Hollywood, CA: Paramount Classics, 2000), DVD; *Mysterious Skin*, Unrated Director's Edition, directed by Gregg Araki (2004; Culver City, CA: Strand Releasing Home Video, 2006), DVD; *Winter's Bone*, directed by Debra Granik (Santa Monica, CA: Lionsgate, 2010), DVD; *Take Shelter*, directed by Jeff Nichols (2011; Culver City, CA: Sony Pictures Home Entertainment, 2012), DVD; *Fargo*, directed by Joel Coen and Ethan Coen (1996; Beverly Hills, CA: Twentieth Century Fox Home Entertainment, 2005), DVD.

8. James R. Shortridge, *The Middle West: Its Meaning in American Culture* (Lawrence: University Press of Kansas, 1989), 27–28, 56.

9. Douglas Rushkoff, "Renaissance Now! Media Ecology and the New Global Narrative," in *Living in the Information Age: A New Media Reader*, 2nd ed., ed. Erik P. Bucy (Belmont, CA: Wadsworth, 2005), 21–32.

10. Frances Cairncross, "The Trendspotter's Guide to New Communications," in *Living in the Information Age: A New Media Reader*, 2nd ed., ed. Erik P. Bucy (Belmont, CA: Wadsworth, 2005), 9–10.

11. Lev Manovich, *The Language of New Media* (Cambridge, MA: MIT Press, 2001), 258.

12. Ibid., 273.

13. Turner, *The Frontier in American History*, 14.

14. Ibid., 186.

15. Svetlana Boym, *The Future of Nostalgia* (New York: Basic Books, 2001), 347.

16. Ibid., 347–348, emphasis added.

17. Jonathan Sterne similarly emphasizes the physically embedded nature of digital technologies. He writes, "In its very name, the Internet signals hardware and infrastructure ... our new media subjects are not only embodied, but they are surrounded by piles and piles of humanmade stuff. Much of this stuff is going to be taken out of service long before it no longer works. It will sit in offices and warehouses. And then it will be trashed." See: Jonathan Sterne, "Out with the Trash: On the Future of New Media," in *Residual Media*, ed. Charles R. Acland (Minneapolis: University of Minnesota Press, 2007), 17.

18. Anthony Harkins provides a thorough analysis of the history of the term "flyover country" being associated with the Midwest. Among other insights, he writes, "The new 'flyover' view of the country ... envisions the nation divided into only two vast and seemingly opposite meta-regions defined almost exclusively in cultural terms."

See: Anthony Harkins, "The Midwest and the Evolution of 'Flyover Country,'" *Middle West Review* 3, no. 1 (2016): 98–99.

19. J. Halberstam, "The Transgender Gaze in *Boys Don't Cry*," *Screen* 42, no. 3 (Autumn 2001): 296, doi: 10.1093/screen/42.3.294.

20. White specifies that the character of Candace (Alicia Goranson) is "a composite character based in part on the third murder victim Lisa Lambert." See: Patricia White, "Girls Still Cry," *Screen* 42, no. 2 (Summer 2001): 220–221, doi: 10.1093/screen/42.2.217.

21. Halberstam, "The Transgender Gaze in *Boys Don't Cry*," 298.

22. Jennifer Devere Brody, "Boyz Do Cry: Screening History's White Lies," *Screen* 43, no. 1 (Spring 2002): 95–96, doi: 10.1093/screen/43.1.91.

23. Johnson, *Heartland TV*, 18, emphasis in original.

24. Brenda Cooper, "*Boys Don't Cry* and Female Masculinity: Reclaiming a Life and Dismantling the Politics of Normative Heterosexuality," *Critical Studies in Media Communication* 19, no. 1 (March 2002): 49, emphasis in original.

25. Lisa Henderson, "The Class Character of *Boys Don't Cry*," *Screen* 42, no. 3 (Autumn 2001): 302, doi: 10.1093/screen/42.3.299.

26. *RoboCop*, directed by Paul Verhoeven (1987; Culver City, CA: Sony Pictures Home Entertainment, 2006), DVD.

27. *Dirty Harry*, directed by Don Siegel (1971; Burbank, CA: Warner Home Video, 2008), DVD.

28. Antonio Machuco similarly observes, "It is as if *Gran Torino*'s narrative structure summarized the careers of the characters once played by Clint Eastwood." See: Kate Stables, review of *Gran Torino*, directed by Clint Eastwood, *Sight & Sound* 19, no. 3 (March 2009): 61; Antonio Machuco, "Violence and Truth in Clint Eastwood's *Gran Torino*," *Anthropoetics* 16, no. 2 (Spring 2011), http://anthropoetics.ucla.edu/ap1602/1602machuco/.

29. Machuco, "Violence and Truth," emphasis in original.

30. Mark W. Roche and Vittorio Hösle present an intriguing reading of Walt's proactive behavior based on his status as a veteran. They write, "Military life has aspects of the frontier mentality, including the need for courage, the willingness to sacrifice, and the temptation to use violence beyond a reasonable measure. Walt still lives that model." While the conception of "military life" offered by Roche and Hosle is a bit limited, their brief linkage of *Gran Torino* to the mythic American frontier is notable. See: Mark W. Roche and Vittorio Hösle, "Cultural and Religious Reversals in Clint Eastwood's *Gran Torino*," *Religion and the Arts* 15 (2011): 668, doi: 10.1163/156852911X596273.

31. Turner, *The Frontier in American History*, 14.

32. Ibid., 39.

33. Ibid., 38.

34. Louisa Schein and Va-Megn Thoj, "*Gran Torino*'s Boys and Men with Guns: Hmong Perspectives," *Hmong Studies Journal* 10 (2009): 14, http://hmongstudies.org/ScheinThojHSJ10.pdf.

35. Ibid., 2–5.

36. Ibid., 2, 16.

37. Ibid., 15–16.

38. Ibid.

39. Bee Vang, interview by Louisa Schein, "*Gran Torino*'s Hmong Lead Bee Vang on Film, Race and Masculinity: Conversations with Louisa Schein," *Hmong Studies Journal* 11 (2010): 3, http://hmongstudies.org/ScheinVangHSJ11.pdf.

40. Ibid., 6.

41. For instance, Roche and Hösle erroneously claim, "In its depiction of the Hmong community, Eastwood's film completely avoids the temptation of idealizing the other culture—which is often simply an instrumentation of the other for one's own purposes." See: ibid., emphasis in original; Roche and Hösle, "Cultural and Religious Reversals," 652.

42. Schein and Thoj, "*Gran Torino*'s Boys and Men with Guns," 29.

43. Ibid.

44. Walt's values are essentially those of Eastwood himself. In a 2016 interview, Eastwood critiques "political correctness" and what he describes as, alternately, the current "kiss-ass generation" and "pussy generation." He remarks, "Everybody's walking on eggshells. We see people accusing people of being racist and all kinds of stuff. When I grew up, those things weren't called racist. And then when I did *Gran Torino*, even my associate said, 'This is a really good script, but it's politically incorrect.' I said, 'Good. Let me read it tonight.' The next morning . . . I said, 'We're starting this immediately.'" Such ideas about language, race, labor, etc. are infused throughout *Gran Torino* (and are exemplified and/or articulated by Walt). See: Clint Eastwood and Scott Eastwood, interview by Michael Hainey, "Clint and Scott Eastwood: No Holds Barred in Their First Interview Together," *Esquire*, August 2016, https://www.esquire.com/entertainment/a46893/double-trouble-clint-and-scott-eastwood/.

45. This visual composition almost seems to be a comment on the obscured contributions of immigrants on Midwestern culture; given the film's many ideological contradictions, it is unclear if such a meaning is intended.

46. When deciding whether or not to reproduce quotes that include racial epithets (as in this instance), I consider the extent to which such language is relevant to the argument at hand. In this case, the quote exemplifies both the film's problematic treatment of race in general and the film's oscillating representation of and attitude toward the Hmong American characters in particular.

47. Schein and Thoj, "*Gran Torino*'s Boys and Men with Guns," 30.

48. For instance, Machuco labels Eastwood as an "accomplished anthropologist." See: Machuco, "Violence and Truth."

49. Roche and Hösle, "Cultural and Religious Reversals," 670.

50. Ibid., 669.

51. Ibid., 656.

52. Stephen Webster, review of *Gran Torino*, directed by Clint Eastwood, "Elegy for the White Man," *American Renaissance*, September 2009, 12.

53. Ibid.

54. Schein and Thoj, "*Gran Torino*'s Boys and Men with Guns," 30.

55. John Wagner, *A History of Violence* (New York: Vertigo, 1997).

56. Cronenberg's ongoing shift to less overt body horror includes films such as *Spider* (2002), *Eastern Promises* (2007), and *A Dangerous Method* (2011). Scott Wilson claims that *A History of Violence* stands as "the first non-Cronenbergian text by Cronenberg, a film . . . in which all of the recognizably Cronenbergian themes (see *Videodrome*) have been so refined as to be only obliquely visible." See: *Spider*, directed by David Cronenberg (2002; Culver City, CA: Sony Pictures Home Entertainment, 2003), DVD; *Eastern Promises*, directed by David Cronenberg (New York City: Focus Features, 2007), film; *A Dangerous Method*, directed by David Cronenberg (New York City: Sony Pictures Classic, 2011), film; Scott Wilson, *The Politics of Insects: David Cronenberg's Cinema of Confrontation* (New York: Continuum, 2011), 200.

57. David Cronenberg, "Audio Commentary," *A History of Violence* (2005; Los Angeles: New Line Home Entertainment, 2006), DVD.

58. William Beard suggests that Cronenberg's films "are full of split or scattered subjects, but none of them can survive in what is inevitably revealed to be an emotionally and psychologically dysfunctional status. All of them yearn for a wholeness that can have no place in the (post)modern world; and the author, too, must be seen as yearning for a wholeness that he fully understands cannot exist." Despite Cronenberg's changing aesthetic mode on display in *A History of Violence*, Beard's summation of the director's troubled characters remains applicable. See: William Beard, *The Artist as Monster: The Cinema of David Cronenberg* (Toronto: University of Toronto Press, 2006), viii–ix.

59. Mark Browning, *David Cronenberg: Author or Film-maker?* (Bristol, UK: Intellect Books, 2007), 37–38, emphasis in original.

60. A map inside the motel office seems to indicate that the scene is taking place in Wisconsin.

61. The cooperation between Tom and the residents of Millbrook is one additional element that further distinguishes *A History of Violence* from much of Cronenberg's work to that point in his career. Michael Grant writes, "There is, in Cronenberg's films, a turning away from the immediacies of communal and social circumstance, a subversion of contour and legible order, in a paradoxical drive to what exists on the far side of humanity." This "turning away" from community and toward isolation in earlier films such as *The Fly* (1986) is attributable to the dehumanizing bodily mutations that occur, whereas the crucial transformation in *A History of Violence* is Joey's prenarrative invention of "Tom." In fact, the "Joey" and "Tom" personas each could be situated on "the far side of humanity," but on opposing ends of a spectrum. See: Michael Grant, *The Modern Fantastic: The Films of David Cronenberg* (Trowbridge, UK: Flick Books, 2000), 7; *The Fly*, directed by David Cronenberg (1986; Beverly Hills, CA: Twentieth Century Fox Home Entertainment, 2005), DVD.

62. The Midwest is regularly presented as a space that imposes restrictions on its inhabitants. Such regional dynamics dovetail with Butler's assertion of "constraint . . . as the very condition of performativity. . . . Moreover, constraint is not necessarily that which sets a limit to performativity; constraint is, rather, that which impels and sustains performativity." See: Judith Butler, *Bodies That Matter: On the Discursive Limits of "Sex"* (1993; repr., New York: Routledge Classics, 2011), 59–60.

63. Ibid., 78.

64. Along these lines, Wilson highlights the strategic element of Tom's identity by observing that "his performance of the town's specific hegemonic, ideological (and, hence, disciplinary) requirements is knowingly and consciously enacted." See: Wilson, *The Politics of Insects*, 204.

65. See: *Roseanne* (New York: ABC, 1988–1997, 2018), broadcast television; *Grace Under Fire* (New York: ABC, 1993–1998), broadcast television.

66. Adam Lowenstein, "Promises of Violence: David Cronenberg on Globalized Geopolitics," *boundary 2* 36, no. 2 (2009): 206, doi: 10.1215/01903659-2009-011.

67. Wilson, *The Politics of Insects*, 207.

68. Tom's drive to the East Coast further affirms this condition, as the time required to travel from Philadelphia to Millbrook seems to be a necessary duration for the alternation of his identities outside of the Indiana town.

5 | Locating Sincerity, Disillusionment, and Paranoia

Svetlana Boym concludes *The Future of Nostalgia* (2001) by reflecting on the perils of endurance. She writes, "Survivors of the twentieth century, we are all nostalgic for a time when we were not nostalgic. But there seems to be no way back."[1] Such sentiments arise from an object of nostalgia more elusive than a general desire for the past. Here, Boym yearns for an indeterminate moment prior to the unsatisfactory conditions that produce nostalgic desire. This longing is for a state of being that likely cannot be restored, as it precedes the foreclosing, restrictive effects of nostalgia. Boym's gloomy perspective on the passage of time strongly corresponds with an element found in some Midwestern narratives around the turn of the new millennium. During this period, the present state of the Midwest is regularly situated as severely wanting in relation to its heavily mythologized past. Within the context of the United States' polarized culture of the twenty-first century, a critical reevaluation of the Midwest's longstanding identity—particularly its linkage with certain forms of white masculinity—emerges through several cinematic portrayals of the region.

This chapter examines Alexander Payne's *About Schmidt* (2002), Jason Reitman's *Up in the Air* (2009), and Jeff Nichols's *Take Shelter* (2011), all of which depict a general sense of loss looming over the Midwest.[2] More precisely, these three films feature white male protagonists who suffer from existential crises that are intertwined with a growing awareness that the Midwest's popular identity is an unsustainable façade. Each film's lead character is burdened with nostalgia and discontentment stemming from the conforming pressures of what has been constructed as standardized Midwestern lifestyles in American culture. The rupturing of personal identity is shown to parallel the Midwest's flickering status as a symbolic space long romanticized as the locus of the "real" or "authentic" America. In this way, regional decline is associated with individualized perceptions of being outmoded. Such personal malaise partly results from desire to nostalgically reenact and restore idealized past images of the region that do not correspond to its degraded contemporary state. How these characters respond to an encroaching sense of purposelessness illuminates the Midwest's general condition in the twenty-first century. A new object of nostalgia thus emerges across these films: the moment just before collapsing Midwestern myths could no longer be sustained. To borrow Boym's phrasing, the protagonists of *About Schmidt*, *Up in the Air*, and *Take Shelter* yearn for a time when they were not nostalgic. As these films reveal, reconstituting a sense of self from the shards of a fractured regional identity is a daunting proposition full of uncertainty.

A palpable sense of disillusionment informs *About Schmidt, Up in the Air,* and *Take Shelter*. As the films unfold, cultural ideals concerning the Midwest, labor, and family are undermined, thereby forcing a reassessment of each protagonist's carefully crafted persona within a region that has a muddled identity. The shaken Midwesterners on display must rebuild their identities in the face of broader regional and global changes. Enduring qualities that heretofore had defined the Midwest since at least the writings of Frederick Jackson Turner have become unsettled in the new millennium. As such, stabilizing the Midwest's fragmented meaning is an ongoing challenge in the early twenty-first century. Interestingly, a heightened national focus on regionalism briefly manifested within a contentious cultural debate that arose in the immediate aftermath of 9/11 and then rapidly faded away. Before returning to this chapter's primary films, it is useful to examine this public discourse on regional identity.

Locating Sincerity

In 2001, as the United States absorbed the trauma of the terrorist attacks that wrought carnage on the East Coast, various media outlets valorized the imagined sense of sincerity and traditionalism long associated with the Midwest, even if direct references to the region remained oblique. This peculiar and short-lived reaction spread through popular media, resulting in hyperbolic declarations of a new era in American culture within the initial days and weeks after 9/11. From high art to the lowbrow, commentators chimed in with predictions that the tone of American culture and its entertainments had undergone an irrevocable transformation. Such proclamations hinged on the elevation of a set of values that overlapped with those perceived as already present in the nation's most central states and, indeed, endemic to those often ignored spaces.

Graydon Carter, editor of *Vanity Fair* and cofounder of the satirical *Spy* magazine, provided perhaps the most cited example of these declarations when he stated, "It's the end of the age of irony. . . . Irony that is cynical and reactive and unserious and detached—I think all of those things will seem foolish and dated."[3] The September 24 issue of *Time* magazine found essayist Roger Rosenblatt similarly opining, "One possible good thing could come from this horror: it could spell the end of the age of irony," a period that the columnist claimed was marked by "detachment and personal whimsy."[4] Another of the most prompt reactions came from Tom Freston, the then-CEO of MTV Networks. In an interview published in the September 21 issue of *Newsweek*, Freston emphasized the importance of the "tone" of popular culture, particularly in relation to "this new reality" that supposedly had come about in the wake of 9/11.[5] Accordingly, the programming for MTV and VH1 temporarily was altered to reflect—or perhaps to support—this predicted turn away from the ironic by playing music videos from exceedingly "sincere" artists such as Bob Marley, Jeff Buckley, and Indiana-native John Mellencamp, a paragon of heartland rock.[6] Don DeLillo—whose December 2001 essay, "In the ruins of the future," marked him as a relative latecomer to this chorus—wrote, "This catastrophic event changes the way we think and act, moment to moment, week to week, for unknown weeks and months to come, and steely years."[7] Above all, these proclamations of change revolved around a belief that all Americans were about to embrace a new era of sincerity and serious-minded public discourse that previously had been lacking outside of isolated and culturally irrelevant sections of the country, such as the Midwest.

These prognostications proved to be little more than emotionally charged overreactions to the intense trauma of 9/11, and a backlash to the supposed death of irony began emerging almost as soon as it was declared. In an October 9 article in the *New York Times*, literary critic Michiko Kakutani reflected on the ways in which past traumas had produced artistic innovations. She wrote, "[t]he belief that the terrorist attacks of Sept. 11 will lead to kinder, gentler entertainment belies the historical record of reactions to earlier tragedies, wars and social upheavals . . . disturbing historical events have tended to elicit not PG-rated displays of inspirational good taste but darker works of art resonating with a culture's deepest fears and forebodings."[8] Regarding the then-current context, Kakutani observed, "As allied air attacks commenced on Afghanistan, and America braced for a possible second wave of terrorist attacks, it was often the fizzier, willfully light cultural offerings that seemed the most irrelevant."[9] On September 25—one day before a piece titled "The End of Irony" appeared in *Newsweek*—*Salon* published an article in which David Beers decried "a cheapened grade of irony" that had supplanted the authentic article in American discourse over the previous several decades.[10] Rather than a defanged concept of irony as "a handy shorthand for moral relativism and self-absorption, for consuming all that is puerile while considering oneself too hip to be implicated in the supply and demand economics of schlock," Beers hoped for a renewed sense of "engaged irony" to develop and then elevate cultural discourse.[11] For Beers, the supposed end of irony was an inherently fallacious claim not only because it was proffered in a moment of trauma, but because "over the past decade ironic farce has been largely consumed as a side dish to sentimental earnestness."[12] If both a coolly ironic disposition and an excessively sincere one were inadequate after 9/11 (and "engaged irony" required a precarious balancing act between the two poles), then how were Americans to determine an appropriate path forward?

Revisiting this short-lived debate nearly two decades later makes it quite clear that the weeks during the immediate aftermath of 9/11 were a period in which an upended nation sought to restore its equilibrium through self-definition. This critical reappraisal of the tone of American culture unearthed dormant conflicts about what constitutes the most authentic and ideal version of the United States. As the commentators on irony circled around questions of what American culture had been and should be, they actually were playing on longstanding estimations of geographically discrete segments of the population and bickering over which region was the most representative of the country. Seemingly for the sake of imagining post-traumatic cultural homogeneity within the United States, these media figures suggested that the nation could be *either* ironic *or* sincere, rather than recognizing that each category roughly corresponds to established associations with different but coexistent sections of the country. In short, the coasts have been framed as trendy and "ironic," while the middle of the country has been imagined as staid and "sincere." Somehow, the supposedly unifying and irony-ending terrorist attacks reactivated a heated discourse about regional hierarchy within the nation, yet voices on both sides of this debate spoke of regional character without precisely using such terminology.

The regional connotations of this cultural debate are strikingly close to the surface and mirror how the Midwest has been envisioned in the American consciousness. For instance, in a discussion of the middle region's historic function as a television market, Victoria Johnson writes, "While the midwestern audience is imagined to be 'low' in terms of taste and cultural sensibility, its 'averageness' is also periodically invoked in ideal terms—as reliably majoritarian, unswayed by fads, and, therefore, allied with stability, traditional values, and the smooth functioning of representative democracy."[13] Midwesterners are constructed as an oppositional category to what Johnson describes as coastal "hipsters" who "represent all that is bright, new, and modern in culture," but who "are also simultaneously criticized as inauthentic and conformist in their slavish attention to consumer trends—icons of misplaced energy and non-productive labor."[14] Clearly, such regional associations are reductive and essentializing, but as Johnson details, they persist in numerous contexts.

To recap, the irony/sincerity exchange began with several media figures predicting that nonironic, exceedingly sincere entertainments would and *should* provide the model for American popular culture post-9/11; a subsequent critique of "willfully light cultural offerings" and "sentimental earnestness" by writers such as Kakutani and Beers then reframed such mindsets as exemplifying precisely what the United States *should not* become: a reactionary culture that produces and consumes blandly positive, uncritical entertainment. The anti-ironists engage in a sort of self-flagellation that frames the terrorist attacks as punishment for their East Coast environs disowning "traditional" American ideals, while the opponents of this stance suggest that anti-irony is a regressive position that returns the United States to a past that it has outgrown or still needs to escape. DeLillo somewhat straddles these competing perspectives. While detailing a dichotomy between what he describes as the future-oriented America and the past-desiring terrorists, DeLillo bluntly declares, "The terrorists of September 11 want to bring back the past."[15] Upon surveying the irony/sincerity debate as a whole, it becomes clear that a preoccupation with space and temporality pervades the divergent perspectives of these commentators.

For my own purposes, the fear of restoring the past (as DeLillo articulates) is a key observation that surreptitiously interrogates the meaning of American regional spaces and cultures. These fears that the past will violently return and subsume the present reflect once again on tensions stemming from how American regions are perceived in relation to one another. For one brief moment, it appeared as though the maligned Midwest might serve as a model for the rest of the nation to emulate in order to cope with a forcibly transformed historical and cultural milieu. Instead, American popular culture generally picked up where it left off, with the facile and vapidly ironic entertainments decried by Rosenblatt and Freston quickly reasserting their resiliency. Meanwhile, the fleeting praise and near-immediate disregard for stereotypical aspects of Midwestern culture signaled the indefinite extension of an identity crisis that has defined the region since the middle of the twentieth century. From the anti-sincerity perspective, to embrace such Midwest-affiliated traits would indicate a regression of American culture to an unsophisticated state that it had outgrown.

Following the Midwest's brief elevation immediately after 9/11, the region soon resumed its slippage in popular estimation. After momentarily being considered as a stable foundation upon which the American populace could regroup from the terrorist attacks, the Midwest rapidly reacquired its status as culturally out-of-touch. Moreover, the sense of cross-regional unity remaining from the autumn of 2001 further dissipated in the wake of the decade's economic disasters, such as the subprime mortgage crisis and the ensuing recession. As these economic catastrophes unfolded in the latter part of the decade, regional antagonisms returned to the fore. Communities across the country became victims of financial malfeasance associated with the East Coast. The Midwest ultimately filled the symbolic role of the nation's helpless and suffering "Main Street"—as opposed to New York City's predatory "Wall Street"—in rhetoric repeated *ad infinitum* during the campaigns and debates of the 2008 and 2012 presidential elections.

Even before being impacted by the worldwide economic crises of the new millennium, the Midwest had been in a state of decay and uncertainty. While reflecting on economic changes to the middle region over the final decades of the twentieth century, journalist Richard Longworth asserts, "How we earn our living determines how we live and who we are. This is true for people, and it's true for towns, and regions, and countries. The Midwest does two big things for a living—farming and heavy industry—and globalization has turned both upside down."[16] Along with destabilizing developments such as the housing crisis, the general conditions outlined by Longworth conspire to force yet another reassessment and revision of the Midwest's identity as the twenty-first century progresses. *About Schmidt*, *Up in the Air*, and *Take Shelter* each express a fundamental sense of uncertainty regarding purpose, meaning, and identity within the Midwest. These three films interrogate the frayed connection between labor and identity through a trio of white, middle class, male protagonists. This privileged demographic has been celebrated and decried—Clint Eastwood's *Gran Torino* (2008) and the novels of Sinclair Lewis, respectively, are notable representatives of such poles on this spectrum—as exemplifying the Midwest's best and worst attributes.[17] In *About Schmidt*, *Up in the Air*, and *Take Shelter*, certain incarnations of white masculinity are presented as obsolete, which reflects upon the Midwest's overall status in the young millennium. Along with examining the impact of economic instability on the region's identity, then, each film also tacitly challenges the sustained predominance of white masculinity in understandings of the Midwest during a crucial turning point within American culture.

About Schmidt

The opening scene of *About Schmidt* shows insurance actuary Warren Schmidt (Jack Nicholson) sitting motionless in his office and stoically staring at the wall clock as it ticks off the remaining minutes before his retirement. Even anticipating the end of the workaday routine, it seems, is an act of labor for Warren. In the next scene, the solemn protagonist dutifully and joylessly endures a retirement party. While delivering a congratulatory speech at the gathering, Warren's best friend Ray Nichols (Len Cariou) drunkenly remarks:

> What means something, what really means something, Warren, is the knowledge that you devoted your life to something meaningful. To being productive and working for a fine company, hell, one of the top-rated insurance carriers in the nation. To raising a fine family, to building a fine home, to being respected by your community, to having wonderful, lasting relationships. At the end of his career, if a man can look back and say, "I did it, I did my job," then he can retire in glory and enjoy riches far beyond the monetary kind. So, all of you young people here, take a good look at a very rich man.

Ray's platitudes neatly encapsulate qualities that have long been associated with the Midwest, including: productivity and steadfastness in terms of work; property ownership; community engagement; the nuclear family as a stabilizing force; and abstract personal "riches" as a goal, rather than (solely) financial wealth. Warren has "achieved" everything on this list, yet he seems a defeated man when his office clock ticks around to five o'clock. As the film makes clear, once Warren is no longer a cog in a routinized daily existence, he loses his sense of self and purpose for living. Without employment as a distraction and a job title as a default identity, Warren quickly becomes aware of the emotional distance between himself and both his wife, Helen (June Squibb), and adult daughter, Jeannie (Hope Davis).

Warren's existential plight stands in for the Midwest as a whole. Like the protagonists of several other Midwestern films from this era (such as *Up in the Air* and *Gran Torino*), Warren perceives himself as having aged out of relevance. His personal crisis and accompanying search for meaning reflect how the Midwest's identity has been similarly unsettled in the late twentieth and early twenty-first centuries. Due, in part, to economic turmoil and changing cultural factors, the region's long decline undermined its traditional image as a site of dedicated labor and family life, as well as its standing as a locus of the most "sincere" components of American culture. This shift in the Midwest's meaning and popular identity is played out through the dramatic arc of *About Schmidt*'s troubled protagonist.

Director Alexander Payne has a career-long preoccupation with putting the daily foibles of Midwesterners onscreen. A native of Nebraska, Payne featured Omaha as the setting for each of his first three films—*Citizen Ruth* (1996), *Election* (1999), and *About Schmidt* (2002)—and he returned to his home state with *Nebraska* (2013).[18] Perhaps it is unsurprising, then, that many critics consider Payne to be a filmmaker marked by a distinctly Midwestern sensibility, as well as a complementary sense of empathy for his characters, however mundane their desires and trials might be. For instance, critic Scott Foundas describes Payne as a "humanist filmmaker" who is "a humble practitioner of smart, grown-up movies about ordinary men and women, their sizable failings and modest victories."[19] Regarding the director's first three features, Foundas writes that they present "a vision of flyover America rarely glimpsed in mainstream movies: Midwestern, middle-class (or lower) lives and the bulk groceries, strip malls, and economy cars that populate them, some of it played for laughs, but never at the expense of the characters' fundamental dignity."[20] Foundas further projects a sense of nondescript Midwestern-ness into the very form of Payne's filmography, which "benefits from a lack of ostentatious stylistic flourishes (except, as in the case of *Election*, when demanded by the material)."[21] Moreover, the film critic identifies regional qualities in Payne's personality and notes, "In person, the native Nebraskan gives off a disarming sense of the Midwestern parvenu still trying to prove himself worthy of the big city."[22] For Foundas, a sense of modesty, the generic, and even self-consciousness about being perceived as unsophisticated are Midwestern traits, and such qualities are evident in Payne's persona, the narratives of his films, and his stylistic techniques.

A. O. Scott of the *New York Times* offers a less reductive assessment of Payne and his films by situating the Nebraska filmmaker within a lineage of literary figures who emerged from the center of the nation to lob critiques back at their places of origin: namely, writers such as Sinclair Lewis and F. Scott Fitzgerald.[23] From Scott's perspective, the "simple change of geography and profession" that the Schmidt character undergoes while being adapted for the screen—in Louis Begley's 1996 source novel, Warren is a New York lawyer—has "a transformative effect" on the material.[24] Scott writes that Payne "has plucked the unsuspecting Schmidt out of one literary tradition and inserted him into another."[25] In this regard, the cinematic Schmidt "is the latest in a long line of sad, comical and heroic embodiments of the ordinary man that have, in loneliness, defeat and occasional glory, populated American novels, plays, movies and television shows for much of the past century."[26] As in Foundas's piece, Scott uses the term "ordinary" to denote Midwestern-ness, which is a revealing slippage that highlights the Midwest's symbolic function in American culture.[27] Again and again, what constitutes the average, common, or ordinary is equated with consumption habits, types of labor, and geographic location—the latter, more often than not, being somewhere within the twelve states of the Midwest.

Given that Payne's version of Schmidt is emblematic of recurring regional associations, *About Schmidt* should be recognized as a commentary on broader understandings of Midwestern identity at the start of the new millennium. Texts such as *Badlands* (1973) and *A History of Violence* (2005) present the Midwest's inhabitants as enacting an illusion of blandness and superficial "normality" through behaviors that reflect stereotypical images of the region.[28] In those films, such regional performances are intended to obscure a culture of dysfunction beneath the sedate surface. Although still present in *About Schmidt*, Warren's regional performativity is tragic rather than serving as a mask for deviant or violent tendencies. Throughout his seemingly unquestioned path through life, Warren has embodied Midwestern stereotypes and drifted into the generic "success" articulated in Ray's retirement speech. Upon retiring, however, Warren turns a critical eye to his personal life and finds it severely lacking. His wife, Helen, habitually irritates him, while his daughter, Jeannie, lives in Colorado and is engaged to Randall Hertzel (Dermot Mulroney), a waterbed salesman who proves susceptible to pyramid schemes. Even more demoralizing, Warren is rebuffed by his youthful replacement at Woodmen of the World Insurance Company. During an aborted return visit to the company, Warren discovers that his archive of work files has been unceremoniously deposited by the garbage. Following this disheartening scene, Helen abruptly dies from a blood clot, but Warren's grief turns to outrage when he discovers a shoebox full of love letters that expose a prior affair between Helen and his best friend Ray.[29] This revelation prompts Warren to embark on an introspective road trip in the Winnebago that Helen had demanded they purchase in anticipation of the married couple's retirement years.

While contending with this personal distress, Warren begins sponsoring Ndugu Umbo, a six-year-old boy in Tanzania, through an international charity organization. Along with monthly checks, Warren also sends letters about himself to Ndugu, which are heard in several voiceover sequences. These letters find Warren habitually revising his life's narrative. For instance, when first departing Omaha, Warren intended to visit Jeannie to help with wedding preparations in Denver, but she curtly rebuffed this offer. In a letter to Ndugu, though, Warren narrates, "Jeannie begged me to come out early and help her with arrangements, but I told her I needed some time to myself. I've decided to visit some places I haven't been to in a long time. So much has happened in my life that I can't seem to remember. Whole sections of my life that are just gone. So, you might say I've been trying to clear a few cobwebs from my memory." The first portion of this statement is one of several moments in which Warren offers a revisionist account of personal rejection. These instances highlight Warren's commitment to maintaining a dignified public exterior while internally absorbing various humiliations such as being rejected by his daughter or spurned by his replacement at Woodmen of the World. Considered through a regional prism, Warren's letters reflect upon ways in which idealized Midwestern narratives gloss over dysfunction and violence in the region.

Warren's purpose for his road trip—which involves visiting sites of personal significance—exemplifies a basic nostalgic undertaking: turning to the past in order to locate a lost sense of identity that is perceived as more authentic than that which exists in the degraded present. Given that Warren's trip is launched by concerns with personal history, identity, and memory, *About Schmidt* functions as another iteration of nostalgic spatiality. As the film progresses, Payne spatializes Warren's nostalgic memories by projecting such past recollections onto physical sites that are revisited during the road trip.[30] To varying degrees, Warren's sequence of stops also produces associations between his personal history and that of the Midwest in general. Beyond the levels of character and narrative,

Warren's road trip may be understood as a parodic replication of the western movement by Turner's valorized frontier pioneers. Payne establishes several ironic juxtapositions between Warren's good-natured curiosity about the Midwest and his obliviousness to the long-lasting repercussions of the United States' western expansion on both Native Americans and the physical terrain itself.

This nostalgic tour of the past—and *into* the past, as it were—brings Warren to the following locales: Holdrege, Nebraska, to see the site of his childhood home; Lawrence, Kansas, to visit his alma mater and former fraternity house; the Custer County Historical Museum in Broken Bow, Nebraska, "to see their fine collection of arrowheads"; and the Buffalo Bill State Historical Park in North Platte, Nebraska. While in Broken Bow, Warren informs Ndugu that he "happened to meet a real Indian or Native American as they like to be called nowadays. We had a nice chat about the history of the area, and he really opened my eyes. Those people got a raw deal, just a raw deal." Warren's acknowledgment of Native American trauma immediately is followed by a trip to the home of Buffalo Bill Cody, who Warren blithely describes as "a remarkable man."

In Holdrege, Warren discovers that his childhood home has been replaced with a tire shop. Despite this spatial transformation, Warren still enters the shop and informs the befuddled attendant, "I used to live here.... My childhood home was right on this spot. In fact, the bedroom would have been right about here, the living room over here, and the dining ... well, that was a long time ago. Before you were born." While speaking, Warren's gestures demarcate the spatial layout of his vanished childhood home within the present-day space of the tire store. At this moment in the film, Warren's nostalgic reminiscing at a site of personal significance begins to collapse barriers between past and present. Payne accentuates this temporal overlap with nondiegetic sounds from Warren's childhood that intrude onto the soundtrack, such as his deceased mother's voice and birthday wishes from a long-past celebration. Tellingly, this moment is one of only a few throughout the film in which Warren's visage relaxes and he seems to be at ease. Simply visiting a nostalgic space, however momentarily, permits Warren to access a time in which his identity was not so muddled.

As *About Schmidt* continues, an awkward encounter with a similarly aged married couple in an RV park unsettles Warren's superficial positivity. He subsequently attempts to stop concealing his disappointment and desires behind revisionist narratives and to renounce the nostalgia that prompted his road trip. In short order, Warren calls Ray in an effort to make amends, apologizes to Helen for being a poor husband during a solitary vigil, and arrives in Denver with the intention of convincing Jeannie to call off her wedding. When Jeannie resists Warren's pleadings, however, he again is reduced to submerging his true desires beneath blandly positive statements, as is evident by a perfunctory wedding toast in which Warren praises his new (and strongly disliked) in-laws. Deflated and defeated, Warren's trip back to Omaha features only a single stop, but one of great significance: the pioneer museum in Kearney, Nebraska. Warren tours the facility, and Payne includes a close-up of a plaque that reads: "THE COWARDS NEVER STARTED/THE WEAK DIED ON THE WAY/ONLY THE STRONG

ARRIVED/THEY WERE THE PIONEERS."[31] The supposedly divine imperative of manifest destiny contrasts sharply with Warren's nostalgia trip through sites of personal history. Moreover, this brief scene reminds viewers that the pioneers' heavily mythologized journey westward continues to inform perceptions of the millennial Midwest.

Turner believed that the effect of frontier closure was cultural stagnation. Following this declaration, Turner situated the Midwest as a space of nostalgia because of its former status as a frontier space in which the *potential* for additional frontiers appeared to be nearly limitless. Hence, this nostalgic vision of the Midwest hinges on a conceptualization of the region as a space in which lost potentialities are visible and possibly accessible. Warren's quest for meaning dovetails with Turner's version of the Midwest in the sense that Warren is nostalgic for a distant past in which numerous potential futures appeared to be available: the youthful period before his identity was fixed in accordance with standardized (and stereotypically Midwestern) forms of family, labor, and masculinity. The ultimate purpose of Warren's road trip thus is to access a forgotten version of himself that contains the potential for alternate life trajectories. Instead of the widespread "perennial rebirth" of "American social development" that Turner describes as the outcome of successive frontier spaces, Warren seeks a more individualized nostalgic rediscovery—and rebirth—of himself.[32] With no vast spatial frontiers available for exploration, Warren's journey is a temporal one—a nostalgic trip inward to access who he once was and, more importantly, who he *might* have been.

After Warren endures numerous failures and indignities over the course of the film, the conclusion of *About Schmidt* finds the protagonist narrating a despairing letter to Ndugu. Unlike the earlier revisionist personal narratives, Warren harshly assesses his life in comparison to the pioneer museum in Kearney:

> Looking at all that history and reflecting on the achievements of people long ago kind of put things into perspective. My trip to Denver, for instance, is so insignificant compared to the journeys that others have taken, the bravery that they've shown, the hardships they've endured. I know we're all pretty small in the big scheme of things. And I suppose the most you can hope for is to make some kind of difference. But, what kind of difference have I made? What in the world is better because of me? [...] I am weak, and I am a failure. There's just no getting around it. Relatively soon, I will die. Maybe in twenty years, maybe tomorrow. It doesn't matter. Once I am dead and everyone who knew me dies too, it'll be as though I never even existed. What difference has my life made to anyone? None that I can think of. None at all.

Throughout the film, Warren becomes more and more cognizant of the fact that his previously unquestioned adherence to Midwestern ideals has resulted in an incomplete identity, and he fixates on missed opportunities to be anything other than the disillusioned figure he now is. What had been the twin pillars of Warren's identity—labor and family—are revealed to be either meaningless or fractured beyond repair. His attempts to nostalgically cling to the past prove unsustainable. With *About Schmidt*, Payne shows that revising the qualities defining the Midwest and its inhabitants is a necessity for the region to not just persist, but to forge a sustainable, more open identity in the new millennium.

Following Warren's gloomy musings to Ndugu, *About Schmidt* ends with a scene that disrupts his personal despair and that also, in a somewhat indirect manner, depicts a possible point of departure from the Midwest's nostalgia-induced malaise. Upon returning home, Warren receives a letter from the nun who is Ndugu's caretaker; she writes that Ndugu wishes Warren happiness and encloses a painting that the boy made, which moves Warren to tears. Until this moment, Warren's correspondence flowed in a single direction, as if the attachment of charity funds entitled him to having Ndugu as a captive audience for his epistolary laments. That said, simply drafting those letters provided Warren with greater clarity about the factors informing his own identity and that of the culture surrounding him. Even with some degree of revisionist narration, Warren articulates his desires and fears more honestly in each letter than in any face-to-face encounter with a fellow Midwesterner. Personal disclosures result in a self-critique that expands into a broader commentary on the Midwest as a whole.

By evaluating his experiences in the letters to Ndugu, Warren comes to recognize the sociocultural conditions that have shaped and restricted the trajectory of his life. This new state of self-awareness is coupled with Warren's expanded, albeit still quite tenuous and incomplete, knowledge of regional history gleaned from his road trip. With these developments, Payne suggests that the limitations created by idealized Midwestern narratives might be circumvented by an altered perspective on the region and its relationship to other spaces. Such a revised understanding of self and place exemplifies Douglas Reichert Powell's concept of "critical regionalism." Along with various other practices, Reichert Powell describes critical regionalism as "a way inhabitants of a place . . . could create visions of their homes, at their best, freed of the limitations of our damagingly nostalgic or abject cultural vocabulary for life on the American geographical margin . . . critical regionalism is about constructing . . . a present out of which could project a better future."[33] *About Schmidt* demonstrates that a shift from embracing regional mythology to understanding actual history—along with an accompanying shift from the insularity and myopia of provincialism to a more extra-regional perspective—may begin to reactivate the seemingly lost potentialities of individual Midwesterners and the region as a whole. Certainly, this future-oriented repositioning would necessitate actions beyond a retired white male financially sponsoring an impoverished African youth while simultaneously exploiting that relationship as an outlet to vent about existential problems. Still, the conclusion of *About Schmidt* indicates that an opening up and evolution of Midwestern culture is achievable. Through Warren's greater degree of critical self-awareness, he comes to recognize the conditioned nature of Midwestern identities. In turn, this revelation undermines conceptions of the Midwest as the site of "ordinary," "average," or "authentic" Americans. Such dynamics are further developed in *Up in the Air*, which also depicts crumbling Midwestern mythologies and identities.

Up in the Air

The Midwestern norms that Warren eventually perceives as having restricted his life are the very same ones against which middle-aged Ryan Bingham (George Clooney) rebels throughout much of *Up in the Air*. Such resistance is made explicit during Ryan's motivational lectures about how to attain professional success. In these presentations—titled "What's In Your Backpack?"—Ryan uses an overstuffed backpack as a strained metaphor for the various personal attachments and obligations that limit aspiring businesspeople. After detailing a litany of commitments, Ryan concludes, "We weigh ourselves down until we can't even move. And make no mistake, moving is living." During a subsequent presentation, Ryan adds, "Make no mistake, your relationships are the heaviest components in your life. . . . All those negotiations and arguments and secrets and compromises. You don't need to carry all that weight. . . . The slower we move, the faster we die." In these two scenes, Ryan articulates his guiding philosophy about life, which revolves around solitary routines: traveling for his job as much as possible and avoiding romantic commitments in favor of casual encounters. As with Warren in *About Schmidt*, Ryan builds his identity in relation to stereotypical Midwestern norms, but in *Up in the Air*, Ryan actively combats the constraints of such cultural pressures.

Along with Ryan's resistance to stereotypical Midwestern ideals of labor and family, *Up in the Air* also addresses the region's uncertain identity in the face of the twenty-first century's economic crises.[34] Ryan works as a job "transition specialist" for an Omaha-based firm that other companies hire to conduct mass firings, typically in Midwestern cities. In fact, director/co-screenwriter Jason Reitman only includes scenes of people being fired in St. Louis, Wichita, Kansas City, Des Moines, Detroit, and Tulsa.[35] Troublingly, Ryan and his coworkers profit from the failure of the region around them. As Ryan's supervisor Craig Gregory (Jason Bateman) observes, "Retailers are down 20%. Auto industry is in the dump. Housing market doesn't have a heartbeat. It is one of the worst times on record for America. This is our moment." For much of *Up in the Air*, Ryan maintains a willfully disconnected attitude toward these circumstances; by the end of the film, though, the firing consultant and part-time motivational speaker is left in a state of self-doubt and uncertainty regarding his own future. Through a dual focus on historical context and the narrative arcs of its primary characters—particularly Ryan—*Up in the Air* interrogates how ideals about labor, gender, and family shape both individual and regional constructions of identity.

Like many other protagonists of Midwestern narratives, Ryan links his identity to the work that he performs and the places that he occupies. Rather than a singular locale, Ryan identifies with the transient spaces of hotel rooms and airport terminals. These attachments are disrupted when twenty-something Natalie Keener (Anna Kendrick), a new coworker at Ryan's company, designs a method of firing people that would replace in-person interactions with communication through computer interfaces. Ryan is apoplectic about Natalie's proposal for two reasons. First, firing people via computers would ground Ryan in Omaha, which he avoids as much as possible in order to sustain his detached lifestyle.[36] Second, Ryan believes in the importance of physical proximity for business dealings and is committed to what he frames as the compassionate decorum of in-person firings. At one point, Ryan explains this philosophy to his supervisor Craig: "What we do here is brutal, and it does leave people devastated, but there is a dignity to the way I do it." By virtue of these apparently outdated work preferences, *Up in the Air* establishes Ryan as something of a contradictory figure. In short, the habitual avoidance of personal attachments contrasts with Ryan's advocacy for intimate human contact when conducting business. Further, Ryan's stated philosophy of detachment masks the fact that some of his fundamental personal principles are very much in line with traditional notions of Midwestern sociality. For instance, even though Ryan claims that he does not "see the value" in getting married or having kids, he still acknowledges the importance of physical proximity to others, especially at times of distress. This devotion to supposedly more dignified face-to-face meetings relates to the localized, place-bound community dynamics in other cinematic depictions of the Midwest around the turn of the twenty-first century. Texts such as *Boys Don't Cry* (1999) and *A History of Violence* imagine the millennial Midwest as a space that remains dependent on geographic proximity for building communities and individual identities.[37] In *Up in the Air*, the impending suspension of constant travel sparks a crisis for Ryan and forces him to reassess the Midwestern identity traits that he has long rejected.

Once Ryan's detached lifestyle is disrupted, he is unable to sustain his contrarian stance toward stereotypical Midwestern norms. This shift begins while traveling with Natalie, who serves as a catalyst for undermining Ryan's identity. Following Natalie's presentation for the new online firing system, Ryan insists that she needs to gain in-person firing experience; supervisor Craig complies and sends them off together like an ersatz odd couple that specializes in downsizing. Their travels take them on a tour of financially ruined Midwestern companies, and Reitman depicts several offices in such states of disarray that they recall sets from post-apocalyptic horror films (see fig. 5.1). Throughout this section of the film, Natalie continually challenges Ryan's disconnection from others, including his casual relationship with Alex Goran (Vera Farmiga), who seems to be a similarly detached business traveler.[38] During one especially contentious exchange, Natalie angrily accuses Ryan of depriving Alex of "[a] chance at something real," which prompts Ryan to respond, "Natalie, your definition of real is going to evolve as you get older." Undeterred, Natalie continues, "You have set up a way of life that basically makes it impossible for you to have any kind of human connection. And now this woman comes along and somehow runs the gauntlet of your ridiculous life choice and comes out on the other end smiling just so you can call her 'casual'?" Essentially, Natalie encourages conformity (and herself yearns to conform) to relationship models often associated with Midwestern culture.

Fig. 5.1. Desolate office spaces used as evocative symbols of economic devastation. Screen captures, *Up in the Air* (2009).

Natalie's critique of Ryan highlights three elements intrinsic to her conception of proper relationships. First, Natalie believes that relationships must be developed strategically in order to satisfy a very precise set of ideals. Earlier in the film, Natalie discusses her ex-boyfriend and how she "could have made it work. He, um, he really fit the bill." Natalie proceeds to describe various qualities that she desires in a male partner and acknowledges that because the ex-boyfriend satisfied many of the items on the list, she could have convinced herself that she loved him. In other words, Natalie would have worked to make the relationship outwardly *appear* successful, regardless of her actual emotional attachment (or lack thereof).

Second, Natalie's view of relationships as labor is further emphasized through her imagined perfect partner, who is a composite of conventional ideals relating to masculinity, socioeconomic status, and consumption practices. Natalie details her preferences: "White-collar, college grad, loves dogs, likes funny movies, 6'1", brown hair, kind eyes, works in finance, but is outdoorsy, you know, on the weekends. I always imagined he'd have a single syllable name like Matt or John or Dave. In a perfect world, he drives a 4Runner. And the only thing he loves more than me is his golden lab. And a nice smile." Although the Midwest traditionally has been linked to blue-collar labor in heavy industry or farming, nondescript white-collar jobs—the sort of positions that are being outsourced throughout *Up in the Air*—also serve as a default image for labor in the region's urban and suburban spaces. On the whole, Natalie's list of desired qualities in a partner reads like a portrait of the generic, an image of masculinity gleaned from a department store clothing catalogue. Rather than Natalie developing personalized criteria for contentment, this list indicates that she is reproducing standardized desires. Furthermore, her preferred masculine type is something of a contemporary substitute for the Midwest's mythic past. Although the white-collar Midwestern labor presented in *Up in the Air* is greatly removed from the ruggedness of Turner's valorized pioneers, Natalie's ideal male would partially embody that archetype by being "outdoorsy" during leisure time and driving a sport utility vehicle. Given that Natalie wishes to have a conformist lifestyle, her hypothetical partner would also be a performative subject who enacts an unmemorable version of regional masculinity whenever possible.

The third element is Natalie's resolute belief that all other women share the same generic desires that she possesses. Although Alex has been happily engaging in a "casual" relationship with Ryan, Natalie presumes that Alex actually seeks a commitment from the determined bachelor. This assumption is proven to be erroneous late in the film when Ryan surprises Alex at her home in Chicago. Upon opening the front door, Alex frowns, children run around in the background, and her off-screen husband asks who rang the doorbell. To this point, Alex has not divulged any information about having a family. Not only is the revelation immensely shocking for Ryan, it also severely undercuts Natalie's assumption about shared desires among Midwestern women. Because Alex already has a family, her affair with Ryan truly is only casual and was not initiated with intent to develop an emotional commitment. In fact, that lack of attachment was precisely what made Ryan so appealing to Alex. During a phone conversation the next day, Alex chides Ryan about his presumptuousness and states that he "could have seriously screwed things up for me. That's my family. That's my real life." Alex elaborates, "I thought our relationship was perfectly clear. I mean, you are an escape. You're a break from our normal lives. You're a parenthesis."

This brief sequence injects complexity into *Up in the Air*'s treatment of sexuality and family formations within the Midwest. Alex's accusation that Ryan almost "screwed things up" creates some ambiguity about the nature of her marriage. Certainly, Alex simply may have been deceiving her husband; it is possible, though, that the pair permits extramarital liaisons, so long as those partners do not intrude upon the domestic home space. More importantly, even as Alex is revealed to have been balancing a family life with a casual sexual affair, she demonstrates a commitment to values that are similar to those held by Natalie. Alex's identification of her family as her "real life" echoes Natalie chastising Ryan about coldly foreclosing a "chance at something real" with Alex. As expressed by Natalie and Alex, to be "real" involves conforming to regional stereotypes—particularly "traditional" family formations. This conception of a Midwestern "real" excludes Ryan, who resists such lifestyle choices for most of the film's duration. Although *Up in the Air* sometimes gestures toward redefining stereotypes about gender, sexuality, and relationships in the Midwest—for instance, in addition to Ryan's devotion to being single, Alex states that she has had relationships with women—the film ultimately reasserts that the middle region is a heteronormative space.

In conjunction with the narrative elements detailed above, a fascinating temporal dynamic emerges in *Up in the Air*: deviance from stereotypical regional norms is framed as being outside of time. For instance, Alex labels Ryan as "a parenthesis" in relation to her "normal" life. Joseph Natoli similarly writes that Ryan "lives a life of 'outplacement': he has consciously placed himself outside the normal itinerary of life, preferring a constantly changing itinerary that puts him more up in the air than on the ground."[39] To expand upon Natoli's observation, Ryan's interstitial status is a result of more than mere divergence from standardized lifestyle norms—he is presented as being temporally out of sync with his fellow Midwesterners. Over the course of the film, this parenthetical condition produces nostalgic longing.

The destabilizing encounter at Alex's doorstep is the end result of Ryan gradually warming to the stereotypical Midwestern lifestyles he had habitually rejected. Of particular note is the way in which this transformation is an outcome of nostalgic spatiality. Immediately following an emotionally charged set of job reductions in Detroit with Natalie, Ryan invites Alex to his sister Julie's (Melanie Lynsky) wedding in Wisconsin. Ryan explains, "Look, I'm not the wedding type, right? But for the first time in my life, I don't want to be that guy alone at a bar. I want a dance partner, I want a 'plus one.'" Initially appearing horrified, Alex reluctantly consents to joining Ryan on what becomes a nostalgic trip similar to that of Warren in *About Schmidt*. In both films, each protagonist's personal history is spatialized across physical sites that house forgotten or misremembered fragments of identity. In Ryan's case, visiting his hometown in Wisconsin alters his personal alignment to the Midwest. Both the context of the visit—that of a family wedding—and the space itself activate Ryan's repressed affinity for "traditional" Midwestern values and lifestyles. At one point, Ryan's older sister Kara (Amy Morton) even enlists him to chat with Julie's fiancé Jim (Danny McBride), who has cold feet about the wedding. In a near-complete reversal of the "backpack" lectures, Ryan observes that individuals are never alone during their "favorite memories" or "most important moments" in life. He concludes, "Life's better with company." After years of extolling the benefits of nonconformity, Ryan's nostalgic return home—an individualized experience of nostalgic spatiality—results in an endorsement of generic platitudes. Ryan now appears to have convinced himself of the appeal of long-term partnerships, which he previously had dismissed.

Prior to visiting his Midwestern hometown, Ryan's identity revolved around his detached lifestyle. After this trip to Wisconsin, he becomes a nostalgic subject who suddenly desires a stable relationship and family life. With the adoption of Natalie's online firing technology, Ryan is forced to live in Omaha when they return from touring the region. Although Ryan has not been fired, he has lost the ability to identify with the labor that he performs; technological changes have seemingly made his preferred in-person interactions obsolete, thereby rendering Ryan himself as outmoded and adrift. This professional upheaval prompts Ryan's attempt to transition the casual relationship with Alex into one that is more committed. From bringing Alex to a wedding to Ryan's "romantic" surprise of appearing unannounced at her doorstep, it is clear that Ryan fully desires to have a monogamous relationship around which he might reconstruct his identity. Ironically, once Ryan embraces the values that he hitherto believed were unnatural constructions, he discovers that they actually might be hollow and performative, as he suspected. By the end of the film, Ryan is unable either to sustain his longtime resistance to normalized Midwestern lifestyles or to satisfy his newfound desire for such circumstances.[40]

In the aftermath of Ryan's disillusionment, rebelling against Midwestern cultural norms seems as meaningless as embracing them. This realization exacerbates Ryan's personal crisis and produces a deeper, more complex nostalgic desire: to return to the moment before his identity was transformed, to a time when conventional lifestyles appeared to be substantive and worth resisting (at least from Ryan's perspective). Like the Stall family at the conclusion of *A History of Violence*, Ryan is left with the recognition that the Midwest's popular identity is propped up by performative behavior that obscures disorder beneath the surface. As Natalie describes, to embody such ideals entails a commitment to "making it work" by embracing superficial signs of conventionality. Without a belief that such normative surfaces are "real" (and not merely the visible products of subjects performing regional stereotypes), Ryan now has no foundation upon which—or against which—he might build an identity.

Following Ryan's newly upended sense of self, he is immediately sent back out on the road as a traveling career transition specialist, due to the failure of Natalie's online firing system. In the final scene of *Up in the Air*, Ryan enters an airport terminal and stares at the departure listing with an ambiguous expression on his face. Although this moment could be viewed as Ryan finally traveling for pleasure by embarking on a personal trip, I read the scene as a reaffirmation of his ambivalence about being forced to continue enacting his contrarian bachelor lifestyle. The norms that Ryan resisted and then embraced have been punctured. Once a self-mythologizing rebel, Ryan is reduced to merely performing the part of a rebellious figure while nostalgically yearning for the recent past in which that role brought contentment. Like Warren, he desires to no longer be nostalgic. Following the portrayals of destabilized identities and regional decline in *About*

Schmidt and *Up in the Air*, a complementary yet unique perspective on the Midwest emerges through *Take Shelter*. In this latter film, personal dissatisfaction results in paranoia and suspicion, rather than the gentler, more introspective disillusionment of Warren and Ryan.

Take Shelter

The protagonists of *About Schmidt* and *Up in the Air* both desire identities outside of those commonly designated as default options for Midwesterners, but the two men find themselves stymied and frustrated, regardless of whether they attempt to conform or revolt. By contrast, writer/director Jeff Nichols's *Take Shelter* features a protagonist who is paranoid that his Midwestern status quo is being threatened by an indeterminate "something." Curtis LaForche (Michael Shannon) is a white, middle-class Midwesterner—the group long elevated as "authentically" American across a century's worth of cultural texts—who experiences delusions of impending apocalyptic doom. Across a series of recurring dreams and visions, such fears manifest as a foreboding storm and shadowy human figures, among other imagery. In the twenty-first century, the Midwest's stature rapidly devolved from that of a comfortingly nonironic American space in the wake of 9/11 to a hopeless victim of economic decline, Wall Street malfeasance, and cultural irrelevancy by the end of the decade. Within this context, Curtis becomes fanatical about issues of home security and goes to extreme lengths in order to alleviate his reactionary fears. Faced with an unstable identity in the new millennium, Curtis engages in a disturbing nostalgic turn to the mythic past by working to prepare his family to be self-sustaining survivalists; in certain ways, achieving this goal necessitates embodying Turner's frontier archetypes of rugged individuals and isolated families.

Take Shelter is set in a small Ohio town, where middle-aged construction worker Curtis has nightmares and waking hallucinations about an apocalyptic storm that rains a strange brownish liquid. Throughout the film, Nichols cuts to these dream/fantasy sequences without clearly indicating that they are subjective images from Curtis's mind. Such seamless transitions imbue the Midwestern setting with a sense of uncertainty and menace. As Curtis's visions become more and more horrific—at different moments, he is attacked by the family dog, anonymous, shadowy figures assault him, the family's living room briefly loses gravity, and even wife Samantha (Jessica Chastain) transforms into a threatening figure—he begins expanding and fortifying a storm shelter in the family's backyard. This increasingly erratic behavior creates tension between Curtis and Samantha, especially after she discovers that he has secretly taken a "risky" home improvement loan from the bank to fund purchases for the shelter. Curtis is fired from his job for borrowing heavy machinery without permission (for use in the construction of the shelter), and the subsequent loss of insurance coverage jeopardizes Samantha's efforts to procure a corrective surgery for their deaf daughter Hannah (Tova Stewart). With these plot points—possibly losing the family home, a lack of employment, and uncertainty about insurance coverage—Nichols links the narrative drama of Curtis's growing paranoia to the daily economic struggles of twenty-first-century Midwestern families.

Following the onset of the troubling dreams and visions, Curtis questions his own sanity, and it is revealed that his mother had been diagnosed with paranoid schizophrenia while also in her thirties. Still, this self-doubt does not deter Curtis from compulsively completing the shelter and stockpiling survival supplies, such as canned food and gasmasks. When a strong storm strikes the Ohio town, Curtis herds Samantha and Hannah into the shelter. The next morning, Curtis is fearful and reluctant to leave the shelter; upon exiting, he discovers clear skies and minimal damage from the storm. A brief scene depicts Curtis and Samantha visiting a psychiatrist (Jeffrey Grover), who suggests that taking a trip would have a therapeutic benefit by providing physical and emotional distance from the storm shelter—the symbol of Curtis's paranoia. Nichols then cuts to Curtis and Hannah making sand castles on a desolate stretch of Myrtle Beach, where all three members of the LaForche family observe the apocalyptic storm from Curtis's dreams as it approaches from the sea. The brownish rain from Curtis's earlier visions begins to fall, and Samantha acknowledges to Curtis that she sees the storm with a solemn nod. In a medium shot, the LaForche family gazes off-screen toward the storm, and the film concludes with a flash of lightning and a roll of thunder as the screen fades to black.

To a large degree, the ideological slant of the entire film hinges on this intentionally ambiguous final scene.[41] At least three interpretations appear plausible. First, it is possible—and perhaps even likely—that this final scene is another vision. Throughout *Take Shelter*, Curtis's visions are presented in an objective manner; that is, Nichols does not use stylistic flourishes to denote a subjective point-of-view, aside from the strange phenomena onscreen. Because of this objective presentation of the visions, many scenes take a few moments before they are revealed to be "reality," dreams, or hallucinations. There are even instances in which it is unclear if Curtis is hallucinating or not, such as when he pulls over to gaze at an electrical storm on the horizon. Samantha and Hannah sleep in the backseat of the family's car, other vehicles are visible on the highway in the background of the shot, and Curtis wonders aloud, "Is anyone seeing this?" Curtis's question remains unanswered—aside from, of course, the film's audience also seeing what Curtis perceives.

The final scene exudes a similar uncertainty, partly because of an abrupt shift in locale after a period of uncertain duration. To this point, the narrative had unfolded solely within its small town setting in Ohio, and the film's chronology appeared to depict each passing day without large jumps forward in time. For the final scene, though, an elliptical edit transfers the LaForche family from Ohio to Myrtle Beach without providing a clear sense of how much time has passed between leaving the psychiatrist's office and arriving at the beach house. As such, this scene is set apart from the temporal and spatial rhythms of the rest of the film. Additionally, *Take Shelter* begins by depicting one of Curtis's dreams, and ending in a similar fashion would provide symmetrical bookends for the narrative. Such an interpretation would potentially indicate that Curtis actually does suffer from some form of mental illness. If this were the case, then the film is more apolitical, since it merely details the struggles of one man contending with the onset of a psychological disorder. Understanding the final sequence exclusively as Curtis's dream or hallucination means that the threatening storm relates primarily to characterization rather than being a symbol with cultural and historical resonances.

A second possibility is that the final storm is an actual occurrence and that all of Curtis's prior dreams and hallucinations were premonitions about this apocalyptic threat of mass destruction. If the storm is "real" within the diegetic world of the narrative, then *Take Shelter* is opened up to broader possible meanings than if it is merely a delusion caused by mental illness. Nick Bradshaw notes that Nichols "began writing [*Take Shelter*] in the summer of 2008—when America was first fixing for the possibility of economic breakdown (to say nothing of manmade climate chaos)."[42] Regarding environmental issues, the onscreen visualization of the storm itself echoes and predicts numerous extreme weather events that occurred across the United States in the twenty-first century, including Hurricane Katrina and Hurricane Sandy, major floods in the South and the Midwest, lengthy droughts in the West, and massive tornadoes that ravaged Midwestern communities such as Joplin, Missouri. Regarding economics, the issue of financial security informs much of *Take Shelter*'s multifaceted exploration of dread in straightforward and more understated ways. Obviously, Nichols's script emphasizes the LaForche family's struggles to maintain gainful employment and insurance coverage, but Bradshaw also calls attention to less overt moments in the film. While discussing the scene in which Curtis wonders if anyone else is seeing a storm in the distance beyond the highway, Bradshaw writes that "it's a question that resonates with the less represented crises of money and morale that isolate struggling people throughout the capitalist world."[43] In this context, the storm could be taken as an abstract symbol of the economic turmoil that threatens Midwesterners not only on the level of personal finances, but also in relation to individual and regional identity formation—which, as suggested by *About Schmidt* and *Up in the Air*, is often attached to labor and family.

Curtis seriously jeopardizes his family's economic security in order to alleviate anxieties relating to perceived—but unsubstantiated—threats. Both the bank loan and Curtis's unapproved use of work equipment introduce risk into what would otherwise be stable elements for the LaForche family: their living space and a steady income that includes a comprehensive insurance policy. Curtis thus sacrifices financial security for the mental security provided by the storm shelter. This substitution demonstrates his valuation of symbolic gestures over pragmatic considerations. It is not enough for Curtis to financially provide for his family; instead, he must assume an antiquated protector role. Like an updated version of Turner's mythical frontier pioneer figure, Curtis uses his physical labor to carve out a secure space for his family within a harsh, threatening environment. By fortifying the storm shelter, Curtis gains an immediate sense of purpose, and, similar to *Gran Torino*, his behavior indicates a desire to return to frontier survival conditions within the twenty-first-century Midwest.

Such a willful regression to past regional archetypes leads to another possible reading of the film's concluding scene.

A third interpretation of the final storm is that the entire LaForche family now is suffering from the delusions that plagued Curtis throughout the narrative. This possibility recognizes the storm as a subjective vision and is contingent on Curtis infecting the family with his own obsessive paranoia. On the film's commentary track, Nichols states, "I'll say this—and I say it in every interview—but, for me, the most important thing about the end of this film is that shot . . . that look between [Curtis and Samantha]. That, to me, is the true resolution in the film, and what happens after that, beyond that, I leave open to interpretation."[44] The "look" referenced by Nichols occurs when Curtis and Samantha meet one another's gaze, and she clearly affirms seeing the apocalyptic storm that only Curtis had perceived prior to this point in the film. Despite Samantha's seemingly straightforward acknowledgement, this onscreen exchange is clouded in ambiguity due to the uncertain status of the scene as dreamscape or diegetic reality. If it is another vision, then Curtis's unconscious mind is merely inventing familial support for his paranoid fears; even if the entire family perceives the storm, the question still remains as to whether it actually is or is not present. The potential exists that the LaForche family is at Myrtle Beach, but experiencing a shared hallucination.

If Samantha and Hannah eventually witness Curtis's visions, then the implication is that his paranoia is contagious. Certainly, Curtis's behavior appears to be erratic and irrational for much of the film. When attempting to describe his frightening visions, Curtis babbles about an imprecise "something" that is rapidly approaching and will produce widespread destruction. Midway through the film, Curtis has a seizure in bed, which prompts him to tell Samantha about his visions. Curtis explains,

> I've been having these dreams. I guess they're more like nightmares. It's why I've been acting like this. They, um, they always start with a kind of storm. Like a real powerful storm. And there's always this, uh, this dark, thick rain, like, like fresh motor oil. And then the things, people, it just makes them crazy. They attack me. . . . It's, it's, it's hard to explain because it's not just a dream. It's a feeling. I'm afraid something might be coming. Something that's not right. I cannot describe it. I just need you to believe me.

During a later scene, Curtis angrily erupts at a community social and warns, "There is a storm coming like nothing you have ever seen! And not a one of you is prepared for it!" (See fig. 5.2.) In both of these moments, Curtis is unable to articulate precisely what the storm is, beyond the fact that it is a portentous harbinger of "something." In an oblique manner, *Take Shelter* thus interrogates the elevation of instinct, belief, and speculation over fact that has marked twenty-first-century American culture. Significantly, the film's nonspecific threat is imagined as a disruption of the middle-class lifestyle enjoyed by the LaForche family.

Curtis's paranoia somewhat aligns him with *Gran Torino*'s Walt Kowalski (Clint Eastwood), who believes that the "old school" ideals he embodies—those

Fig. 5.2. An enraged Curtis flips a table at the community social. Screen capture, *Take Shelter* (2011).

relating to masculinity, labor, race, and family dynamics—are threatened by the mere presence of ethnically diverse inhabitants in his formerly homogeneous neighborhood. In *Take Shelter*, Curtis's life is thrown into disarray by simply imagining (or predicting) the arrival of a disruptive force. Much as *Gran Torino* posits an ongoing cultural and economic assault on "white" America—one that, importantly, creates the impetus for a white savior figure to intervene—so too does Curtis envision a vague "something" that necessitates the utilization of his masculine protectionist abilities in the twenty-first century. *Take Shelter*'s impending storm could symbolize a variety of anxieties within the millennial Midwest, including those related to employment, health, economics, environmental issues, and home security. Regardless of the possible interpretations of the mysterious storm and the other visions, a powerful sense of paranoia causes Curtis to embrace a contemporary version of a frontier survivalist mentality with a particular emphasis on self-sufficiency and isolation.

As is evident by these three possible readings of *Take Shelter*'s final scene, the ideology of the film is quite debatable. Depending on the interpretation, *Take Shelter* could be understood as generally apolitical, as a progressive-minded warning about the repercussions of the global economy on middle class families and the dangers of environmental irresponsibility, or as a paranoid, reactionary, and conservative fable about an imprecise "something" threatening the region's traditional identity as a white, heteronormative space. Due to Nichols's intentional ambiguity, it is difficult to determine which, if any, of the above interpretations is most appropriate. Mirroring the variable ways in which the Midwest itself has been and continues to be understood, *Take Shelter* permits viewers to extract whichever meanings they choose from the film. Such is the nature of the millennial Midwest, as its popular identity is malleable enough to support a number of conflicting positions; mere belief in a particular incarnation of the Midwest is seemingly all that is required to appropriate regional images and narratives for purposes across the political and ideological spectrum in American discourse (as exemplified by the post-9/11 "death of irony" debate).

Take Shelter examines the contentious and muddled status of the United States in the early twenty-first century within a decidedly Midwestern context. Even if Nichols's film lacks explicit references to outsourcing, the collapse of the housing market, and the ensuing recession, *Take Shelter* still dutifully details the daily economic hardships facing numerous Midwesterners and other Americans during this period. Alternately, by considering the film as a rumination on white male paranoia, *Take Shelter* demonstrates how a fanatical belief that "traditional" Midwestern identities are being threatened—rather than already vanished or never even existent—results in extreme efforts to ward off the extinction of those long-held regional associations. *About Schmidt*, *Up in the Air*, and *Take Shelter* all share this dynamic: once the Midwest's surface cohesion is shattered, an identity crisis follows, and the illusory sense of stability generated by traditional regional images is desired anew. To varying degrees, *About Schmidt*'s Warren and *Up in the Air*'s Ryan are cognizant of Midwestern mythology and the discontent that it may produce, but these two protagonists also lack a fully formed identity outside of this regional discourse. Both characters are forced to confront the trauma of losing past markers of identity in the wake of Midwestern decay. For his part, *Take Shelter*'s Curtis preemptively seeks to protect his family by physically isolating them from imagined threats in a storm shelter. This paranoid endeavor jeopardizes the family's home and his job, which are their actual sources of stability and economic security.

Following the celebration of the Midwest as a site of sincerity and authenticity in the immediate wake of 9/11, the region quickly reacquired its diminished status, which proved to be a recurring topic of interest in popular culture. In particular, *About Schmidt*, *Up in the Air*, and *Take Shelter* spotlight the disconnect between the Midwest's traditional image and its identity in the twenty-first century. More than a century earlier, Turner imagined that the western frontiers provided a "perennial rebirth" for the pioneers who ventured into such territories.[45] In the millennial Midwest, however, Curtis's attempted frontier re-enactment and the sentimental journeys of Warren and Ryan offer no such revitalization. Instead, these nostalgic actions reveal the exhaustion of Midwestern myths; in a geographic and cultural realm where "sincere" folks presumably once resided, there now are desperate Midwesterners clumsily attempting to prop up unsustainable and outdated images of the region. By representing such dynamics, these three films demonstrate how the nostalgic prospect of restoring—or at least of preserving—idealized incarnations of self and spaces is a powerful force that has the potential to deeply influence behaviors and beliefs. Here, traditional Midwestern narratives are shown to be alluring because they produce a semblance of fixed identities on individual and regional levels. Undermining that appeal are lingering doubts that such stability remains possible. This state of uncertainty results in the disillusionment and paranoia that, to varying degrees, define the characters of Warren, Ryan, and Curtis. As the next chapter will illustrate, negative outcomes such as nostalgic violence and the malaise on display in these three films are not the exclusive effects of contending with faltering Midwestern narratives. Instead, contemporary dissatisfaction may bring about nostalgic atonement, which is a more measured assessment of (and progressive response to) the impacts of the past within the present.

Notes

1. Svetlana Boym, *The Future of Nostalgia* (New York: Basic Books, 2001), 355.
2. *About Schmidt*, directed by Alexander Payne (2002; Los Angeles: New Line Home Entertainment, 2003), DVD; *Up in the Air*, directed by Jason Reitman (2009; Hollywood, CA: Paramount Pictures, 2010), DVD; *Take Shelter*, directed by Jeff Nichols (2011; Culver City, CA: Sony Pictures Home Entertainment, 2012), DVD.
3. David D. Kirkpatrick, "A Nation Challenged: The Commentators; Pronouncements on Irony Draw a Line in the Sand," *New York Times*, September 24, 2001, https://www.nytimes.com/2001/09/24/business/nation-challenged-commentators-pronouncements-irony-draw-line-sand.html.
4. Roger Rosenblatt, "The Age of Irony Comes to an End," *Time*, September 24, 2001.
5. *Newsweek* Staff, "Terror's Cultural Fallout," *Newsweek*, September 21, 2001, http://www.newsweek.com/terrors-cultural-fallout-151937.
6. See: ibid.; David Bauder, "'The Holy or the Broken' by Alan Light Traces Odd Journey of Leonard Cohen's Song 'Hallelujah,'" *Washington Examiner*, December 3, 2012, https://www.washingtonexaminer.com/book-traces-odd-journey-of-cohens-song.
7. Don DeLillo, "In the Ruins of the Future," *The Guardian*, December 21, 2001, https://www.theguardian.com/books/2001/dec/22/fiction.dondelillo.
8. Michiko Kakutani, "Critic's Notebook: The Age of Irony Isn't Over After All; Assertions of Cynicism's Demise Belie History," *New York Times*, October 9, 2001, https://www.nytimes.com/2001/10/09/arts/critic-s-notebook-age-irony-isn-t-over-after-all-assertions-cynicism-s-demise.html.
9. Ibid.
10. See: David Beers, "Irony Is Dead! Long Live Irony!," *Salon*, September 25, 2001, https://www.salon.com/2001/09/25/irony_lives/; *Newsweek* Staff, "The End of Irony," *Newsweek*, September 26, 2001, http://www.newsweek.com/end-irony-152295.
11. Beers, "Irony."
12. Ibid.
13. Victoria E. Johnson, *Heartland TV: Prime Time Television and the Struggle for U.S. Identity* (New York: New York University Press, 2008), 12.
14. Ibid., 17.
15. DeLillo's reading of the Al-Qaeda terrorist attacks as a past-oriented assault roughly corresponds to the concept of "nostalgic violence." Fully exploring such a linkage would require a more extensive commentary than this space permits. For now, it will suffice to note that, at its most basic level, nostalgic violence refers to violent acts perpetrated in order to restore an idealized sense of the past within the present. In a highly general way, the events of September 11th may be understood as nostalgic violence writ large—as acts intended to reshape American physical, cultural, and ideological landscapes. As DeLillo writes, "Now a small group of men have literally altered our skyline. We have fallen back in time and space." See: DeLillo, "In the Ruins of the Future."
16. Richard C. Longworth, *Caught in the Middle: America's Heartland in the Age of Globalism* (2008; repr., New York: Bloomsbury, 2009), 2.

17. *Gran Torino*, directed by Clint Eastwood (2008; Burbank, CA: Warner Home Video, 2010), DVD; Sinclair Lewis, *Main Street* (1920; repr., New York: The New American Library, 1980); Sinclair Lewis, *Babbitt* (1922; repr., New York: Bantam Classic, 2007).

18. *Citizen Ruth*, directed by Alexander Payne (Los Angeles: Miramax, 1996), film; *Election*, directed by Alexander Payne (Hollywood, CA: Paramount Pictures, 1999), DVD; *Nebraska*, directed by Alexander Payne (Los Angeles: Paramount Vantage, 2013), film.

19. Scott Foundas, "Small Is Beautiful," *Film Comment* 47, no. 6, November/December 2011, 24.

20. Ibid., 25.

21. Girish Shambu similarly comments on the form of *About Schmidt* by noting that it "has an invisible, functional style that does not call attention to itself. . . . This Spartan approach makes every stylistic gesture stand out in bold relief." Whereas critics such as Foundas attribute Payne's modest formal style to his Midwestern roots, Shambu considers the possibility that such restraint is used in a strategic manner to impact audiences. See: ibid., 24; Girish Shambu, "*About Schmidt*: Is That All There Is?," *Senses of Cinema* 25 (2003), http://sensesofcinema.com/2003/feature-articles/about_schmidt/.

22. Foundas, "Small Is Beautiful, 24.

23. A. O. Scott, "That Mythic American Hero: The Regular Guy," *New York Times*, December 8, 2002, https://www.nytimes.com/2002/12/08/movies/film-that-mythic-american-hero-the-regular-guy.html.

24. *Election* and *About Schmidt* each were adapted from novels that originally took place on the East Coast. Begley wrote a response to changes in the screenplay by Payne and Jim Taylor. The novelist noted that his "fancy New York lawyer" version of Schmidt "had surely never set foot" in Omaha. Despite such alterations, Begley acknowledged that he was pleased with the screen adaptation because his "most important themes were treated with great intelligence and sensitivity." See: ibid.; Louis Begley, "My Novel, the Movie: My Baby Reborn; 'About Schmidt' Was Changed, But Not Its Core," *New York Times*, January 19, 2003, https://www.nytimes.com/2003/01/19/movies/my-novel-the-movie-my-baby-reborn-about-schmidt-was-changed-but-not-its-core.html.

25. Scott, "That Mythic American Hero."

26. Ibid.

27. Stephen Holden similarly describes Schmidt as "a staid Middle American everyman" and claims, "The Warren Schmidts of this world and their friends and families . . . constitute a quietly humming, stabilizing collective engine in American society. An out-of-date term that might still be applied to these decent middle-class folk who work hard, respect their neighbors, attend church and obey the law is the Silent Majority." See: Stephen Holden, "An Uneasy Rider on the Road to Self-Discovery," *New York Times*, September 27, 2002, https://www.nytimes.com/2002/09/27/movies/film-festival-review-an-uneasy-rider-on-the-road-to-self-discovery.html.

28. *Badlands*, directed by Terrence Malick (1973; Burbank, CA: Warner Home Video, 2010), DVD; *A History of Violence*, directed by David Cronenberg (2005; Los Angeles: New Line Home Entertainment, 2006), DVD.

29. A literal compartmentalization of extramarital sexual desire also appears in Payne's *Election*. Schoolteacher Jim McAllister (Matthew Broderick) hides a stash of pornography inside a trunk in his basement. Both scenes remind viewers that Payne is invested in exposing how the surface of Midwestern imagery may obscure deviance from the values associated with the region.

30. Regarding this trip, Holden provides a metatextual consideration by observing that "it is impossible not to compare this excursion to the cross-country jaunt Mr. Nicholson made in *Easy Rider* 33 years ago." Whereas that film ventured "into the sunrise of a drug-enlightened future," Holden specifies that Warren's trip is "a psychic journey into the twilight and the past." Notably, the protagonists in *Easy Rider* symbolically embark on their trip in the west and head eastward, as opposed to the historical expansion of the United States that steadily progressed from the East Coast across the continent. See: Holden, "An Uneasy Rider on the Road to Self-Discovery."

31. Of this scene, Shambu writes, "The parallel with Schmidt's own life, in which the demands of work and family and outward respectability turned him into a passive, remote creature, lacking any meaningful actions of individual will, could not be more clear." See: Shambu, "*About Schmidt*: Is That All There Is?."

32. Frederick Jackson Turner, *The Frontier in American History* (1920; repr., Charleston, SC: BiblioBazaar, 2008), 14.

33. Douglas Reichert Powell, *Critical Regionalism: Connecting Politics and Culture in the American Landscape* (Chapel Hill: University of North Carolina Press, 2007), 28.

34. Among other factors, this period is marked by the continuation of what Longworth describes as "white-collar outsourcing.... The old globalization dealt with money, goods, and factory jobs; the new globalization deals with all this, and with service jobs, too.... Basically, any job that does not require face-to-face contact with a customer can be outsourced." See: Longworth, *Caught in the Middle*, 11.

35. According to the United States Census Bureau, Oklahoma technically is not one of the twelve states of the Midwest, but it often is associated with the region and considered to be "Midwestern" in terms of culture. Johnson, for example, includes Oklahoma in her conception of the "Heartland." See: United States Census Bureau, "Census Regions and Divisions of the United States," United States Census Bureau, last modified February 9, 2015, https://www2.census.gov/programs-surveys/sahie/reference-maps/2015/us-regdiv.pdf; Johnson, *Heartland TV*, 174–199.

36. In the previous year, Ryan claims that he "spent 322 days on the road, which means I had to spend 43 miserable days at home."

37. *Boys Don't Cry*, directed by Kimberly Peirce (1999; Beverly Hills, CA: Twentieth Century Fox Home Entertainment, 2000), DVD.

38. Alex bluntly informs Ryan, "I am the woman that you don't have to worry about.... Just think of me as yourself, only with a vagina." Even when expressing flexible attitudes about sexual encounters and commitment, Alex reasserts somewhat conventional attitudes about gender identity.

39. Joseph Natoli, "The Perils of Being *Up in the Air*," *Senses of Cinema* 54 (2010), http://sensesofcinema.com/2010/feature-articles/the-perils-of-being-up-in-the-air/.

40. As a brief overview, the following individuals shatter the pretense that "traditional" Midwestern relationships are easily attainable: Kara, who Ryan labels as the "glue" of the Bingham family, is separated from her husband; Natalie, the most vocal advocate of relationships providing "something real," has been dumped by the boyfriend for whom she first moved to Nebraska and now is pursuing a career in San Francisco; Alex, the casual partner who became Ryan's object of monogamous desire, has revealed herself to be both exemplary of Midwestern domesticity and a brash refutation of such values through her extramarital relationship with Ryan.

41. The DVD commentary track features director Nichols and star Shannon, but neither individual offers a definitive statement about the scene. Nichols coyly states, "People would probably want us to talk about this ending, but I don't think, uh, I don't think we

should say anything other than, 'Yeah, this is the ending.'" See: Jeff Nichols and Michael Shannon, "Audio Commentary," *Take Shelter*, directed by Jeff Nichols (2011; Culver City, CA: Sony Pictures Home Entertainment, 2012), DVD.

42. Nick Bradshaw, review of *Take Shelter*, directed by Jeff Nichols, *Sight & Sound* 21, no. 12 (December 2011): 77.

43. Ibid.

44. Nichols and Shannon, "Audio Commentary."

45. Turner, *The Frontier in American History*, 14.

6 | Nostalgic Atonement

Midway through David Lynch's *The Straight Story* (1999), a young man asks protagonist Alvin Straight (Richard Farnsworth) to explain "the worst part about being old."[1] Without a pause, the septuagenarian replies, "Well, the worst part of bein' old is rememberin' when you was young." An emphasis on the lingering presence of the past—especially the ongoing impacts of prior circumstances and occurrences that an individual such as Alvin might wish to forget—propels the film's narrative. *The Straight Story* is a fictionalized account of the true story of Alvin's lengthy journey across two Midwestern states on a riding lawnmower; he embarks upon this trip in order to reconcile with his estranged brother. Through the cinematic portrayal of these events, Lynch presents viewers with an intriguingly optimistic outcome of nostalgia: that nostalgic desire may function as an impetus for making amends and atoning for the past. In this sense, *The Straight Story* is about coming to terms with the condition of the present by acknowledging and working to revise negative aspects of personal and collective history. At age seventy-three, Alvin is near death, but he stubbornly persists on a laboriously paced mission to repair the damaged fraternal relationship looming over his flawed present. In doing so, he seeks to reconnect with his nostalgically remembered childhood. Within a regional framework, Alvin's physically decrepit state also reflects that of the Midwest as it slogged into the twenty-first century.[2] Like Alvin's failing body, the region's established identity was strained and faltering around the dawn of the millennium, as memorably depicted in *Up in the Air* (2009), *About Schmidt* (2002), and *Boys Don't Cry* (1999), to list a few films.[3] Given the despair and violence on display in so many texts that depict the millennial Midwest, it may seem difficult or perhaps even naïve to imagine a progressive potential for nostalgia. Yet, such a possibility emerges through *The Straight Story* and several other complementary texts.

This chapter continues to examine films produced during the years surrounding the turn of the twenty-first century, which was a tumultuous and traumatic period that found the Midwest scrambling to forge a new identity in American culture. I begin by considering how a nostalgic engagement with the past might be productive, rather than debilitating, violent, restrictive, and so on. My concept of "nostalgic atonement" envisions a turn to the past for the purpose of "correcting" the temporally distant elements that negatively affect the present. While introducing what nostalgic atonement entails, I again revisit Svetlana Boym's work on nostalgia—her notion of "restorative nostalgia" is of particular importance—and briefly address Debra Granik's *Winter's Bone* (2010) and Gregg Araki's *Mysterious Skin* (2004).[4] Both of these films revolve around past traumas that are brought to light and reckoned with in order to reshape the experience of the present and, potentially, to open up what otherwise would have been a foreclosed future.

After delineating some conceptual parameters of nostalgic atonement, I turn my attention to Sofia Coppola's *The Virgin Suicides* (1999) and Lynch's *The Straight Story*.[5] These two films are inundated with nostalgia-drenched memories. The protagonists believe that a meaningful existence in the present may be achieved only by accessing lost identities perceived as being located solely in the past. Both films showcase variations of the forms that nostalgic atonement might take. *The Virgin Suicides* features characters who collectively fetishize a nostalgic vision of the past, especially the youthful versions of themselves, their neighbors, and the space of their neighborhood. By contrast, *The Straight Story* depicts an individualized nostalgic voyage into the past that is simultaneously internal and, crucially, a physical journey across the Midwestern landscape. Lynch's film thus serves as a prime example of both nostalgic spatiality—a reconfiguration of how space is understood, perceived, and/or experienced in a manner that relates to a nostalgic sense of time—and nostalgic atonement. Unlike texts such as *Sister Carrie* (1900) and Terrence Malick's *Badlands* (1973), the nostalgic spatiality of *The Straight Story* enables rather than inhibits Alvin's ability to enter the past in order to change his present status.[6]

In conjunction with the thematic ways in which nostalgia is treated in the narratives of *The Virgin Suicides* and *The Straight Story*, I also address the aesthetics that Coppola and Lynch utilize to visually represent nostalgia. Elsewhere in this book, I discuss how nostalgic spatiality is depicted onscreen through a variety of formal elements including mise-en-scène, shot length, and editing. Such examples of nostalgic spatiality include the seemingly untraversable space of the badlands in *Badlands*, the looping imagery and graphlike camera movements in Werner Herzog's *Stroszek* (1977), and the disorienting long take that opens *A History of Violence* (2005) and creates the impression of the camera moving along—and deviating from—a linear timeline.[7] Here, I analyze the pervasive use of dissolves in *The Virgin Suicides* and *The Straight Story*. Coppola and Lynch each deploy this editing technique to blend images in a manner that creates a sense of temporal simultaneity—a collapse of the past and the present, however briefly, within the frame. Across both films, form and narrative align and produce an immersive experience of nostalgia for viewers. Overall, this chapter further considers the aesthetics of nostalgic spatiality and expands on the previous two chapters by continuing to unravel the complicated, often contradictory, representations of the millennial Midwest produced during this period of turbulence for the region's identity and meaning in American culture.

Nostalgic Atonement

The term "atonement" contains a set of temporal relations. Broadly defined, atonement recognizes that an occurrence (or multiple events) from the past remains unresolved in the present, which necessitates action (whether in the immediate or distant future). In short, the lingering impacts of the past require acknowledgement and response. Within religious contexts, atonement features variable meanings; it may refer to a renewed relationship between humanity and a deity or simply the correction of past wrongdoing. This reconciled state is often dependent upon or achieved through acts of confession, restitution, and/or repentance. On the level of national history (as well as communities of other scales), one version of atonement involves compensation that is more material in nature. In particular, financial reparations constitute an official recognition of the historical disenfranchisement and marginalization suffered by certain groups of people, such as Japanese Americans who were held in internment camps during World War II.[8] Regarding the possibility of reparations paid to African Americans, Ta-Nehisi Coates asserts, "Reparations would mean a revolution of the American consciousness, a reconciling of our self-image as the great democratizer with the facts of our history."[9] Because reparations would entail "the full acceptance of our collective biography and its consequences," Coates envisions that such developments would produce "a national reckoning that would lead to spiritual renewal."[10] Across these varying contexts, an act of atonement brings about a realignment of an individual, communal, or even national relationship to the past, as well as an accompanying rejuvenation of the present.

Tracing the long and complicated histories of atonement's theological connotations and sociohistorical manifestations exceeds the scope of my project. I briefly reference these contexts so as to distinguish my use of the phrase "nostalgic atonement," which I conceptualize as a framework for analyzing particular types of temporal relationships within textual objects, particularly works of film and literature. Although my concept's primary applications involve textual analysis, there is certainly some overlap between nostalgic atonement and broader cultural contexts including those mentioned above. In this chapter, though, I focus on using nostalgic atonement to make sense of ways in which selected texts establish a potentially progressive linkage of the past and present on narrative, thematic, and/or formal levels. Films such as *The Straight Story* depict a reparatory attitude toward the past that counters and inhibits the often reactionary yearnings of nostalgia.

I develop the concept of nostalgic atonement in relation to Svetlana Boym's theories of nostalgia and through readings of the climactic scenes in *Winter's Bone*, set in Missouri, and *Mysterious Skin*, set in Kansas. In *The Future of Nostalgia* (2001), Boym theorizes two forms of nostalgia: reflective nostalgia and restorative nostalgia. Boym explains:

> Two kinds of nostalgia are not absolute types, but rather tendencies, ways of giving shape and meaning to longing. Restorative nostalgia puts emphasis on *nostos* and proposes to rebuild the lost home and patch up the memory gaps. Reflective nostalgia dwells in *algia*, in longing and loss, the imperfect process of remembrance. The first category of nostalgics do not think of themselves as nostalgic; they believe that their project is about truth. This kind of nostalgia characterizes national and

nationalist revivals all over the world, which engage in the antimodern myth-making of history by means of a return to national symbols and myths and, occasionally, through swapping conspiracy theories. Restorative nostalgia manifests itself in total reconstructions of monuments of the past, while reflective nostalgia lingers on ruins, the patina of time and history, in the dreams of another place and another time.[11]

To somewhat oversimplify Boym's two nostalgic "tendencies," reflective nostalgia is a subjective contemplation of the past and memory, while restorative nostalgia is a damaging process in which individuals and groups attempt to restore essentialized and partly (or entirely) fictional accounts of history within the present. As Boym goes on to explain, "Restorative nostalgia knows two main narrative plots—the restoration of origins and the conspiracy theory. . . . 'Home,' imagine extremist conspiracy theory adherents, is forever under siege, requiring defense against the plotting enemy."[12] Of particular note is Boym's association of restorative nostalgia with myth and narrative. Rather than simply functioning as an internal reaction, this form of nostalgia spreads outward into the cultural sphere, where it plays upon reactionary fears.

Boym's concepts have greatly impacted my own theoretical consideration of nostalgia. For instance, nostalgic violence has certain correspondences with restorative nostalgia. The nostalgic violence on display in Midwestern texts such as *Gran Torino* (2008) and *A History of Violence* is enacted by each film's protagonist in response to perceived threats to their respective homes.[13] In this way, nostalgic violence sometimes—but not always—may refer to actions that are the outcome of desires produced by restorative nostalgia. That said, the nostalgic violence of, say, *A History of Violence*'s Tom Stall (Viggo Mortensen) features an intentionally performative component that is seemingly absent from the individuals who deny the nostalgic nature of their restorative agendas, as Boym suggests. Such distinctions are worth making in order to more fully recognize the complex and multifarious forms of nostalgia.

After detailing the many ways in which nostalgia may have deleterious outcomes, I am interested in examining how a reparatory attitude toward the past can push nostalgia in more progressive directions. Similar to nostalgic violence, the notion of nostalgic atonement is something of a response to Boym's restorative nostalgia. Nostalgic atonement is not a critique of or replacement for restorative nostalgia, but rather functions as the flipside to Boym's concept. As with restorative nostalgia, nostalgic atonement is a mode of interacting with the past that exceeds mere internal reflection and is expressed partly through actions. Nostalgic atonement, however, emerges through an inverse view of how the past and present relate to one another. Instead of the degraded present being reshaped in the image of a mythic version of the past as with restorative nostalgia, a perspective informed by nostalgic atonement emphasizes how the flaws of the past unsettle the present. Consequently, a nostalgic journey into the past must be undertaken in order to repair—or at least acknowledge the existence of—the damage that continues to weigh on the present and impinge on the future.

Before turning to *The Virgin Suicides* and *The Straight Story*, two brief examples will help to illustrate how nostalgic atonement may appear in film. *Winter's Bone* and *Mysterious Skin*—which are adaptations of novels by, respectively, Daniel Woodrell and Scott Heim—share a thematic emphasis on atonement across their narratives.[14] In both films, characters are haunted by past traumas that linger in the present through their multitudinous, harmful effects. Although definitively resolving such conflicts proves to be difficult, the characters populating *Winter's Bone* and *Mysterious Skin* are able to confront the past, and this tentative act of nostalgic atonement enables them to imagine or even to begin realizing lives outside of those burdened by traumatic history.

Set in the deeply impoverished Ozarks of southern Missouri, *Winter's Bone* shines a light on a decidedly troubled section of the Midwest. Director Granik shot the film on location, and she presents viewers with a mise-en-scène that gives the impression of being simultaneously documentarylike and expressionistic.[15] The harsh Midwestern landscape is marked by detritus and natural elements, such as trees and fog, that exude sinister overtones (see fig. 6.1). Of the setting, James Bell writes that "the rugged landscape of the Ozarks lends the film a southern gothic quality. The grey skies, the bleached colours, the wooden houses with their yards strewn with old furniture, cars and junk—all are deeply expressive of a community with a distinct sense of its own ancestry, for better or worse. The isolated mountains seem haunted by inhabitants of times past...."[16] At the beginning of *Winter's Bone*, teenage protagonist Ree Dolly (Jennifer Lawrence) is tasked with providing for her two younger siblings and catatonic mother due, in part, to the absence of her father Jessup, a local crystal meth cook who has abandoned the family. The Dolly family's already precarious status is further jeopardized because Jessup has put their home and land up as bond after being arrested; when he fails to appear in court, Ree has only a few days to locate her father before the family is evicted from their residence. Finding Jessup—or just proof that he is dead—becomes Ree's dangerous mission, and she singlemindedly hikes across the rural terrain to question known members of the local criminal community, many of whom are blood relatives.

Ree especially pursues Thump Milton (Ron "Stray Dog" Hall), who runs the area's various criminal activities and for whom Jessup had worked. After first being turned away, Ree is later beaten by three women in Thump's family, including Merab (Dale Dickey). As Thump and his associates deliberate about whether or not to kill Ree, she pleads her case: "If Dad has done wrong, then Dad has paid, and whoever killed him, I don't need to know all that. But I can't forever carry them kids and my Mom, not without that house." Several scenes later, Merab and her sisters appear at Ree's home, and the former announces, "We're goin' to fix your problem for you.... We'll take you to your daddy's bones." The sisters then bring Ree to a pond where Jessup's body is submerged beneath the surface; Ree is told to pull up her father's arms, which Merab removes with a chainsaw. After bringing Jessup's arms to the police station, the film concludes with the remaining members of the Dolly family sitting together outside of the home that, for the moment, is resecured.

Fig. 6.1. Ree hikes across the simultaneously stark and cluttered Ozark landscape. Screen capture, *Winter's Bone* (2010).

Ultimately, the fate of the Dollys hinges on a gruesome act of compassion by Merab and possibly Thump, although the latter's role in the decision to reveal the location of Jessup's body is not depicted onscreen. Regardless, this gesture recognizes that Thump's conflict had been with Jessup, not his destitute wife and children. Because the past retribution enacted against Jessup—who was apparently going to become an informant for the police—spills over into the present for the innocent members of the Dolly family, Merab and her sisters acknowledge the hidden murder of Jessup by literally dredging up his body in order to help Ree, her siblings, and her mother. In a peculiar way, then, providing Ree with access to Jessup's arms is an act of nostalgic atonement, one intended to cease the lingering harm resulting from the legal repercussions of Jessup's disappearance. Through this most grotesque dismemberment, the past is revisited so that the present may be repaired.

Mysterious Skin revolves around a different sort of past trauma than *Winter's Bone*, but similarly builds to a climactic moment of demystification that serves as an example of nostalgic atonement. Following the opening credits sequence, *Mysterious Skin* begins with a title card that designates the period as "Summer 1981." From off-screen, teenager Brian Lackey (Brady Corbet) narrates, "The summer I was eight years old, five hours disappeared from my life. Five hours. Lost. Gone without a trace." Over the course of the film, it is revealed that Brian's "lost" time covers the evening in which he and Neil McCormick (played as a teenager by Joseph Gordon-Levitt) were sexually abused by the coach of their baseball team in Hutchinson, Kansas. "Coach" (Bill Sage) abuses Neil over the entirety of the summer. As a teenager, Neil, who narrates that he was attracted to men prior to encountering Coach, disturbingly recalls, "What happened that summer—it's a huge part of me. No one ever made me feel that way, before or since. Like I . . . I was special . . . he really loved me . . . I was his one true love." By this time in late 1991, Neil has been a prostitute in Hutchinson and since moved to New York City, where he continues to perform sex work. Brian, on the other hand, is seemingly asexual and remains in Hutchinson. For much of the narrative, Brian obsesses over his missing memories, which he suspects are the result of being abducted by aliens.

Director Araki—a key filmmaker in the movement that B. Ruby Rich describes as "New Queer Cinema"—uses a lush, vibrant color palette for the scenes set in the early 1980s, and the aesthetic produces a sense of exaggerated nostalgic memory.[17] These childhood scenes are narrated by the teenage versions of Neil and Brian, and this dynamic further muddles how viewers process the images onscreen, which clearly do not appear to be objective depictions of the past. Early in the film, for instance, Brian watches a UFO fly over his home, and Araki regularly inserts shots of the younger Brian lying on a metal slab as if aboard a spaceship. Such moments constitute a visual slippage between Brian's repressed memories of abuse and the alien abduction fantasies that he concocts as a coping mechanism. Similarly, Araki occasionally intercuts brief shots of Coach's face within Neil's narrated memories, as if to demonstrate the ongoing influence of the abuse on the latter's psychological state.

The climax of *Mysterious Skin* revolves around a more clinical account of the abuse that Neil and Brian collectively experienced. After Neil is brutally assaulted in New York City, he returns to Hutchinson for Christmas at the end of 1991. During the previous several months, Brian realized that another boy was in his abduction visions: childhood baseball teammate Neil, who Brian arranges to meet on Christmas Eve. In a distressing variation of the nostalgic journeys undertaken in *About Schmidt* and *Up in the Air*, Neil brings Brian to Coach's former house, which was the site of their abuse.[18] With the current residents away, Neil and Brian enter through a rear window. In the living room, Neil announces, "Well, this is it, right?" Neil then claims that he could only remember Brian as a "hazy picture in my head. Like a static-y TV." Throughout this scene, Brian recognizes elements that his mind had transformed into the alien abduction scenario, such as a blue light on the front porch. Neil states that Coach disappeared after that summer and tragically insists, "I was his favorite . . . when it first started happening, I felt honored." In addition to the other dynamics of this scene, the mapping of memory and emotion onto a precise structure situates the conclusion of *Mysterious Skin* within the purview of nostalgic spatiality.

As the scene progresses, Brian demands that Neil disclose the exact details of their abuse. While Brian breaks down in tears and shakes with uncontrollable convulsions, Neil holds him and gently caresses his head. In a final voiceover sequence, Neil states,

> I wanted to tell Brian it was over now and everything would be okay. But that was a lie. Plus, I couldn't speak, anyway. I wish there was some way for us to go back and undo the past. But there wasn't. There was nothing we could do. So I just stayed silent and [tried] to telepathically communicate how sorry I was about what had

happened. And I thought of all the grief and sadness and fucked up suffering in the world, and it made me want to escape. I wished with all my heart that we could just leave this world behind. Rise like two angels in the night and magically disappear.

Despite Brian's emotional collapse and Neil's emphasis on the unchangeable nature of the past, this concluding scene contains a measure of tenuous, elusive hope. For both Brian and Neil, the moment is a direct confrontation with the unadorned past: a recognition of actual occurrence, rather than the former's alien fictions or the latter's reframing of the abuse as a loving relationship. It is, in other words, what I would label as an instance of nostalgic atonement, however partial or still unfolding it might be.

The traumatic past cannot be undone, but what can be changed is one's relation to that history. Throughout *Mysterious Skin*, Brian is tormented by the knowledge that something horrific happened to him during his "lost" hours, and Neil engages in risky, self-destructive behavior from which he attempts to shield himself by adopting a detached, cold persona. As Neil's longtime "soulmate," Wendy (Michelle Trachtenberg), bluntly states, "Where normal people have a heart, Neil McCormick has a bottomless black hole." Following their reunion, both Brian and Neil appear to be altered in potentially beneficial ways that tentatively point toward paths of recovery. In a sense, Brian's memory is now repaired; by learning the facts of his repressed trauma, perhaps he might be able to process those events through therapy and to move beyond his lifelong obsession with those missing hours—"to dream about something else for a change," as he tells Neil. Having only previously discussed Coach with Wendy, Neil is also subtly transformed after recounting the abuse to Brian and witnessing his distraught reaction. Here, Neil's hard exterior softens as he admits to feeling remorse and seems to finally recognize the devastating nature of Coach's actions, rather than fondly remembering the abuse. As *Mysterious Skin* ends, the past is not rewritten and neither character is recovered. Yet, the mere acknowledgement of the actual past and its lasting effects is a significant gesture. Through this act of nostalgic atonement, the past becomes increasingly demystified, which begins to unburden the teens' present and future states from the shadow of their traumatic history.

The Virgin Suicides

In *Flashbacks in Film: Memory and History* (1989), Maureen Turim explains that, through cinematic flashbacks, "a juncture is wrought between present and past and two concepts are implied in this juncture: memory and history."[19] The tension between these latter two terms—memory and history—deeply informs Sofia Coppola's *The Virgin Suicides*, which is an adaptation of Jeffrey Eugenides's 1993 novel.[20] The film depicts the unreliable collective recollections of a group of adult men reminiscing about growing up in a Detroit suburb in the 1970s. This period inaugurated their lifelong fixation on the five suicidal Lisbon sisters. With two brief exceptions, the film's images consist entirely of stylized representations of the 1970s, while the soundtrack features ongoing commentary by a single, unnamed narrator (voiced by Giovanni Ribisi) in the present. Coppola continually emphasizes the unknowable nature of the past through the narrative and film style. Essentially, *The Virgin Suicides* is a feature-length flashback that reveals the limitations of memory, while also troubling a masculine compulsion to attain unambiguous knowledge of the past and of the internal lives of the Lisbon girls. Rather than demystifying the past, the film evinces a negative repercussion for disregarding nostalgic atonement: an ongoing inability to untether history from recollection and desire.

An overtly nostalgic treatment of memory and history defines *The Virgin Suicides*, particularly through the film's reimagining of the past as a destination or precise locale, instead of a moment lost to the steady progression of time. Interestingly, Boym discusses how nostalgic subjects seek to spatialize the flow of time so that it might become navigable. She writes, "At first glance, nostalgia is a longing for a place, but actually it is a yearning for a different time—the time of our childhood, the slower rhythms of our dreams. In a broader sense, nostalgia is rebellion against the modern idea of time, the time of history and progress. The nostalgic desires to obliterate history and turn it into private or collective mythology, *to revisit time like space*, refusing to surrender to the irreversibility of time that plagues the human condition."[21] *The Virgin Suicides* clearly corresponds to Boym's commentary on the nostalgic transformation of a temporal moment into a spatial coordinate. Again and again, the unnamed present-day narrator and his nostalgic cohorts scrutinize their foggy memories and collection of mementos in a futile effort to revisit the past. It is through this jumbled perspective that all of the narrative events are filtered.

Although teenage versions of the film's collective male voice appear onscreen throughout *The Virgin Suicides*, it is unclear precisely which, if any, of the boys is the younger version of the adult narrator.[22] Debra Shostak discusses the "unusual first-person plural narrative voice" featured in Eugenides's source novel, and her comments also are applicable to the voiceover narration in Coppola's adaption.[23] Shostak writes, "Eugenides's use of the collective voice enables a kind of perspectival vertigo. Because the voice is plural, it promises to offer a more reliable point of view than one might expect from a single voice, and the assumptions that determine its interpretations would, for the same reason, seem to have social legitimacy. Yet the authority conferred by numbers is undermined by the narrators' confession of their common puzzlement. . . . Indeed, rather than merging the multiplicity of conflicting interpretations through an implied coincidence of viewpoints, the "we" exacerbates the indeterminacy of the text."[24] For the vast majority of *The Virgin Suicides*, Coppola visualizes memories of the 1970s, but the film does not actually take place in that decade. Instead, as Bree Hoskin explains, "the film's representation of the sisters, and the past in general, reside[s] in the collective memory of the boys, a memory that both informs and is informed by their subjective longings in the present, manifested in their dreams."[25] As such, the true "present" of the narrative is approximately the year of the film's release: 1999. From this temporally distant vantage point, the film's male characters review the origins of their obsession with the five Lisbon sisters: thirteen-year-old Cecilia (Hanna Hall), fourteen-year-old Lux (Kirsten Dunst), fifteen-year-old Bonnie (Chelse Swain), sixteen-year-old Mary (A. J. Cook), and seventeen-year-old Therese (Leslie Hayman).

As *The Virgin Suicides* opens, Coppola's camera lingers over the mundane routines of the suburban neighborhood (such as watering the lawn or grilling food in a driveway) until a cut to the inside of the Lisbon home reveals Cecilia in a bathtub with slit wrists. Although Cecilia is resuscitated, she later succeeds in killing herself by plunging from a second-story window onto a spiked metal fence in the front lawn during a party hosted by her sisters. When school resumes in the fall, high school hunk Trip Fontaine (Josh Hartnett) becomes smitten with Lux, and he convinces the Lisbon parents to permit their daughters to attend the homecoming dance. After the dance, Trip seduces and then abandons Lux, causing her to miss curfew. Mrs. Lisbon (Kathleen Turner), the family's repressive matriarch, subsequently pulls all of the girls out of school and cloisters them in the house. The group of boys and the Lisbon girls begin communicating via Morse code and telephone calls, but the remaining four sisters eventually all commit suicide on the same evening within the walls of their house-turned-prison—but only after inviting several of the boys over to witness the gruesome spectacle.

Immediately following the opening scene and title sequence, "MICHIGAN 25 YEARS AGO" appears across the screen. The narrator states, "Everyone dates the demise of our neighborhood from the suicides of the Lisbon girls. People saw their clairvoyance in the wiped-out elms, the harsh sunlight, and the continuing decline of our auto industry. Even then, as teenagers, we tried to put the pieces together. We still can't. Now, whenever we run into each other at business lunches or cocktail parties, we find ourselves in the corner going over the evidence one more time—all to understand those five girls, who, after all these years, we can't get out of our minds." Here, the disembodied narrator's commentary reminds viewers that the onscreen imagery is not the present, but rather a reimagined version of the past. Crucially, the film's images and soundtrack are quickly exposed as the product of a temporal and spatial disjuncture. The mise-en-scène and sound design represent the adult men's collective memory of their childhood, not the "objective" history of the neighborhood. History and memory are separated by an ever-expanding distance, which frustrates the men's obsessive (and problematic) efforts "to understand" the Lisbon sisters and, presumably, to make the present more satisfactory through a more complete knowledge of the past.

The true present of *The Virgin Suicides*—the time during which the adult men "still" cannot process the events of their childhood—only makes a brief, but remarkable appearance onscreen. Twice, Coppola cuts to a scene with an older version of Trip Fontaine (Michael Pare) sitting at a table in a rehabilitation clinic. In addition to the juxtaposition of actors Hartnett and Pare, the formal elements used to depict the present are jarring in relation to all of the film's other scenes. Throughout most of *The Virgin Suicides*, nondiegetic noises intrude upon the soundtrack, from pop songs to ambient rumblings. When shifting to the present's rehabilitation facility setting, though, all nondiegetic music abruptly drops from the sound design, with only diegetic background noises detectable.

Similarly, Coppola uses a variety of fluid camera movements to capture the past (or at least how the narrator remembers the past), as well as a mixture of shot types, including many extreme close-ups. In the present, the older Trip is shown only in a stationary medium shot that recalls a talking head interview in a documentary. The literally and figuratively sobering quality of this brief view of the present reflects a nostalgic subject's perspective on the progression of time. Once an emblem of youthful beauty, now Trip exists as a reminder that everything and everyone decays as time passes; for the nostalgic individual, the present can only be a drab, empty husk of the vibrant past, where the authentic and idealized version of one's self is believed to be located. Transcending the degraded present thus is the goal of the narrator and his nostalgic peers.

In the rehabilitation scenes, Trip appears haggard while recounting his memories of Lux. Both cuts to this scene disrupt the stability of the nostalgic visualization of the past that comprises the majority of *The Virgin Suicides*. Although there are several overt fantasy sequences in the film, those moments are presented as concurrent with the past; that is, the fantasies are established as being imagined by the boys in the past, rather than being conjured up by their adult selves. Notably, the first instance in which Coppola cuts to middle-aged Trip establishes the diegetic existence of a tangible present outside of the narrative events located in the past. Although the narrator clearly is temporally distant from the onscreen proceedings, the first cut to the rehabilitation center confirms that there is an exterior to the film's immersion in nostalgic memory.[26] Cutting to older Trip simultaneously configures the imagined past as a fictive construction and as a more preferable spatial and temporal locale than the dreary present.

Due to its placement in *The Virgin Suicides*, the second cut to the present further undermines the coherence of the film's nostalgic visual, aural, and narrative elements. The second scene at the rehabilitation facility is sequenced just after the 1970s homecoming dance sequence. After the dance, Trip and Lux have sex on the football field, while the other Lisbon sisters and their dates return home. Coppola then cuts to Lux waking up alone on the grass and taking a taxi back to her house. Despite nearly the entirety of the film being a nostalgic flashback, prior to this moment, the past had been presented in what appeared to be chronological order. After Lux arrives at home, however, Coppola cuts backwards in time to the moment when Trip abandons his date. As young Trip is shown exiting the football field alone and then sitting in his bedroom, older Trip's voiceover appears on the soundtrack, and a cut returns viewers to the rehabilitation facility in the present. The sequence in which these scenes are edited together introduces a flashback within the flashback that constitutes most of the film. This disruption of narrative linearity reemphasizes that all of the film's images (except for the depictions of older Trip) are nostalgic reconstructions of the past generated by subjective perspectives and unreliable memories. Yet, this clearly false portrait of the past—a product of misinformation, uncertain recollection, and nostalgic yearning—is presented as an object of desire for the narrator, albeit one that is acknowledged as unattainable.

Intriguingly, there is one other instance that denotes a temporal moment outside of the film's imagined past: a brief bit of voiceover by Mrs. Lisbon near the end of the film. After all of the Lisbon girls have killed themselves, Mr. and Mrs. Lisbon are shown leaving their house and driving away. In voiceover, Mrs. Lisbon says, "None of my daughters lacked for any love. There was plenty of love in our house. I never understood why." This intrusion of Mrs. Lisbon's ruminations onto the voiceover track is peculiar. Aside from the narrator, it is the only voiceover in *The Virgin Suicides* that is not attributed to an individual located in a specific time and place (such as the older Trip in a rehabilitation facility). The film's audience is given no information about when or where Mrs. Lisbon makes these statements. Did the narrator (and/or the collective group of adult men from the neighborhood) interview the mother? Did these men gain access to an archived recording of a deposition by Mrs. Lisbon? Do these statements come from the same "present" as occupied by the narrator and adult Trip? If not, are they made in the interim between the present and the 1970s? No definite resolution is provided by Coppola, which further clouds the treatment of time and memory in *The Virgin Suicides*.

In an effort to satisfy their desire to occupy the imagined past, the boys (and their adult selves) fetishize mementos once possessed by the Lisbon girls. Regarding nostalgic objects, Hoskin writes, "This process of locating authenticity in material objects is . . . a legitimate means of attempting to satisfy nostalgic desire, acting, like dreams, as a medium through which the temporal disjunctions that constitute nostalgia are resolved through their dissolution. For an instant, desire is fulfilled."[27] Although examining the Lisbon girls' personal property functions as a short-lasting salve for nostalgia, Coppola shows that such objects direct the boys away from lived experience and into a realm of fanciful imagination. One exception to this dynamic is the figure of middle-aged Trip, who himself exists as something of a nostalgic object. As "the only reliable boy who actually got to know Lux," the narrator explains that the boys turn to Trip for clarification about their memories and the girls' identities. Crucially, the older Trip's inability to explain his motives for abandoning Lux on the football field reinforces the interpretability of the past. Even with Trip talking about situations in which he was involved, the motivations for his younger self's behavior remain inscrutable, just as with so many of the past events shown in the film. Moreover, rather than acknowledging some degree of complicity for the fates of the Lisbon sisters, Trip evades any sense of nostalgic atonement by selfishly focusing on how Lux affected his own identity, despite the devastating ramifications of his actions.

Every scene in which one or more of the boys scrutinizes an item owned by the Lisbon girls is accompanied by a fantasy that is visualized onscreen. Early in *The Virgin Suicides*, for instance, Peter Sisten is invited to the Lisbon household for dinner. Peter excuses himself to use the bathroom, where he examines the girls' personal beauty products and toiletries. While smelling a lipstick tube, Peter closes his eyes and Coppola cuts to a close-up of Lux waving her hair around in bright sunlight and tilting her head back as if experiencing pleasure. This fantasy, tellingly, is interrupted by Lux herself knocking at the door. After the girls' suicides, the narrator states, "We, of course, took the family photos that were put out with the trash. In the end, we had pieces of the puzzle, but no matter how we put them together, gaps remained, oddly shaped emptiness mapped by what surrounded them, like countries we couldn't name. What lingered after them was not life, but the most trivial list of mundane facts." In these two scenes, the boys/men seem to believe that exposure to the girls' possessions will produce intimate knowledge of the girls themselves—a fully repaired and coherent understanding of the past. Such objects, though, merely spark fantasies about the girls and accentuate the untraversable distance between past and present, between the male friends and the Lisbon sisters.

In another scene during which the boys inspect the girls' belongings, images of memory and fantasy dissolve into one another in a decidedly cinematic representation of nostalgia (see fig. 6.2). After Cecilia's death, the boys acquire her diary, and the narrator explains that by reading it, they came "to hold collective memories of times we hadn't experienced." As the boys read the diary onscreen, Cecilia's voice provides narration from beyond the grave, and Coppola inserts a sequence of shots that overlap and rapidly dissolve into one another. The material in these shots includes the boys reading the diary, what appears to be a home video of Lux, the girls in a golden field of wheat with warm lighting, and other images inspired by Cecilia's writings, including a unicorn. The content of this montage blends the adult men's memories of reading the diary with the fantastical impressions of the Lisbon girls that they concocted as teenagers.

This sequence functions as a variation on what Jennifer A. González describes as an "autotopography." González specifies, "In the creation of an autotopography—which does not include all personal property but only those objects seen to signify an 'individual' identity—the material world is called upon to present a physical map of memory, history, and belief. The autobiographical object therefore becomes a prosthetic device: an addition, a trace, and a replacement for the intangible aspects of desire, identification, and social relations."[28] Rather than using artifacts as a "prosthetic device" for individual identity, however, the boys (and, later, as adult men) use the Lisbon girls' belongings to construct a group identity. Further complicating matters is the fact that this shared identity is predicated upon, as the narrator describes, "collective memories of times we hadn't experienced." In order to access the past, the male characters problematically invent imagined memories for the Lisbon sisters through the act of fetishizing objects pilfered from the girls' home and waste in the wake of the five suicides. This masculine desire to control the past—and, by proxy, to possess intimate knowledge of the Lisbons—results in a collective self-definition based on unstable, likely false memories. In this way, Coppola progressively reveals how what seemingly began as an effort to nostalgically repair incoherent memories is actually much closer to the regressive behavior that Boym describes as constitutive of restorative nostalgia. These men build their sense of identity through the troubling creation of a mythic past based on the dubious interpretation of objects that belonged to others. This version of the past obscures any culpability

Fig. 6.2. Nostalgia is visualized with images dissolving into one another. Screen captures, *The Virgin Suicides* (1999).

that the boys might have for the Lisbon sisters' deaths and, as with Trip's recollections, closes off the possibility for nostalgic atonement.

Coppola's aesthetic choices for the fantasy sequences—such as the diary-reading scene described above—produce a sense of overlapping but discrete temporalities within the Midwestern setting of *The Virgin Suicides*. In particular, her use of the dissolve as an editing device results in a superimposition of images that illustrates the continually elusive stability of these temporalities. The recurring uncertainty as to which images represent a memory, a fantasy, or an actual occurrence further highlights the futility of the men's efforts to reconcile their faulty memories and projected desires into a comprehensive narrative. Even at the film's end, this project remains unfinished. The narrator reflects, "So much has been said about the girls over the years, but we have never found an answer. It didn't matter in the end how old they had been or that they were girls, but only that we had loved them, and that they hadn't heard us calling, still do not hear us calling them out of those rooms, where they went to be alone for all time, and where we will never find the pieces to put them back together." In this voiceover commentary, the narrator emphasizes the nostalgic nature of the journey into memory and history by spatializing the temporally removed location of the Lisbon girls. Paradoxically, he explains that the girls still reside in the space of the Lisbon home, but remain out of reach when the men search it for artifacts that might produce a singular and ordered narrative of the past. In this way, the Lisbon home and its surrounding Midwestern suburb are configured as environments that do not correspond to the linear flow of time. Instead, those who enter this space occupy the in-between temporality of nostalgia, forever apart from what is desired.

In *The Virgin Suicides*, the potential for nostalgic atonement dissipates within flawed memories, as do desperate, self-serving attempts to restore an imagined version of the past. On the cusp of the new millennium, Coppola's film shows how the power of nostalgic memory may strand individuals and, potentially, regional spaces in a liminal state between past and present. When nostalgic atonement is neglected and restorative nostalgia proves to be unachievable, the male characters are forced to commence what the present-day narrator describes as "the impossible process of trying to forget"—in essence, a disavowal of nostalgia, memory, and history. Surrounded by the physical structures in which the past was once present—the houses, streets, and sidewalks of the neighborhood—*The Virgin Suicides* concludes with four of the boys staring intently at the Lisbon home as Coppola's camera slowly tracks away from them. What remains is a lingering awareness that the past and the lives of others remain outside of the material spaces and objects that the men collectively scrutinize.

The Virgin Suicides exemplifies an obsession with knowing and/or controlling the past that recurs in twenty-first-century Midwestern narratives. On the surface, *The Straight Story* might appear to fit within this trend, as it features an aged white male protagonist who yearns to recreate the idealized past within the present. Moreover, he seeks to do so by travelling across the physical landscape of the Midwest. Despite these shared qualities, *The Straight Story* instead offers a hopeful outcome for the frequently destructive experience of nostalgia found in many texts that represent the millennial Midwest.

The Straight Story

Inspired by actual events, David Lynch's *The Straight Story* presents the superficially simplistic story of seventy-three-year-old Alvin Straight traveling well over two hundred miles on a riding lawnmower to reunite with his estranged brother Lyle (Harry Dean Stanton).[29] As in *Winter's Bone* and *Mysterious Skin*, Alvin engages in an act of nostalgic atonement. In Lynch's film, Alvin acknowledges how certain elements of his personal history were damaged as the result of his own failings, and he wishes to make amends. It is this desire that launches his deceptively linear trek through Iowa and Wisconsin. Eventually, Alvin successfully bridges the present and the pretraumatic past that he nostalgically desires via a conciliatory perspective. An additional outcome of Alvin's steady progression across the Midwest extends beyond merely repairing a relationship: within the logic of Lynch's film, the journey transcends its ostensibly "straight" spatial trajectory by reversing linear temporality and functioning as an excursion into the nostalgically remembered past. *The Straight Story* thereby connects nostalgic spatiality and nostalgic atonement on the levels of narrative, theme, and aesthetics.

At the start of the film, Alvin's doctor speculates that the septuagenarian may have diabetes and emphysema. The physician warns that "serious consequences" will result if Alvin does not change his lifestyle. Near death, Alvin learns that Lyle has suffered a stroke, which prompts Alvin to devise a plan to visit the ailing brother with whom he has not spoken in a decade. Despite "being blind and lame at the same time," as Alvin later describes himself, he dismisses the concerns of his adult daughter Rose (Sissy Spacek) with a simple explanation: "I've gotta make this trip on my own." Midway through the journey, Alvin repeats this sentiment when his mower breaks down. Danny (James Cada) and Darla Riordan (Sally Wingert) befriend Alvin and offer to drive him the rest of the way. Once again, Alvin insists on completing the journey alone and replies, "Well, I appreciate that, but I wanna finish this one my own way." Clearly, the arduous and deliberate nature of Alvin's transportation is intended to display contrition for his past conflict with Lyle, who indeed is moved to the point of speechlessness when Alvin appears outside his Wisconsin home.[30] Because of this purpose, the trip constitutes an act of nostalgic atonement.

Throughout Alvin's time on the road, he encounters a variety of Midwesterners who more or less embody the positive stereotype of the region's inhabitants as fundamentally friendly, decent people. Lynch's idyllic portrait of the Midwest sharply deviates from the many troubled Midwesterners on display in other millennial-era films depicting the region. Film scholar Todd McGowan assesses the nature of these positive regional images and writes, "Lynch presents his mythical image of the heartland not as reality, but as the result of an extreme fantasmatic distortion."[31] Audiences perceive "the physical beauty of Iowa fields and the moral beauty of the American small town . . . not because [this beauty] actually exists but because, as viewers of the film, we are looking through the lens of Alvin's fantasy."[32] McGowan suggests that Alvin transforms the physical space upon which his journey takes place—the very Midwestern landscape that viewers might recognize as a realistic environment—into "the world of fantasy" because the aged protagonist "embodies the full commitment to one's fantasy."[33] For McGowan, "The relatively tame and habitable public world depicted in *The Straight Story* results from Alvin's complete commitment to his fantasy. By committing himself to his fantasy, Alvin alters the way that he perceives and interacts with the external world, and this has the effect of changing it."[34] This reading of *The Straight Story* positions the film as being in line with the dream logic that marks nearly the entirety of Lynch's output as a filmmaker.

I expand on McGowan's insights about the fantasmatic nature of the landscape in *The Straight Story* by calling attention to the temporal dimension of Alvin's nostalgic revision of the Midwest. In short, the transformation of space on display in Lynch's film is a prime example of nostalgic spatiality. *The Straight Story* is one of many texts that present Midwestern imagery through a nostalgic prism, and the distinctive temporality of nostalgia strongly informs the film's narrative and style. Lynch's film is distinguished by its depiction of Alvin's fantasy world in what appears to be an objective manner—that is, there are almost no formal elements indicating that the regional space onscreen is distorted in some way. By contrast, in *The Virgin Suicides*, the color scheme and sound design constantly remind audiences that the film's images are, in fact, unreliable representations of nostalgic memories. Coppola also utilizes dissolves in order to create an atemporal blending of memory, fantasy, and the actual past, but only in scenes during which the boys' imaginations are activated by objects formerly owned by the Lisbon girls. Lynch and film editor Mary Sweeney, on the other hand, regularly use dissolves throughout *The Straight Story*, and this editing technique produces a curious sense of overlapping spatiality and temporality within the Midwestern setting.[35]

The dissolve edit exemplifies Boym's brief observation about ways in which nostalgia might be represented through filmic aesthetics. Boym writes, "A cinematic image of nostalgia is a double exposure, or a superimposition of two images—of home and abroad, past and present, dream and everyday life. The moment we try to force it into a single image, it breaks the frame or burns the surface."[36] Rather than omitting stretches of time via elliptical cuts, the dissolve blends images into one another and collapses time (and space) into brief moments of simultaneity. What would otherwise be clearly discrete shots and scenes instead occupy the same frame, however fleeting that instant might be. In this way, the basic desire of the nostalgic subject—to access and revisit the past within the present—is momentarily realized through the merging effect of the dissolve. For much of *The Straight Story*, the repeated use of dissolves disrupts the apparent linear trajectory of Alvin's journey by imbuing the Midwest with nostalgic spatial and temporal properties that suggest uncertain physical parameters and a distorted experience of time; Lynch thus renders Midwestern space as abstract and the region's temporality as comprised of an indeterminate duration and nonlinear flow (see fig. 6.3). Alvin may appear to be traveling across the regional landscape, but this movement is actually a slowly unfolding nostalgic manipulation of space and time.

Late in the film, Alvin enters Wisconsin, where he camps out in a cemetery. During this scene, Alvin explains to a local priest (John Lordan) the nostalgic impetus for embarking on his slow journey:

> [Lyle] and I used to sleep out in the yard every summer night if it wasn't pourin'. Nine months of winter, and we couldn't get enough of the summer. We'd bunk

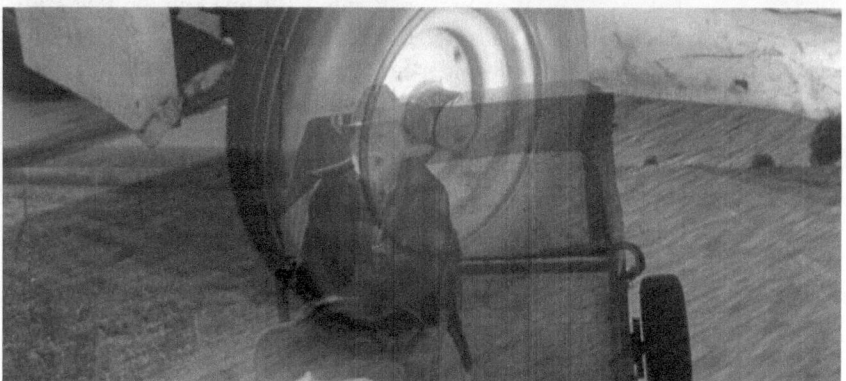

Fig. 6.3. The dissolve edit produces a sense of spatial and temporal simultaneity. Screen captures, *The Straight Story* (1999).

down when the sun went down, and we'd talk to each other until we went to sleep. We'd talk about the stars and whether there might be somebody else like us out in space, and places we wanted to go, and it made our trials seem smaller. Yeah, we pretty much talked each other through growin' up . . . [we] haven't spoken in ten years. Well, whatever it was that made me and Lyle so mad, it don't matter anymore. I wanna make peace. I wanna sit with him, look up at the stars like we used to do so long ago.

The ultimate goal of the journey is not simply to reconcile with Lyle, but also for the two brothers to recreate the experiences that Alvin nostalgically associates with their childhood relationship. In the film's final scene, Alvin achieves this desire, as the elderly siblings sit beside one another and gaze at the sky with tearful eyes. Lynch frames Alvin in a close-up, and the camera tilts upward; at this moment, one final dissolve is used as a transition to a shot of a star field, and the camera slowly begins to advance through this celestial space. This sequence of shots is significant for multiple reasons. First, the reunion between Alvin and Lyle occurs while it is still daylight, so the subsequent shot of stars cannot be an eyeline match, as viewers might expect. Again, the dissolve indicates an uncertain duration between these two shots. Second, the film opens with a nearly identical shot of a star field, although the camera's movement through space is a bit slower than in the final shot. Beginning and ending the film with these two shots has the peculiar effect of establishing celestial bookends that open up the regional narrative to a cosmic scale.

In early pressings of the DVD edition of *The Straight Story*, an insert is included with a quote from Lynch to explain why there are no "chapters" on the disc: "I know that most DVDs have chapter stops. It is my opinion that a film is not like a book—it should not be broken up. It is a continuum and should be seen as such. Thank you for your understanding."[37] Putting aside Lynch's preferences regarding how films should be experienced, his choice of the word continuum is especially meaningful in relation to this particular text. In addition to the first and last shots of *The Straight Story*, Lynch prominently sprinkles shots of stars—and, importantly, shots of Alvin gazing at them—throughout the film. These moments link the vast cosmos with what seems to be a highly provincial environment and story. Furthermore, stargazing may be understood as an inherently nostalgic practice, or at least an excellent metaphor for nostalgia.[38] Due to the speed of light, to look at the night sky is to literally gaze upon the past, to see a glow that no longer matches the present state of the stars that long ago emanated the light only now perceptible to the human eye. By connecting the expanse of outer space to a precise geographic territory, Lynch indicates that Alvin's Midwest exists as a continuum, a self-contained universe in which the past is visible in—or perhaps even concurrent with—the present. Any borders placed upon the suddenly nebulous Midwest are as arbitrary as the film frame around a random selection of the night sky; in the nostalgic domain of *The Straight Story*, neither the region nor the cosmos have terrestrial spatial and temporal boundaries. Once Alvin takes to the road in *The Straight Story*, he occupies a nearly uninterrupted nostalgic state, habitually stargazing at night while fixating on his ultimate destination: a reunion with Lyle during which the brothers will reenact their childhood contemplation of the night sky.

Within the context of the millennial Midwest's heightened sense of decline and decay, Alvin nostalgically attempts to reoccupy the past and succeeds in doing so. His relationship to the past contrasts with the narrator and his peers in *The Virgin Suicides*, all of whom are trapped within an unsatisfactory present characterized by unrelenting nostalgic longing. Because Alvin is able to avoid this emotionally paralytic state, *The Straight Story* exemplifies conceptions of the Midwest as a space of nostalgia at its logical extreme. Here, Lynch presents the region as an embodiment of how numerous commentators and texts—such as James Shortridge's description of the Midwest as a nostalgia museum—have imagined the territory.[39] In *The Straight Story*, the Midwest is an anachronistic space in which the spatiotemporal logic of nostalgia deeply affects the lives of Midwesterners. The region is depicted as a site of simultaneous, overlapping temporalities. For Lynch, though, the region's innate nostalgic character dispels the disillusionment, paranoia, violence, and impotent longing that affect the fictional Midwesterners found in other films from this period. This more hopeful vision of the Midwest is brought forth through nostalgic atonement. In Lynch's film, nostalgic atonement is represented as meaningful, progressive movement across the region's surface—a more introspective variation on the heavily mythologized spatial trajectories found in Frederick Jackson Turner's frontier writings.

The nostalgic spatial and temporal dynamics of *The Straight Story* produce a surprising twenty-first-century connection between an influential pair of thinkers who emerged in the late nineteenth century: Turner and French philosopher Henri Bergson. I develop the notion of nostalgic spatiality by arguing that Turner's geographic model of western expansion mirrors the temporal model of nostalgia: steady, linear progression to a certain point—for Turner, this point is when there are no longer any remaining frontier spaces within the continental United States—and then a looping turn backwards or inwards, as the case might be. By virtue of the Midwest's central location, the region operates as the fulcrum for Turner's claim that the nation "is now thrown back upon itself" on the cusp of the twentieth century.[40] This geographic positioning situates the region as a space of nostalgia in American culture. Remarkably, over one hundred years after the last western frontier purportedly was closed, the rejuvenating qualities that Turner attributes to those spatial frontiers manifest in *The Straight Story*. Alvin's slow journey across a segment of the Midwest repairs his damaged relationship with Lyle and, more importantly, ends with both brothers gazing contemplatively at the starlight emitted in the distant past. This final image of the Straight brothers suggests a positive outcome for nostalgic desire and has correspondences with Bergson's notion of duration.

Bergson first outlines the complex conditions of duration in *Time and Free Will* (1889). He writes that when "restored to its original purity, [duration] will appear as a wholly qualitative multiplicity, an absolute heterogeneity of elements which pass over into one another."[41] As such, "real duration is made up of moments inside one another."[42] The overlapping and blending temporality of Bergson's duration is evident in Lynch's depiction of the Midwest in *The Straight Story*. Lynch consistently blurs distinctions between particular locations and obfuscates the passage of time with the repeated use of dissolves. Furthermore, the final scene that shows Alvin and Lyle silently sitting together is, in essence, a visualization of the experience of duration. Regarding ways in which duration may be recognized, Bergson advocates that "[we] carry ourselves back in thought to those moments of our life when we made some serious decision, moments unique of their kind, which will never be repeated . . . if these past states cannot be adequately expressed in words or artificially reconstructed by a juxtaposition of simpler states, it is because in their dynamic unity and wholly qualitative multiplicity they are phases of our real and concrete duration, a heterogeneous duration and a living one."[43] Beyond the stated goal of atonement, Alvin's quest to reach Lyle and to reenact their childhood stargazing is also an attempt to reaccess the experience of duration that Alvin remembers from his past. At film's end, Alvin has successfully carried himself "back in thought" to a past state that is not a repetition, but instead is a renewal—an escape from a nostalgic foreclosure of the present and future. The disconnect that Alvin felt from his ideal childhood self has been repaired, and Lynch leaves audiences with an image of the aged protagonist contentedly nestled within a durational convergence of overlapping temporalities.

Throughout *The Straight Story*, Alvin strains to account for what caused the rift with Lyle, and a precise explanation is never provided. Alvin recalls past moments that are meaningful to him, but these instances (such as staring at the starry sky) seem to resonate simply for having occurred in his youth. Ultimately, the true focus of Alvin's nostalgia is revealed to be moments of duration in which he experienced a cosmic elevation from the burdens of provincial spaces and linear time. In this sense, *The Straight Story* serves as a less unsettling counterpart to the looping temporality featured in Lynch's more overtly unconventional films, such as *Lost Highway* (1997).[44] Alvin's reparatory trek across the Midwest permits him to access a fantastical space where a state of duration is achieved. Indeed, by the end of the film, Lynch—particularly through his repeated use of the dissolve—suggests that the entire region may be transformed into something approaching a realm of pure duration. Whereas the Midwest has often been perceived as a void in the middle of the country, *The Straight Story* reimagines the region as an arena in which nostalgia has the potential to enable a correction of the flawed past, rather than merely perpetuating nostalgic longing in the present. After more than a century of Midwestern identity being bound to an oppressive sense of nostalgia, Lynch both embraces and revises such regional associations. *The Straight Story* paradoxically suggests that a nostalgic perception of space and time is endemic to the Midwest while also being the very mechanism that may transcend geographic limitations.

The millennial Midwest is continually presented as a site of conflict and contradiction in popular culture. As the second half of *The American Midwest in Film and Literature* demonstrates, the region's status fluctuates dramatically in the American consciousness during the early years of the twenty-first century. Over roughly two decades, the Midwest rapidly shifts from being celebrated as a region of sincerity and authenticity to being exposed as a space that houses restrictive ideologies about identity categories such as race, gender, sexuality, and class. A recurring narrative element involves Midwesterners grasping for meaning, failing, and then lapsing into disillusionment, paranoia, and/or violence. *Boys Don't Cry, Gran Torino*, and *A History of Violence* present the Midwest as a performative space that is out of sync with contemporary American culture. Consequently, its inhabitants are constrained in their efforts to generate meaningful identities. Within these films, nostalgic violence is used to enforce regressive norms relating to masculinity, race, and regional identity in general. *About Schmidt, Up in the Air,* and *Take Shelter* explore a profound sense of disillusionment resulting from what has been framed as traditional Midwestern lifestyles. In the wake of economic turmoil, the recognition of the unsustainable nature of ideals about labor and family in the Midwest, and a subsequent destabilization of both individual and regional identity, the white male protagonists of *About Schmidt* and *Up in the Air* undertake nostalgic journeys into their personal histories. *Take Shelter*'s damaged, paranoid protagonist experiences visions of impending destruction and resorts to enacting a survivalist scenario in a backyard storm shelter. The actions showcased in these three films fail to provide comfort or relief for the various protagonists.

Concurrent with these narratives of Midwestern gloom and despair are films that feature nostalgic atonement. Through texts such as *Winter's Bone, Mysterious Skin, The Virgin Suicides,* and *The Straight Story*, more progressive ways of engaging with the past come into focus. Obviously, even across these four texts, there are substantial disparities in terms of the degree to which they depict positive outcomes of nostalgia. In *Winter's Bone*, an act of nostalgic atonement enables the Dolly family to keep their home (for the moment), but they remain trapped within an environment that promises, at best, ongoing economic struggles. The men of *The Virgin Suicides* fixate on trying to understand the actions and internal lives of the long-deceased Lisbon sisters, yet prove unable—or unwilling—to fully critique the self-involved purpose of their collective remembrances, which results in the potential for nostalgic atonement to slip away. Slivers of cautious optimism more clearly emerge in *Mysterious Skin*. At the conclusion of Araki's film, the traumatic past has been illuminated in an unvarnished, clear-eyed manner, and this acknowledgement is what seems to be the starting point of a release from the weight of that history. Finally, *The Straight Story* functions as an overt example of nostalgic atonement through its depiction of Alvin's attempt to alleviate the lingering repercussions of past misdeeds and conflicts. Rather than enacting regressive ideals or creating a monumental and ahistorical mythology of the past, Lynch shows that the possibility of returning to a desired lost moment may hinge upon conciliatory gestures, such as Alvin's journey to repair the fractured relationship with his brother Lyle. In undertaking this quest, Alvin merges nostalgic spatiality and nostalgic atonement, thus revealing the progressive potential of nostalgia in the millennial Midwest.

Notes

1. *The Straight Story*, directed by David Lynch (1999; Burbank, CA: Walt Disney Home Video, 2000), DVD.

2. As a slight coincidence, the widespread recognition of the Midwest as a discrete space in American culture developed in relatively close proximity to Alvin's birth. According to James Shortridge, the regional label "Middle West" attained popular usage around 1912, only a decade or so before Alvin was born. See: James R. Shortridge, *The Middle West: Its Meaning in American Culture* (Lawrence: University Press of Kansas, 1989), 24.

3. *Up in the Air*, directed by Jason Reitman (2009; Hollywood, CA: Paramount Pictures, 2010), DVD; *About Schmidt*, directed by Alexander Payne (2002; Los Angeles: New Line Home Entertainment, 2003), DVD; *Boys Don't Cry*, directed by Kimberly Peirce (1999; Beverly Hills, CA: Twentieth Century Fox Home Entertainment, 2000), DVD.

4. Svetlana Boym, *The Future of Nostalgia* (New York: Basic Books, 2001); *Winter's Bone*, directed by Debra Granik (Santa Monica, CA: Lionsgate, 2010), DVD; *Mysterious Skin*, Unrated Director's Edition, directed by Gregg Araki (2004; Culver City, CA: Strand Releasing Home Video, 2006), DVD.

5. *The Virgin Suicides*, directed by Sofia Coppola (1999; Hollywood, CA: Paramount Classics, 2000), DVD.

6. Theodore Dreiser, *Sister Carrie*, ed. Claude Simpson (1900; repr., Boston: Houghton Mifflin, 1959); *Badlands*, directed by Terrence Malick (1973; Burbank, CA: Warner Home Video, 2010), DVD.

7. *Stroszek*, directed by Werner Herzog (1977; Troy, MI: Anchor Bay Entertainment, 2001), DVD; *A History of Violence*, directed by David Cronenberg (2005; Los Angeles: New Line Home Entertainment, 2006), DVD.

8. Bilal Qureshi, "From Wrong to Right: A U.S. Apology for Japanese Internment," NPR, National Public Radio, August 9, 2013, https://www.npr.org/sections/codeswitch/2013/08/09/210138278/japanese-internment-redress.

9. Ta-Nehisi Coates, *We Were Eight Years in Power: An American Tragedy* (New York: One World, 2017), 202.

10. Ibid.

11. Boym, *The Future of Nostalgia*, 41, emphasis in original.

12. Ibid., 43.

13. *Gran Torino*, directed by Clint Eastwood (2008; Burbank, CA: Warner Home Video, 2010), DVD.

14. Daniel Woodrell, *Winter's Bone* (2006; repr., New York: Back Bay Books, 2007); Scott Heim, *Mysterious Skin* (1995; repr., Harper Perennial, 2005).

15. James Bell similarly observes that "the film is as much a stylised backwoods *noir* as a realist portrayal of a little-known pocket of the American underclass." See: James Bell, "Meth and the Maiden," *Sight & Sound* 20, no. 10 (October 2010): 28, italics in original.

16. Ibid.

17. Rich initially developed the term "New Queer Cinema" to describe the increasing amount of independent films that focused on LGBTQ+ issues and characters in the late 1980s and early 1990s. See: B. Ruby Rich, "New Queer Cinema," *Sight & Sound* 2, no. 5 (1992): 30–37; B. Ruby Rich, *New Queer Cinema: The Director's Cut* (Durham, NC: Duke University Press, 2013).

18. Of this reunion at Coach's house, Kylo-Patrick R. Hart writes that it is one of numerous "lengthy scenes that play out in real time in order to heighten their emotionality" throughout Araki's filmography. See: Kylo-Patrick R. Hart, *Images for a Generation Doomed: The Films and Career of Gregg Araki* (Plymouth, UK: Lexington Books, 2010), 80.

19. Maureen Turim, *Flashbacks in Film: Memory and History* (New York: Routledge, 1989), 1.

20. Jeffrey Eugenides, *The Virgin Suicides* (New York: Picador, 1993).

21. Boym, *The Future of Nostalgia*, xv, emphasis added.

22. The group of boys shifts in number and composition, although some of them garner more screen time and appear more frequently than the rest: Tim Weiner (Jonathan Tucker), Chase Buell (Anthony DeSimone), Peter Sisten (Chris Hale), and Parker Denton (Noah Shebib).

23. Debra Shostak, "'A Story We Could Live With': Narrative Voice, the Reader, and Jeffrey Eugenides's *The Virgin Suicides*," MFS Modern Fiction Studies 55, no. 4 (Winter 2009): 808, doi: 10.1353/mfs.0.1642.

24. Ibid., 809.

25. Bree Hoskin, "Playground Love: Landscape and Longing in Sofia Coppola's *The Virgin Suicides*," Literature Film Quarterly 35, no. 3 (2007): 216.

26. Coppola occasionally includes voiceover narration by the older Trip, but in these instances, his commentary is used as a sound bridge during edits that shift from the past to the present scene in the rehabilitation center.

27. Hoskin, "Playground Love," 217.

28. Jennifer A. González, "Autotopographies," in *Prosthetic Territories: Politics and Hypertechnologies*, eds. Gabriel Brahm Jr. and Mark Driscoll (Boulder, CO: Westview, 1995), 134.

29. The precise distance of the journey varies according to the source. The DVD packaging lists the distance as 260 miles, while Chris Rodley cites the distance as three hundred miles. Within the film, Alvin's adult daughter Rose (Sissy Spacek) estimates that Lyle lives 370 miles away, and an article in the *Des Moines Register* identifies the distance traveled by the real-life Alvin as 240 miles. Given the film's nostalgic abstraction of space and time, the specific mileage is incidental and merely a point of trivia. See: Chris Rodley, ed., *Lynch on Lynch*, revised edition (London: Faber and Faber, 2005), 245; Tom Longden, "Alvin Straight," *The Des Moines Register*, https://data.desmoinesregister.com/famous-iowans/alvin-straight.

30. Tim Kreider and Rob Content describe Alvin's insistence on visiting Lyle without assistance as "an ordeal ritual, its rigors and privations rigidly maintained as a form of self-flagellation." Kreider and Content offer a distinctly dark reading of the film based upon the revelation that Rose's children were taken away by the state. During an encounter with a runaway teen, Alvin explains, "One night, somebody else was watchin' the kids, and there was a fire. Her second boy got burned real bad." For Kreider and Content, Alvin's stories about his past are "full of conspicuous gaps and contradictions," which leads them to extrapolate that Alvin's negligence is what caused Rose to lose her children—that he is the "someone else" in the story. From this perspective, Alvin's "journey . . . of atonement" is not simply undertaken for Lyle; it is an act of penance for the entirety of Alvin's lifetime of regrettable behavior, including accidentally killing an American soldier in World War II, his subsequent alcoholism, and the possibility that he caused his grandchildren to be injured and taken from Rose. See: Tim Kreider and Rob

Content, review of *The Straight Story*, by David Lynch, *Film Quarterly* 54, no. 1 (Autumn 2000): 27, 31, doi: 10.2307/1213799.

31. Todd McGowan, *The Impossible David Lynch* (New York: Columbia University Press, 2007), 179.

32. Ibid., 190.

33. Ibid., 184–185.

34. Ibid., 192.

35. In their respective texts, McGowan and Kreider and Content highlight particular scenes in which dissolves are used. McGowan writes about a scene depicting Alvin waiting for an undefined period of time after his mower stalls just before reaching Lyle's home, while Kreider and Content note that Lynch illustrates one of Alvin's stories about his past with "a series of dissolves from one allusive image of abandonment and emptiness to another." See: ibid., 189; Kreider and Content, Review of *The Straight Story*, 27.

36. Boym, *The Future of Nostalgia*, xiii–xiv.

37. David Lynch, statement on DVD chapter stops, *The Straight Story*, directed by David Lynch (1999; Burbank, CA: Walt Disney Home Video, 2000), DVD insert.

38. The relationship between nostalgia and stargazing is especially emphasized in Chilean filmmaker Patricio Guzmán's documentary *Nostalgia for the Light* (2010), which features a dual focus on the work of astronomers and the search for the missing bodies of victims of political violence in the Atacama Desert. See: *Nostalgia for the Light*, directed by Patricio Guzmán (Brooklyn, NY: Icarus Films, 2010), film.

39. Shortridge, *The Middle West*, 67–68.

40. Frederick Jackson Turner, *The Frontier in American History* (1920; repr., Charleston, SC: BiblioBazaar, 2008), 186.

41. Henri Bergson, *Time and Free Will: An Essay on the Immediate Data of Consciousness*, trans. F. L. Pogson (1889; repr., London: George Allen & Unwin, 1950), 229.

42. Ibid., 232.

43. Ibid., 238–239.

44. *Lost Highway*, directed by David Lynch (1997; Universal City, CA: Universal Studies Home Entertainment, 2008), DVD.

Conclusion: Nostalgic Frontiers

I began *The American Midwest in Film and Literature* by relating how the satirical newspaper *The Onion* had humorously announced the "discovery" of the Midwest in the late 1990s. In that article, the Midwest was framed as a mysterious realm that baffled outside observers with its "backwards" culture and "vast" space.[1] With a nod toward symmetry, I open this concluding chapter by returning to *The Onion* for further insights regarding popular perceptions of the region. As with many of the texts considered in this book, a 2011 article in *The Onion* establishes the Midwest as an atemporal space that entraps people who enter its nebulous borders. Entitled "30 Years of Man's Life Disappear in Mysterious 'Kansas Rectangle,'" this piece details the story of a Chicago man who, despite being a Midwesterner himself (albeit one from the Midwest's unofficial urban capital, which is frequently exempted from regional tags and associations), vanishes in Kansas after being "drawn there to investigate tales of cheap tuition."[2] This victim hardly is unique, as he "is only one of hundreds of people who, for unknown reasons, have had years or even decades of their lives utterly fade away in the mystifying region. . . . The few known photos from inside the rectangle show only a flat, blank emptiness, stretching unremarkably to the horizon."[3] Even individuals who have successfully exited this abnormal space describe sensory confusion: "The most frequent occurrence reported by those who have survived the Kansas Rectangle is extreme disorientation and an unsettling perception of time distortion."[4] Beyond simply being a comical description of the Midwest as an eerie Bermuda Triangle–like locale, this article's conception of the region matches the spatiotemporal qualities on display in numerous other Midwestern texts such as *Badlands* (1973) and *The Straight Story* (1999).[5] Again and again, across genre, medium, and period, popular texts render the middle region as a "blank" domain that is inseparable from the transformative spatial and temporal dynamics of nostalgia.

Throughout this project, I theorize multiple forms of nostalgia and uncover how Midwestern identity has been envisioned, shaped, and contested by a variety of texts spanning roughly 125 years. Regarding the former objective, I introduce and delineate the concepts of nostalgic spatiality, nostalgic violence, and nostalgic atonement in order to make sense of narrative conventions and aesthetics that recur in representations of nostalgia. Regarding the latter objective, I work to bring regional studies—in the form of the scholarly study of the Midwest—into extended contact with film and literary studies. I particularly expose how critical engagement with the Midwest is submerged yet sustained within American cinema since the beginning of the sound era. From studio system–produced

Technicolor musicals of the 1940s to independent horror cinema of the 1970s to the wide-ranging filmic depictions of the millennial Midwest, an undercurrent of regionalism is detectible in ways both overt and subtle across a diverse array of films. Notably, films with Midwestern content frequently occupy overlapping positions of significance within the histories of cinema and region. Many iconic examples of genre and period—for instance, *Meet Me in St. Louis* (1944) and *Halloween* (1978) fit the categories listed above—also sit easily within established regional discourses and reflect certain preexisting conventions for representing the Midwest.[6] In short, cinema serves as an essential forum for critically exploring the contours of regional identity.

To make sense of the interplay between regionalism and nostalgia, I situate my primary textual objects within historico-cultural contexts. Although I largely focus on fictional narrative films, I also consider the treatment of the Midwest in selected literary texts and in other studies of the region, such as the work of Frederick Jackson Turner and Robert S. Lynd and Helen Merrell Lynd's sociological study, *Middletown: A Study in Modern American Culture* (1929).[7] In tandem with this cross-medium set of materials, *The American Midwest in Film and Literature* has a bifurcated structure that is partly based upon time period. The chapters in "Part I: Twentieth-Century Narratives of Nostalgia and the Midwest" examine an eclectic selection of texts produced or set during three key periods in the twentieth century, and the chapters in "Part II: The Millennial Midwest on Film" provide a more focused study of films from the past two decades. With this combination of textual objects and methodology, a more complex portrait of the Midwest emerges, thereby illuminating how the region's popular identity is marked by continuity *and* continued evolution. The Midwest is a cultural construct that remains in flux, rather than retaining a stable meaning since the region first gained widespread recognition as a discrete space in the early twentieth century.

As I argue over the preceding chapters, Turner's theories about the frontier and regional spaces heavily influence the initial development of the Midwest's identity, various Midwestern narratives produced over the course of the twentieth century, and even how the region continues to be understood in the twenty-first century. In essence, Turner discusses the Midwest in ways that are explicitly nostalgic, as he asserts that the middle region houses the lost culture and values of frontier spaces. Variations of these ascribed regional attributes reappear in many Midwestern texts. Furthermore, by rereading Turner as a nostalgia writer, I conceptualize nostalgic spatiality, which underpins the entirety of this project. I identify a nostalgic dimension to Turner's notion that the cessation of the United States' western expansion resulted in the nation being "thrown back upon itself."[8] According to Turner, linear progression changes into a coiling return inward. This movement is a spatial version of the temporal operation of nostalgic desire. Hence, the concept of nostalgic spatiality refers to nostalgia's looping desire circuit as it is projected onto physical landscapes, which generates effects that permeate the cultural sphere.

I recognize multiple iterations of nostalgic spatiality manifesting within a variety of Midwestern texts on the levels of narrative, theme, and/or aesthetics.

My first two case studies, Theodore Dreiser's *Sister Carrie* (1900) and *Meet Me in St. Louis*, both revolve around the negative impacts of spatial relocations to the East Coast and a strong nostalgic attachment to Midwestern cities: Chicago and St. Louis, respectively.[9] Nostalgic spatiality is evident through the two texts' shared emphasis on tensions between movement and stability. In Dreiser's novel, protagonists Caroline Meeber and George Hurstwood flee to New York City following the latter's impulsive theft of a large sum of money; escaping into the West is never considered as a possibility, as the pair immediately embark eastward. By the novel's end, Carrie has become a theater star, while George is impoverished and has slipped into a delirious state in which he experiences nostalgic memories of Chicago as if they are actually happening in the present. Spatial dislocation results in a debilitating nostalgic reverie that ends only with George's death. By contrast, *Meet Me in St. Louis* details the lives of the Smith family who, with the exception of patriarch Alonzo (Leon Ames), are wary of disrupting their idealized present condition in which they joyfully anticipate the arrival of the 1904 World's Fair. When Alonzo shares that he intends to move the family, discontentment ensues. Essentially, the Smith family desires to maintain their suddenly endangered status quo, and this is expressed as nostalgia for geographic stasis—that is, nostalgia for spatial immobility. In anticipation of future nostalgia for the present, the various family members transform their contemporary moment into a period of continual longing in which the object of desire is the fleeting present itself. Both *Sister Carrie* and *Meet Me in St. Louis* show how nostalgic spatiality may emerge through a sustained emotional linkage to particular spatiotemporal coordinates.

From this opening examination of nostalgic spatiality, I proceed to identify its shifting forms in a disparate set of Midwestern texts. On the levels of narrative and theme, nostalgic spatiality may be quite overt, as in *About Schmidt* (2002) and *Up in the Air* (2009).[10] These two films depict their respective protagonists nostalgically revisiting sites of personal significance; such journeys qualify as straightforward and somewhat mundane examples of nostalgic spatiality. *Halloween* details the grisly homecoming of Michael Myers and his efforts to nostalgically transform various spaces—from the specific sites of his childhood home and the Wallace house to the town of Haddonfield more generally—into venues in which symbols of his past violence are visibly present. In *Native Son* (1940), Richard Wright associates racial segregation with a regressive nostalgic attitude through the character of the wealthy white landlord Mr. Dalton, who flippantly remarks that rental discrimination is "an old custom."[11] Here, Wright frames racist housing practices as an especially contemptible type of nostalgic spatiality in which powerful white figures map their prejudice onto a cityscape. Director Sofia Coppola's *The Virgin Suicides* (1999) reflects on what it means for a location—the neighborhood of the collective narrator's youth—to be understood entirely through a temporally distant state of nostalgic longing.[12] The film's flashback narrative and commentary on memory exemplify nostalgic spatiality, as the adult narrator reduces a physical site and its inhabitants to the status of nostalgically remembered phantasms.

Like the levels of narrative and theme, the aesthetics of nostalgic spatiality are variable and may differ from text to text. *The Virgin Suicides* merges all three ways in which nostalgic spatiality might be rendered within a given textual object. Coppola creates a dreamlike environment with a stylized color palette and lighting scheme, and she showcases dated visual elements such as 1970s attire and party decorations. Yet Coppola undercuts the status of the mise-en-scène as a representation of the actual past by continually reminding viewers that nearly the entirety of the film is a highly subjective flashback. Voiceover narration establishes the images as visualizations of the collective narrator's present-day memories, and Coppola twice cuts to a scene in the present, which contrasts the drab contemporary moment with the vibrancy of the nostalgia-saturated past. Similar to *The Virgin Suicides*, in *Mysterious Skin* (2005), director Gregg Araki plays on cultural nostalgia for the years stretching from the early 1980s to the early 1990s.[13] Araki emphasizes the film's period-specific props, costumes, and audiovisual technologies (such as VCRs and the grainy production values of a television program on alien abductions). He also uses colors and lighting that, at times, are almost expressionistic in their heightened lushness. This onscreen depiction of the film's Midwestern setting is explicitly framed as corresponding to the traumatic and disturbingly nostalgic recollections of Brian Lackey (Brady Corbet) and Neil McCormick (Joseph Gordon-Levitt), who discuss their past experiences in voiceover narration from an unspecified later date. Despite these two films' substantially different subject matter, both *The Virgin Suicides* and *Mysterious Skin* present the past as especially vivid and colorful in order to match the reminiscing of the characters and, among viewers of certain ages, the nostalgic memories of audience members.

It is worth qualifying that past-oriented narrative premises or the mere presence of nostalgic objects within the mise-en-scène do not confirm the existence of nostalgic spatiality in a film. Simply representing a past milieu does not, in and of itself, denote nostalgic spatiality. One element that separates a standard period picture from a film that does contain some aspect of nostalgic spatiality is an emphasis on the subjective rendering or understanding of the represented space. In *The Virgin Suicides* and *Mysterious Skin*, stylized and often-unrealistic aesthetics push both films from simply being representations of their narratives' respective time periods to operating within the parameters of nostalgic spatiality.

Beyond the aesthetics discussed above, nostalgic spatiality may be visualized in additional ways. Nearly the entirety of *The Straight Story* qualifies as a rather distinctive example of nostalgic spatiality in which Lynch transforms the film's seemingly naturalistic regional setting into an abstract terrain. Throughout *The Straight Story*, Lynch utilizes the dissolve edit to produce a visual merging of past and present. In this way, the Midwestern landscape is presented as a space of temporal simultaneity—the very condition desired by nostalgic subjects such as the film's aged protagonist, Alvin Straight (Richard Farnsworth). Coppola also makes use of dissolves during several fantasy sequences in *The Virgin Suicides*, which has the similar effect of unsettling the stability of the film's vision of the past. Films such as *Badlands* and Werner Herzog's *Stroszek* (1977) engender nostalgic spatiality via a combination of elements in the mise-en-scène and camerawork.[14] *Stroszek* immerses viewers inside a regional environment of looping circles that reflect the halted, atemporal status of the film's titular protagonist upon arrival in Wisconsin. Both the mise-en-scène—with its frozen ponds and circling farmers—and several graphlike camera movements suggest a spatial dynamic informed by nostalgia's nonlinear desire mechanism. In *Badlands*, Kit Carruthers (Martin Sheen) and Holly Sargis (Sissy Spacek) are unable to successfully navigate through the regional borderland during their attempted flight from the Midwest. Malick portrays the Badlands as a space that seems to continually expand as Kit and Holly drive across its sparse surface. Despite the apparent linearity of the pair's movements—many shots feature their car travelling either in a parallel or perpendicular line in relation to the bottom of the frame—Malick's depiction of the Badlands is filtered through the prism of nostalgia. As is evident by the many permutations detailed above, nostalgic spatiality is a flexible concept that appears in numerous forms.

Along with locating nostalgic spatiality in various Midwestern texts, I also draw attention to the recurrence of violence in many of those narratives. By examining the restrictive, violent effects of nostalgic spatiality, the concept of nostalgic violence emerges. Nostalgic violence describes acts of violence that are compelled by regressively nostalgic ideals about the identities, behaviors, and cultural mythologies of a place and its inhabitants. *Badlands* provides an exemplary case study of nostalgic violence, as Kit repeatedly commits violent acts in conjunction with ritualistic and symbolic gestures. For instance, Kit kills individuals (such as Holly's father and a group of bounty hunters) who threaten to disrupt his relationship with Holly and their performative enactment of domesticity in the wilderness. Kit's nostalgic violence supports the pair's bewildering efforts to conform to conventional values, particularly those concerned with gender identity, relationships, and class. In *Halloween*, Michael Myers's murderous acts are disturbing reenactments of the formative killing of his sister as a child. This commemorative function clearly situates such actions as instances of nostalgic violence.

Whereas *Badlands* and *Halloween* present viewers with nostalgic violence being deployed for individually meaningful purposes, other films illustrate how nostalgic violence may be used as a cultural regulatory mechanism with broader symbolic ramifications. Kimberly Peirce's *Boys Don't Cry* (1999) depicts the usage of nostalgic violence to brutally assert the primacy of heteronormative gender roles through the film's fictionalized account of a real-life incident in which a transgender man, Brandon Teena (Hilary Swank), was assaulted and murdered in Nebraska.[15] In *Gran Torino* (2008), protagonist Walt Kowalski (Clint Eastwood) responds to the changing demographics in his Detroit neighborhood with hostility and resentment.[16] As the film progresses, Walt espouses reductive values about masculinity and commits acts of nostalgic violence in order to preserve a racial hierarchy that elevates whiteness in American culture. With *A History of Violence* (2005), director David Cronenberg exposes how the mundane surface of normality in a small Indiana community is actually dependent upon nostalgic violence for its maintenance.[17] The superficial stability of the Stall family is propped up by the exceptionally violent faculties of protagonist Tom Stall (Viggo Mortensen), whose bland Midwestern persona masks a background as a vicious Philadelphia gangster. As these three films demonstrate, textual representations of nostalgic violence often engage with—either directly or metaphorically—the structures and ideologies that perpetuate various inequalities along the lines of race, gender, and sexuality. Such narrative occurrences are also attached to nostalgic mythologies about regional identity.

Nostalgic atonement is a much different relationship to the past than that of nostalgic violence. Rather than working to actualize nostalgia-based ideals within the present, nostalgic atonement recognizes the ongoing impacts of the damaged past and seeks to alleviate such detrimental repercussions. Doing so necessitates that individuals revisit the past and acknowledge actual historical circumstances instead of embracing myths and ideologies that uncritically celebrate the past. *The Straight Story* is an especially overt example of nostalgic atonement. The narrative revolves around Alvin Straight's slow, laborious journey to visit his ailing brother. At multiple points in the film, Alvin openly comments on his own culpability for the brothers' long period of estrangement; consequently, his trip is cast as a conciliatory act—a symbolic gesture to make amends for the past. In more compartmentalized ways, *Mysterious Skin* and *Winter's Bone* (2010) exhibit narrative developments that are aligned with the corrective goals of nostalgic atonement.[18] The resolution of each film involves a changed relationship to past traumas that, in part, stems from the unshrouding of those events. By virtue of unvarnished disclosures, the burden of the past is loosened, and the future opens to a broader set of tentatively hopeful potentialities.

Two works of literature offer further examples of ways in which nostalgia may produce a less restrictive or even progressive relationship to the past within Midwestern contexts. While not quite falling within the category of nostalgia atonement, Sandra Cisneros's *The House on Mango Street* (1984) and Kao Kalia Yang's *The Latehomecomer: A Hmong Family Memoir* (2008) both are distinguished by sophisticated, nuanced forms of nostalgia.[19] Each text treats the past as a lingering presence, but not necessarily as an idealized object of nostalgia or as moments to be nostalgically restored. Esperanza Cordero, the fictional protagonist of *The House on Mango Street*, expresses a profound ambivalence toward the Chicago neighborhood and home of her youth. At the conclusion of the novel, Esperanza imagines that she "will say goodbye to Mango" and eventually "go away," but she still envisions a nostalgic return in the future: "[Friends and neighbors] will not know I have gone away to come back. For the ones I left behind. For the ones who cannot out."[20] For Cisneros, nostalgic memory appears to be something of an obligation to one's own history as well as to that of others. Similar to nostalgic atonement, such acts of memory and narration enable a partial release from the grip of the past. *The Latehomecomer: A Hmong Family Memoir* also features an idea of "home" that remains in flux for Yang's family and other Hmong Americans in the Midwest. Yang was born in a refugee camp in Thailand, and she explains her impetus for writing a family history as "slowly unleash[ing] the flood of Hmong into language, seeking refuge not for a name or a gender, but a people."[21] In completing this task, Yang shares her family's experiences as they settle in Minnesota. The memoir concludes with a lengthy description of the traditional Hmong funeral for Yang's beloved grandmother, during which a guide ceremoniously "teach[es] Grandma's soul the way back to the place where she was born."[22] As Yang details, the guide narrates a route from the Midwest back to the grandmother's birthplace in Laos that is based on personal history. By retracing the spatial trajectory of the deceased's life, this deeply personal ritual may be understood as a form of nostalgic spatiality—a distinctive iteration that is at once mournful and celebratory. In both of these texts, then, Cisneros and Yang present readers with nostalgia that is purposeful and that exceeds individualistic longing in ways that have possible benefit for larger communities.

By studying the nostalgic mythologies and facets of the Midwest in film, literature, and assorted other materials, the region comes into greater focus as a site of contradictory meanings and symbolic functions in American culture. Portrayals of the Midwest as a blank space simultaneously obscure and illuminate the nostalgic spatial and temporal dimensions that are intrinsic to the region's identity. The past-oriented fixation that pervades Midwestern culture—at least as conceptualized in many regional texts and discourses—contributes to reductive conceptions of the Midwest as a static, unchanging domain. Nostalgia, however, is a dynamic force, and its effects vary considerably. In Midwestern narratives, nostalgia manifests in forms that are spatially constrictive (as in *Native Son* and *The Miracle of Morgan's Creek* [1944]), violently regressive (as in *Halloween* and *Boys Don't Cry*), frustratingly ambivalent (as in *Gran Torino* and *Take Shelter* [2011]), or potentially transcendent (as in *The Straight Story*).[23] Across a diverse range of textual objects, I have sought to demonstrate how the relationship between the Midwest and nostalgia is modulated in response to changing historical circumstances. Ultimately, through sustained critical attention to the operations of nostalgia within both representations of the region and actual Midwestern culture, the constraints upon regional identity might be loosened so that a more desirable Midwest can emerge—a version that escapes a nostalgic future by not being bound so closely to mythologized conceptions of the past. The nostalgic desire for simultaneity is a yearning for spatiotemporal collapse: that is, a reconnection of the past and present within a particular locale. Perhaps, though, the state of simultaneity might be reimagined as, to appropriate Turner's phrase, a mode of "perennial rebirth" that opens up the Midwest's popular identity to reflect its actual heterogeneity and that moves beyond the curtailed meanings that long have defined the region.[24]

Notes

1. "'Midwest' Discovered Between East, West Coasts," *The Onion*, September 4, 1996, https://www.theonion.com/midwest-discovered-between-east-west-coasts-1819564009.

2. "30 Years of Man's Life Disappear in Mysterious 'Kansas Rectangle,'" *The Onion*, June 30, 2011, https://local.theonion.com/30-years-of-mans-life-disappear-in-mysterious-kansas-re-1819572765.

3. Ibid.

4. Ibid.

5. *Badlands*, directed by Terrence Malick (1973; Burbank, CA: Warner Home Video, 2010), DVD; *The Straight Story*, directed by David Lynch (1999; Burbank, CA: Walt Disney Home Video, 2000), DVD.

6. *Meet Me in St. Louis*, directed by Vincente Minnelli (1944; Burbank, CA: Warner Home Video, Inc., 2004), DVD; *Halloween*, directed by John Carpenter (1978; Troy, MI: Anchor Bay Entertainment, 2000), DVD.

7. Frederick Jackson Turner, *The Frontier in American History* (1920; repr., Charleston, SC: BiblioBazaar, 2008); Robert S. Lynd and Helen Merrell Lynd, *Middletown: A Study in Modern American Culture* (1929; repr., San Diego, CA: Harcourt Brace Jovanovich, 1957).

8. Turner, *The Frontier in American History*, 186.

9. Theodore Dreiser, *Sister Carrie*, ed. Claude Simpson (1900; repr., Boston: Houghton Mifflin, 1959).

10. *About Schmidt*, directed by Alexander Payne (2002; Los Angeles: New Line Home Entertainment, 2003), DVD; *Up in the Air*, directed by Jason Reitman (2009; Hollywood, CA: Paramount Pictures, 2010), DVD.

11. Richard Wright, *Native Son* (1940; repr., New York: Harper Perennial Modern Classics, 2005), 327.

12. *The Virgin Suicides*, directed by Sofia Coppola (1999; Hollywood, CA: Paramount Classics, 2000), DVD.

13. *Mysterious Skin*, Unrated Director's Edition, directed by Gregg Araki (2004; Culver City, CA: Strand Releasing Home Video, 2006), DVD.

14. *Stroszek*, directed by Werner Herzog (1977; Troy, MI: Anchor Bay Entertainment, 2001), DVD.

15. *Boys Don't Cry*, directed by Kimberly Peirce (1999; Beverly Hills, CA: Twentieth Century Fox Home Entertainment, 2000), DVD.

16. *Gran Torino*, directed by Clint Eastwood (2008; Burbank, CA: Warner Home Video, 2010), DVD.

17. *A History of Violence*, directed by David Cronenberg (2005; Los Angeles: New Line Home Entertainment, 2006), DVD.

18. *Winter's Bone*, directed by Debra Granik (Santa Monica, CA: Lionsgate, 2010), DVD.

19. Sandra Cisneros, *The House on Mango Street* (1984; repr., New York: Vintage Contemporaries, 2009); Kao Kalia Yang, *The Latehomecomer: A Hmong Family Memoir* (Minneapolis, MN: Coffee House, 2008).

20. Cisneros, *The House on Mango Street*, 110.

21. Yang, *The Latehomecomer*, 4.

22. Ibid., 252.

23. *The Miracle of Morgan's Creek*, directed by Preston Sturges (1944; Hollywood, CA: Paramount Pictures, 2005), DVD; *Take Shelter*, directed by Jeff Nichols (2011; Culver City, CA: Sony Pictures Home Entertainment, 2012), DVD.

24. Turner, *The Frontier in American History*, 14.

Afterword: Regionalism and Politics

During the months preceding and following the 2016 presidential election, a recurring topic of inquiry in news outlets and among cultural commentators revolved around understanding the appeal of Donald Trump to rural, white Americans, especially those living in the center of the nation.[1] Trump, a celebrity businessperson whose public identity had long been associated with New York City and the East Coast, waged a campaign structured on his outsized force of personality and inflammatory statements directed at a broad range of targets, from immigrants to political rivals in the Republican Party. For the purposes of my project, it is particularly notable that Trump's rhetoric of resentment and stigmatization was—and continues to be—filtered through a blustery performance of hypermasculinity and packaged within a decidedly nostalgic slogan: "Make America Great Again!"[2] This promise to elevate the United States from its supposedly degraded present by returning the nation to an idealized past condition exemplifies the ahistorical, paranoid, conspiratorial, and nationalistic qualities of what Svetlana Boym describes as "restorative nostalgia."[3] To "Make America Great Again!" thus may be translated as a nostalgic agenda that envisions a future in which a lost state of affairs, imagined or actual, is miraculously restored to the benefit of Trump's predominantly white base.[4]

Interpretations of the motives and values of Trump's supporters have generally tended to fall into two broad categories. Given the demographics denigrated by Trump, many observers opined that deeply engrained racist, misogynistic, and xenophobic attitudes within American culture were responsible for his allure to certain white voters. Others suggested that economic anxiety was a sufficient explanation for the passionate support of his base. In this afterword, I review a sampling of these assessments and then connect them to a regional context: cultural narratives about the Midwest. Trump's rhetorical conflation of ahistorical declarations about a lost condition of greatness, accusations of contemporary failure (in economic and cultural realms, among others), and widespread resentment of demographics that are not white corresponds with popular understandings of the Midwest across medium and time period. These very dynamics—again, the interrelationships among nostalgia, failure, and resentment—have appeared in numerous Midwestern texts since at least the late nineteenth century and are visible in documentaries produced over the past three decades. By examining a short story by Hamlin Garland and a small selection of films, the interplay of regional mythologies, nostalgia's powerful cultural impacts, and contemporary political developments comes into greater focus. In addressing such topics, I also seek to accentuate how regional scholarship provides insights about multiple facets of American culture. A region is a geographic territory, the lives and culture within those borders, *and* the narratives told about that space. Studying these areas in conjunction with one another necessitates an approach that oscillates between analyses of textual representations and actual historical circumstances. As a way to reveal further applications for the primary arguments of *The American Midwest in Film and Literature*, I consider additional points of contact among cultural nostalgia, narratives about the Midwest's identity and meaning, and the lived experiences of the region's inhabitants. Of extra note, many of this afterword's primary materials more narrowly engage with the state of Wisconsin, which has been one of the Midwest's most intense staging grounds for ideological clashes in recent years.

Nostalgia, Failure, and Resentment

Just two months prior to the 2016 election, *The Atlantic* published an article by Alex MacGillis and ProPublica that details a "general aura of decline that hangs over towns" near the border of Ohio and Kentucky.[5] MacGillis and ProPublica outline a linkage of despair, nostalgia, and political views within such communities:

> The fatalism is clear: Things were much better in an earlier time, and no future awaits in places that have been left behind by polished people in gleaming cities. The most painful comparison is not with supposedly ascendant minorities—it's with the fortunes of one's own parents or, by now, grandparents. The demoralizing effect of decay enveloping the place you live cannot be underestimated. And the bitterness—the "primal scorn"—that Donald Trump has tapped into among white Americans in struggling areas is aimed not just at those of foreign extraction. It is directed toward fellow countrymen who have become foreigners of a different sort, looking down on the natives, if they bother to look at all.[6]

This passage's commentary on race and national identity is striking, especially in the final sentences. Here, the brief equivalence of the term "natives" and "white Americans in struggling areas" recalls a similar phrasing in Robert S. Lynd and Helen Merrell Lynd's influential sociological study, *Middletown: A Study in Modern American Culture* (1929).[7] As I discuss in the second chapter, when selecting a locale for their study, the Lynds sought a city comprised of "a relatively constant native American stock"—a description that they use to denote white Americans.[8] Even as passing references, these parallel framings of "native" status in texts produced nearly ninety years apart highlight the symbolic importance and ongoing elevation of whiteness within cultural mythologies of American regions, particularly the Midwest.[9]

MacGillis and ProPublica touch upon several other topics that reappear in commentary on the 2016 election, such as a sense of being "left behind" among poor (and often rural) white populations and an accompanying growth of resentment toward other demographics. The nostalgic contrast of a favorable past with an uncontrollable present and a dire future is a hallmark of economic interpretations of Trump's victory. For instance, two weeks after the election, economist Robert Schiller notes that Trump's "most enthusiastic support tended to come from those with average and stagnating incomes and low levels of education."[10] Schiller speculates that such loyalists were motivated by "a sense of economic powerlessness, or a fear of losing power," although he concludes that Trump is "highly unlikely to deliver . . . an increase in workers' economic power."[11] Significantly, economic readings of the election consistently stress perceptions of limited power and influence among Trump's supporters, which is also a common feature of interpretations based upon white attitudes about race and location.

For observers such as Ta-Nehisi Coates, focusing on economic explanations obfuscates the racial dimensions of the 2016 election outcome, as well as the history and culture of the United States in general. While reminding readers that Trump achieved "dominance across nearly every white demographic," Coates insists that "escapism" is the reason why "Trump is pawned off as a product of the white working class as opposed to a product of an entire whiteness."[12] Coates later argues that "an imagined white working class remains central to our politics and our cultural understanding of those politics, not simply when it comes to addressing broad economic issues but also when it comes to addressing racism."[13] Like Coates, political scientist Diana C. Mutz dismisses the "dominant narrative explaining the outcome of the 2016 presidential election [which is] that working class voters rose up in opposition to being left behind economically."[14] Instead, in a 2018 study of the election results, Mutz asserts, "Evidence points overwhelmingly to perceived status threat among high-status groups as the key motivation underlying Trump support."[15] More precisely, "because white male Christians are seen as most prototypically 'American,'" Mutz explains that this group has "the most to lose psychologically if they perceive America and/or whites to be no longer dominant."[16] In short, Mutz contends that these latter two fears account for Trump's success among white voters.

Another element shaping American culture and politics—one that bridges many of the economic, racial, and spatial dynamics detailed above—is what political scientist Katherine J. Cramer describes as a "rural-versus-urban divide" that produces "resentment toward our fellow citizens."[17] Notably, Cramer's invaluable study was published several months before the 2016 election, and her research stretches back to 2007.[18] While detailing the results of her roughly ten-year study of shifting political sentiments in rural Wisconsin communities, Cramer outlines critical frameworks for processing this spatio-cultural schism. Cramer writes, "A politics of resentment arises from the way social identities, the emotion of resentment, and economic insecurity interact. In a politics of resentment, resentment toward fellow citizens is front and center. People understand their circumstances as the fault of guilty and less deserving social groups, not as the product of broad social, economic, and political forces."[19] According to Cramer, resentment is a common feature of what she conceptualizes as "rural consciousness," which has "three elements: (1) a belief that rural areas are ignored by decision makers, including policy makers, (2) a perception that rural areas do not get their fair share of resources, and (3) a sense that rural folks have fundamentally distinct values and lifestyles, which are misunderstood and disrespected by city folks."[20] Essentially, Cramer suggests that "an identity as a rural person" supersedes other factors that influence political views.[21] This geography-based sense of self prompts resentment of those who are perceived as not sharing rural values and somehow benefiting from their different spatial location and lifestyles: namely, urban dwellers.

Cramer acknowledges racialized aspects of the "rural consciousness" that she detects in Wisconsin. Because "cities are often shorthand for people who are not white," Cramer writes that "the urban-versus-rural-divide is undoubtedly in part about race."[22] That said, Cramer emphasizes that much of the rural resentment that she witnessed was "almost always directed at white people: government bureaucrats and faculty members at the flagship public university."[23] Along with these groups, other primary targets of resentment include public employees who are "actually residents of a rural community," but who are believed to be "controlled by urban concerns and values."[24] Due to these factors, Cramer qualifies that "antiurban resentment is not simply resentment against people of color. At the same time, given the way arguments against government redistribution in the United States have historically been made by equating deservingness with whiteness, these conversations are about race even when race is not mentioned."[25] Although this complicated cultural resentment does not exclusively hinge on racial prejudice, it is an intermingling of rural white attitudes about race with "antigovernment attitudes and preferences for small government," among other elements.[26] As a brief aside, education scholar Mara Casey Tieken reminds, "There's another rural America that exists beyond [the] rural white America. Nearly 10.3 million people, about one-fifth of rural residents, are people of color."[27] Tieken explains that such residents embrace different values and political affiliations than the "rural white America" that has received heightened attention in academic studies and the media. This is not to challenge Cramer's conclusions—which, again, are based on the study of a single Midwestern state, rather than the entire nation—but merely to recognize that the United States' rural populations are not homogeneous.

The works surveyed above address many of the most significant factors shaping the United States' polarized political climate in the twenty-first century. By examining these varying perspectives in relation to one another, it becomes clear that both the propelling force of nostalgia and deeply entrenched ideas about regional identity may be used to mobilize what Cramer would describe as a politics of resentment. Given that Trump has been able to successfully foment and harness a distinct brand of nostalgia-oriented resentment—which is attached to accusations of widespread failure and the habitual vilification of people of color (ranging from immigrants and asylum seekers from Central America and elsewhere to Democratic congresswomen)—it is worth reiterating the conditions that enable such messages to carry powerful impacts. Regarding Trump's support among white Americans, Mutz observes that "dominant group status threat" results in "conservatism surg[ing] along with a nostalgia for the stable hierarchies of the past."[28] Here, Mutz directly posits a linkage between nostalgia and reactionary political views based upon racist fears and attitudes. Coates ruminates on the symbolic value of the white working class across all of American culture.

The ideological meanings of this demographic have often been projected onto the specific territory of the Midwest. As referenced elsewhere in my project, Victoria E. Johnson argues, "The persistent association of 'midwesternness' *as* 'white' is critical to the region's revaluation—particularly in moments of social upheaval and trauma—as 'home' of 'authentic' cultural populism and traditional U.S. values."[29] The connective threads among these various authors illuminate how contemporary American politics are related, either explicitly or implicitly, to popular understandings of regional identity. In this sense, Trump's rhetoric of nostalgia, failure, and resentment seems to have been adapted from preexisting regional narratives, especially those about the Midwest. Such ideas about Midwestern identity extend backward in history. For instance, in the early 1890s— around two decades before the term "Midwest" came to denote the geographic territory to which it now refers—Hamlin Garland's *Main-Travelled Roads* (1891) depicts cultural tensions and political views within the middle region that are quite comparable to those manifesting in the twenty-first century.[30] More than a fascinating coincidence, Garland's collection of short stories helps to illustrate how textual objects may track historico-cultural change and continuity across eras, as well as the contemporary relevance of regional study.

One short story in *Main-Travelled Roads*—"Up the Coulé: A Story of Wisconsin"—is exceptionally pertinent to the present discussion. This story explores how location affects identity, and Garland gives particular attention to issues of class, race, gender, and politics. "Up the Coulé" details the acrimonious reunion of two adult brothers in rural Wisconsin: Howard, who now lives in New York City and works in the theater industry, and younger brother Grant, an impoverished farmer who is the provider for their aging mother, Mrs. McLane, and his own family. After "an absence of ten years," Howard's stylish, expensive attire and precise elocution brand him as an outsider within his childhood community.[31] His fumbling attempts to reintegrate into the family—which include "dropping back into [local] colloquialisms" and wearing a "knockabout costume" that Mrs. McLane assumes is a "special suit"—merely accentuate his unwelcome status.[32] Mrs. McLane also dismisses Howard's guilt-induced suggestion that she move to New York City so that he might give more proximate support. She remarks that she "couldn't live in a big city," which prompts Howard to directly comment on her "truly rural mind."[33]

Woven throughout "Up the Coulé" is an emphasis on the resentment of urbanites by rural people, as well as commentary on perceptions of failure in the latter space. Grant exudes hostility and explicitly critiques Howard's urban lifestyle and career by contrasting it with his own hardships. While discussing the family's desperate condition, Grant declares, "Everybody is [poor] that earns a living. We fellers on the farm have to earn a livin' for ourselves and you fellers that don't work. I don't blame you. I'd do it if I could."[34] The next day, Grant further expresses his resentment by mockingly asking, "Singular we think the country's goin' to hell, we fellers, in a two-dollar suit, wadin' around in the mud or sweatin' around in the hay-field, while you fellers lay around New York and smoke and wear good clothes and toady to millionaires?"[35] At the conclusion of the narrative, Howard offers to repurchase the family farm that has been lost to foreclosure, but Grant refuses: "I tell you, I don't ask your help. You can't fix this thing up with money. If you've got more brains'n I have, why, it's all right. I ain't got any right to take anything that I don't earn."[36] Despite Howard's protestations that random circumstances produced his own good fortunes and caused Grant's struggles, the younger brother grimly states that "life ain't worth very much to me. . . . I'm a dead failure. I've come to the conclusion that life's a failure for ninety-nine per cent of us. You can't help me now."[37] For Grant, despair produces resentment, yet ideals about labor, entitlements, what is rightfully earned, and individualism prevent him from accepting Howard's financial assistance.

Along with the class-based tensions between Howard and Grant, Garland also touches on issues of gender and race in "Up the Coulé." The story's female characters are stymied in their personal aspirations by burdensome marriages (or a lack of marriage prospects), as well as by gendered limitations on economic and geographic mobility. Laura, Grant's neglected and overworked wife, states that she "was a fool for ever marrying."[38] While contrasting her past and present circumstances, Laura laments, "I made a decent living teaching, I was free to come and go, my money was my own. Now I'm tied right down to a churn or a dishpan, I never have a cent of my own."[39] During an earlier social gathering, Rose, a childhood acquaintance of Howard, similarly speaks to the lack of opportunities for women in the community. A self-proclaimed "old maid" at age twenty-five, Rose explains, "Marriage is a failure these days for most of us. We can't live on a farm, and can't get a living in the city, and there we are."[40] Many of the community's men "have gone West," but local women are trapped by far more limited options.[41] With the characters of Laura and Rose, Garland emphasizes that women's ability to generate their own income is a necessity in order to escape some of the gendered restrictions within rural Wisconsin. In addition to the lengthier commentary on gender, Garland includes a fleeting depiction of racist attitudes among the white characters. At the same social gathering that introduces Rose, Grant nostalgically complains that "farmin' ain't so free a life as it used to be."[42] He then proceeds to compare the status of impoverished white farmers to the enslavement of African Americans. Using racial epithets, Grant states, "This cattle-raisin' and butter-makin' makes a nigger of a man. Binds him right down to the grindstone and he gets nothin' out of it—that's what rubs it in. He simply wallers around in the manure for somebody else. I'd like to know what a man's life is worth who lives as we do? How much higher is it than the lives the niggers used to live?"[43] With this passage, Garland exposes how men like Grant hold expectations of preserving a certain socioeconomic status by virtue of being white, as well as concurrent fears that such a privileged status has been lost for rural white people.[44] In tandem with economic struggles, Grant is frustrated by perceptions of declining racial stature.

Remarkably, at the end of the nineteenth century, Garland crafts a portrait of a rural Midwestern community shaped by nostalgia for the past, perceptions of failure, and resentment toward multiple groups—those very dynamics impacting American politics more than a century later. What Cramer later identifies as "rural consciousness," a "rural-versus-urban divide," and the "politics of resentment" clearly encapsulate the anger that Grant expresses toward urbanites on the East Coast. Moreover, Grant's racism and concern that poor rural white people will no longer be "higher" than African Americans is of a kind with the white fears of declining status discussed by Coates and Mutz. Finally, the entirety of "Up the Coulé" features a sense of perpetual despair stemming from the community's seemingly irreversible economic decline. For the twenty-first-century reader, one of the most striking aspects of Garland's story is how contemporary it feels. With little change, much of Grant's dialogue and the central conflicts of the story could easily unfold in the present. Hence, an instructive lesson of "Up the Coulé" is that textual representations of place have the potential to illuminate under-recognized continuities linking seemingly disparate eras.

As evidenced by the connections between analyses of the 2016 presidential election and Garland's nineteenth-century short story, critical understandings of place-identity in multiple contexts are crucial for more fully comprehending American culture. To glean further insights about contemporary politics and culture, I now turn to Midwestern documentaries produced over the past three decades. Rather than engaging in lengthy analyses of these documentaries, my intention is to concisely delineate another important way in which the Midwest is interrogated in American cinema. Given the content of this opening section, I feel obliged to specify that I am not implying that the subjects featured in the following documentaries (or the filmmakers themselves) embrace the reactionary political views discussed above; indeed, most of these films highlight issues of racial injustice and/or economic inequality that clash with Trump's expressed values. Instead, I am sketching out—in abbreviated form—ways in which some of the Midwestern cultural dynamics spotlighted in the build-up to and wake of the 2016 presidential election have already been given significant coverage by documentary filmmakers over an extended period. In documenting the Midwest, this corpus of films collectively reveals pieces of the historical occurrences and cultural developments that have produced the region's tumultuous status in the second decade of the millennium.

Documenting the Midwest

In January of 2016, a state of emergency was declared in Flint, Michigan, and its surrounding county because of a major public health threat from toxic levels of lead in the water supply. Despite being horrific in its own right, this water crisis was but the latest trial for the long-suffering residents of Flint. Following the economic devastation stemming from deindustrialization over the latter half of the twentieth century, Flint's twenty-first century has been marked by a series of municipal financial crises, high rates of violent crimes, depopulation, and spiking unemployment rates.[45] Through the very publicized decline and decay of this once-prosperous city, Flint—along with Detroit and other former industrial hubs across the region—has become a symbol of Midwestern failure within the American popular imagination.

Filmmaker Michael Moore grew up in Flint and has diligently documented his hometown's continuing struggles, most famously in his debut feature, *Roger & Me* (1989).[46] This documentary revolves around Moore's frustrated attempts to meet with Roger Smith, the then-current chairman of General Motors, who had overseen massive layoffs and numerous plant closings in Flint. While tracking Smith through corporate office buildings and private clubs, Moore nostalgically reflects on his childhood memories of living in a former hub of the automobile industry, and he provides a general overview of Flint's labor history with a particular emphasis on past disputes between workers and GM management. On a formal level, Moore's influential documentary is distinguished by an ironic appropriation of vintage advertisements, promotional materials, and footage of parades and other civic events from Flint's glory years.

Beyond the tragic fact that the general subject matter of *Roger & Me*—the now-interminably abject status of Flint due to corporate greed and government malfeasance—remains relevant, I return to Moore's film because of its position within an expanding tradition of documenting the Midwest in cinema. In hindsight, *Roger & Me* functions as something of an opening salvo for what has become a distinct subset of documentaries focusing on problems and challenges faced by the Midwest in the late twentieth and early twenty-first centuries. Covering urban centers, rural communities, and parts in-between, Midwestern documentaries from recent decades explore the region's fractured identity. As with many fictional Midwestern texts produced since the 1970s, these documentaries capture a frequently nostalgic Midwest that is trapped in an unsatisfactory present. For instance, Heidi Ewing and Rachel Grady's *Detropia* (2012) is a contemplative and, at times, almost impressionistic documentary that surveys Detroit's physical ruins while following a diverse set of residents who seek to improve their city.[47] Again and again, documentaries such as *Detropia* highlight the vulnerability of individual Midwesterners and communities throughout the region. Across the various locales and circumstances covered by these films, the Midwest collectively appears to be searching for a renewed sense of purpose and a redefined identity.

Before taking an extended look at a few films, it is worth highlighting several notable contributions to this growing Midwestern documentary tradition. In the decades after *Roger & Me*, documentaries regularly inspect the Midwest through the prisms of race, gender, sexuality, and/or class. Since collaborating with Frederick Marx and Peter Gilbert on *Hoop Dreams* (1994), Steve James has been one of the most established and influential documentarians working on Midwestern subject matter.[48] Along with *Hoop Dreams*, James has documented Chicago life and culture over several projects, including *The Interrupters* (2011), *Life Itself* (2014), and *America to Me* (2018).[49] James's films often relate Chicago-specific dimensions of a larger Midwestern story of systematized racial injustice. Additional facets of the region's notoriously segregated cities have been investigated by other documentarians. For instance, Chad Freidrichs's *The Pruitt-Igoe Myth* (2011) provides valuable historical context about structural discrimination faced by impoverished people of color in the Midwest; while surveying the history and legacy of St. Louis's infamous public housing complex, Pruitt-Igoe, the film explains how such public housing programs were designed to exacerbate segregation in the city.[50] Sabaah Folayan and Damon Davis's *Whose Streets?* (2017) and Erik Ljung's *The Blood is at the Doorstep* (2017) detail demonstrations and political activism in the wake of two high profile cases of unarmed African Americans being killed by police officers in Midwestern cities: eighteen-year-old Michael Brown in Ferguson, Missouri, and Dontre Hamilton, a schizophrenic man who had been sleeping in a park and was shot fourteen times during an encounter with a Milwaukee police officer.[51] Keith McQuirter's *Milwaukee 53206: A Community Serves Time* (2016) explores "the ZIP code that incarcerates the highest percentage of black men in America"; within this community, "62% of men have spent time in prison by the time they are 34."[52] LGBTQ+ subject matter has received attention in documentaries such as Susan Muska and Gréta Olafsdóttir's *The Brandon Teena Story* (1998), which examines the events surrounding the 1993 rape and murder of Brandon Teena, a transgender man, in Nebraska.[53] On a much broader scale, Roger Ross Williams uncovers the far-reaching impacts of Midwest-originating prejudice toward LGBTQ+ people in *God Loves Uganda* (2013).[54] Williams shows how the Kansas City–based International House of Prayer (IHOP) has played a role in developing anti-LGBTQ+ legislation and fomenting an overall culture of intolerance for LGBTQ+ individuals in Uganda. Concerns with class permeate most of the films listed above and are a major component of Tracy Droz Tragos and Andrew Droz Palermo's *Rich Hill* (2014), which follows three teenage boys—Andrew, Harley, and Appachey—living in the impoverished and primarily white town of Rich Hill, Missouri.[55]

While producing fictional depictions of economic instability and poverty in the Midwest, some filmmakers have adopted documentarylike methods. For example, the narratives of Debra Granik's *Winter's Bone* (2010) and Harmony Korine's *Gummo* (1997) are set within, respectively, the rural Ozarks in southern Missouri and the city of Xenia, Ohio.[56] During the production of *Winter's Bone*, Granik shot on location, used nonprofessional actors, and closely collaborated with the local community; members of this latter group assisted with ensuring that the script's language and dialect was authentic. In addition to showcasing area musicians and other aspects of Ozark culture, one scene even features a local army recruiter, Sergeant Russell Schalk, responding to protagonist Ree Dolly (Jennifer Lawrence) in a partly improvised manner based on his real-life work. Like *Winter's Bone*, *Gummo* focuses on the lives unfolding in an impoverished Midwestern community; the narrative takes place after a tornado has devastated Xenia. Korine also makes prominent use of nonprofessionals and their actual homes, which are frequently cluttered, dilapidated, and/or infested with bugs.[57] Given their thematic content and production methods, *Winter's Bone* and *Gummo* could almost be described as "Midwestern neorealism," to borrow and modify the label for the Italian film movement of the 1940s and 1950s.[58] Along with the narrative events depicted in *Winter's Bone* and *Gummo*, the struggles and challenges of the Midwest in the late twentieth and early twenty-first centuries are embedded within the very mise-en-scène of each film.

Even the glossier, mainstream film *Up in the Air* (2009) includes a few sequences that borrow documentary filmmaking conventions.[59] Director/co-screenwriter Jason Reitman blurs distinctions between the fictional narrative and its twenty-first-century setting by incorporating actual Midwesterners into the film. At multiple moments in *Up in the Air*, Reitman includes montages of white-collar workers making statements in response to notifications that they have been fired. Shot in a basic documentary interview style, these individuals are non-actors who had recently become unemployed during the Great Recession. In an interview, Reitman states, "Except for a few recognisable actors, everyone who gets fired in this movie is someone who lost their job. They're from St. Louis, Detroit—non-actors who answered an ad in the paper and came in and went on camera. They were incredibly authentic and said the kind of things you never think of as a writer."[60] Although the firing scenes are staged reenactments, the onscreen despair of these newly unemployed people brings a heightened sense of veracity to the film's themes. Within *Up in the Air*, Reitman sequences the testimonials to create an affirmative narrative arc that emphasizes personal attachments outside of work. Just after the opening credits, the first montage finds the fired workers lamenting new financial and emotional challenges; one man remarks, "On a stress level, I've heard that losing your job is like a death in the family. But, personally, I feel more like the people I worked with were my family and I died." By contrast, the final montage nostalgically affirms the role of family and friends—rather than identifying with one's job—in making life meaningful. This last montage concludes with a man asserting, "My kids are my purpose, my family." Whether in fictional films or documentaries, the millennial Midwest is consistently presented as a precarious space that offers uncertainty in terms of emotional stability and financial security.

The fusion of nostalgia and failure is a potent combination featured in multiple Midwestern narratives and contexts. To bring this afterword to a close, I consider two documentaries that—as with Garland's nineteenth-century story, "Up the Coulé"—spotlight how nostalgia shapes notions of success and failure. Fraught economic conditions and frustrated ambitions define the experiences of the Milwaukee-area working class individuals featured in *American Movie* (1999) and *Two American Families* (2013).[61] In the former, director Chris Smith follows Mark Borchardt as he works a number of blue collar jobs (including custodial work at a cemetery), shoots a low-budget horror film titled *Coven*, and attempts to secure funding and begin preproduction for *Northwestern*, his long-imagined dream project. Roger Ebert memorably describes *American Movie* as "a documentary about someone who wants to make a movie more than you do. Mark Borchardt may want to make a movie more than anyone else in the world."[62] From the outset of the documentary, though, such aspirations brush up against a variety of limitations. *American Movie* begins with Mark ruminating on the nature of failure and opportunity:

> I was a failure. I was a failure, and I get very sad and depressed about it. And I can't be that no more. Cause I really feel like I've betrayed myself, big-time. Because I think when I, I know when I was growing up I had all the potential in the world.

Now I'm back to being Mark who, who has a beer in his hand and is thinking about the great American script and the great American movie. And this time I cannot fail, I won't fail, it's not in me. You don't get second chances and mess them up, you'd be a fool to. Not just finishing films or in the long run gettin' some money, but it's right now I feel like it's, like I said, five, ten, fifteen years ago, and now I've got the same options again, and this time, I'm not gonna fail. This time, it's most important not to fail, just to drink and dream, but rather to create and complete.

Here, as in so many Midwestern stories, Mark's monologue interweaves a nostalgic narrative of his past (which contained "all the potential in the world") with fears about the insecure nature of the present in which failure is an ever-looming possibility. Throughout *American Movie*, Mark is continually frustrated by limited finances, family conflicts, and unprepared or disinterested collaborators. Despite such circumstances, Mark later comments, "The American dream stays with me each and every day." This oscillation between despair and hope, fatigue and persistence reappears across numerous Midwestern texts and is strongly evident in the subjects whose lives are documented in *Two American Families*.

Near the conclusion of *Two American Families*, journalist Bill Moyers poses a question to Jackie Stanley, a resilient, hardworking mother of five: "Do you feel like a failure today?" Jackie somberly affirms, "Yes." Elsewhere in the documentary, Terry Neumann, matriarch of the other titular Milwaukee family, similarly confesses, "I felt, like, a sense of failure because I've always been able to get back up on my feet. I've always found a way or the money to fix it. And I just couldn't fix it anymore." Like an intimate Midwestern version of British filmmaker Michael Apted's *Up* series, Moyers revisits the white Neumann family and the African American Stanley family multiple times over a twenty-two-year span. By highlighting the trials of the Stanleys and Neumanns, Moyers narrates a larger story about the changing identity of the Midwest in the decades surrounding the turn of the millennium, particularly as experienced in the region's deindustrialized urban spaces—in this case, Milwaukee. Further, *Two American Families* functions as a condemnation of the devastating effects of neoliberalism on the middle and working classes. While examining the challenges faced by these families, Moyers reveals how economic ruin produces a sense of temporal dislocation that is nostalgic in nature. It is as though financial crisis reactivates—or perhaps accentuates—a nostalgic longing to return to a lost or imagined past state.

Two American Families initially aired as a feature-length episode of *Frontline* and is the fourth PBS documentary since the early 1990s to pick up the story of these Midwestern families.[63] Moyers begins *Two American Families* with footage from 1991, just after Claude Stanley and Tony Neumann have been laid off from union jobs at A. O. Smith and Briggs and Stratton, respectively. These two firms had been cornerstones of the local manufacturing industry that once provided families such as the Stanleys and Neumanns with steady employment and the means for a middle class lifestyle. As Moyers explains, though, forty thousand jobs had already been lost from the Milwaukee area during the 1980s, including four thousand from Briggs and Stratton. This reduction of full-time

Afterword 221

manufacturing jobs was one of the outcomes of accelerated outsourcing and weakened unions. Across Milwaukee, the majority of employment opportunities for laborers such as Claude and Tony increasingly consisted of lower paying nonunion positions in manufacturing and the service industry—most of which lacked benefits. The Stanleys also face the added challenge of racial discrimination. Jackie and her supervisor note that her real estate career has been impeded by restrictions on the areas in which she is permitted to sell properties and by prospective white clients who are resistant to working with an African American agent. For Jackie, the racist practice of redlining is reproduced in the limited opportunities that she receives in the real estate business.

One of the most troubling and fascinating aspects of *Two American Families* is the way that the documentary demonstrates how the neoliberal logic of success and failure has been internalized by the middle and working classes. In *A Brief History of Neoliberalism* (2005), David Harvey provides background on the ideals and policies that inform neoliberal economic theory. Harvey especially underscores the individualized burdens that accompany such a system:

> Privatization and deregulation combined with competition, it is claimed, eliminate bureaucratic red tape, increase efficiency and productivity, improve quality, and reduce costs, both directly to the consumer through cheaper commodities and services and indirectly through reduction of the tax burden....
>
> While personal and individual freedom in the marketplace is guaranteed, each individual is held responsible and accountable for his or her own actions and well-being. This principle extends into the realms of welfare, education, health care, and even pensions.... Individual success or failure are interpreted in terms of entrepreneurial virtues or personal failings (such as not investing significantly enough in one's own human capital through education) rather than being attributed to any systemic property (such as the class exclusions usually attributed to capitalism).[64]

Although the Stanleys and Neumanns often acknowledge the systemic conditions that have contributed to their hardships, they still own an unshakable sense of individual failure. This is another insidious layer to the tragedy that Moyers brings to light: these industrious families claim, at least in part, personal culpability for their struggles within an economic system that actually produces their financial ruination.

Growing debt accompanies the families' mutual inability to secure adequate employment and exacerbates their struggles. Over the duration of *Two American Families*, the Neumanns fight to stay caught up with the mortgage payment for their home, and they are eventually forced to vacate. Amidst the ongoing financial stresses, Terry and Tony grow apart, and their marriage ends in divorce. By the mid-1990s, the Stanleys are trapped beneath a mound of credit card debt, partly because of large medical bills that were not covered by Claude's nonunion job. Moyers bluntly narrates, "The Stanleys were like millions of others trying to survive the good times of the nineties. Living on credit became a way of life. Over that decade, credit card debt for the average American family increased by 53 percent. For low-income families, it was 184 percent. And the paychecks weren't getting any bigger." *Two American Families* also shows how these conditions have lasting impacts on the Neumann and Stanley children in their adulthood. When Moyers revisits the families in 2012, only the oldest of the five Stanley siblings (thirty-five-year-old Keith) has a bachelor's degree, and just the youngest of the three Neumann siblings (twenty-six-year-old Karissa) has an associate degree. As adults, many of the children have difficulty procuring jobs and keeping housing while trying to provide for their own dependents.

Despite their dire multidecade financial circumstances, the Neumanns and Stanleys resist government aid and charitable support when possible. Both families simply wish to work their way back to the middle class comforts they had so recently enjoyed. After Claude loses his job in 1991, he defiantly proclaims, "When I got laid off, they wanted me to go on welfare, but I could not stand in that line. I just said, 'It's not me. This is not me.... I got my strength, my health, I will find me a job.'" Following Tony first being laid off, Terry admits, "It really bothers us that we have to depend on other people. I just want to get up and do what I have to do, just go in the car and go grocery shopping and have a normal life again. I don't like having to go and ask and say, 'I have no food in the house or something, can you help me out?'" With high paying jobs being systematically replaced by part-time or temporary positions that barely permit subsistence living, an inability to thrive is the resultant condition for families such as the Stanleys and Neumanns. Yet, a sense of personal failure stubbornly persists.

Given this perception of failure, perhaps it is unsurprising that members of both families—particularly Claude and Terry—continually deny that their present status is an authentic reflection of their identities. In other words, the Neumanns and Stanleys frame the present as merely a temporary bubble between the increasingly distant past of regular employment and the indefinitely deferred future restoration of that nostalgic idyll. In 1991, Terry desperately states, "I just feel it's just a tough time, and if we can just get through this, you know, then we'll be back to the life that we had before." Terry's prediction is undermined by a cut to the Neumanns attending church, where Tony silently breaks down in tears. As mentioned above, Claude Stanley dissociates himself from the state of being unemployed when first laid off in 1991; even after two decades of setbacks, he persistently asserts his belief that a better future awaits. For the Neumanns and Stanleys, there is an ongoing temporal and, at times, spatial dislocation of desire that I would identify as nostalgic. The present is a period of estrangement from their "true" selves, which the families desperately believe may someday be restored.

Such faith is fostered and perpetuated by the caretakers of the neoliberal economy. *Two American Families* highlights this role with the inclusion of excerpts from presidential speeches that span four administrations. For instance, at Bill Clinton's inauguration, he announces, "Today we celebrate the mystery of American renewal." More than a decade later, George W. Bush proclaims,

"A future of hope and opportunity begins with a growing economy. And that is what we have." These statements suggest that only by "renewing" the past or looking to the future may the nation find relief from the inadequate present. For families such as the Stanleys and Neumanns, the nostalgic disavowal of the present is a designed outcome of navigating an economy that offers the working class fewer and fewer opportunities for a stable, livable income.

As detailed throughout this book, fictional and nonfictional Midwestern texts alike present the geographically in-between region undergoing profound transitions.[65] In the young millennium, the Midwest is suspended between its vanishing past identity and an uncertain future. Economic changes have undermined foundational components of how the region is understood within the broader American consciousness. *Two American Families* provides an insightful portrait of such conditions, but it lacks an accompanying map for regional recovery. How does the Midwest escape the economic "failure" brought about by globalization and neoliberalism? What new forms might Midwestern "success" take as the twenty-first century unfolds? At the end of *Two American Families*, Terry predicts, "I don't think anybody is going to be financially secure, truthfully.... And we'll just work until we collapse and keel over and die." By contrast, Claude proclaims, "I still believe there's something for us." Jackie provides context for their faith and diligence by pragmatically adding, "I would interject and say, 'What else?' We have no other choice." Clearly, many questions about the Midwest's future require answers.

The Midwestern documentaries stretching from *Roger & Me* to *Two American Families* and beyond comprise variegated lenses through which to view and evaluate the region's complicated millennial status. Of further importance, by making visible the ongoing linkage of nostalgia and failure, this set of documentaries has correspondences with contemporary politics. Collectively, these films expose preexisting notions of place-identity that have been readily appropriated for a variety of political agendas. For instance, a Midwestern narrative of decline and despair has been harnessed and channeled into what Cramer describes as a "politics of resentment" on local and national levels. Even in such a dilapidated condition, however, the Midwest's oft-repeated identity as the supposed most American of regions remains intact—after all, Moyers elevates two unmistakably Midwestern families as representatives of an entire class of American workers. As goes the Midwest, Moyers ominously suggests, so goes the nation. This prediction has been borne out by recent political developments, such as the results of the 2016 presidential election. Ideological associations with regional spaces have once again come to the fore and are shaped by nostalgia-influenced notions of authenticity. Consequently, it is an essential task to analyze and respond to the cultural forms—including film, literature, and television—that evince the powerful impacts of nostalgia and regional narratives. Among its many implications, then, the current political climate reaffirms the significance and outright necessity of ongoing critical engagement with nostalgia and region in a variety of historico-cultural contexts.

Notes

1. Portions of this chapter have been previously published in *Middle West Review*. See: Adam Ochonicky, review of *Frontline*, season 31, episode 14, "Two American Families," written by Kathleen Hughes and Bill Moyers, featuring Bill Moyers, July 9, 2013, PBS, https://www.pbs.org/wgbh/frontline/film/two-american-families/; *Middle West Review* 1, no. 1 (Fall 2014): 161–164, doi: 10.1353/mwr.2014.0005.

2. Trump, of course, is not the first politician to use this slogan (or some variation thereof). For instance, just a few decades earlier, Ronald Reagan featured a version of the slogan in campaign materials for the 1980 presidential election.

3. Svetlana Boym, *The Future of Nostalgia* (New York: Basic Books, 2001), 41–45.

4. Trump's running mate and subsequent vice president, former Indiana governor Mike Pence, had previously signed into law the state's "Religious Freedom Restoration Act." Critics denounced this act as a reactionary attempt to legally sanction discrimination against the LGBTQ+ community by business owners. As with Trump's campaign slogan, the nostalgic rhetoric of this piece of legislation—evidenced by the term "restoration"—implies the present-day loss or restriction of conservative values that supporters believed were more openly expressed and enacted in the nostalgically imagined past—presumably sometime before the increased, but still incomplete, acceptance of LGBTQ+ people in the United States. For a more detailed examination of the Religious Freedom Restoration Act, see: Garrett Epps, "What Makes Indiana's Religious-Freedom Law Different?," *The Atlantic*, March 30, 2015, https://www.theatlantic.com/politics/archive/2015/03/what-makes-indianas-religious-freedom-law-different/388997/.

5. Alec MacGillis and ProPublica, "The Original Underclass," *The Atlantic*, September 2016, https://www.theatlantic.com/magazine/archive/2016/09/the-original-underclass/492731/.

6. Ibid.

7. Robert S. Lynd and Helen Merrell Lynd, *Middletown: A Study in Modern American Culture* (1929; repr., San Diego, CA: Harcourt Brace Jovanovich, 1957).

8. Ibid., 8.

9. As with the Lynds' study, this connection of whiteness and "native" status again conjures up associations with the long history of nativist ideologies and movements in American history. See: David H. Bennett, *The Party of Fear: From Nativist Movements to the New Right in American History* (Chapel Hill: University of North Carolina Press, 1988).

10. Robert Schiller, "Why Did US Voters Back Trump? Economic Powerlessness," *The Guardian*, November 22, 2016, https://www.theguardian.com/business/2016/nov/22/why-did-americans-support-trump-economic-powerlessness.

11. Ibid.

12. Ta-Nehisi Coates, *We Were Eight Years in Power: An American Tragedy* (New York: One World, 2017), 346–347.

13. Ibid., 354.

14. Diana C. Mutz, "Status Threat, not Economic Hardship, Explains the 2016 Presidential Vote," *PNAS* 115, no. 19 (2018): E4330, doi: doi.org/10.1073/pnas.1718155115.

15. Ibid.

16. Ibid., E4332.

17. Katherine J. Cramer, *The Politics of Resentment: Rural Consciousness in Wisconsin and the Rise of Scott Walker* (Chicago: University of Chicago Press, 2016), 5.

18. Cramer's work may be extrapolated to make sense of broader Midwestern and national developments, such as the 2016 presidential election. Indeed, in the week after the election, Cramer herself contributed a short piece to the *Washington Post* that considered the wider relevance and applicability of her research on Wisconsin culture and politics. See: Katherine Cramer, "How Rural Resentment Helps Explain the Surprising Victory of Donald Trump," *Washington Post*, November 13, 2016, https://www.washingtonpost.com/news/monkey-cage/wp/2016/11/13/how-rural-resentment-helps-explain-the-surprising-victory-of-donald-trump/.

19. Cramer, *The Politics of Resentment*, 9.

20. Ibid., 12.

21. Ibid., 5–6.

22. Ibid., 85.

23. Ibid., 86.

24. Ibid., 131.

25. Ibid., 86.

26. Ibid. 87.

27. Mara Casey Tieken, "There's a Big Part of Rural America that Everyone's Ignoring," *Washington Post*, March 24, 2017, https://www.washingtonpost.com/opinions/theres-a-big-part-of-rural-america-that-everyones-ignoring/2017/03/24/d06d24d0-1010-11e7-ab07-07d9f521f6b5_story.html.

28. Mutz, "Status Threat," E4331.

29. Victoria E. Johnson, *Heartland TV: Prime Time Television and the Struggle for U.S. Identity* (New York: New York University Press, 2008), 18, emphasis in original.

30. Hamlin Garland, *Main-Travelled Roads* (1891; repr., New York: Holt, Rinehart and Winston, 1965).

31. Ibid., 49.

32. Ibid., 59, 66.

33. Ibid., 94.

34. Ibid., 63.

35. Ibid., 70.

36. Ibid., 98–99.

37. Ibid., 101.

38. Ibid., 92.

39. Ibid.

40. Ibid., 81–82.

41. Ibid.

42. Ibid., 86.

43. Ibid., 86–87. Regarding this quote, I was reluctant to reproduce a passage with such derogatory, hateful language. In order to more precisely show how the story connects racism to Grant's rural identity and economic fears, however, I felt that it was necessary to directly reference Garland's original language in this particular instance.

44. Coates discusses the historical relationship of the "black working class" and the "white working class," which features dynamics echoed by Grant's comments. "By the eighteenth century," Coates writes, "a bargain emerged—the descendants of indenture would enjoy the full benefits of whiteness, the most definitional benefit being that they would never sink to the level of the slave. But if the bargain protected white workers from slavery, it did not protect them from near-slave wages nor backbreaking labor to attain them, and always there lurked a fear of being degraded to the level of 'black' slave labor." See: Coates, *We Were Eight Years in Power*, 348.

45. For an overview of the Flint water crisis, see: Merrit Kennedy, "Lead-Laced Water in Flint: A Step-By-Step Look at The Makings of a Crisis," NPR, National Public Radio, Inc., April 20, 2016, https://www.npr.org/sections/thetwo-way/2016/04/20/465545378/lead-laced-water-in-flint-a-step-by-step-look-at-the-makings-of-a-crisis; Anna Clark, "'Nothing to Worry About. The Water Is Fine.': How Flint Poisoned Its People," *The Guardian*, July 3, 2018, https://www.theguardian.com/news/2018/jul/03/nothing-to-worry-about-the-water-is-fine-how-flint-michigan-poisoned-its-people.

46. *Roger & Me*, directed by Michael Moore (1989; Burbank, CA: Warner Home Video, 2003), DVD.

47. *Detropia*, directed by Heidi Ewing and Rachel Grady (New York: Loki Films, 2012), film.

48. *Hoop Dreams*, directed by Steve James (1994; New York: Criterion Collection, 2005), DVD; This documentary has elicited a great deal of praise, as well as more critical reactions. For instance, historian Matthew E. Stanley observes that *Hoop Dreams* "reveals the interconnecting levels of oppression in American inner cities: the self-perpetuating cycle of racial, gender, and economic disadvantage; the bevy of peddlers and opportunists (some well-meaning); and the improbable hope of breaking free." Further, Stanley writes that the film "reminds that the failures of [impoverished and segregated] neighborhoods are the failures of postwar urban theorists, bankers, and policymakers. It also reminds—through a subtext of ghettoization, redlining, block busting, white flight, disinvestment and shrinking municipal services, and deindustrialization and the loss of good paying jobs—that the fulfilled dreams of some Americans have always depended on the deferred dreams of other Americans." For bell hooks, though, the production and reception of *Hoop Dreams* has several problematic elements. Along with emphasizing that the documentary does not go far enough in its critique of young black men being exploited, hooks suggests that white praise of *Hoop Dreams* demonstrates, in part, "the extent to which blackness has become commodified in this society—the degree to which black life, particularly the lives of poor and underclass black people, can become cheap entertainment even if that is not what the filmmakers intended." As such, hooks asserts, "The lure of *Hoop Dreams* is that it affirms that those on the bottom can rise in this society, even as it is critical of the manner in which they rise." See: Matthew E. Stanley, review of *Hoop Dreams*, directed by Steve James, *Middle West Review* 3, no. 1 (2016): 193, 196–197; bell hooks, *Reel To Real: Race, Sex, and Class at the Movies* (New York: Routledge, 1996), 78–79.

49. *The Interrupters*, directed by Steve James (Chicago: Kartemquin Films, 2011), *Frontline*, season 30, episode 6, February 14, 2012, PBS, https://www.pbs.org/wgbh/frontline/film/interrupters/; *Life Itself*, directed by Steve James (New York: Magnolia Pictures, 2013), film; *America to Me*, directed by Steve James (Meridian, CO: Starz, 2018), broadcast television. *The Interrupters* highlights the efforts of the CeaseFire Chicago organization—later renamed as Cure Violence—to stop community violence by treating it as a communicable disease. For further information on this organization, see http://cureviolence.org. *Life Itself* is a biography and celebration of famed Chicago film critic (and Illinois native) Roger Ebert. *America to Me* is a docuseries that covers one year at Oak Park and River Forest High School (OPRF), which is a racially and economically diverse school in the Chicago area. See: "*America to Me*," Kartemquin Films, Kartemquin Educational Films, http://kartemquin.com/films/america-to-me/about.

50. *The Pruitt-Igoe Myth*, directed by Chad Freidrichs (2011; New York: First Run Features, 2012), DVD.

Afterword 227

51. *Whose Streets?*, directed by Sabaah Folayan and Damon Davis (New York: Magnolia Pictures, 2017), film; *The Blood Is at the Doorstep*, directed by Erik Ljung (Studio City, CA: September Club, 2017), film.

52. *Milwaukee 53206: A Community Serves Time*, directed by Keith McQuirter (Transform Films, 2016), *America Reframed*, April 3, 2018, PBS, https://www.pbs.org/video/milwaukee-53206-abaext/; *Milwaukee 53206*, Mass Incarceration Project LLC, https://www.milwaukee53206.com. Early in the documentary, a title card specifies, "On Milwaukee's north side, in the ZIP code 53206, 62% of men have spent time in prison by the time they are 34."

53. *The Brandon Teena Story*, directed by Susan Muska and Gréta Olafsdóttir (1998; New York: Zeitgeist Films, 2000), VHS.

54. *God Loves Uganda*, directed by Roger Ross Williams (New York: Variance Films, 2013), film.

55. *Rich Hill*, directed by Tracy Droz Tragos and Andrew Droz Palermo (2014; Pacific Palisades, CA: Dinky Pictures, 2015), DVD.

56. *Winter's Bone*, directed by Debra Granik (Santa Monica, CA: Lionsgate, 2010), DVD; *Gummo*, directed by Harmony Korine (1997; Los Angeles: New Line Home Video, 2001), DVD.

57. Despite the narrative's Midwestern setting, it should be noted that this location shooting took place in Tennessee.

58. Certainly, there are vast differences that distinguish the historical and cultural contexts of mid-twentieth century Italy and the millennial-era Midwest. As such, I hesitate to draw too close of a connection between the work of, say, Vittorio De Sica or Roberto Rossellini and these Midwestern films of Granik and Korine. Further, these latter films do not necessarily feature the formal elements that influential film critic André Bazin associates with realism, such as lengthier shots, minimal editing, and deep focus within the frame. For Bazin's discussion of Italian neorealism, see: André Bazin, *What Is Cinema? Volume II*, trans. Hugh Gray (1971; repr., Berkeley: University of California Press, 2005).

59. *Up in the Air*, directed by Jason Reitman (2009; Hollywood, CA: Paramount Pictures, 2010), DVD.

60. Nick James, "No Place Like Home," *Sight & Sound* 20, no. 2 (February 2010): 33.

61. *American Movie*, directed by Chris Smith (1999; Culver City, CA: Sony Pictures Classics, 2000), DVD; *Frontline*, season 31, episode 14, "Two American Families," written by Kathleen Hughes and Bill Moyers, featuring Bill Moyers, July 9, 2013, PBS, https://www.pbs.org/wgbh/frontline/film/two-american-families/.

62. Roger Ebert, review of *American Movie*, directed by Chris Smith, *RogerEbert.com*, Ebert Digital, modified on January 21, 2000, https://www.rogerebert.com/reviews/american-movie-2000.

63. The other three documentaries are *Minimum Wages: The New Economy*, directed by Tom Casciato, January 8, 1992, PBS, https://billmoyers.com/content/minimum-wages/; *Frontline*, season 14, episode 6, "Living on the Edge," written by Tom Casciato, Kathleen Hughes, and Bill Moyers, December 12, 1995, PBS, https://billmoyers.com/content/living-on-the-edge/; *Surviving the Good Times*, directed by Tom Casciato and Kathleen Hughes, March 28, 2000, PBS, https://billmoyers.com/content/surviving-the-good-times/.

64. David Harvey, *A Brief History of Neoliberalism* (2005; repr., Oxford: Oxford University Press, 2009), 65–66.

65. For example, even a mainstream comedy such as *Bridesmaids* (2011) engages with the Midwest's unsettled status and shaken identity. Of relevance for the present discussion, *Bridesmaids* features a protagonist whose boutique bakery in Milwaukee failed during the Great Recession. See: *Bridesmaids*, directed by Paul Feig (Universal City, CA: Universal Pictures, 2011), film.

BIBLIOGRAPHY

About Schmidt. Directed by Alexander Payne. 2002; Los Angeles: New Line Home Entertainment, 2003. DVD.
Aguirre, The Wrath of God. Directed by Werner Herzog. New York: New Yorker Films, 1972. Film.
Ahearn, Edward J. *Urban Confrontations in Literature and Social Science, 1848–2001: European Contexts, American Evolutions*. Burlington, VT: Ashgate, 2010.
Altman, Rick. *The American Film Musical*. Bloomington: Indiana University Press, 1987.
America to Me. Directed by Steve James. Meridian, CO: Starz, 2018. Broadcast television.
"America to Me." Kartemquin Films. Chicago: Kartemquin Educational Films, 2018. http://kartemquin.com/films/america-to-me/about.
American Movie. Directed by Chris Smith. 1999; Culver City, CA: Sony Pictures Classics, 2000. DVD.
Anderson, Benedict. *Imagined Communities: Reflections on the Origin and Spread of Nationalism*. 1983. Reprint, London: Verso, 2006.
Anderson, Sherwood. *Winesburg, Ohio*. 1919. Reprint, New York: Viking, 1967.
Badlands. Directed by Terrence Malick. 1973; Burbank, CA: Warner Home Video, 2010. DVD.
Bauder, David. "'The Holy or The Broken' by Alan Light Traces Odd Journey of Leonard Cohen's Song 'Hallelujah.'" *Washington Examiner*, December 3, 2012. https://www.washingtonexaminer.com/book-traces-odd-journey-of-cohens-song.
Bazin, André. *What Is Cinema? Volume II*. Translated by Hugh Gray. 1971. Reprint, Berkeley: University of California Press, 2005.
Beard, William. *The Artist as Monster: The Cinema of David Cronenberg*. Toronto: University of Toronto Press, 2006.
Beers, David. "Irony Is Dead! Long Live Irony!" *Salon*, September 25, 2001. https://www.salon.com/2001/09/25/irony_lives/.
Begley, Louis. "My Novel, the Movie: My Baby Reborn; 'About Schmidt' Was Changed, But Not Its Core." *New York Times*, January 19, 2003. https://www.nytimes.com/2003/01/19/movies/my-novel-the-movie-my-baby-reborn-about-schmidt-was-changed-but-not-its-core.html.
Bell, James. "Meth and the Maiden." *Sight & Sound* 20, no. 10 (October 2010): 28–29.
Bennett, David H. *The Party of Fear: From Nativist Movements to the New Right in American History*. Chapel Hill: University of North Carolina Press, 1988.
Bergson, Henri. *Time and Free Will: An Essay on the Immediate Data of Consciousness*. Translated by F. L. Pogson. 1889. Reprint, London: George Allen & Unwin, 1950.
Berman, Marshall. *All That Is Solid Melts into Air: The Experience of Modernity*. 1982. Reprint, New York: Penguin Books, 1988.
Black Christmas. Directed by Bob Clark. 1974; Toronto: Critical Mass Releasing, 2001. DVD.
Blok, Anton. "The Enigma of Senseless Violence." In *Meanings of Violence: A Cross Cultural Perspective*, edited by Göran Aijmer and Jon Abbink, 23–38. Oxford: Berg, 2000.

The Blood Is at the Doorstep. Directed by Erik Ljung. Studio City, CA: September Club, 2017. Film.

Blow, Charles M. "Trump's Rural White America." *New York Times*, November 14, 2016, https://www.nytimes.com/2016/11/14/opinion/trumps-rural-white-america.html.

Bonnie and Clyde. Directed by Arthur Penn. 1967; Burbank, CA: Warner Home Video, 2008. DVD.

Boym, Svetlana. *The Future of Nostalgia*. New York: Basic Books, 2001.

Boys Don't Cry. Directed by Kimberly Peirce. 1999; Beverly Hills, CA: Twentieth Century Fox Home Entertainment, 2000. DVD.

Bradshaw, Nick. Review of *Take Shelter*, directed by Jeff Nichols. *Sight & Sound* 21, no. 12 (December 2011): 77.

The Brandon Teena Story. Directed by Susan Muska and Gréta Olafsdóttir. 1998; New York: Zeitgeist Films, 2000. VHS.

Bridesmaids. Directed by Paul Feig. Universal City, CA: Universal Pictures, 2011. Film.

Brody, Jennifer Devere. "Boyz Do Cry: Screening History's White Lies." *Screen* 43, no. 1 (Spring 2002): 91–96. doi: 10.1093/screen/43.1.91.

Browning, Mark. *David Cronenberg: Author or Film-maker?* Bristol, UK: Intellect Books, 2007.

Butler, Judith. *Bodies That Matter: On the Discursive Limits of "Sex."* 1993. Reprint, New York: Routledge Classics, 2011.

Cairncross, Frances. "The Trendspotter's Guide to New Communications." In *Living in the Information Age: A New Media Reader*. 2nd ed. Edited by Erik P. Bucy, 7–10. Belmont, CA: Wadsworth, 2005.

Campbell, Neil. "The Highway Kind: *Badlands*, Youth, Space and the Road." In *The Cinema of Terrence Malick: Poetic Visions of America*, edited by Hannah Patterson, 37–49. London: Wallflower, 2004.

Candyman. Directed by Bernard Rose. 1992; Culver City, CA: Columbia TriStar Home Entertainment, 2004. DVD.

Carroll, Noël. "Horror and Humor." *The Journal of Aesthetics and Art Criticism* 57, no. 2 (Spring 1999): 145–160.

Cather, Willa. *O Pioneers!*. 1913. Reprint, New York: Vintage Classics, 1992.

Cayton, Andrew R. L. "The Anti-region: Place and Identity in the History of the American Midwest." In *The Midwest: Essays on Regional History*, edited by Andrew R. L. Cayton and Susan E. Gray, 140–159. Bloomington: Indiana University Press, 2001.

Cayton, Andrew R. L., and Susan E. Gray. "The Story of the Midwest: An Introduction." In *The Midwest: Essays on Regional History*, edited by Andrew R. L. Cayton and Susan E. Gray, 1–26. Bloomington: Indiana University Press, 2001.

Chow, Rey. *Ethics After Idealism: Theory—Culture—Ethnicity—Reading*. Bloomington: Indiana University Press, 1998.

Cisneros, Sandra. *The House on Mango Street*. 1984. Reprint, New York: Vintage Contemporaries, 2009.

Citizen Ruth. Directed by Alexander Payne. Los Angeles: Miramax, 1996. Film.

Clark, Anna. "'Nothing to Worry About. The Water Is Fine.': How Flint Poisoned Its People." *The Guardian*, July 3, 2018. https://www.theguardian.com/news/2018/jul/03/nothing-to-worry-about-the-water-is-fine-how-flint-michigan-poisoned-its-people.

Clover, Carol J. *Men, Women, and Chain Saws: Gender in the Modern Horror Film*. Princeton, NJ: Princeton University Press, 1992.

Coates, Ta-Nehisi. *We Were Eight Years in Power: An American Tragedy.* New York: One World, 2017.

Cohen, Richard. "'Real America' Is Its Own Bubble." *Washington Post*, December 12, 2016. https://www.washingtonpost.com/opinions/real-america-is-its-own-bubble/2016/12/12/e8ba60c2-c09f-11e6-b527-949c5893595e_story.html.

Cook, Pam. *Screening the Past: Memory and Nostalgia in Cinema.* London: Routledge, 2005.

Coontz, Stephanie. *The Way We Never Were: American Families and the Nostalgia Trap.* 1992. Reprint, New York: Basic Books, 2000.

Cooper, Brenda. "*Boys Don't Cry* and Female Masculinity: Reclaiming a Life and Dismantling the Politics of Normative Heterosexuality." *Critical Studies in Media Communication* 19, no. 1 (March 2002): 44–63.

Cramer, Katherine J. "How Rural Resentment Helps Explain the Surprising Victory of Donald Trump." *Washington Post*, November 13, 2016. https://www.washingtonpost.com/news/monkey-cage/wp/2016/11/13/how-rural-resentment-helps-explain-the-surprising-victory-of-donald-trump/.

———. *The Politics of Resentment: Rural Consciousness in Wisconsin and the Rise of Scott Walker.* Chicago: University of Chicago Press, 2016.

Creed, Barbara. *The Monstrous-Feminine: Film, Feminism, Psychoanalysis.* 1993. Reprint, London: Routledge, 2007.

Cronenberg, David. "Audio Commentary." *A History of Violence.* 2005; Los Angeles: New Line Home Entertainment, 2006. DVD.

Cure Violence. Cure Violence. http://cureviolence.org.

A Dangerous Method. Directed by David Cronenberg. New York: Sony Pictures Classic, 2011. Film.

de Certeau, Michel. *The Practice of Everyday Life.* Translated by Steven Rendall. 1984. Reprint, Berkeley: University of California Press, 1988.

Deleuze, Gilles. *Cinema 2: The Time-Image.* Translated by Hugh Tomlinson and Robert Galeta. 1985. Reprint, Minneapolis: University of Minneapolis Press, 2010.

DeLillo, Don. "In the Ruins of the Future." *The Guardian*, December 21, 2001. https://www.theguardian.com/books/2001/dec/22/fiction.dondelillo.

Detropia. Directed by Heidi Ewing and Rachel Grady. New York: Loki Films, 2012. Film.

Dickos, Andrew. *Intrepid Laughter: Preston Sturges and the Movies.* Metuchen, NJ: Scarecrow, 1985.

Dickstein, Morris. "Depression Culture: The Dream of Mobility." In *Radical Revisions: Rereading 1930s Culture*, edited by Bill Mullen and Sherry Lee Linkon, 225–241. Urbana: University of Illinois Press, 1996.

Dika, Vera. *Recycled Culture in Contemporary Art and Film: The Uses of Nostalgia.* Cambridge: Cambridge University Press, 2003.

———. "The Stalker Film, 1978–81." In *American Horrors: Essays on the Modern American Horror Film*, edited by Gregory A. Waller, 86–101. Urbana: University of Illinois Press, 1987.

Dirty Harry. Directed by Don Siegel. 1971; Burbank, CA: Warner Home Video, 2008. DVD.

Dreiser, Theodore. *Sister Carrie.* Edited by Claude Simpson. 1900. Reprint, Boston: Houghton Mifflin, 1959.

Drop Dead Gorgeous. Directed by Michael Patrick Jann. Los Angeles: New Line Home Entertainment, 1999. DVD.

Eastern Promises. Directed by David Cronenberg. New York: Focus Features, 2007. Film.

Ebert, Roger. Review of *American Movie*, directed by Chris Smith. *RogerEbert.com.* Ebert Digital LLC. Modified on January 21, 2000. https://www.rogerebert.com/reviews/american-movie-2000.

Elder, Matthew. "Social Demarcation and the Forms of Psychological Fracture in Book One of Richard Wright's *Native Son*." *Texas Studies in Literature and Language* 52, no. 1 (Spring 2010): 31–47.

Election. Directed by Alexander Payne. Hollywood, CA: Paramount Pictures, 1999. DVD.

Encounters at the End of the World. Directed by Werner Herzog. 2007; Chatsworth, CA: Image Entertainment, 2008. DVD.

Epps, Garrett. "What Makes Indiana's Religious-Freedom Law Different?" *The Atlantic*, March 30, 2015. https://www.theatlantic.com/politics/archive/2015/03/what-makes-indianas-religious-freedom-law-different/388997/.

Eugenides, Jeffrey. *The Virgin Suicides.* New York: Picador, 1993.

Faragher, John Mack. Afterword to *Rereading Frederick Jackson Turner: "The Significance of the Frontier in American History" and Other Essays*, by Frederick Jackson Turner. Edited by John Mack Faragher, 225–241. New York: Henry Holt, 1994.

———. Introduction to *Rereading Frederick Jackson Turner: "The Significance of the Frontier in American History" and Other Essays*, by Frederick Jackson Turner. Edited by John Mack Faragher, 1–10. New York: Henry Holt, 1994.

Fargo. Directed by Joel Coen and Ethan Coen. 1996; Beverly Hills, CA: Twentieth Century Fox Home Entertainment, 2005. DVD.

Fisher, Philip. "Looking Around to See Who I Am: Dreiser's Territory of the Self." *ELH* 44, no. 4 (Winter 1977): 728–748.

Fitzcarraldo. Directed by Werner Herzog. 1982; Troy, MI: Anchor Bay Entertainment, 1999. DVD.

The Fly. Directed by David Cronenberg. 1986; Beverly Hills, CA: Twentieth Century Fox Home Entertainment, 2005. DVD.

Foundas, Scott. "Small Is Beautiful." *Film Comment* 47, no. 6, November/December 2011, 22–27.

Frank, Thomas. *What's the Matter with Kansas? How Conservatives Won the Heart of America.* 2004. Reprint, New York: Henry Holt, 2005.

Frontline. Season 14, episode 6, "Living on the Edge." Written by Tom Casciato, Kathleen Hughes, and Bill Moyers. December 12, 1995, PBS. https://billmoyers.com/content/living-on-the-edge/.

———. Season 31, episode 14, "Two American Families". Written by Kathleen Hughes and Bill Moyers. Featuring Bill Moyers. July 9, 2013, PBS. https://www.pbs.org/wgbh/frontline/film/two-american-families/.

Garland, Hamlin. *Main-Travelled Roads.* 1891. Reprint, New York: Holt, Rinehart and Winston, 1965.

Genné, Beth. "Vincente Minnelli's Style in Microcosm: The Establishing Sequence of 'Meet Me in St. Louis.'" *Art Journal* 43, no. 3 (1983): 247–254.

Geyh, Paula. "From Cities of Things to Cities of Signs: Urban Spaces and Urban Subjects in *Sister Carrie* and *Manhattan Transfer*." *Twentieth-Century Literature* 52, no. 4 (Winter 2006): 413–442.

Giant. Directed by George Stevens. 1956; Burbank, CA: Warner Home Video, 2003. DVD.

Gjerde, Jon. "Middleness and the Middle West." In *The Midwest: Essays on Regional History*, edited by Andrew R. L. Cayton and Susan E. Gray, 180–195. Bloomington: Indiana University Press, 2001.

God Loves Uganda. Directed by Roger Ross Williams. New York: Variance Films, 2013. Film.

González, Jennifer A. "Autotopographies." In *Prosthetic Territories: Politics and Hypertechnologies*, edited by Gabriel Brahm Jr. and Mark Driscoll, 133–150. Boulder, CO: Westview, 1995.

Grace Under Fire. New York: ABC, 1993–1998. Broadcast television.

Gran Torino. Directed by Clint Eastwood. 2008; Burbank, CA: Warner Home Video, 2010. DVD.

Grant, Michael. *The Modern Fantastic: The Films of David Cronenberg*. Trowbridge, UK: Flicks Books, 2000.

Grease. Directed by Randal Kleiser. Hollywood, CA: Paramount Pictures, 1978. Film.

Grindon, Leger. *The Hollywood Romantic Comedy*. Hoboken, NJ: Wiley-Blackwell, 2011.

Gummo. Directed by Harmony Korine. 1997; Los Angeles: New Line Home Video, 2001. DVD.

Hainey, Michael. "Clint and Scott Eastwood: No Holds Barred in Their First Interview Together." *Esquire*, August 2016. https://www.esquire.com/entertainment/a46893/double-trouble-clint-and-scott-eastwood/.

Halberstam, J. "The Transgender Gaze in *Boys Don't Cry*." *Screen* 42, no. 3 (Autumn 2001): 294–298. doi: 10.1093/screen/42.3.294.

Halloween. Directed by John Carpenter. 1978; Troy, MI: Anchor Bay Entertainment, 2000. DVD.

Halloween: Unmasked. Directed by Mark Cerulli. 1999; Troy, MI: Anchor Bay Entertainment, 2000. DVD.

Hansberry, Lorraine. *A Raisin in the Sun*. 1959. Reprint, New York: Vintage Books, 1994.

Happy Days. New York: ABC, 1974–1984. Broadcast television.

Harkins, Anthony. "The Midwest and the Evolution of 'Flyover Country.'" *Middle West Review* 3, no. 1 (2016): 97–121.

Harris, Martin. "You Can't Kill the Boogeyman: *Halloween III* and the Modern Horror Franchise." *Journal of Popular Film and Television* 32, no. 3 (Fall 2004): 98–109.

Hart, Kylo-Patrick R. *Images for a Generation Doomed: The Films and Career of Gregg Araki*. Plymouth, UK: Lexington Books, 2010.

Harvey, David. *A Brief History of Neoliberalism*. 2005. Reprint, New York: Oxford University Press, 2009.

Harvey, James. *Romantic Comedy in Hollywood, from Lubitsch to Sturges*. 1987. Reprint, New York: Da Capo, 1998.

Hauze, Emily. "Keyed Fantasies: Music, The Accordion and the American Dream in *Stroszek* and *Schultze Gets the Blues*." *German Life and Letters* 62, no. 1 (January 2009): 84–95. doi: 10.1111/j.1468-0483.2008.01450.x.

Heim, Scott. *Mysterious Skin*. 1995. Reprint, New York: Harper Perennial, 2005.

Henderson, Lisa. "The Class Character of *Boys Don't Cry*." *Screen* 42, no. 3 (Autumn 2001): 299–303. doi: 10.1093/screen/42.3.299.

Herzog, Werner, and Norman Hill. "Audio Commentary." *Stroszek*, DVD. Directed by Werner Herzog. 1977; Troy, MI: Anchor Bay Entertainment, 2001.

Higgins, Scott. "Color at the Center: Minnelli's Technicolor Style in *Meet Me in St. Louis*." *Style* 32 no. 3 (Fall 1998): 449–470.

Hinderaker, Eric. "Liberating Contrivances: Narrative and Identity in Midwestern History." In *The Midwest: Essays on Regional History*, edited by Andrew R. L. Cayton and Susan E. Gray, 48–68. Bloomington: Indiana University Press, 2001.

A History of Violence. Directed by David Cronenberg. 2005; Los Angeles: New Line Home Entertainment, 2006. DVD.

Holden, Stephen. "An Uneasy Rider on the Road to Self-Discovery." *New York Times*, September 27, 2002. https://www.nytimes.com/2002/09/27/movies/film-festival-review-an-uneasy-rider-on-the-road-to-self-discovery.html.

hooks, bell. *Reel To Real: Race, Sex, and Class at the Movies*. New York: Routledge, 1996.

Hoop Dreams. Directed by Steve James. 1994; New York: Criterion Collection, 2005. DVD.

Hoose, Eric Van. "Native Sun: Lightness and Darkness in *Native Son*." *The Black Scholar* 41, no. 2 (Summer 2011): 46–54.

Hoskin, Bree. "Playground Love: Landscape and Longing in Sofia Coppola's *The Virgin Suicides*." *Literature Film Quarterly* 35, no. 3 (2007): 214–221.

The Interrupters. Directed by Steve James. Chicago: Kartemquin Films, 2011. *Frontline*. Season 30, episode 6. February 14, 2012, PBS. https://www.pbs.org/wgbh/frontline/film/interrupters/.

Jaeckle, Jeff. "Dreiser's Universe of Imbalance in *Sister Carrie*." *Dreiser Studies* 33, no. 2 (Fall 2002): 3–20.

Jaffe, Greg, and Juliet Eilperin. "Tom Vilsack's Lonely Fight for a 'Forgotten' Rural America." *Washington Post*, September 26, 2016. https://www.washingtonpost.com/politics/tom-vilsacks-lonely-fight-for-a-forgotten-rural-america/2016/09/26/62d7ee64-7830-11e6-ac8e-cf8e0dd91dc7_story.html.

James, Nick. "No Place Like Home." *Sight & Sound* 20, no. 2 (February 2010): 30–33.

Jameson, Fredric. *Postmodernism: or, The Cultural Logic of Late Capitalism*. Durham, NC: Duke University Press, 1991.

Johnson, Brian. "Violence Hits Home." *Maclean's* 118, no. 42, October 17, 2005.

Johnson, Jenna. "This Deeply Blue Wisconsin Village Still Seems Surprised It Voted for Trump." *Washington Post*, January 19, 2017. https://www.washingtonpost.com/politics/this-deeply-blue-wisconsin-village-still-seems-surprised-it-voted-for-trump/2017/01/19/9e9777ca-dd26-11e6-918c-99ede3c8cafa_story.html.

Johnson, Victoria E. *Heartland TV: Prime Time Television and the Struggle for U.S. Identity*. New York: New York University Press, 2008.

———. "The Persistence of Geographic Myth in a Convergent Media Era." *Journal of Popular Film and Television* 38, no. 2 (July 2010): 58–65. doi: 10.1080/01956051.2010.483341.

Kakutani, Michiko. "Critic's Notebook: The Age of Irony Isn't Over After All; Assertions of Cynicism's Demise Belie History." *New York Times*, October 9, 2001. https://www.nytimes.com/2001/10/09/arts/critic-s-notebook-age-irony-isn-t-over-after-all-assertions-cynicism-s-demise.html.

Kennedy, Merrit. "Lead-Laced Water in Flint: A Step-By-Step Look at the Makings of a Crisis." NPR. National Public Radio, April 20, 2016. https://www.npr.org/sections/thetwo-way/2016/04/20/465545378/lead-laced-water-in-flint-a-step-by-step-look-at-the-makings-of-a-crisis.

Kirkpatrick, David D. "A Nation Challenged: The Commentators; Pronouncements on Irony Draw a Line in the Sand." *New York Times*, September 24, 2001. https:// www.nytimes.com/2001/09/24/business/nation-challenged-commentators-pronouncements-irony-draw-line-sand.html.

Kreider, Tim, and Rob Content. Review of *The Straight Story*, by David Lynch. *Film Quarterly* 54, no. 1 (Autumn 2000): 26–33. doi: 10.2307/1213799.

Kruse, Michael. "'What Do You Do if a Red State Moves to You?': Letter from Pepin County." *Politico*, January/February 2017. https://www.politico.com/magazine/story/2017/01/blue-red-state-democrats-trump-country-214647.

Lassiter, Luke Eric, Hurley Goodall, Elizabeth Campbell, and Michelle Natasya Johnson, eds. *The Other Side of Middletown: Exploring Muncie's African American Community*. Lanham, MD: AltaMira, 2004.

Lauck, Jon K. *From Warm Center to Ragged Edge: The Erosion of Midwestern Literary and Historical Regionalism, 1920–1965*. Iowa City: University of Iowa Press, 2017.

———. *The Lost Region: Toward a Revival of Midwestern History*. Iowa City: University of Iowa Press, 2013.

Leeder, Murray. *Horror Film: A Critical Introduction*. New York: Bloomsbury Academic, 2018.

Leonard, Robert. "Why Rural America Voted for Trump." *New York Times*, January 5, 2017. https://www.nytimes.com/2017/01/05/opinion/why-rural-america-voted-for-trump.html.

Lesy, Michael. *Wisconsin Death Trip*. New York: Pantheon Books, 1973.

Lewis, Sinclair. *Babbitt*. 1922. Reprint, New York: Bantam Classic, 2007.

———. *Main Street*. 1920. Reprint, New York: The New American Library, 1980.

Life Itself. Directed by Steve James. New York: Magnolia Pictures, 2013. Film.

Lim, Bliss Cua. *Translating Time: Cinema, the Fantastic, and Temporal Critique*. Durham, NC: Duke University Press, 2009.

Lindsay, Jane. "I Am a Democrat in Rural, Red-State America. My Party Abandoned Us." *The Guardian*, November 15, 2016. https://www.theguardian.com/commentisfree/2016/nov/15/rural-america-working-class-voters-democrats-donald-trump.

Linthicum, Kate. "'I Feel Forgotten': A Decade of Struggle in Rural Ohio." *The New Yorker*, October 2016. https://www.newyorker.com/culture/photo-booth/i-feel-forgotten-a-decade-of-struggle-in-rural-ohio.

Longden, Tom. "Alvin Straight." *The Des Moines Register*. https://data.desmoinesregister.com/famous-iowans/alvin-straight.

Longworth, Richard C. *Caught in the Middle: America's Heartland in the Age of Globalism*. 2008. Reprint, New York: Bloomsbury, 2009.

Lost Highway. Directed by David Lynch. 1997; Universal City, CA: Universal Studios Home Entertainment, 2008. DVD.

Lowenstein, Adam. "Promises of Violence: David Cronenberg on Globalized Geopolitics." *boundary 2* 36, no. 2 (2009): 199–208. doi: 10.1215/01903659-2009-011.

Lutz, Tom. *Cosmopolitan Vistas: American Regionalism and Literary Value*. Ithaca, NY: Cornell University Press, 2004.

Lynch, David. Statement on DVD chapter stops. *The Straight Story*. Directed by David Lynch. 1999; Burbank, CA: Walt Disney Home Video, 2000. DVD insert.

Lynd, Robert S., and Helen Merrell Lynd. *Middletown: A Study in Modern American Culture*. 1929. Reprint, San Diego, CA: Harcourt Brace Jovanovich, 1957.

———. *Middletown in Transition: A Study in Cultural Conflicts*. 1937. Reprint, New York: Harcourt Brace Jovanovich, 1965.

Ma, Jean. *Melancholy Drift: Marking Time in Chinese Cinema*. Hong Kong: Hong Kong University Press, 2010.

MacGillis, Alec, and ProPublica. "The Original Underclass." *The Atlantic*, September 2016. https://www.theatlantic.com/magazine/archive/2016/09/the-original-underclass/492731/.

Machuco, Antonio. "Violence and Truth in Clint Eastwood's *Gran Torino*." *Anthropoetics* 16, no. 2 (Spring 2011). http://anthropoetics.ucla.edu/ap1602/1602machuco/.

MacKinnon, Kenneth. *Hollywood's Small Towns: An Introduction to the American Small-Town Movie*. Metuchen, NJ: Scarecrow, 1984.

Mad Men. New York: AMC, 2007–2015. DVD.

The Magnificent Ambersons. Directed by Orson Welles. 1942; Burbank, CA: Warner Home Video, 2011. DVD.

Manalansan IV, Martin F., Chantal Nadeau, Richard T. Rodríguez, and Siobhan B. Somerville. "Queering the Middle: Race, Region, and a Queer Midwest." *GLQ* 20 no. 1–2 (2014): 1–12. doi: 10.1215/10642684-2370270.

Manovich, Lev. *The Language of New Media*. Cambridge, MA: MIT Press, 2001.

Markov, Nina. "Class, Culture, and Capital in *Sister Carrie*." *Dreiser Studies* 36, no.1 (Summer 2005): 3–27.

Marshall, Kate. "Sewer, Furnace, Air Shaft, Media: Modernity Behind the Walls in *Native Son* and *Manhattan Transfer*." *Studies in American Fiction* 37, no. 1 (Spring 2010): 55–80.

Martin, Adrian. "Things to Look Into: The Cinema of Terrence Malick." *Rouge* 10 (2007). http://www.rouge.com.au/10/malick.html.

McGowan, Todd. *The Impossible David Lynch*. New York: Columbia University Press, 2007.

Meet Me in St. Louis. Directed by Vincente Minnelli. 1944; Burbank, CA: Warner Home Video, 2004. DVD.

The Middle. New York: ABC, 2009–2018. Broadcast television.

Middletown. Arlington, VA: PBS, 1982. Broadcast television.

"'Midwest' Discovered Between East, West Coasts." *The Onion*, September 4, 1996. https://www.theonion.com/midwest-discovered-between-east-west-coasts-1819564009.

"'Midwest' Discovered Between East and West Coasts." *The Onion*, July 6, 2005. https://www.theonion.com/midwest-discovered-between-east-and-west-coasts-1819567923.

Milwaukee 53206. Mass Incarceration Project LLC. 2018. https://www.milwaukee53206.com.

Milwaukee 53206: A Community Serves Time. Directed by Keith McQuirter. Transform Films, 2016. *America Reframed*. April 3, 2018, PBS. https://www.pbs.org/video/milwaukee-53206-abaext/.

Minimum Wages: The New Economy. Directed by Tom Casciato. January 8, 1992, PBS. https://billmoyers.com/content/minimum-wages/.

The Miracle of Morgan's Creek. Directed by Preston Sturges. 1944; Hollywood, CA: Paramount Pictures, 2005. DVD.

Morrison, Toni. *Beloved*. 1987. Reprint, New York: Vintage International, 2004.

Mouton, Jan. "Werner Herzog's *Stroszek*: A Fairy-Tale Film in an Age of Disenchantment." *Literature Film Quarterly* 15, no. 2 (1987): 99–106.

Mutz, Diana C. "Status Threat, Not Economic Hardship, Explains the 2016 Presidential Vote." *PNAS* 115, no. 19 (2018): E4330-E4339. doi: doi.org/10.1073/pnas.1718155115.

Mysterious Skin. Unrated Director's Edition. Directed by Gregg Araki. 2004; Culver City, CA: Strand Releasing Home Video, 2006. DVD.

Naremore, James. *The Films of Vincente Minnelli*. Cambridge: Cambridge University Press, 1993.
Natoli, Joseph. "The Perils of Being *Up in the Air*." *Senses of Cinema* 54 (2010). http://sensesofcinema.com/2010/feature-articles/the-perils-of-being-up-in-the-air/.
Nebraska. Directed by Alexander Payne. Los Angeles: Paramount Vantage, 2013. Film.
Newsweek Staff. "The End of Irony." *Newsweek*, September 26, 2001. http://www.newsweek.com/end-irony-152295.
———. "Terror's Cultural Fallout." *Newsweek*, September 21, 2001. http://www.newsweek.com/terrors-cultural-fallout-151937.
Nichols, Jeff, and Michael Shannon. "Audio Commentary." *Take Shelter*. Directed by Jeff Nichols. 2011; Culver City, CA: Sony Pictures Home Entertainment, 2012. DVD.
Nostalgia for the Light. Directed by Patricio Guzmán. Brooklyn, NY: Icarus Films, 2010. Film.
O'Brien, Tim. *In the Lake of the Woods*. 1994. Reprint, New York: Penguin Books, 1995.
Ochonicky, Adam. "The Millennial Midwest: Nostalgic Violence in the Twenty-First Century." *Quarterly Review of Film and Video* 32, no. 2 (2015): 124–140. doi: 10.1080/10509208.2013.780937.
———. Review of *Frontline*. Season 31, episode 14. *Two American Families*. Written by Kathleen Hughes and Bill Moyers. Featuring Bill Moyers. July 9, 2013, PBS. https://www.pbs.org/wgbh/frontline/film/two-american-families/. *Middle West Review* 1, no. 1 (Fall 2014): 161–164. doi: 10.1353/mwr.2014.0005.
Oman, Patricia. "'Here Comes the Show Boat!': *Show Boat* and the Case for Regionalism," *Cinema Journal* 56, no. 1 (Fall 2016): 63–87.
———. "Judy Garland and MGM's Nostalgic Midwestern Home." *Middle West Review* 4, no. 1 (Fall 2017): 209–229.
Parks and Recreation. New York: NBC, 2009–2015. DVD.
———. Season 2, episode 9, "The Camel." Directed by Millicent Shelton. November 12, 2009, NBC. DVD.
Patterson, Hannah. "Two Characters in Search of a Direction: Motivation and the Construction of Identity in *Badlands*." In *The Cinema of Terrence Malick: Poetic Visions of America*, edited by Hannah Patterson, 24–36. London: Wallflower, 2004.
Phillips, Kendall R. *Dark Directions: Romero, Craven, Carpenter, and the Modern Horror Film*. Carbondale: Southern Illinois University Press, 2012.
———. *Projected Fears: Horror Films and American Culture*. Westport, CT: Praeger, 2005.
Prager, Brad. *The Cinema of Werner Herzog: Aesthetic Ecstasy and Truth*. London: Wallflower, 2007.
The Pruitt-Igoe Myth. Directed by Chad Freidrichs. 2011; New York: First Run Features, 2012. DVD.
Psycho. Directed by Alfred Hitchcock. 1960; Universal City, CA: Universal Studios Home Entertainment, 2008. DVD.
The Public Enemy. Directed by William A. Wellman. 1931; Burbank, CA: Warner Home Video, 2005. DVD.
Qureshi, Bilal. "From Wrong to Right: A U.S. Apology for Japanese Internment." National Public Radio, August 9, 2013. https://www.npr.org/sections/codeswitch/2013/08/09/210138278/japanese-internment-redress.
Radavich, David. "Midwestern Dramas." In *In the Middle of the Middle West: Literary Nonfiction from the Heartland*, edited by Becky Bradway, 186–190. Bloomington: Indiana University Press, 2003.

Rafter, Nicole. *Shots in the Mirror: Crime Films and Society.* New York: Oxford University Press, 2006.

Rebel Without a Cause. Directed by Nicholas Ray. 1955; Burbank, CA: Warner Home Video, 2010. DVD.

Reichert Powell, Douglas. *Critical Regionalism: Connecting Politics and Culture in the American Landscape.* Chapel Hill: University of North Carolina Press, 2007.

Relyea, Sarah. *Outsider Citizens: The Remaking of Postwar Identity in Wright, Beauvoir, and Baldwin.* New York: Routledge, 2006.

Rentschler, Eric. "How American Is It: The U.S. as Image and Imaginary in German Film." *The German Quarterly* 57, no. 4 (Autumn 1984): 603–620. doi: 10.2307/404701.

Rich, B. Ruby. "New Queer Cinema." *Sight & Sound* 2, no. 5 (1992): 30–37.

———. *New Queer Cinema: The Director's Cut.* Durham, NC: Duke University Press, 2013.

Rich Hill. Directed by Tracy Droz Tragos and Andrew Droz Palermo. 2014; Pacific Palisades, CA: Dinky Pictures, 2015. DVD.

RoboCop. Directed by Paul Verhoeven. 1987; Culver City, CA: Sony Pictures Home Entertainment, 2006. DVD.

Roche, David. *Making and Remaking Horror in the 1970s and 2000s: Why Don't They Do It Like They Used To?.* Jackson: University Press of Mississippi, 2014.

Roche, Mark W., and Vittorio Hösle. "Cultural and Religious Reversals in Clint Eastwood's *Gran Torino*." *Religion and the Arts* 15 (2011): 648–679. doi: 10.1163/156852911X596273.

Rodley, Chris, ed. *Lynch on Lynch.* Rev. ed. London: Faber and Faber, 2005.

Roger & Me. Directed by Michael Moore. 1989; Burbank, CA: Warner Home Video, 2003. DVD.

Romell, Rick. "In Western Wisconsin, Trump Voters Want Change." *Milwaukee Journal Sentinel,* November 27, 2016. https://www.jsonline.com/story/news/politics/elections/2016/11/26/western-wisconsin-trump-voters-want-change/94436384/.

Roseanne. New York: ABC, 1988–1997, 2018. Broadcast television.

Rosenblatt, Roger. "The Age of Irony Comes to An End." *Time,* September 24, 2001.

Rottenberg, Dan, ed. *Middletown Jews: The Tenuous Survival of an American Jewish Community.* Bloomington: Indiana University Press, 1998.

Rushkoff, Douglas. "Renaissance Now! Media Ecology and the New Global Narrative." In *Living in the Information Age: A New Media Reader.* 2nd ed., edited by Erik P. Bucy, 21–32. Belmont: Wadsworth, 2005.

Sargeant, Jack. "Killer Couples: From Nebraska to Route 666." In *Lost Highways: An Illustrated History of Road Movies,* edited by Jack Sargeant and Stephanie Watson, 147–168. London: Creation Books, 1999.

Scarface. Directed by Howard Hawks. 1932; Universal City, CA: Universal Studios Home Entertainment, 2007. DVD.

Schein, Louisa, and Va-Megn Thoj. "*Gran Torino*'s Boys and Men with Guns: Hmong Perspectives." *Hmong Studies Journal* 10 (2009): 1–52. http://hmongstudies.org/ScheinThojHSJ10.pdf.

Schiller, Robert. "Why Did US Voters Back Trump? Economic Powerlessness." *The Guardian,* November 22, 2016. https://www.theguardian.com/business/2016/nov/22/why-did-americans-support-trump-economic-powerlessness.

Schotland, Sara D. "Breaking Out of the Rooster Coop: Violent Crime in Aravind Adiga's *White Tiger* and Richard Wright's *Native Son*." *Comparative Literature Studies* 48, no. 1 (2011): 1–19.

Scott, A. O. "That Mythic American Hero: The Regular Guy." *New York Times*, December 8, 2002. https://www.nytimes.com/2002/12/08/movies/film-that-mythic-american-hero-the-regular-guy.html.

Shambu, Girish. *"About Schmidt*: Is That All There Is?." *Senses of Cinema* 25 (2003). http://sensesofcinema.com/2003/feature-articles/about_schmidt/.

Sharrett, Christopher. "The Horror Film in Neoconservative Culture." *Journal of Popular Film and Television* 21, no. 3 (Fall 1993): 100–110.

Shortridge, James R. *The Middle West: Its Meaning in American Culture*. Lawrence: University Press of Kansas, 1989.

Shostak, Debra. "'A Story We Could Live With': Narrative Voice, the Reader, and Jeffrey Eugenides's *The Virgin Suicides*." *MFS Modern Fiction Studies* 55, no. 4 (Winter 2009): 808–832. doi: 10.1353/mfs.0.1642.

A Simple Plan. Directed by Sam Raimi. 1998; Hollywood, CA: Paramount Pictures, 1999. DVD.

Sinclair, Upton. *The Jungle*. 1906. Reprint, New York: The Modern Library, 2006.

Slotkin, Richard. *The Fatal Environment: The Myth of the Frontier in the Age of Industrialization, 1800–1890*. 1985. Reprint, Middletown, CT: Wesleyan University Press, 1986.

Spider. Directed by David Cronenberg. 2002; Culver City, CA: Sony Pictures Home Entertainment, 2003. DVD.

Spigel, Lynn. "Postfeminist Nostalgia for a Prefeminist Future." *Screen* 54, no. 2 (Summer 2013): 270–278. doi: 10.1093/screen/hjt017.

Sprengler, Christine. *Screening Nostalgia: Populuxe Props and Technicolor Aesthetics in Contemporary American Film*. 2009. Reprint, New York: Berghahn Books, 2011.

Stables, Kate. Review of *Gran Torino*, directed by Clint Eastwood. *Sight & Sound* 19, no. 3 (March 2009): 61–62.

Stanley, Matthew E. Review of *Hoop Dreams*, directed by Steve James. *Middle West Review* 3, no. 1 (2016): 193–197.

Sterne, Jonathan. "Out with the Trash: On the Future of New Media." In *Residual Media*, edited by Charles R. Acland, 16–31. Minneapolis: University of Minnesota Press, 2007.

Stewart, Jacqueline. "Negroes Laughing at Themselves? Black Spectatorship and the Performance of Urban Modernity." *Critical Inquiry* 29, no. 4 (Summer 2003): 650–677.

Stewart, Susan. "The Epistemology of the Horror Story." *The Journal of American Folklore* 95, no. 375 (1982): 33–50. doi: 10.2307/540021.

———. *On Longing: Narratives of the Miniature, the Gigantic, the Souvenir, the Collection*. 1993. Reprint, Durham, NC: Duke University Press, 2007.

The Straight Story. Directed by David Lynch. 1999; Burbank, CA: Walt Disney Home Video, 2000. DVD.

Stroszek. Directed by Werner Herzog. 1977; Troy, MI: Anchor Bay Entertainment, 2001. DVD.

Suner, Asuman. *New Turkish Cinema: Belonging, Identity and Memory*. London: I. B. Tauris, 2010.

Surviving the Good Times. Directed by Tom Casciato and Kathleen Hughes. PBS, March 28, 2000. https://billmoyers.com/content/surviving-the-good-times/.

Take Shelter. Directed by Jeff Nichols. 2011; Culver City, CA: Sony Pictures Home Entertainment, 2012. DVD.

Takeuchi, Masaya. "Bigger's Divided Self: Violence and Homosociality in *Native Son*." *Studies in American Naturalism* 4, no. 1 (Summer 2009): 56–74.

Tavernise, Sabrina. "Many in Milwaukee Neighborhood Didn't Vote—and Don't Regret It." *New York Times*, November 20, 2016. https://www.nytimes.com/2016/11/21/us/many-in-milwaukee-neighborhood-didnt-vote-and-dont-regret-it.html.

Telotte, J. P. "Self and Society: Vincente Minnelli and Musical Formula." *The Journal of Popular Film and Television* 9, no. 4 (1982): 181–193.

"30 Years of Man's Life Disappear in Mysterious 'Kansas Rectangle.'" *The Onion*, June 30, 2011. https://local.theonion.com/30-years-of-mans-life-disappear-in-mysterious-kansas-re-1819572765.

Tieken, Mara Casey. "There's a Big Part of Rural America that Everyone's Ignoring." *Washington Post*, March 24, 2017. https://www.washingtonpost.com/opinions/theres-a-big-part-of-rural-america-that-everyones-ignoring/2017/03/24/d06d24d0-1010-11e7-ab07-07d9f521f6b5_story.html.

Trencansky, Sarah. "Final Girls and Terrible Youth: Transgression in 1980s Slasher Horror." *Journal of Popular Film and Television* 29, no. 2 (Summer 2001): 63–73.

Turim, Maureen. *Flashbacks in Film: Memory and History*. New York: Routledge, 1989.

Turner, Frederick Jackson. *The Frontier in American History*. 1920. Reprint, Charleston, SC: BiblioBazaar, 2008.

United States Census Bureau. "Census Regions and Divisions of the United States." United States Census Bureau, last modified February 9, 2015. https://www2.census.gov/geo/maps/general_ref/pgsz_ref/CensusRegDiv.pdf.

Up in the Air. Directed by Jason Reitman. 2009; Hollywood, CA: Paramount Pictures, 2010. DVD.

Vang, Bee. Interview by Louisa Schein. "*Gran Torino*'s Hmong Lead Bee Vang on Film, Race and Masculinity: Conversations with Louisa Schein." *Hmong Studies Journal* 11 (2010): 1–11. http://hmongstudies.org/ScheinVangHSJ11.pdf.

The Virgin Suicides. Directed by Sofia Coppola. 1999; Hollywood, CA: Paramount Classics, 2000. DVD.

Vonnegut, Kurt. "To Be a Native Middle-Westerner." Indiana Humanities Council. NUVO Cultural Institute. 1999. http://www.indianahumanities.org/pdf/Vonnegut.pdf.

Wagner, John. *A History of Violence*. New York: Vertigo, 1997.

Walker, Beverly. "Malick on Badlands." *Sight and Sound* 44, no. 2 (Spring 1975): 82–83.

Webster, Stephen. Review of *Gran Torino*, directed by Clint Eastwood. "Elegy for the White Man." *American Renaissance*, September 2009, 10–12.

Wells, Paul. *The Horror Genre: From Beelzebub to Blair Witch*. 2000. Reprint, London: Wallflower, 2004.

White, Patricia. "Girls Still Cry." *Screen* 42, no. 2 (Summer 2001): 217–221. doi: 10.1093/screen/42.2.217.

Whose Streets?. Directed by Sabaah Folayan and Damon Davis. New York: Magnolia Pictures, 2017. Film.

Williams, Raymond. *Keywords: A Vocabulary of Culture and Society*. Rev, ed. New York: Oxford University Press, 1985.

Wilson, Scott. *The Politics of Insects: David Cronenberg's Cinema of Confrontation*. New York: Continuum, 2011.

Winfrey-Harris, Tamara. "Stop Pretending Black Midwesterners Don't Exist." *New York Times*, June 16, 2018. https://www.nytimes.com/2018/06/16/opinion/sunday/black-midwesterners-trump-politics.html.

Winter's Bone. Directed by Debra Granik. Santa Monica, CA: Lionsgate, 2010. DVD.
The Wizard of Oz. Directed by Victor Fleming. 1939; Burbank, CA: Warner Home Video, 2009. DVD.
Wood, Robin. *Hollywood from Vietnam to Reagan . . . and Beyond*. Rev ed. 1986. Reprint, New York: Columbia University Press, 2003.
Woodrell, Daniel. *Winter's Bone*. 2006. Reprint, New York: Back Bay Books, 2007.
Worland, Rick. *The Horror Film: An Introduction*. 2007. Reprint, Malden: Blackwell, 2011.
Wright, Richard. "How 'Bigger' Was Born." In *Native Son*, 431–462. 1940. Reprint, New York: Harper Perennial Modern Classics, 2005.
——. *Native Son*. 1940. Reprint, New York: Harper Perennial Modern Classics, 2005.
Yang, Kao Kalia. *The Latehomecomer: A Hmong Family Memoir*. Minneapolis, MN: Coffee House, 2008.
Žižek, Slavoj. *Violence*. New York: Picador, 2008.

INDEX

Page numbers in *italics* indicate figures.

9/11, 124; post-9/11 debate about irony and sincerity, 19, 152–155, 173
1950s: "1950s suburban family," mythology of, 51n24; "Fifties" as "nostalgic construct," 106; nostalgic associations with, 106, 109, 117n62. See also Sprengler, Christine

About Schmidt (novel), 157. See also Begley, Louis
About Schmidt (film), 19, 151–152, 155, 156–162, 173, 178; and *Easy Rider*, 176n30; labor and identity, treatment of, 156, 158, 160, 199; nostalgia, aesthetics of, 159; nostalgic spatiality in, 158, 160, 166, 205; personal revisionism theme, 158, 159, 161; and western expansion, 159–160. See also Nicholson, Jack; Payne, Alexander
acting: performance of Midwestern traits, 138, 140–145; slapstick, 65–67; voice elements, 140, 143. See also Mortensen, Viggo
African Americans: exclusion from Midwestern label, 4, 61–62; Midwestern population, 4; in Milwaukee, 9, 219, 221–224; perceptions of "black rurality," 81n65; representation of, 70–77 (*Native Son*), 128–129 (*Boys Don't Cry*, film); violence against, 124, 219
Aguirre, The Wrath of God, 99. See also Herzog, Werner
Altman, Rick, 48; gender and region, associations with, 45; musical as "cultural problem-solving device," 42–43; temporality of musicals, 42–43
America to Me, 218, 227n49. See also James, Steve
American Midwest. See Midwest
American Movie, 220–221. See also Borchardt, Mark; Smith, Chris
Anderson, Benedict: newspapers and national identity, 80n58
Anderson, Sherwood, 1–2, 57, 59, 70, 76. See also *Winesburg, Ohio*
Apted, Michael, 221. See also *Up* (documentary series)
Araki, Gregg, 20, 178–179, 183–185; "real time," use of, 201n18. See also *Mysterious Skin*

Atlantic, The (magazine): 2016 presidential election, 9, 212–213
"autotopography," 190–191. See also González, Jennifer A.

Babbitt, 57–58, 66. See also Lewis, Sinclair
Badlands, 18, 84–85, 88–98, *91*, *92*, 100, 105, 106, 111–112, 203; blankness of protagonists, 91–96; treatment of conformity, 89, 95–97, 113n19, 207; nostalgia, aesthetics of, 90–92, *91*, *92*, 179, 206–207; nostalgic spatiality in, 91, 97, 179, 206–207; nostalgic violence in, 96–97, 207; performativity in, 93–98, 105, 113n24, 114n25, 114n26, 115n32, 157, 207. See also Malick, Terrence
Bazin, André, 228n58
Beers, David, 153, 154
Begley, Louis, 157; on the film adaptation of *About Schmidt* (novel), 175n24
Beloved (novel), 2. See also Morrison, Toni
Bergson, Henri, 197–198
Berman, Marshall: on modernity, 56–57
Black Christmas, 118n65
Blok, Anton: "senseless violence," 96
Blood Is at the Doorstep, The, 219. See also Ljung, Erik
Bonnie and Clyde (film), 96
Borchardt, Mark, 220–221. See also *American Movie*; *Coven*
Boym, Svetlana: internet, materiality and temporality of, 126–127; nostalgia, cinematic aesthetics of, 194; nostalgia, spatiotemporal aspects of, 186; "reflective nostalgia," 10, 32, 127, 180–181; "restorative nostalgia," 10, 14, 20, 32 (and Frederick Jackson Turner), 39 (and *Sister Carrie*), 53n57, 178, 180–181, 190, 211 (and American politics); on yearning for pre-nostalgic state, 151. See also nostalgia
Boys Don't Cry (film), 14, 19, 124, 128–130, *131*, 139, 145–146, 163, 178; DeVine, Phillip, omission of, 128–129; Midwestern setting of, 128, 129–130; nostalgic violence in, 128, 129, 199, 207, 209. See also *Brandon Teena Story, The* (documentary); Peirce, Kimberly; Teena, Brandon
Brandon Teena Story, The (documentary), 219. See also *Boys Don't Cry* (film); Muska, Susan; Olafsdóttir, Gréta; Teena, Brandon

Bridesmaids, 229n65
Brown, Michael, 124, 219. See also *Whose Streets?*
Buckley, Jeff, 152
Bush, George W., 8, 223–224
Butler, Judith, 140, 150n62

Cabrini-Green Homes, 72
Cairncross, Frances: "death of distance," effects of 126, 127
Candyman, 72. See also Rose, Bernard
Capra, Frank, 63
Carpenter, John, 18, 85, 104–111; and frontier mythology, 111; on horror sequels, 108. See also *Halloween*
Carter, Graydon, 152
Cather, Willa, 58–59, 70, 76. See also *O Pioneers!* (novel)
Cayton, Andrew R. L.: "anti-region," 7; perceptions of the Midwest, 7; regional identity and "regionality," 5
Chicago (IL), 125; Cabrini-Green Homes, 72; CeaseFire Chicago organization/Cure Violence, 227n49; in films of Steve James, 218, 227n48; in gangster films, 69; in *The House on Mango Street*, 208–209; in *The Jungle* (novel), 59; in *Native Son*, 70–77; in *Sister Carrie*, 37, 205; Turner's conception of, 34
Chow, Rey, 15
cinema: American film, 16, 203–204; documentaries, 20–21, 217–224; gangster film, 69; geographic contexts and scales, 15; Hong Kong cinema, 15; horror films, 72, 104–112, 204; international cinema, 15–16; *Native Son*, cinematic aspects of, 73–75, 83n84; Italian neorealism, 219, 228n58; "Midwestern neorealism," 219, 228n58; New German Cinema, 98 (see also *Stroszek*); New Queer Cinema, 184, 200n17; nostalgia, aesthetics of (*see* nostalgia, aesthetics of; *and individual titles of films*); "nostalgia films," 89; romantic comedies, 65, 80n57; small towns in Hollywood films, 79n43; and temporality, 15–17; Turkish cinema, 15–16; World War II and Hollywood, 65. See also acting; dissolve as film editing technique; flashbacks, cinematic; horror films; long take; musicals; *titles of individual films*; tracking shot
Cisneros, Sandra, 208–209. See also *House on Mango Street, The*
Citizen Ruth, 156. See also Payne, Alexander
class: in *Badlands*, 95–97, 115n35; in frontier thesis, 35, 38; in *Sister Carrie*, 38; in *Two American Families*, 221–224. See also economic decline; labor and identity; Midwest
Clinton, Bill, 223
Clinton, Hillary, 8
Clover, Carol, 105; on horror sequels, 107–108; "Terrible Place" in horror, 110
Coates, Ta-Nehisi: on class and race, 226n44; on reparations, 180; on whiteness, 22n12, 213, 214, 217, 226n44
Coen, Ethan, 125. See also *Fargo*
Coen, Joel, 125. See also *Fargo*
Cook, Pam: nostalgia and cinema, 15–16.
Coontz, Stephanie: frontier families and the "1950s suburban family," mythologies of, 51n24
Coppola, Sofia, 20, 179, 185–192, 205. See also *Virgin Suicides, The* (film)
Coven, 220. See also *American Movie*; Borchardt, Mark
Cramer, Katherine J.: on the 2016 presidential election, 226n18; "politics of resentment," 213–214, 216–217, 224; "rural consciousness," 213–214, 217; "rural-versus-urban divide," 213–214, 217. See also resentment
Creed, Barbara, 105
critical regionalism, 161. See also regionalism; Reichert Powell, Douglas
Cronenberg, David, 14, 19, 123–125, 138–146, 207; filmography, recurring elements in, 138, 149n56, 150n58, 150n61; on idealized Midwestern imagery, 123, 138–139. See also *History of Violence, A* (film)

Dangerous Method, A, 149n56. See also Cronenberg, David
Davis, Damon, 219. See also Folayan, Sabaah; *Whose Streets?*
de Certeau, Michel: "paradox of the frontier," 13; story/narrative as spatial practice, 5
De Sica, Vittorio, 228n58
Dean, James, 91, 94–95, 96, 105, 114n28
Deleuze, Gilles: on musicals and Vincente Minnelli, 41
DeLillo, Don: "In the Ruins of the Future," 152–153, 154, 174n15
Democratic Party. See elections, presidential (United States)
Detroit (MI), 125, 217, 220; in *Detropia*, 218; in *Gran Torino*, 131–138; in *RoboCop*, 131; in *The Virgin Suicides* (film), 185–192
Detropia, 218. See also: Ewing, Heidi; Grady, Rachel
Dickos, Andrew: on *The Miracle of Morgan's Creek*, 63–65

digital culture and technology, 19, 123–124, 125–128, 145; materiality of, 126–127, 147n17
Dika, Vera: on *Badlands*, 89, 90, 113n24, 114n28; nostalgia and American cinema, 16, 89; "stalker" versus "slasher" terms (horror subgenre), 118n70; "two-part temporal structure" of slasher films, 108. *See also* horror films
Dirty Harry, 131. *See also* Eastwood, Clint
discrimination, housing, 72, 76, 205. *See also Native Son*; redlining; segregation
dissolve as film editing technique: nostalgic aesthetics of, 20, 42, 179, 190–192, *191*, 194–196, *195*, 206. *See also* nostalgia, aesthetics of; *individual titles of films*
documentaries, 20–21, 217–224. *See also titles of individual films*
Dreiser, Theodore, 17, 37, 48, 86, 205. *See also Sister Carrie*
Drop Dead Gorgeous, 125
duration, 197–198. *See also* Bergson, Henri; *Straight Story, The*

East (American region), 1, 7, 13, 211; contrast with Midwest in media/press, 11–12, 125, 152–155; frontier spaces, relationship to, 31–32, 36; *A History of Violence*, treatment in, 138, 143–144; *Meet Me in St. Louis* (film), treatment in, 45–47; Wall Street, associations with, 19, 155. *See also* region; regionalism; movement; New York City
Eastern Promises, 149n56. *See also* Cronenberg, David
Eastwood, Clint, 19, 124, 131–138, 155, 207; on "political correctness" and racism, 149n44. *See also Gran Torino*
Ebert, Roger, 220, 227n49. *See also Life Itself*
economic decline: and American politics, 211–215, 224; in the Midwest, 19, 21, 155, 212–213, 217, 221–224; in the twenty-first century, 124, 155, 176n34; *Two American Families*, discussion in, 221–224; *Up in the Air*, depiction in, 162–163, *164*, 220. *See also* class; labor and identity; neoliberalism
Election, 156, 157, 175n29. *See also* Payne, Alexander
elections, presidential (United States): media coverage of the Midwest, 8–9, 212–213; 2000 election, 8; 2004 election, 8; 2008 election, 8, 155; 2012 election, 8, 155; 2016 election, 8–9, 20, 211–217, 224, 226n18. *See also* politics; swing states
electoral map: and regional identity, 8

Encounters at the End of the World, 98. *See also* Herzog, Werner
entrapment. *See* movement; spatial constriction
Eugenides, Jeffrey, 185. *See also Virgin Suicides, The* (film); *Virgin Suicides, The* (novel)
Ewing, Heidi, 218. *See also Detropia*; Grady, Rachel

failure: Midwest, associations with, 20–21, 211–213, 214–215, 217; and neoliberalism, 222; perceptions/treatment of, 58–59 (in *O Pioneers!*, novel), 64 (in *The Miracle of Morgan's Creek*), 160 (in *About Schmidt*, film), 162 (in *Up in the Air*), 215–217 (in "Up the Coulé: A Story of Wisconsin"), 220–221 (in *American Movie*), 221–224 (in *Two American Families*), 227n48 (in *Hoop Dreams*); and political rhetoric, 211–212, 214–217. *See also* resentment
Fargo, 125. *See also* Coen, Joel and Ethan
femininity: and rural limitations, 216 ("Up the Coulé: A Story of Wisconsin"); and social order, 64–67 (*The Miracle of Morgan's Creek*); transgender masculinity (*Boys Don't Cry*, film), relation to, 128. *See also* gender
Ferguson, Missouri. *See Whose Streets?*
film. *See* cinema; *titles of individual films*
Fitzcarraldo, 98. *See also* Herzog, Werner
Fitzgerald, F. Scott, 157
flashbacks, cinematic, 185. *See also* Turim, Maureen; *Virgin Suicides, The* (film)
Flint (MI), 217–218
Fly, The, 150n61. *See also* Cronenberg, David
"flyover country": in films of Alexander Payne, 157. *See also* Harkins, Anthony; Midwest
Folayan, Sabaah, 219. *See also* Davis, Damon; *Whose Streets?*
Ford, John, 63
Frank, Thomas, 8; Kansas as test market, 78n30
Freidrichs, Chad, 218–219. *See also Pruitt-Igoe Myth, The*
Freston, Tom, 152, 155
Friday the 13th (franchise), 108. *See also Halloween*; horror films
frontier: American identity, impact on, 30–32; "nostalgic frontier," 13; "paradox of the frontier," 13; "perennial rebirth" effect, 31, 126, 160, 173, 209; reversal of mythology in John Carpenter films, 111; self-sufficient settlers, debates concerning, 34–35, 38, 51n24; as set of conditions, 31, 50n3; and "virtual space," 126–128, 145. *See also* de Certeau, Michel; Midwest; nostalgic spatiality; space; Turner, Frederick Jackson

Index 247

Frontline (PBS), 221. See also *Two American Families*
Fugate, Caril Ann, 88. See also *Badlands*; Starkweather, Charles

gangster film, 69. See also *Public Enemy, The*; *Scarface* (1932)
Garland, Hamlin, 20, 59, 211, 215–217, 220. See also *Main-Travelled Roads*; "Up the Coulé: A Story of Wisconsin"
Garland, Judy: in *Meet Me in St. Louis* (film), 42, 46, 48, 55; in *The Wizard of Oz* (film), 55
gender: American regions, associations with, 45 (*Meet Me in St. Louis*, film); gender roles, attitudes about, 58, 64–67 (*The Miracle of Morgan's Creek*); and horror, 105; performance of, 19, 130, 132, 135. See femininity; masculinity; performativity; transphobia; white masculinity
General Motors, 218. See also *Roger & Me*
geography: contexts for film analysis, 15–16. See also region; regionalism
Giant, 114n28. See also Dean, James
Gilbert, Peter, 218. See also *Hoop Dreams*
Gjerde, Jon: lingering influence of Frederick Jackson Turner, 31
GLQ (journal): special issue on "Queering the Middle," 7
God Loves Uganda, 219. See also Williams, Roger Ross
González, Jennifer A.: "autotopography," 190–191
Grace Under Fire (ABC), 141
Grady, Rachel, 218. See also *Detropia*; Ewing, Heidi
Gran Torino, 10, 19, 124, 127–128, 131–138, 145–146, 155, 209; contrasting interpretations of, 136–137; and frontier mythology, 132–133, 135–136; masculinity, treatment of, 132–135, 138, 171–172; nostalgic violence in, 136, 138, 181, 199, 207; race, treatment of, 132–138, 207; white savior figure, 132, 134, 145, 172. See also Detroit (MI); Eastwood, Clint; Hmong Americans; Vang, Bee
Granik, Debra, 20, 178–179, 182–183, 219, 228n58. See also *Winter's Bone* (film)
Gray, Susan E.: perceptions of the Midwest, 7; regional identity and "regionality," 5
Grease (film), 106
Great Depression, 17, 18, 55, 76; Midwestern identity, impact on, 47
Great Recession, 124, 155, 229n65
Griffith, D. W., 63

Guardian, The (newspaper): 2016 presidential election, 9
Gummo, 219; shooting location of, 228n57. See also Korine, Harmony
Guzmán, Patricio, 202n38. See also *Nostalgia for the Light*

Halberstam, Jack, 128–129
Halloween, 2, 18, 85, 98, 104–112, 204, 209; Michael Myers, blankness of, 105–106, 111; Michael Myers, mask of, 117n57; Midwest and nostalgia, association of, 105–106, 110–111; nostalgia, critique of, 106–107, 109, 110; nostalgic spatiality in, 205; nostalgic violence in, 105, 107, 109–111, 207; and temporality of horror, 107–108. See also Carpenter, John; horror films
Hamilton, Dontre, 219. See also *Blood Is at the Doorstep, The*
Hansberry, Lorraine, 72, 73. See also *Raisin in the Sun, A* (play)
Happy Days (ABC), 106
Harkins, Anthony: American regions and "flyover" view, 147n18
Harvey, David: on neoliberalism, 117n60, 222
Harvey, James: entrapment in romantic comedies, 80n57; World War II and Hollywood, 65
"Heartland myth." See Johnson, Victoria E.; Midwest
Heim, Scott, 182. See also *Mysterious Skin*
Herzog, Werner, 18, 85, 98–104, 179; circle motif, use of, 99, 101–104, *103*, 116n52, 206–207; commentary on the Midwest, 98, 99. See also *Stroszek*
heteronormativity: and Midwestern identity, 9, 14, 124–125, 129–130, 166
Hill, Debra, 105, 107. See also *Halloween*
Hinderaker, Eric: "liberating contrivances," 61
history: and "liberating contrivances," 61; mythical conceptions of, 12, 186; nostalgia as against history, 186 (see also Boym, Svetlana: restorative nostalgia); reflections on, 86–88; regional mythologies, relation to, 161
History of Violence, A (film), 2, 14, 19, 123–125, 127–128, 131, 138–146, *141*, *146*; long take, use of, 139–140, 179; Midwestern temporality, depiction of, 139, 141; nostalgia, aesthetics of, 139–140, 179; nostalgic violence in, 139, 142–144, 181, 199, 207–208; performance of Midwestern traits, 138, 140–145, 157, 167, 199; region and identity, relationship of, 139–141, 163; tracking shot, use of, 139–140, 179.

See also Cronenberg, David; Mortensen, Viggo
History of Violence, A (novel), 138
Hmong Americans: *Gran Torino*, problematic depiction in, 133–137; in *The Latehomecomer: A Hmong Family Memoir*, 208–209
hooks, bell: critique of *Hoop Dreams*, 227n48
Hoop Dreams, 218, 227n48. See also Gilbert, Peter; James, Steve; Marx, Frederick
horror films, 72, 104–112, 204; political contexts of, 106–107, 118n64; repetition in, 107–108, 118n65; "stalker" versus "slasher" terms, 118n70; temporality of, 107–108. See also titles of individual films
House on Mango Street, The: nostalgia, treatment of, 208–209. See also Cisneros, Sandra

Illinois, 4: in *Halloween*, 104–112 See also Chicago (IL)
In the Lake of the Woods, 18, 86–88, 90. See also O'Brien, Tim
Indiana, 4; in *A History of Violence* (film), 138–146; Muncie, 18, 59–62; in *Parks and Recreation* (NBC), 2, 6. See also *Middletown: A Study in Modern American Culture*; Religious Freedom Restoration Act
Interrupters, The, 218, 227n49. See also James, Steve
Iowa, 4; and presidential elections, 8; in *The Straight Story*, 192–199
irony: post-9/11 debate about irony and sincerity, 19, 152–155, 173

James, Steve, 218, 227n49. See also *America to Me*; *Hoop Dreams*; *Interrupters, The*; *Life Itself*
Jameson, Fredric: 1950s as nostalgic object, 106; "nostalgia film," 89
Johnson, Victoria E.: "Heartland myth," 11, 24n46, 129; Midwest as television market, 78n30, 154; race and Midwestern identity, 70–71, 124–125, 215; regionalism and media studies, 4
Jungle, The (novel). See also Sinclair, Upton

Kakutani, Michiko, 153, 154
Kansas, 4; in *Mysterious Skin*, 183–185; in *The Onion*, 203; as test market, 78n30; in *The Wizard of Oz* (film), 55
Korine, Harmony, 219, 228n58. See also *Gummo*

labor and identity: in *About Schmidt* (film), 156, 158, 160; in *Badlands*, 91–93, 96, 114n26,

114n28; in *Gran Torino*, 132; and regional identity, 1, 23n38, 34–35, 58–59, 60, 124, 155, 156, 165, 170, 224; in *Sister Carrie*, 37–38; in *Up in the Air*, 162–163, 167, 199, 220; in "Up the Coulé: A Story of Wisconsin," 215–216. See also class; economic decline
Latehomecomer: A Hmong Family Memoir, The: and nostalgic spatiality, 208–209. See also Yang, Kao Kalia
Lauck, Jon K.: critique of "revolt thesis" in literature, 77n13; Midwest as "lost region," 7
Leeder, Murray: sound design of *Halloween*, 119n77; terminology of "slasher" subgenre, 118n70
Leone, Sergio, 131
Lesy, Michael, 18, 86–88. See also *Wisconsin Death Trip*
Lewis, Sinclair, 9, 35–36, 57–59, 66, 70, 76, 155, 157; American culture, critique of, 78n26. See also *Babbitt*; *Main Street*
LGBTQ+ population: discrimination against, 14, 128–130, 219, 225n4; New Queer Cinema, 184, 200n17. See also queerness; titles of individual films; transphobia
Life Itself, 218, 227n49. See also Ebert, Roger; James, Steve
Lim, Bliss Cua, 16
literature: critique of "revolt thesis," 77n13; Midwestern literature of the 1910s and 1920s, 57–59, 69; naturalism (see *Sister Carrie*); "revolt from the village" writers, 57, 59. See also titles of individual works
Ljung, Erik, 219. See also *Blood Is at the Doorstep, The*
long take: in *A History of Violence* (film), 139–140, 179; in *The Miracle of Morgan's Creek*, 68–69
Longworth, Richard C., 7, 155; on nostalgia and Midwestern identity, 23n38
Lost Highway, 198. See also Lynch, David
Lutz, Tom: modernity and *O Pioneers!* (novel), 59; "revolt from the village" writers, 57
Lynch, David, 10, 14, 20, 178–179, 192–199, 207; dream logic, 194; on film as "a continuum," 196. See also *Straight Story, The*
Lynd, Robert S. and Helen Merrell, 18, 55, 59–62, 76, 204, 212, 225n9. See also *Middletown: A Study in Modern American Culture*

Ma, Jean, 15
MacGillis, Alex, 212–213
Mad Men (AMC), 16

Magnificent Ambersons, The (film), 69. *See also* Welles, Orson

Main Street, 9, 35–36, 57–58; critique of American culture, 78n26. *See also* Lewis, Sinclair

"Main Street": as shorthand for middle America, 19

Main-Travelled Roads, 20, 215–217. *See also* Garland, Hamlin; "Up the Coulé: A Story of Wisconsin"

Malick, Terrence, 18, 84–85, 88–98, 100; displacement in filmography of, 115n41; on nostalgia, 88. *See also Badlands*

Manalansan IV, Martin F. *See GLQ* (journal)

Manovich, Lev: virtual space and frontiers, 126, 127–128

Marley, Bob, 152

marriage: in *The Miracle of Morgan's Creek*, 64–66; in *Up in the Air*, 163; in "Up the Coulé: A Story of Wisconsin," 216

Martin, Adrian: on filmography of Terrence Malick, 115n41

Martin, Trayvon, 124

Marx, Frederick, 218. *See also Hoop Dreams*

masculinity: in *Babbitt*, 58; in *Boys Don't Cry* (film), 14, 128–130, 145; in *Gran Torino*, 132–135, 138, 145; hypermasculinity, performance of, 211; in *The Miracle of Morgan's Creek*, 65–67; in *Up in the Air*, 165. *See also* gender; nostalgic violence; performativity; white masculinity

McQuirter, Keith, 219. *See also Milwaukee 53206: A Community Serves Time*

Meet Me in St. Louis (film), 2, 17–18, 30, 36, 41–49, 46, 55, 69, 204; fear of moving, 43–47, 55; gender and region, associations with, 45; Halloween scene, 54n62; "Have Yourself a Merry Little Christmas" (song), 46, 54n66; nostalgia, aesthetics of, 42, 46, 53n58; nostalgic spatiality in, 41, 46–47, 48–49, 205; temporality of/in, 42, 45, 46–49; "Meet Me in St. Louis" (title song), 43, 48, 54n70. *See also* Minnelli, Vincente; movement; musicals

Mellencamp, John, 152

memory: in cinema, 15–17; cultural memory, 15, 21; *In the Lake of the Woods*, treatment in, 87–88; *The Virgin Suicides* (film), treatment in, 185–192. *See also* "autotopography"; history; nostalgia

Middle, The (ABC), 9

Middletown (PBS), 78n27

Middletown: A Study in Modern American Culture, 17, 18, 55, 59–62, 76, 204, 212; follow-up study, 78n27; nostalgic spatiality in, 61. *See also* Lynd, Robert S., and Helen Merrell; Muncie, Indiana

Midwest: as absence or blank/vacant space, 1, 7, 18, 29, 36, 76, 84, 90, 203, 209; American/national identity, associations with, 7, 8, 9, 12, 19, 34–36, 59–62, 64, 67–68, 85–86, 129, 153–154, 215, 224; anachronistic culture of, 9, 11, 18, 21, 56 (*see also* modernity), 67, 99, 125, 139, 197; as "average," "normal," or "authentic," 7, 9, 59–62, 71, 76, 78n30, 151, 154, 157, 161, 175n27, 199; class, associations with and representations of, 19–20, 224 (*see also* labor and identity); documentaries about, 217–224; expansive definition of, 5; failure, associations with, 20–21, 211–213, 214–215, 217, 221–224; "flyover country," 1, 127, 147n18; frontier mythology, relation to, 13, 29–30, 33–37, 62, 70, 111, 127–128, 204; as fulcrum/pivot of nation, 32–33, 71, 81n59, 197; gender, associations with, 4, 45, 58, 124–125, 129; "Heartland myth," 11, 24n46, 129, 193 (*see also* Johnson, Victoria E.); malleable meanings of, 60, 138, 172–173; as nebulous space, 84–85, 87–88, 89, 97–98, 104, 111, 113n23, 127, 196, 203; as nostalgia museum, 12, 13, 85–86, 88, 90, 110, 111, 123, 146, 197; nostalgic identity of, 2–3, 9–15, 21, 29–30, 33–34, 49, 85–86, 110–111, 146, 160, 197, 198, 209; as "pastoral ideal," 11–12, 34, 70, 76, 111, 125; political uses of Midwestern imagery and narratives, 7, 172–173, 211–212, 214–215, 224; and presidential elections (*see* elections, presidential; politics; swing states); racial perceptions of, 4, 19, 59–62, 70–71, 76, 94, 124–125, 129, 133–135, 155, 212, 215 (*see also* African Americans; Native Americans; white masculinity; whiteness); rural, associations with, 47, 70; satirical depiction of, 1–2, 6, 63–70, 203; stereotypes about, 1, 7, 140–141, 157, 166, 193–194; temporality of, 9, 11–12, 13–15, 21, 42, 49, 76, 84, 101, 127, 139, 194, 197, 203, 209; term (Midwest), early uses of, 12, 25n55, 34, 35; twelve state definition of, 4, 12, 24n46, 176n35; uncertain identity/boundaries, 1–2, 4, 6–7, 24n46, 24n50; urban spaces, dissociation from, 11–12, 70, 77, 125; violence, associations with, 10, 111–112, 139, 143–145 (*see also* nostalgic violence; white masculinity). *See also* nostalgic spatiality; region; regional identity; regionalism

Midwesterners: as blank slates, 18, 84–85, 91–96 (*Badlands*), 105–106 (*Halloween*), 112; and performativity, 85, 93–97 (*Badlands*)

Michigan, 4; and presidential elections, 8. *See also* Detroit (MI); Flint (MI)
Milwaukee 53206: A Community Serves Time, 219. *See also* McQuirter, Keith
Milwaukee (WI): African American population, 9, 219, 221–224; in *American Movie*, 220–221; in *The Blood Is at the Doorstep*, 219; in *Milwaukee 53206: A Community Serves Time*, 219; in *Two American Families*, 21, 221–224. *See also* Wisconsin
Minnelli, Vincente, 17, 30, 36, 41–49, 55. *See also Meet Me in St. Louis* (film)
Minnesota, 4; in *In the Lake of the Woods*, 87–88; in *The Latehomecomer: A Hmong Family Memoir*, 208–209
Miracle of Morgan's Creek, The, 18, 56, 63–70, 69, 76, 209; gender, treatment of, 64–67, 80n50; nostalgia, aesthetics of, 68–69, 69; nostalgic spatiality in, 68–69; private and public matters, linkage of, 64; slapstick elements, 65, 67; tracking shot, use of, 63, 68–69. *See also* Sturges, Preston
Missouri, 4; in *Rich Hill*, 219. *See also* Ozarks; St. Louis, Missouri
modernity: Marshall Berman on, 56–57; "infrastructural modernity," 82n75; mass culture of, 74–75; Midwest as "antimodern," 18, 47, 56, 59, 67, 76–77; and *O Pioneers!* (novel), 59
Moore, Michael, 20, 218. *See also Roger & Me*
Morrison, Toni, 2. *See also Beloved* (novel)
Mortensen, Viggo: performance elements in *A History of Violence* (film), 140, 142, 143
movement: entrapment in romantic comedies, 80n57; in "fantasy culture of the 1930s," 74; fear of moving, 43–47 (*Meet Me in St. Louis*, film), 55 (*Sister Carrie*); from Midwest to the East, 30, 37–38 (*Sister Carrie*), 41–47 (*Meet Me in St. Louis*, film), 55, 143–144 (*A History of Violence*, film), 184 (*Mysterious Skin*), 205; frontier spaces and potential for movement, 33; Midwestern isolation, 61, 76–77, 130; nostalgia and restriction of mobility (Marshall Berman), 56; physical movement and slapstick conventions, 65–66; and segregation, 73; and spatial abstraction, 194–196 (*The Straight Story*); tracking shot, 63, 68–69. *See also* frontier; space; spatial constriction; Turner, Frederick Jackson; western expansion
Moyers, Bill, 221–224. *See also Two American Families*
MTV, 152

Muncie, Indiana: African American population of, 79n34; Jewish population of, 79n34. *See also* Indiana; *Middletown: A Study in Modern American Culture*
musicals, 204: as "cultural problem-solving device," 42–43; regional and historical contexts of MGM musicals, 55; temporality of, 41, 42–43. *See also* Altman, Rick; *Meet Me in St. Louis* (film)
Muska, Susan, 219. *See also Brandon Teena Story, The* (documentary); Olafsdóttir, Gréta
Mutz, Diana C.: on the 2016 presidential election, 213, 214, 217
Mysterious Skin, 20, 125, 178–179, 180, 183–185; as adaptation, 182; nostalgia, aesthetics of, 184, 206; nostalgic atonement in, 182, 184–185, 192, 199, 208; nostalgic spatiality in, 184. *See also* Araki, Gregg

Nadeau, Chantal. *See GLQ* (journal)
national cinemas. *See* cinema
Native Americans: frontier mythology, treatment within, 32, 61–62, 124, 132–133, 135; omission from Midwestern narratives, 29, 64; representation of, 102, *103* (*Stroszek*)
Native Son, 2, 10, 18, 55, 70–77, 209; and cinema, 73–74, 83n84; nostalgic spatiality in, 73, 205; performativity in, 72, 81n74. *See also* segregation; spatial constriction; Wright, Richard
nativism, 62, 79n41, 211, 225n9
naturalism (American literature). *See* Dreiser, Theodore; *Sister Carrie*
Nebraska, 4, 88; in *Boys Don't Cry* (film), 14, 128–130; in *O Pioneers!* (novel), 58–59. *See also* Omaha (NE); Payne, Alexander
Nebraska, 156. *See also* Payne, Alexander
neoliberalism, 21, 117n60, 221, 222, 223–224; and nostalgia, 21, 221, 224. *See also* Harvey, David
New York City, 30, 211; Midwestern locales, contrast with, 37–38, 44–47, 58–59, 155, 215–217. *See also* East (American region)
New York Times, The (newspaper): 2016 presidential election, 9; post-9/11 irony/sincerity debate, 153
newspapers: American culture, relationship to, 67; business class, support of, 80n58; national identity, relationship to, 80n58
Newsweek (magazine): post-9/11 irony/sincerity debate, 152, 153
Nichols, Jeff, 19, 151–152, 168–173; commentary on *Take Shelter*, 171, 176n41. *See also Take Shelter*

Index 251

Nicholson, Jack: in *About Schmidt* (film), 156–162; *Easy Rider*, 176n30
Nightmare on Elm Street, A (franchise), 108. See also *Halloween*; horror films
North America: perceptions of vacancy, 29, 32, 33, 61–62. See also Native Americans; racism
North Dakota, 4
Northeast (American region). See East (American region)
nostalgia: aesthetics of (*see* nostalgia, aesthetics of; *individual titles of films*); and cinema, 15–17, 89, 106 (*see also* cinema; *titles of individual films*); as debilitating disorder, 30, 39–40; definition of, 9–10; in frontier mythology, 13, 32–34; and the future, 93–94, 205, 209; history and myth, relation to, 12, 16–17; ideological properties of, 10; looping desire/temporality of, 13, 30, 33, 36, 47, 48, 69, 84, 98, 99, 103, 197; and modernity, 56–57; "nostalgia films," 89; and American politics, 211–215, 224; preemptive nostalgia, 93–94; purpose of studying, 15, 16–17, 209, 224; simultaneity, desire for, 39, 49, 87, 97, 107 (and horror), 179, 194 (and dissolve edit), 197–198 (and duration), 206, 209; spatiotemporal properties of, 9–10, 12, 16, 99, 186, 192; as stabilizing element, 30, 41; and stargazing, 196–197, 202n38; the study of, contexts/frameworks for, 3, 9–10. *See also* Boym, Svetlana; nostalgic atonement; nostalgic spatiality; nostalgic violence; Stewart, Susan
nostalgia, aesthetics of, 20, 179, 194 (Svetlana Boym), 206–207; in *About Schmidt* (film), 159; in *Badlands*, 90–92, *91*, *92*, 179, 206–207; in *A History of Violence* (film), 139–140, 179; in *Meet Me in St. Louis* (film), 42, *46*, 53n58; in *The Miracle of Morgan's Creek*, 68–69, *69*; in *Mysterious Skin*, 184, 206; in *The Straight Story*, 20, 179, 194–196, *195*, 206; in *Stroszek*, 99–101, *100*, *103*, 104, 179, 206–207; in *The Virgin Suicides* (film), 20, 179, 187–188, 190–192, *191*, 206. See also cinema; *individual titles of films*; nostalgia; nostalgic spatiality
Nostalgia for the Light, 202n38
nostalgic atonement, 10, 15, 21, 174, 178–181, 199, 203; definition of, 3, 14, 20, 181, 208; and restorative nostalgia, 180–181, 190, 192. See also *individual titles of films and literature*
nostalgic spatiality, 10, 15, 17–18, 21, 203–207; aesthetics of, *46*, 68–69, *69*, 90–92, *91*, *92*, 99–101, *100*, 104, 179, 194–196, *195*, 206–207; definition of, 3, 10–11, 29, 204, 206; development in Midwestern narratives and contexts, 10–14, 86; frontier mythology, relation to, 13, 32–34, 36; manifestation across mediums, 49; and segregation, 73; and tracking shots, 68–69. See also *individual titles of films and literature*
nostalgic violence, 10, 15, 18–19, 21, 85, 111–112, 123, 125, 144, 146, 199, 203; definition of, 3, 14, 84, 124, 207; and gender identity, 129–130; and restorative nostalgia, 181. See also *individual titles of films and literature*

O Pioneers! (novel) 58–59. See also Cather, Willa
Obama, Barack, 8
O'Brien, Tim, 18, 86–88. See also *In the Lake of the Woods*
Ohio, 4; in *Beloved* (novel), 2; and presidential elections, 8, 212; in *Take Shelter*, 168–173; in *Winesburg, Ohio*, 1–2
Olafsdóttir, Gréta, 219. See also *Brandon Teena Story, The* (documentary); Muska, Susan
Omaha, Nebraska: in *About Schmidt* (film), 156–162; in filmography of Alexander Payne, 156; in *Up in the Air*, 162, 163
Oman, Patricia: "black rurality," perceptions of, 81n65; on modernity and regional identity, 57; on regional and historical contexts of MGM musicals, 55
Onion, The, 1, 3, 8, 10, 203
Ozarks: in *Winter's Bone*, 182–183, 219

Palermo, Andrew Droz, 219. See also *Rich Hill*; Tragos, Tracy Droz
Parks and Recreation (NBC), 2; "The Camel" episode and Midwestern narratives, 6, 7
past: as narrative and idea, 15; in "nostalgia film," 89. See also memory; nostalgia
pastoralism. See Midwest; Shortridge, James R.
Payne, Alexander, 19, 151–152, 156–162; Midwest, associations with, 52n41, 156–157; Midwestern aesthetics of, 157, 175n21; Omaha in filmography, depiction of, 156. See also *About Schmidt* (film)
Peirce, Kimberly, 14, 19, 124, 128–130, 207. See also *Boys Don't Cry* (film)
Penn, Arthur, 96. See also *Bonnie and Clyde* (film)
performance (film). See acting; *individual titles of films*; Mortensen, Viggo
performativity, 19, 66, 112, 123, 130, 142–143; Butler, Judith, 140, 150n62; hypermasculinity, performance of, 211; and Midwestern traits, 138, 140–145, 157–158, 165, 167, 199; violence and nostalgia, association with, 144–145, 199. See also

individual titles of films and literature; Midwesterners

Phillips, Kendall R.: frontier mythology in John Carpenter's filmography, 111; *Halloween* and the Gothic, 118n66

politics: American politics, polarization of, 124, 214; Midwestern imagery and narratives, political uses of, 7, 172–173, 211–212, 214–215, 224; and nostalgia, 211–215, 224; and regional identity, 215; and "rural consciousness," 213–214; "rural-versus-urban divide," 213–214. *See also* elections, presidential (United States); electoral map; failure; resentment; swing states

Presley, Priscilla, 94

ProPublica, 212–213

Pruitt-Igoe Myth, The, 218–219. *See also* Freidrichs, Chad

Psycho (1960), 118n65

Public Enemy, The, 69

public housing. *See* Cabrini-Green Homes; *Pruitt-Igoe Myth, The*

queerness: and Midwestern identity, 7; New Queer Cinema, 184, 200n17. *See also* LGBTQ+ population; *titles of individual films*; transphobia

race: and American politics, 211–215; Midwest, associations with, 4, 19, 59–62, 70–71, 124–125, 133–135, 212; and "rural consciousness," 214. *See also* African Americans; Hmong Americans; Native Americans; white masculinity; whiteness

racism: American culture and regional identity, 70–71, 129, 211–217; in frontier thesis, 32, 61–62, 124, 133; representation of, 6, 72, 135, 216

Radavich, David, 6

Raisin in the Sun, A (play), 72, 73. *See also* Hansberry, Lorraine

Reagan, Ronald, 225n2

Rebel Without a Cause, 114n28. *See also* Dean, James

redlining, 72–73, 222, 227n48. *See also* discrimination, housing; segregation

reflective nostalgia. *See* Boym, Svetlana

region: definition of, 4–6, 211; regional mythologies/narratives, 3–4, 5, 215, 224; regional stereotypes, 1; and storytelling, 4–5. *See also* critical regionalism; *names of individual regions*; Reichert Powell, Douglas; regionalism

regional identity: American regions and authenticity, 19, 153–154, 215, 224; definition of, 4–5, 211; and "flyover" view, 147n18; performance of, 140 (*see also individual titles of films and literature*; performativity); and sincerity/irony, 152–155. *See also* labor and identity; *names of individual regions*

regionalism: methods of regional study, 4–5, 203–204, 211–212, 215; outcomes/purpose of regional study, 3, 204, 209, 217, 224; in/ and textual objects, 2–3, 21. *See also* critical regionalism; *names of individual regions*; Reichert Powell, Douglas

Reichert Powell, Douglas: critical regionalism, 161; on region and regional identity, 5

Reitman, Jason, 19, 151–152, 162–168, 220. *See also Up in the Air*

Religious Freedom Restoration Act: nostalgic rhetoric of, 225n4

Republican Party. *See* elections, presidential (United States)

resentment: and American politics, 9, 211–217; "politics of resentment," 213–214, 216–217, 224; in rural communities, 9, 213–217, 226n18. *See also* Cramer, Katherine J.; failure; politics

restorative nostalgia. *See* Boym, Svetlana

Rich, B. Ruby, 184, 200n17

Rich Hill, 219. *See also* Palermo, Andrew Droz; Tragos, Tracy Droz

RoboCop, 131. *See also* Verhoeven, Paul

Rodríguez, Richard T. *See GLQ* (journal)

Roger & Me, 20, 218, 224. *See also* Moore, Michael

romantic comedies, 65, 80n57. *See also Miracle of Morgan's Creek, The*

Rose, Bernard, 72. *See also Candyman*

Roseanne (ABC), 141

Rosenblatt, Roger, 152, 155

Rossellini, Roberto, 228n58

Rouge, 15

"rural consciousness." *See* Cramer, Katherine J.; politics

"rural-versus-urban divide." *See* Cramer, Katherine J.; politics; "Up the Coulé: A Story of Wisconsin"

Rushkoff, Douglas, 126

St. Louis (MO): in *Meet Me in St. Louis* (film), 41–49, 205; in *The Pruitt-Igoe Myth*, 218–219; in *Up in the Air*, 162, 220. *See also* Missouri

Scarface (1932), 69

Schiller, Robert, 212–213

Scott, A. O., 157

segregation: in Midwestern cities, 218–219, 227n48; *Native Son*, depiction in, 72–73, 76, 205

September 11th. *See* 9/11

Shortridge, James R.: Midwest, negative associations with, 47, 69; nostalgia museum, Midwest as, 12, 85–86, 197; "pastoral ideal," 11–12, 34, 70, 125; term "Midwest," emergence of, 12, 25n55, 34, 200n2; uncertain identity/boundaries of the Midwest, 24n50

Show Boat (novel and films), 57, 81n65

Simple Plan, A, 125

sincerity: post-9/11 debate about irony and sincerity, 19, 152–155

Sinclair, Upton, 59. *See also Jungle, The* (novel)

Sister Carrie, 2, 10, 17–18, 30, 36–41, 49, 86; "evolution and dissolution," theme of, 52n39; Hurstwood and nostalgia, 39–40, 55; nostalgic spatiality in, 37, 40–41, 179, 205. *See also* Dreiser, Theodore

Slotkin, Richard: on history and myth, 12

Smith, Chris, 220–221. *See also American Movie*; Borchardt, Mark

Smith, Roger. *See Roger & Me*

sociology: *See Middletown: A Study in Modern American Culture*

Somerville, Siobhan B. *See GLQ* (journal)

South (American region), 6, 170. *See also* Ozarks; region; regionalism

South Dakota, 4; in *Badlands*, 84–85, 89

space. *See* frontier; geography; movement; nostalgic spatiality; region; regionalism; spatial constriction

Spacek, Sissy: in *Badlands*, 84, 89–98, 113n19; 113n20, 114n29; in *The Straight Story*, 193

spatial constriction: in frontier mythology, 31–33; and the Midwest, 57, 111, 209; in *The Miracle of Morgan's Creek*, 18, 56, 63, 66, 68–69; in *Native Son*, 18, 56, 70–74; nostalgia, relation to, 56; and nostalgic spatiality, 29, 32–34; psychological effects of, 73–74, 76–77; racial dimensions of, 56, 72–74; stability, resulting from, 55; in *Stroszek*, 99. *See also* movement

Spider, 149n56. *See also* Cronenberg, David

Spigel, Lynn: nostalgia and American television, 16

Sprengler, Christine: 1950s and "Fifties" as "nostalgic construct," 106, 117n62; nostalgia and American cinema, 16

Starkweather, Charles, 88. *See also Badlands*; Fugate, Caril Ann

Stewart, Susan: on horror narratives, 107; nostalgia, 10, 32, 50n5

Straight Story, The, 10, 14, 20, 178–179, 192–199, *195*, 203, 209; dissolves, use in, 194–196, *195*, 198, 202n35, 206; duration, depiction of 197–198; fantasy elements of, 193–194; nostalgia, aesthetics of, 20, 179, 194–196, *195*, 206; nostalgic atonement in, 179, 192–193, 197, 198, 199, 208; nostalgic spatiality in, 179, 192–193, 194–196, 197, 199, 206. *See also* Lynch, David

Stroszek, 18, 85, 98–104, *100*, *103*, 105, 111–112, 179; circle motif, 99, 101–104, *103*, 116n52, 207; concluding sequence, 102–104; as "fairy tale," 116n45; nostalgia, aesthetics of, 99–101, *100*, *103*, 104, 179, 206–207; nostalgic spatiality in, 99–101, *100*, 103–104, 206–207; space and time, treatment of, 98, 99–100; soundtrack and acts of translation, 101–102, 116n49. *See also* Herzog, Werner

Sturges, Preston, 18, 56, 63–70; American culture, critique of, 63–64, 65–66, 76. *See also Miracle of Morgan's Creek, The*

Suner, Asuman, 15–16

Sweeney, Mary, 194. *See also* dissolve as a film editing technique; *Straight Story, The*

swing states, 8–9. *See also* elections, presidential (United States); politics

Take Shelter, 19, 125, 151–152, 155, 168–173, *172*, 209; economic contexts of, 168–169, 170, 172; environmental contexts of, 170, 172; final scene, interpretations of, 169–172; and frontier mythology, 170, 172; paranoia and masculinity, 168, 171–172, 173, 199. *See also* Nichols, Jeff

Teena, Brandon, 128–130, 207. *See also Boys Don't Cry* (film); *Brandon Teena Story, The* (documentary)

television: nostalgia in, 16. *See also* titles of *individual series*

Telotte, J. P.: on individualism and collectivity in *Meet Me in St. Louis* (film), 45

Tieken, Mara Casey, 214

time/temporality. *See* cinema; duration; memory; nostalgia; past

Time (magazine), 152

tracking shot: in *A History of Violence* (film), 139–140, 179; in *The Miracle of Morgan's Creek*, 63, 68–69; and nostalgic spatiality, 68–69

Tragos, Tracy Droz, 219. *See also* Palermo, Andrew Droz; *Rich Hill*

254 *Index*

transphobia, 14, 124, 128–130, 207
Trump, Donald, 8, 211–215, 217, 225n2, 225n4. *See also* elections, presidential (United States); resentment
Turim, Maureen: on cinematic flashbacks, 185
Turner, Frederick Jackson, 2, 4, 17–18, 59, 76, 94, 152; critique of, 31, 50n10; frontier and class/economics, 35, 38, 64, 124; frontier closure, 13, 30, 31–33, 50n10, 56, 111; frontier mythology, 12–13, 30–36, 133; on Midwestern identity, 14–15, 33–37, 49, 56, 70, 110, 124, 160, 204, 209; movement, emphasis on, 30–33, 197, 204; Native Americans, treatment of, 32, 61–62, 124, 132–133, 135; and nostalgic spatiality, 12–14, 17–18, 29–30, 33–34, 48, 197, 204; "Problem of the West," 31–32; on regional identity, 12, 30, 50n5; as theorist of nostalgia, 12–13, 17, 29, 32–34, 204; twenty-first century, lingering influence in, 123, 125–128, 132–133 (in *Gran Torino*), 170, 204; United States as "thrown back upon itself," 13, 32, 40, 56, 126, 197, 204; "witches' kettle" image, 32, 37, 56, 76. *See also* frontier
Twain, Mark, 2, 59
Two American Families, 21, 220, 221–224. *See also* failure; *Frontline* (PBS); Moyers, Bill; neoliberalism

United States: in film and television, 16 (*see also* titles of individual films and series); post-9/11 irony/sincerity debate, 152–155. *See also* East (American region); elections, presidential; frontier; Midwest; South (American region); West (American region); western expansion
United States Census Bureau, 4; twelve-state definition of Midwest versus "Heartland" label, 24n46, 176n35
Up (documentary series), 221. *See also* Apted, Michael
Up in the Air, 19, 151–152, 155, 162–168, *164*, 173, 178; documentary elements in, 220; labor and identity, treatment of, 162–163, 167, 199, 220; nostalgic spatiality in, 166–167, 205; philosophy of detachment in, 162, 163; relationships, commentary on, 163–167. *See also* Reitman, Jason
"Up the Coulé: A Story of Wisconsin," 20, 215–217, 220. *See also* Garland, Hamlin; *Main-Travelled Roads*

Vang, Bee: on problematic representation of Hmong characters, 134, 136. *See also Gran Torino*; Hmong Americans

Verhoeven, Paul, 131. *See also RoboCop*
Vietnam War, 106; and horror genre, 118n65; in *In the Lake of the Woods*, 87
violence: mass shootings, 124; "senseless violence," 96; "zero-level protest," 96. *See also* individual titles of films and literature; Midwest; nostalgic violence; white masculinity
Virgin Suicides, The (novel), 185: narration style, 186
Virgin Suicides, The (film), 20, 125, 179, 185–192, *191*, 197; as adaptation, 185; dissolves, use of, 190–192, *191*, 194, 206; flashback structure of, 186, 187–188, 205–206; narration, use of, 186–189, 190, 192, 201n26, 206; nostalgia, aesthetics of, 20, 179, 187–188, 190–192, *191*, 206; nostalgic atonement in, 189–191, 199; nostalgic spatiality in, 205. *See also* Coppola, Sofia
Vonnegut, Kurt: "To Be a Native Middle-Westerner," 29, 33

Washington Post, The (newspaper): 2016 presidential election, 9
Welles, Orson, 69. *See also Magnificent Ambersons, The* (film)
West (American region), 1, 7, 13, 30, 170; frontier spaces, relationship to, 31–33; progress, association with, 47; as set of conditions, 31. *See also* region; regionalism; Turner, Frederick Jackson; western expansion
western expansion, 12, 30–31; and nostalgia, 18, 29, 31, 33, 36; parody of, 159 (*About Schmidt*, film); and "virtual space," 126. *See also* frontier; Turner, Frederick Jackson; West (American region)
white masculinity: and Midwestern identity, 4, 14, 19–20, 124, 130, 133–135, 137, 151–152, 155; and nostalgic violence, 14, 18, 97, 105, 124, 129; and paranoia (in *Take Shelter*), 19, 168, 171–173, 199; and "perceived status threat," 213, 214, 217; and politics, 211, 213; and resentment, 211–212, 215–217
whiteness: and American culture and history, 22n12; and Midwestern identity, 4, 61–62, 70–71, 133–135, 137, 212, 215; as "native American," 62, 64, 212, 225n9; and politics, 211–215; and "rural consciousness," 213–214; white supremacy, 124, 137. *See also* white masculinity
Whose Streets?, 219. *See also* Davis, Damon; Folayan, Sabaah
Williams, Raymond: on "region," 5

Index 255

Williams, Roger Ross, 219. See also *God Loves Uganda*
Winesburg, Ohio, 1–2, 57. See also Anderson, Sherwood
Winfrey-Harris, Tamara, 4
Winter's Bone (film), 20, 125, 178–179, 180, 182–183, *183*; as adaptation, 182; documentarylike elements, 219; nostalgic atonement in, 182–183, 192, 199, 208. See also Granik, Debra
Wisconsin, 4; as ideological battleground, 212; and presidential elections, 8, 9; "rural consciousness" and "politics of resentment," 213–214; in *The Straight Story*, 192–199; in *Stroszek*, 98–104; in "Up the Coulé: A Story of Wisconsin," 215–217. See also Milwaukee, Wisconsin
Wisconsin Death Trip, 18, 86–88. See also Lesy, Michael

Wizard of Oz, The (film), 55, 57
Wood, Robin, 105, 118n66
Woodrell, Daniel, 182. See also *Winter's Bone* (film)
World War II, 17, 18, 55, 67, 76, 180; as context for film production, 65; impact on Midwestern identity, 47
Wright, Richard, 18, 55, 70–77, 205; Chicago as national "pivot," 71; "How 'Bigger' Was Born," 71, 74, 75. See also *Native Son*

Xenia, Ohio: in *Gummo*, 219

Yang, Kao Kalia, 208–209. See also *Latehomecomer: A Hmong Family Memoir, The*

Žižek, Slavoj: violence and "zero-level protest," 96, 115n39

ADAM R. OCHONICKY is Lecturer of English at the University of Wisconsin Oshkosh. He is the Media Review Editor of *Middle West Review*.

www.ingramcontent.com/pod-product-compliance
Lightning Source LLC
Chambersburg PA
CBHW031805220426
43662CB00007B/532